Holywood Star

Holywood Star

The Life and Times
of a
Rock and Roll Misadventurer

Eamon Nancarrow

SHOWCASE UK

First published in the United Kingdom in 2009
by Showcase UK
www.showcaseuk.tv
www.eamonnancarrow.com

ISBN 978-0-9563900-0-4

Produced by
The Choir Press
www.thechoirpress.co.uk

Contents

Foreword

There are many roads that enter Belfast and, thanks to the laws of map making, the same amount will take you away from the city.

One such highway is the A2. It takes you east along the southern shore of Belfast Lough to Bangor. If you travel down that wholesome stretch of tarmac you will see signs for the town of Holywood which the inhabitants pronounce 'Hollywood'.

The reason I found it hard to believe such a place existed in Northern Ireland was that Eamon Nancarrow delivered this nugget of information. Eamon is one of the funniest people I've ever met and someone who found me a pleasure to tease. He was also backed up by his friend for life Ken Heaven.

Eamon and Ken took me to Holywood a couple of times: I visited 'Ned's', the small but heroic bar; stood next to the maypole in the centre of town; I also visited 'the Shore' from which some people swam when it was warm and others gathered to drink when it was legally impossible.

We also went to the working men's club at Sunday lunchtime where I was able to witness the lining up of half-poured Guinnesses in anticipation of the imminent arrival of thirsty churchgoers.

There is nothing about Holywood that would stop a family, or heavy drinker, settling there. But for teenagers with energy, talent and ambition, its sleepy nature would have given them impetus to leave.

It was also the time of the 'Troubles', which to the ignorant sounds like a touch of indigestion – but to the people of Northern Ireland, the sectarian divide caused agony, anger and frustration in every home. However in times of hardship humanity seems to find resilience through humour and none more so than in Eamon, Ken and their families.

I'll always remember saying goodnight to Eamon's mother Molly on her doorstep when we heard a 'crump' sound in the distance. 'That'll be a bomb,' Molly told me quite casually. The Troubles were never far away.

My first glimpse of Eamon Nancarrow was through the frosted glass of a front door. I had recently moved to London and decided to give the notion of 'fame through rock and roll' one last blast.

I placed a free advertisement on a radio station, declaring to all and sundry that a bass player was available for gigs and fun. As I had such a memorable name I decided to use a pseudonym to avoid seeming uncool for placing an advert.

Unfortunately I didn't realise my availability would be read out by the inimitable Tommy Vance during one of his legendary rock shows. At the time rock was a style of music I was generally unfamiliar with.

And I definitely didn't expect that in the whole of London's millions the only musicians in need of a bass player would live around the corner. Looking back you assume this was either divine intervention or divine retribution, but either way a meeting was organised and there I was walking towards this frosted glass, pseudonym in hand, looking at the outline of a definite rock person and wondering if I should deny all knowledge of anything.

Like jumping into a cold swimming pool there was a point of no return and I opened the door to reveal Eamon Nancarrow who, it transpired, was a fantastic singer, a brilliant storyteller, and as you will discover, a very funny author.

This book is his life as a musician on the rocky road to fame, a road that quite happily contravenes the laws of normal ordnance surveying.

Eamon's life is entwined with that of the mercurial Ken Heaven, one of the best guitarists I have ever seen or heard. Why the 'Tinsel Twins' thought I was necessary to their plans is still beyond my comprehension.

Eamon always had the ability to keep a crowd in stitches with his stories. It might seem impossible that someone has so many funny things happening in their daily life but I firmly believe we all have similar occasions, it's just that we don't recognise them and, if we do, we don't remember them well enough to form such a great narrative.

All these tales are true. Some, however, have tweaks to save blushes, a few have dimmed through time and there is the occasional embellishment to amaze and confound, but what you will discover is something that Eamon taught me through example: no matter how bad things get, and no matter how desperate your situation, there is always a funny side to your plight. It's a thread I try to keep running through my life and hopefully, you'll be able weave into yours.

Having seen this book develop over the past two years I feel honoured to be part of Eamon's misadventure as a Holywood Star.

Xan 'Fingal' Phillips
August 2009

Acknowledgements

It all sounded so simple. 'Write a book about the band,' said Big Xan Phillips. 'Not on your Nellie,' said I. Being slap bang in the middle of an MSc, having two kids in the house under three, holding down a full time job, recording a new album and gigging every Saturday night, I just didn't have the time or energy.

Then the babies decided that they didn't need to sleep at night, therefore neither did I. A horrendously bad sleeper anyway, once awake I needed something to do. Romance was out of the question: we already had the kids, and I think that if I had roused my exhausted partner from her much needed slumber I might never have woken from the hiding she would've inflicted upon my person. So what to do?

In the wee small hours the memories were collated in my insomniacal brain and then put down on computer chip in combinations of 1s and 0s when and where I could. I know that my name appears on the cover but it was a team effort.

Many thanks to:

Firstly my beautiful kids Teelin and Tara for not sleeping, although at the time I could've killed them. I love them more than life itself.

Donna my beautiful, long-suffering, partner in life needs special mention for her love and support while I continually bite off more than I can chew and also for letting me know, in her own honest way, that she didn't like what I was writing.

My friend for life Ken Heaven. Read the book and you'll know why.

My family, bandmates, friends, the wonderful people of

Holywood County Down throughout the years and the many characters that I've encountered on my Rock and Roll journey – all of whom have provided me with the material with which to fill these pages. To all of them I owe a debt of gratitude because without their lunacy there would've been nothing to write.

All the bands and musicians that have filled my world with Rock and Roll and inspired me. These include: The Rolling Stones, AC/DC, Motorhead, Thin Lizzy, Judas Priest, Queen, Deep Purple, Black Sabbath, Journey, John Waite, Glen Hughes and Elvis Presley.

Rosemary Cassidy and Fari at Knockbracken Library for all their help with the MSc and for taking some of the pressure off me.

Paul Kane for proofreading and not being too cruel about my grammar and spelling.

Special thanks must go to Lorraine Moreland who typed and retyped all the numerous changes I made and still laughed.

Dr Hugh Webb, Ray Kendall and his family, my cousin Marty Tolan and Amy Bradley for reading the rough drafts without complaint.

Dr Paul Boreland for his keen eye in finding mistakes.

Legal advice was provided very kindly free of charge by the wonderful Gráinne Brady.

Arty Magee for all his expertise.

Fiona Thornton for editing the book with style and grace. And to Miles Bailey from Choir Press for guidance and advice.

Jenny Rainbird, Big Xan's beautiful partner, for the support she has given him and for her artistic bent.

But most of all thanks must go to Xan Phillips because he believed when I didn't and said my ramblings were funny when I couldn't see it. Cheers mate – this is really your book because without you it would never have happened.

This book is dedicated to my Mum and Dad who made me who I am, but especially my Mum, Molly Nancarrow who, having faced all the trials and tribulations that bringing up six kids and holding down three jobs brings, should be enjoying a well-earned rest. Instead she now faces her biggest challenge – go on ya girl ya, you can do it. A true Holywood Star.

CHAPTER ONE

A Holywood Star is Born

'She's heavy with child, is there no way we can bunk to the front of the queue?' So asked Marcus Nancarrow, holding onto the hand of his visibly pregnant new wife of nine months, Molly. The usher took pity on them, it was September 1965 and the weather was cold and wet – although the month didn't matter, it is always cold and wet in Belfast. There were hundreds of people pushing and shoving trying to get into the ABC Theatre where what would turn out to be the greatest Rock and Roll band of all time were about to play. The couple were led past the less than pleased throngs. There were shouts of, 'Check under yer woman's coat for a cushion,' and, 'My wife's bunions are giving her gip – any chance we can get in?'

Once inside Marcus dragged Molly to the very front of the stage. She wasn't complaining: she was a big fan of the Stones and a little thing like being seven and half months pregnant was not going to stop her from witnessing the raw R&B power of the dirtier Beatles. Marcus loved music; he was a veteran of many a showband and had played guitar in groups with the young Van Morrison, so there wasn't even the slightest twinge of guilt that he had used his wife's condition to enable them to get the best spot in the house.

The lights dimmed, the hairs on the backs of necks rose, and in a flash London's finest hit the boards. The crowd went mad, surging forward. Marcus had to stand behind Molly to protect her from bouncing the fruit of his loins off the stage. 'Route 66' rattled out of the speakers followed closely by the old Chuck Berry number 'Oh Carol'. Hit after hit got the joint jumping. Keith then let rip with the opening riff to 'Satisfaction' and the crowd responded by going berserk. Jagger was doing that funny little dance he used to do, the one where he would shake his head from side to side, just enough to get some movement into his establishment-baiting long hair. Brian Jones stood virtually motionless, his Vox Teardrop guitar sitting slightly too high. Charlie did what Charlie always does, like clockwork. Wyman picked out the bass lines that rattled the windows of the room. Molly loved it, but as Bill's bass mimicked Keith's phrasing she felt a little stirring down below: the vibrations travelled along the floor of the stage, dissipating in the amniotic fluid that surrounded her offspring. Luckily it was to be the last song of the night. She didn't want to miss anything but she was starting to feel a little queasy – the baby was turning somersaults.

They travelled back to the seaside town of Holywood, a suburb of Belfast, in Marcus's old Ford Thames van; he had had the good sense, or was persuaded by his young bride, to leave his AJS 650 motorbike behind. Molly suddenly announced that, 'It might be a good idea to fetch the doctor when we get back' – she wasn't feeling great. This did nothing for the state of Marcus's already frayed nerves and his ability to remain within the speed limit.

The woken-from-his-sleep and slightly pissed-off medic said that the expectant mum had 'overdone it gyrating to the jungle rhythms of those long-haired louts'. I assume he was expressing his misgivings about the cultural changes taking place in 60s, less than liberal, North of Ireland. He then went on, 'She needs rest, otherwise the baby will arrive prematurely.'

Sure enough a couple of short weeks later and a month ahead of schedule, at just over five pounds, I was born. My parents were as proud as punch; however, they were slightly concerned that every time the Stones came on the wireless I would giggle, try to roll off the sofa and soil my nappy. They were and still are convinced that Bill Wyman had paved a path that was to lead me on a life full of Rock and Roll adventure/misadventure. If music be the food of love pull up a chair, tuck the tablecloth into the front of your shirt and chow down.

A fine estate of affairs

About a year or so after my early arrival the North Down Borough Council gave my parents the good news that we could have a house in the White City housing estate on the outskirts of Holywood Town. With it being a predominantly Protestant development, and with political tensions on the rise everywhere, my Catholic Ma and Da were obviously apprehensive. But with another little one on the way the one bedroom flat, above Bernie Toner's House in the town centre, was way too small and with money being as short as the mini skirts of the time there was just no alternative.

Our new estate was run by Loyalist paramilitaries who did a great job of dividing people who, if they had been left to their own devices, probably would've just got on with each other. For some reason these bastions of public and religious decency felt that it was their duty to turn their area into a virtual no-go area for Catholics; the flags and red, white and blue painted kerbstones were less than welcoming.

The political tensions came to a head over a two-week period in May of 1974 when the Loyalist workers' strike took place. The cause for this act of defiance was the Sunningdale Agreement, which would have given the Republic of Ireland a direct say in the running of the Province. Nobody was allowed to go to work or school, which as kids, and not knowing the gravity of the situation, we thought was great. We were also deprived of food, except for unpasteurised milk, supplied from the back of a lorry, that gave everyone the shits. There was no water, no electricity, no gas and no transport, effectively bringing the Six Counties to its knees. Nowhere else in the British Isles would this have been tolerated, but it was allowed to carry on, with no intervention from the army or police, leaving the likes of our estate in the hands of balaclava-wearing, pickaxe-handle-carrying, thugs and drunks in combat gear.

A barricade, set up at the bottom of our street, was manned by the local militia, one of whom was a well-known character who sported a beard that came down to below his chest; it wouldn't have looked out of place on Dusty Hill or Billy Gibbons from ZZ Top. My Da, who had never missed a day's work in his life, decided that no one was going to prevent him from going out to earn a crust to feed his family. He drove up to the blockade and demanded to be let through. The balaclava-clad 'sharp dressed man' informed him, while stroking his whiskers, that if he didn't turn around, and enjoy a holiday for Queen and Country, the car would be taken off him and burnt. My Da saw red and blasted, 'For

Chrissakes Roy, who's gonna pay the rent?' Roy stood for a minute in shock and then asked, 'How did you know it was me Marcus?'

You're probably wondering why I'm telling you all this – after all there's not a lot about music – but it's to set the scene of the times and is to highlight that we were all acutely aware of the threatening nature of men wearing combat uniforms. One day when I saw a guy with long jet-black hair, wearing an army jacket and who was not from our street, walking towards me, I felt slightly wary. As he reached me I half expected to get a clip round the ear, or worse, but he just said, 'All right son?' and walked on. When I saw the back of his jacket I burst out laughing. There was no Red Hand of Ulster or paramilitary emblem, as was the fashion of the day. Instead, there big and bold was painted a daisy. Ladies and gentlemen, let me introduce Ken Heaven – one of the most intelligent, funny and talented people I have ever met. Unfortunately, he is also one of the most infuriating.

The events of the Loyalist workers' strike made my Ma and Da's minds up; the family would be better off out of the estate. There was also the fact that there were now five kids and another one on the way – Catholics eh!! Their three-bedroom house was getting smaller by the day. My Da went to college at night and educated himself to a standard whereby he was able to secure a job in the laboratories of the Bass Ireland Brewery on the Glen Road in Belfast. Being a life-long appreciator of the fruit of the hop he was on cloud nine: one of his jobs even entailed him taste-testing the beers for microbiological impurities. As good as this was, it was the salary that the position provided that gave the greatest benefit: the family could move to a five-bedroom, three-storey house in the middle of Holywood Town.

Maybe my memory is rose tinted, but I recall my life on the estate at 15 Abbey Ring as being wonderful fun. There were some truly decent people who lived there; unfortunately there were also gangsters and bullies. Our house was always full of laughter and the music of my Da's bands that would rehearse in our front room. Looking back it strikes me as bizarre that 'The Galway Shawl' and 'The Black Velvet Band' could be rattling the windows while a bonfire right across the street was sitting ready to burn an effigy of the Pope and a Tricolour, but at the time it just seemed normal. Don't get me wrong, there were a few horrors that stick in the mind, like the time a guy was shot right outside our house. A neighbour and lifelong friend, Derek McFarland, braved the bullets to administer first aid and attempted to stem the blood flow. As bad as that was the worst thing to happen to me personally was that following a trip to Germany, my Nan returned with a pair of leather lederhosen. I was made to wear these, camp as Christmas, little garments by my sadistic parents.

The White City was not renowned for its appreciation of other European cultures; the kids couldn't quite believe their luck when the skinny little blond boy from the bottom of the estate took to dressing up like Hansel from the Brothers Grimm fairytale. I don't know if my Ma and Da saw in me the promise of a prosperous career in professional sports, but I'll tell you this for nothing: those tight little shorts and bib, after I got used to the chafing, turned me into one of the fastest runners around. In spite of these mishaps, if you can call attempted murder and a laughing mob chasing a child to the point of exhaustion mishaps, it was with heavy hearts that we left our friends, the Divers, the Crieghtons and especially the McFarlands behind when we relocated to 18 Park Avenue, one and a half miles away.

Heaven and hell

Funnily enough it was only after our family left the estate that Ken Heaven and myself crossed paths on a more regular basis. I had taken to walking around the town carrying a plastic bag with Whitesnake's 'Live in the Heart of the City', AC/DC's 'If You Want Blood' and The Rolling Stones' 'Love You Live' albums contained within. Why, you may ask? Well the reasons were twofold. One, you never knew when you might be in the same room as a stereo that needed rescuing from the Osmonds or some other crap of the era. Secondly, I lived in hope that someone would ask me what I had in the bag, thus giving me the opportunity to show off my superior taste in music; sad really.

I was always slightly in awe of Ken. He was about three years older than me, he was allowed to grow his hair (my parents wouldn't let me) and I had heard he could play the guitar; this gave him God-like status in my eyes. One day, out of the blue, he stopped me in the High Street and asked me what was in my ever-present Stewarts Supermarket shopping bag. I was over the moon. He would now realise I was just like him, a rocker. He took one look at the Whitesnake and Stones albums, declaring them crap; he did however say that the AC/DC album was a gem. I must admit that I was a little deflated by his first comments – I loved those records. But he liked 'If You Want Blood', which meant we were kindred spirits, whether he liked it or not, and consequently we were mates, again, whether he liked it or not. I remember telling my schoolmates later that night that Ken Heaven and myself had been discussing music, and we both agreed that AC/DC's live album was a classic. They couldn't really care less what I and the local hippy thought – they had no interest in Rock music. Their apathy went right over my head: I thought I was the bee's feckin' knees.

Ken was in a band called the Blue Malaysian Rogues with Kevin 'Lado' Morrow on lead vocals, probably one of the most naturally gifted singers the world has ever known. I would put him up there with Paul Rodgers, Glen Hughes, Steve Perry and Stevie Wonder: in short, a genius. Joining these two were Martin 'Specky Beard' MaCaffery on the bass and Davy 'Miss the Cymbal' Kennedy who occupied the drum stool: two really lovely guys but they looked and probably were slightly out of place. When everyone was out, they would rehearse, without permission, in the attic of Lado's parent's house. I couldn't believe my luck when Ken invited me down to one of their secret sessions. I was now hanging out with a band; there must be no cooler feeling in the world, apart from actually being in one, I assumed.

You had to climb up a ladder to get into the attic. Once up I noticed that the place was a mess – to me however, it was heaven on earth. Music could be made here and rock stars nurtured. Before the band had even plugged in they had run into a hitch. Ken didn't have a plectrum; he asked me if I had one. Normally I did, I had taken to messing about with my Da's acoustic guitar, but for some reason, on the very day that I could've impressed, by nonchalantly whipping one from my pocket, I had left the damn thing back in the bloody house. Ken then asked me to run home to get one, adding, 'That is if you really have any.' Was he implying that I might have been lying about having a guitar myself? Which I was of course. 'I'll show the bastard' I thought.

I ran the whole way there and back, like some star-struck teenager, which when you think about it is exactly what I was. This was a chance to gain brownie points with a band for Chrissakes – stuff the O levels, this was a real achievement. On my return I was puzzled to hear the band cranking out a deafening version of Saxon's 'Wheels of Steel'. Could you finger pick a song of such metallic majesty? I didn't think so. Climbing back up the ladder, I started to get the feeling that I had been had. When I poked my head through the trapdoor, Ken held up a plectrum and smiled. I swore I would get my own back; I wouldn't let this happen again. I may have been younger than them but I was not thick. As Ian Hunter of Mott the Hoople wrote: 'Once bitten twice shy'.

I hid my embarrassment by turning the colour of a baboon's arse and settled down in the corner to watch the band in silent wonder. In retrospect they were actually terrible. Lado was a star and Ken was good but rough around the edges. The rhythm section, however, were absolutely horrendous: I got the feeling that they really didn't love Rock music the way they should have. But at that time I didn't care about the quality of their musicianship; they were playing music, therefore they were blessed. The band took a break after three songs. I thought that it was to smoke cigarettes and drink bottles of Irish stout, because that's actually what they did. However what I didn't know, at the time, was that they only knew that number of songs. Their policy was to rest after playing them once through. Obviously trying to tighten them up by repeated playing would have been too tiring; there was definitely no Protestant work ethic going on here folks.

As they conserved their energies, all talk was of their first gig, which was to be held in the local High School youth club. The plan was to bulk out their meagre repertoire by playing 'Hey Joe' about five times longer than it normally takes. Now that the problem of lack of material was sorted out, they could return to smoking and drinking – no need to waste valuable sweat trying to learn a few more songs.

While they had been sitting around doing nothing, Lado's Da, Big Harry, had come home from work early with a headache and retired to his bed, which was situated just below where the band were planning how to con the public. A couple more fags and few more bottles of Guinness later and they were ready to get back to some good old-fashioned hard work. Below their feet the big man, and local police sergeant, dragged his sore head into a fitful sleep.

Back in the attic the band thundered into 'Wishing Well'. This was at the height of the so-called 'Troubles', and being a police officer was a risky business to say the least. The sound that caused his rude awakening must have resembled a bomb going off: this was almost verified when the weakened plaster above his bed decided that it had had enough of the violent vibrations caused by the ridiculous volume rattling through the rafters, and loosened its grip. The ceiling came crashing down onto the migraine-addled head of Sergeant Morrow.

The trapdoor opened and Paul Rodgers' pro-peace lyrics – 'throw down your gun you might shoot yourself' – now had the added line of 'Shit, there's ma Da!' thrown in. Lado, on seeing his father's dust-encrusted head, decided to increase the blood supply to his vital organs, a classic response by the body to a threat, when all non-essential blood is drawn to where it is of most use. The colour drained from the singer's face. The air was filled with expletives that would've made a Tourette's sufferer blush. The Mighty Rogues lost their rehearsal space and were lucky not to lose a few teeth into the bargain – the big man was not happy.

With the gig being only a week away, to say they were under-rehearsed would've been an understatement, but they were young and cocky so really there was no problem. That is until they were told, on the night, that they would be expected to play for an hour. Three songs do not sixty minutes make – even Hendrix wouldn't have had the gall to drag 'Hey Joe' out to fifty minutes. There was however a solution at hand: Ken had the brainwave of playing 'Free-bird', the rebel anthem of the gods of southern rock Lynyrd Skynyrd.

Following Ken's suggestion there was a stunned silence from the rhythm section. Specky Beard revealed that neither he nor Miss the Cymbal had ever heard the song; I knew they weren't true rock fans. Ken reasoned that this wouldn't be a problem, they would just watch his hands for the chord changes in the slow bit (music theory anyone?), and then they could just rock out for the final mighty lead break – another hitch successfully analysed and sorted. I must admit that I had my misgivings, the song had numerous twists and turns that were integral to the flow of the finale, but these guys were a band – they obviously knew what they were doing.

The first three songs went pretty well, Lado and Ken shining, the other two making heavy work of it. But then it was time for the Skynyrd classic. I held my breath; could they really pull this off? Well no actually they couldn't. The start was a shambles; Specky was unable to see Ken's hands because he had taken his substantially thick glasses off in a failed attempt to look cooler on stage. He faffed about with whatever notes came into his head. The drummer kept changing the rhythm and tempo insanely trying to stay apace of Specky's jazz noodlings. I have never heard, and never want to hear again, this classic song played Reggae and Bosa Nova style at the same time. There was a further problem; Lado had neglected to tell anyone that he didn't know the words; so to cover his lyrical short-comings he took to mumbling like a drunken Elvis. Those in attendance, who were friends, relatives, the kids that frequented the club and the youth leaders (who were all Christians) were confused, appalled, frightened and in one poor child's case, sick.

There was worse to come. Ken announced the start of the lead break by jumping in the air and shouting '1,2,3,4!' The rhythm section charged into a cacophony of noise that had neither rhyme nor reason. Lado staggered off the stage, glad that his participation in the whole debacle was over. Ken went on to play the whole 'One More from the Road' twenty-minute version of the song note for note. Its excellence was lost to the public however due to the abomination that was going on behind him. The guitar hero was undeterred, rounding off the proceedings by playing the guitar with his teeth, and then he tried to smash his axe over a pool table.

The robust six-string stayed intact. The games table however collapsed, much to the horror and disgust of the Holy Joes, one of whom tried to throw a punch at Ken (let him that is without sin and all that). After the second attempt the guitar finally gave up the ghost and disintegrated on the floor of the stage, accompanied by a wall of feedback. Ken 'The Fastest' Heaven walked off stage to the open-mouthed astonishment of those that bore witness. It was one of the worst spectacles and noises I had ever encountered but I loved every single abominable second of it. 'This is what I am going to do with my life,' I said to myself while bending down to pick up the scratch plate from the matchwood that was now Ken's guitar. It would hang on my wall for years to come.

I told my Ma and Da, the next morning, that I wanted an electric guitar for Christmas. My Da, being a musician, was delighted; his acoustic would be left alone. My Ma, who was not a musician but married to one, was horrified. We weren't well off financially but we were rich as far as love was concerned. It must have been an economic strain when on Christmas morning I was greeted with a Hondo 2 Les Paul copy and a Vox AC 30 amp. Up to this point it was the best present I had ever received. I still have the guitar; the amp, however, blew up due to excessive volume only a few months into the New Year. Matchetts music shop would see my Da on a monthly basis for the next couple of years as he paid off the hire purchase agreement.

I struggled to learn the instrument; I was never a natural the way Ken was. My Da must have been frustrated, him being a natural too, but I persevered and got reasonably good. Good enough, I thought, to make a recording. I persuaded my cousin, Martin Tolan, who was staying with us one summer, to play the bass line of 'Smoke on the Water' on the low strings of my Da's acoustic, while I hammered out the guitar parts and sang. A microphone from the one-speaker recorder was fixed to the handle of a stand-up Hoover with sticky tape. To get down low enough to sing into it I had to spread my legs to the point where I nearly gave myself an inguinal hernia.

Over and over the song was played, but each effort was spoiled by a mistake. After about fifteen attempts we were finally reaching the end of the song, without a hitch, and it looked like we were going to commit our art to tape. As the last chorus began my brother Mark, who was about four at the time, and my Granny, who was about seventy-four, walked in through the door to inform us that our lunch was ready. Over the racket they were told in no uncertain terms to clear off. Seeing as it was the closest we had actually got to completing the song, and because we were starving, it remained the final cut. My cousin says he has a copy of the tape somewhere and on occasion he threatens to unleash it on an unsuspecting and uninterested public. I don't think he really has the offending item, he just wants to scare me, but there is the odd night in the early hours when the ghosts of guilty secrets return to haunt me that I can almost hear the words 'Smoke on the water' ... 'Your beans on toast are ready!'... 'a fire in the sky'. Please don't let that tape exist.

The Rogues only played one more gig before splitting: it was at the Savoy Hotel in Bangor. Again it was brilliantly shambolic and I loved it. There was, however, one sickening incident. I had left my 'cut off' denim jacket, the back of which had just been freshly painted with the cover of Whitesnake's 'Lovehunter' album, in the band's changing room. To my horror 'Specky' came walking out on stage wearing it; even scarier he was bare-chested below. Here was a man who would sweat if he sneezed, so I was not best pleased when it was handed back to me in a state that would have been drier if he had walked through a monsoon. The artwork, which was supposed to depict a naked woman straddling a snake, now looked like a big pink jelly baby sitting on an anaemic, undercooked sausage. My Ma preferred it, and the parish priest had an extra half hour to himself each week, knowing that he no longer had to pray for my soul.

Holywood's Mick and Keef

Now that the Rogues were no more (musical differences were cited – two could play music, two couldn't), Ken was at a loose end and obviously desperate. He knew that I had recently come into possession of an electric guitar and that I played a bit of rhythm, so he invited me to form a band with him. This heralded the birth of 'Captain Scarlet and the Pink Malaysian Rogues', one of the most unfortunate things to ever happen to the world of the arts. I was over the moon, proudly telling everyone who would listen, which let's face it was really only my family. Ken said we could jam in his bedroom. His plan, he said, was to get a set together before we recruited other members. With hindsight, I now realise it was just an excuse to get me to strum rhythm parts while he played lead breaks over the top.

Ken's house was about a mile and a half from mine and I carried my guitar and amp the whole way. I was so excited, the fact that my arms were now an inch longer than they had been and aching like I had done a hundred press-ups, caused me no concern at all. On arrival at the house I was shown into the front room by his mum, Kay, a stunner in her day. She told me that Ken was upstairs and would be with me in a minute. I could hear an argument going on hot and heavy and I knew one of the voices was Ken's; I just assumed that he would be down when things had calmed down. His mum and dad – 'Big Sid', a true gent – were sharing a bottle of QC Sherry, which they warmed by the open fire. They kindly offered me a swig. I refused: I was not eighteen yet and didn't want my chance of being in a band with Ken scuppered by arriving home smelling of fortified grape juice.

When the fight upstairs had finished, I patiently awaited the arrival of 'Captain Scarlet' himself. While doing so I couldn't help but notice that the family's black Labrador, Darkie, was sitting on top of the TV. It was watching the screen by leaning forward and looking down through its front legs. In our house we had never had the ingenious idea of using our pets as ornaments. I asked why the dog was up there, but as the final words of the question slipped from my lips I realised that I didn't really want to know.

Ken's brother Harry, I was told, would order the poor animal up there, in an attempt to entertain, mesmerise and shock visitors. Barnum and Bailey he was not. Unfortunately for the poor mutt, Harry would sometimes forget to get him back down before going out for the night, and the dog, who only obeyed his master, would dutifully stay put, growling at anyone who tried to move him. Sometimes it would be the early hours of the morning before Harry returned, usually after everyone had gone to bed. I couldn't help but think that if a burglar had broken in with the intention of nicking the telly he would be in for one hell of a surprise. The blasé way that the whole situation was accepted and explained to me, made me come to a decision that I should ask no more questions: I knew not what I might hear. I had a feeling that there were adventures and stories to be told about this household and I was proved right over the next few years.

I sat silent as the minutes and then hours passed. After about two hours, with nobody taking me, or the dog, under their notice – the latter I thought was quite difficult seeing as the animal was sitting legs akimbo and on occasion would decide that it was bath time, making sure that its lipstick was well cleaned if you know what I mean – I plucked up the courage to ask the whereabouts of my lead guitar player. Sid shouted up the stairs. When there was no answer he called his daughter Susan, whom I assumed was the one Ken had had the fight with and asked her where Ken was. She came down and announced that following their disagreement her brother had packed his bags and left home. 'There you go,' his Dad said, 'he's gone,' and that was that, first rehearsal over. I bid the Heavens a fond farewell and carried my guitar and amp all the way home without striking a note. This time the pain was excruciating and the next day I was able to tie my laces without bending down.

Despite that first disastrous attempt at rehearsing Ken and I became very close friends; in fact for many years we were inseparable. We would spend many nights consuming under-age bottles of Strongbow and discussing what life was going to be like when we became rich and famous. One night following a drink or two Ken invited me back to his house for a bite to eat. Being 2am it was way too early to go home so I accepted his gracious offer. The chip pan was put on and the frying pan was laden heavy with sausages and bacon. I buttered a few slices of bread and settled down in anticipation of a meal that would lie heavy in the stomach, as all meals at that time of the night/day should.

Ken asked me if I wanted a fried egg. Never one to pass up an opportunity to dunk a chip, again I accepted. When the food was set down in front of me I noticed that Ken didn't have an egg on his plate. 'You not having one?' I asked pointing to mine.

'No,' he said. 'We only had one left and as a guest it was only good manners to offer it to you.' Very civil, I thought, but there was a smirk on his face that didn't sit easy with me. The feeling however didn't last long and I got stuck into the gastronomic delight – it was just what the doctor hadn't ordered.

Halfway through the fat feast the back door opened and in walked a guy I had never seen before. 'This is my brother Harry,' Ken announced.

I stood up, transferred some of the grease from my hands onto my jeans and said, 'Pleased to meet you.' I held out my right mit to be shaken, as is the done thing when gentlemen are being introduced. The gesture, however, was totally ignored. I then heard the question 'Is that my egg?' slur from his moustachioed mouth. I said, 'I don't quite know what you mean.'

His gaze never left my plate. 'I wasn't talkin' to you numb nuts, I was talkin' to him,' he said pointing to his younger brother.

'What are you worried about? Sure you have a carryout,' Ken said nodding at the Chinese takeaway in Harry's hand.

'You knew I was saving it for my breakfast you dickhead,' Harry shouted.

And so the debate carried on, back and forth, one witty riposte countered by another, until Ken reached the zenith of his argument with, 'Was your name on it?'

'*What*?' screamed Harry, starting to get a tad agitated.

Ken was on a roll. 'When the chicken laid that egg did it have Harry Heaven, Oakley Avenue, Holywood printed on it?' He went on, 'Was it then whisked off, post-haste, by RAF helicopter to be deposited in our fridge to await your chosen moment of consumption?'

Harry's face went a sort of purple colour; he turned around and opened the doors of a cupboard which was attached to the wall. I thought he was looking for something within. I guess I was mistaken, because the next thing I knew he had ripped the doors from their hinges, opened the back door and thrown them into the garden.

I must admit that at this point I was a little bit frightened. I had never seen a confrontation settled by inanimate objects being torn asunder. I couldn't help thinking that, seeing as it was me that had been responsible for eating the feckin' egg in the first place, that there might be bits of me ripped off and thrown out to join the cupboard doors. A cold sweat broke on me when I reasoned that the severed items may well be my, what did Harry call them? Oh yes, 'numb nuts'.

Following the rather unorthodox bout of DIY Harry calmed down immediately; the carnage must have acted like a pressure release valve. He turned around and offered his hand saying, 'Sorry about that kid but I was really lookin' forward to that egg.'

I said, 'No, I'm sorry, I didn't know it was yours.' As I was speaking I was thinking, 'Ken, you git, you knew all along this was going to happen.' I had been done up like a kipper again.

Harry then asked, while still shaking my hand, 'Did you feed Darkie?'

I said, 'Sorry, I don't quite know what you mean,' to which he responded, 'Not you numb nuts, I was talking to him.' There was a feeling of déjà vu.

Ken asked, 'Why should I feed him? He's your dog.' And so it started again. As violent and upsetting as the climax of their last argument was, it was nothing compared to what was to follow.

After about ten minutes, Harry realised that this argument was un-winnable. He didn't have the intellect to challenge someone with Ken's wit, and his attention returned to the now door-less cupboard. I thought he was going to rip the whole thing off the wall, but no, he reached in and took about five slices of bread from a bag, he then rolled them into a ball. What happened next seemed to occur in slow motion. Harry walked over to the recently used chip pan and, in an attempt to moisten the bread for the poor dog, he plunged his hand into the still bubbling fat. There was a sickening sizzle, closely followed by a blood curdling scream and shortly after that the smell of frying human flesh. For some reason I started to feel a little queasy.

Harry stood running his rapidly swelling, blistering hand under the cold tap. I marvelled at the fact that he was not shedding a tear; if it had been me I would've been wailing like a baby. I told him that he needed to see a doctor. None of us could drive so it was suggested that we call an ambulance. Unfortunately the phone was not working, so myself and Ken ran next door. Luckily they were already up – something to do with furniture being smashed, shouting, hair-raising screams and the smell of somebody cooking pork or something, coming from the Heavens' house. There was an air of resignation from the poor unfortunates huddled in their nightwear, like this had not been the first time that they had seen the sun rise due to a disturbance from next door.

We phoned 999 and ran back to let Harry know assistance was on its way. I was fully expecting to see him crumpled on the floor in agony, but what I was greeted with was the sight of him sitting in an armchair, watching a video, his frazzled hand in a saucepan of cold water, while he was feeding himself chicken chow mien with his good hand. I made a mental note never to cross this man again; he was obviously made of sterner stuff than me. I also swore never to accept anything to eat from Ken unless I was sure there was more than one of them in the fridge. Sleep didn't come that night/morning: it could have been the drink, it could have been the gut busting food, but I think it was the image of a man deep-fat-frying his own hand that appeared every time I closed my eyes.

Underwear under where?

As mates you get to know things about people, sometimes too much. Like most young men Ken was very proud of his sexual appendage and on the few unfortunate occasions that I saw it, I would have to say that he had more reason for pride than most. He would refrain from wearing underwear, he says for comfort, I say to show off or advertise. He would inform anyone who would listen, that being of ample proportions made him very popular with the ladies. This I found puzzling, as there never seemed to be that many offers that came his way. Well, there was one, of sorts.

He was once playing the fruit machine at the local roller disco, when the town gay, Brendan, came over and said, 'Hold your plums.' Ken was convinced that this was an offer made to his 'invitation to treat'. I on the other hand thought that it was a tactical instruction concerning the state of play on the one-armed bandit. I pointed out that Brendan may have been advising him that he would be in a better position to beat the laws of probability if he put the purple pieces of fruit depicted on the spinning wheels on hold. Ken actually seemed a little disappointed when the penny finally dropped; attention after all is attention no matter where it comes from.

One of the drawbacks of not wearing underwear is that after going to the toilet there is the tendency to have the odd dribble, which to be honest is the last thing a young man, who is obviously proud of his physical appearance, in that department at least, wants. I mean there is nothing sexy about resembling a seventy-year-old man with a weak bladder and restrictively enlarged prostate; damp patches near the groin area are not a good look. Ken came up with an ingenious solution.

Dear reader I have agonised over how I should describe this next piece and I have come to the conclusion that I must bite the bullet and just get on with it – anyone with a weak stomach fast forward to the next paragraph. His technique was to roll back his foreskin, wrap a piece of toilet paper around the tip and roll the wrinkled flesh back again; if toilet paper were not available he would improvise. In a blind moment of lunacy Ken even contemplated getting a patent for his creation; he thought that there must be millions of men around the world who had thrown away the restrictive undergarments that society dictates decent gentleman wear. He even got as far as giving the product a name. I would have loved to have been in Her Majesty's registration of names and copyright office, when the application came in for 'Knob Roll®'.

At times Ken's unique form of sanitary brief would get him in a spot of bother. On one such occasion, when he had cause to visit the doctor, I don't know why, I didn't ask and I have no desire to ever know, he was asked to drop his trousers. Following the unveiling, the doctor exclaimed 'Jesus Christ!!' Ken, thinking he was shocked by the length and girth said, 'I know, it is quite impressive isn't it?' The doctor then shouted, 'It's not the size you idiot, it's the colour.' Ken looked down and seeing what he was referring to offered the hapless medic the comforting explanation that it was not anything serious – it was only a green bookies' docket poking out. At least we can take small consolation in that the horse didn't come in. I would have pitied the poor bookie that had to accept the soggy documentation, which would have needed to be peeled away in order for Ken to collect his winnings.

Crash in the attic

As Ken was a couple of years older than me he was able to frequent the bars of Holywood long before I could. Charitably he would accompany me for a few drinks 'down the shore' (as the beach in Holywood was known), no matter what the weather. Later I would stand like a faithful puppy dog, outside whichever hostelry he decided to use. I would remain there until closing time or Ken's money ran out, whichever came first, then we would seek entertainment wherever we could.

If the weather was very good we would forget about the pubs altogether and just stay down the shore. One such night saw all of Ken's family join us, including his parents who were in their late fifties.

The end of the drunken night, or should I say morning, saw us playing leap-frog. Ken's dad tried to jump over his mum; he failed, hitting the ground with a sickening crack. A couple of days later, after walking around on it, the pain in his leg caused Sid to attend A&E, where he was found to have a fractured tib and fib. He was promptly put into a full leg cast, given super-strength painkillers and told not to weight-bear.

It was Sunday however, so he went straight from the hospital to the Holywood Social Club where he joined myself (it was one of the only places that I could get into being under-age as they didn't know how old I was), Ken, his brothers Harry and Trevor and their brother-in-law, John. Sid washed down the painkillers with copious amounts of Mackeson's milk stout. Ken and I stayed until we had no money left, which was not very long, and went to my house for something to eat before Ken headed home.

On his arrival home Ken discovered an empty home, something that rarely happened in the Heaven household. He decided to make the most of it and settled down with a cup of tea and the racing pages of the *Daily Mirror*. While he was picking out the winners that were going to lose him all his money, he heard a noise that seemed to come from upstairs. He called up to see who he had missed when he came in. There was no answer, so he climbed the stairs and looked around the rooms; there was still no sign of anyone.

Around that time there was a rather disturbing trend on the estate, where the local hoods would break into empty houses, climb into the attic with a hammer and chisel then knock a hole through the wall. They would then climb into the roof space of the occupied house next door, wait for everyone to leave, and then rob them blind. Quite ingenious really – it's a pity the little scumbags hadn't used their brains for something constructive. But hey, it was an easy way of terrorising the local community, getting drug money and then handing it over to the paramilitary drug lords, who would use their ill-gotten gains to move out of the area into a plush house in the suburbs. The thieving kids were left with drug habits and the residents, who couldn't just pack up and leave, were left frightened and broke.

The noise did indeed seem to be coming from the attic; Ken thought to himself that these hoods must have been extraordinarily thicker than usual, because the Heavens' house was not one that any sane human being would rob, well not unless they wanted to keep their windpipe that is. Ken ran downstairs and picked up the poker from the fireplace before running back up again. As he reached the landing he heard his mum and sister coming in. He shouted down to them, in a voice that could easily be heard by the toerags above, 'Phone the police!' and in an equally loud voice his mum shouted, 'I can't, they cut us off over a week ago.' With the thieves now painfully aware that the cops wouldn't be joining the party there was only one thing for Ken to do. He would just have to take the law into his own hands.

Ken shouted, 'Come down you rascals and offer yourselves up to a beating you so richly deserve' or some other phrase with perhaps a little more swearing involved. There was no response, so he started to shout again but was cut off mid-sentence by a dragging sound accompanied by guttural groaning. Just then the trapdoor started to open. Ken braced himself, raised the poker above his head. These boys were going to be very sorry that they chose this house to thieve from, he thought.

The door opened to its full aperture, and something started to come through. Ken swung the poker, more through reflex than anything else. Just as he was about to make contact, something triggered in his head to pull back. The heavy, turned metal weapon whizzed just inches past a white object that looked vaguely familiar. As Ken was following through he realised, to his horror, that the object was a plaster of Paris.

A full leg cast emerged from the sky and then the ashen face of Big Sid peered down from between his legs. Ken, his mother and sister struggled to help their father out of the attic. He emerged mumbling gibberish about waking up, finding himself dead. The poor man, when quizzed about what he meant, said he thought he had been in hell because there had been no light and it was boiling hot. He went on that he had found himself lying on a surface that offered no source of comfort; each movement encountered ever more four-foot gaps with only a couple of inch slats to rest his head and lower limbs. If that was not bad enough there were violent voices screaming that they were going to perpetrate violence upon his person. Then out of the pitch black there came a crack of light.

Sid reasoned that it was obviously the Lord Jesus guiding him away from Hades to a place that offered a sanctuary from the eternal damnation that he was destined for. He summoned up the last ounce of strength that was left within his battered body and mind. He dragged himself over peak and trough until he reached the light, he grabbed at it with such force that his fingernails were nearly ripped from their beds; it was his last-gasp attempt to save his soul.

The head of the house was put to bed where he slipped into a sleep filled with horrible visions. When the rest of the family returned from the club they were told of the incredible strength that their father had displayed, in dragging himself up the walls of the landing and into the attic. Not only was this extraordinary, in light of his age and heart condition, but it was all achieved with multiple fractures and no ladder. The story was greeted, not with astonished silence, as it should have been, but with gales of laughter.

When Ken asked why his brothers found the idea of their invalid father traversing the landing walls in a leg cast, being imprisoned within a cell of horror-movie proportions and inflicting numerous cuts and abrasions upon himself so funny, he was told that his dad had actually passed out in the club after consuming a fair few stouts and handfuls of analgesics. A taxi was called; Harry and Trevor accompanied him home. As they carried their helpless father up the path to the front door a fiendish plan developed. The two sons decided that it would be hilarious to drag their beloved pater up into the roof space, leave him there alone to wake up, believe he had died and gone to hell, and thus become the source of great merriment for many years to come. Thank Christ they loved him, and believe me they really did, but God knows what would have happened if they had hated him. The boys had actually toyed with the idea of removing the cast and putting it on his good leg; we can only be grateful that common sense, if you can use such a phrase in this instance, prevailed.

A man called Fish

Roughly around the same time that I was being corrupted by the influence of Ken Heaven I was becoming friendly with a kid who lived in our street. We were at number 18, he lived in number 10. His

name was Andrew Fisher; he was also known by a variety of nicknames including Fishy, Berty, The Fishmeister or as I have always
called him, just Fish. While I was tall, blond and as skinny as a rake,
sounds good but really I was a drip, he was short dark haired, and a
little on the heavy side. His hair was sort of down to his collar and
cut in a bowl style; he looked like a chubby Johnny Ramone. I don't
think we hit it off straight away but when we did it was a friendship
that was destined to last.

Fish was very keen on motorbikes, cars and all things mechanical,
something he inherited from his father who was a genius when it
came to engines and tinkering. I on the other hand hated the idea of
taking the skin off my knuckles while trying to tighten a nut on the
ice-cold, hard metal bits of a battered old Robin Reliant. I preferred
to kick a football around a freezing pitch and have two of my teeth
broken by the studs of a flying boot. Fish hated soccer, and all sports
for that matter, which is why it came as such a shock when many
years later he started playing for the Holywood Rugby Club. I think
the social life and a subsidised bar may have played an important
role in his decision to eventually break a sweat.

As you are beginning to see, Fish and myself didn't have that
many things in common; we would argue over differences of
opinion, and still do to this day. Subjects that would get us hot under
the collar were fox hunting, the role of the military and class structure, or specifically the royal family, all of which Fish is an enthusiast
of and I oppose with equal vigour. The fact that we both came from
opposite sides of the, so called, political/religious divide may have
nurtured these differences but we always agreed to disagree and
these issues never came between us – well we never came to blows,
let's just put it that way.

Anyway let's get back to the subject of bikes; Fish had a very small
blue moped-type thing that he would ride up and down the alley that
ran along the back of our houses. One Saturday afternoon he
persuaded me to take a spin on the contraption; he told me it would
be a piece of cake as there were no gears to worry about. I reluctantly
got on to the 'midget of death' and following Fish's detailed instructions of 'Just turn that thing on the handlebar and you'll move
forward,' I set out on my journey towards the top of the alley and
our hedge. Fish had been very open about the lack of gears but less

so about the lack of brakes. He was also slightly remiss in not telling me that to stop I had to return the throttle, for that is what that thing on the handlebar was called, to its original position. Furthermore and probably the most dangerous of his omissions, he neglected to tell me that when the throttle was fully opened up it stuck. I did, however, find this out for myself, as did my Da who was digging up the vegetable patch in our back garden.

I was launched into the air when I hit a plank that sat along the herbaceous border at the foot of our hedge. I flew through the thickets just missing the auld lad's head by inches. I lay in the garden, with the bike still running beside me, my Da enquiring as to my wellbeing by using foul and abusive language, clutching his chest, and turning grey.

Money was very tight at home. There were six kids to feed and clothe and a mortgage to pay, and as a consequence my Ma and Da never went out. As chance would have it, that very night was the first time in many years that they were going to spend an evening away from the madness that was our household. I was made to promise that I wouldn't get on that 'bloody thing' again, which of course I swore to and then, thanks to more encouragement from Fish, I did exactly the opposite.

I travelled up and down the alley getting used to the rather unorthodox workings of 'Old Blue'. As my confidence rose, familiarity bred contempt and I got the throttle stuck again, and again I hurtled towards our already damaged hedge. I thought, I can't go through it again, my Da would kill me, so I tried to avoid death at the hands of my father by attempting to do it myself. I took a sharp left and crashed into the wall that ran the length of the alley. I was dragged along its jutting stones taking a fair proportion of the skin off my right arm and the side of my face, before being thrown to the ground. I watched the now riderless bike career off and finally stop by colliding with a neighbour's garage.

Fish came running up the alley. I stupidly thought he was coming to my aid; however he stopped somewhat short of my battered and bleeding body. Looking down at his lifeless pride and joy, and the instrument of my near-death experience, he turned and shouted with a tear in his eye, 'Look what you've done to my fecking bike.' Thank God it was his brother who became the paramedic, that's all I can say. I struggled to my feet and I think I even issued an apology before nearly passing out.

We had, that night, babysitting for us a teenage neighbour, and I knew that if I didn't tidy myself up that my misdemeanour would be her first topic of conversation on my parents' return. To avoid this I asked Fish to get me something to clean up the mess. The blood loss was quite substantial so I was hoping for a couple of towels or something to stop the bleeding and make me look a little less like someone who works in an abattoir. My mate returned carrying three squares of toilet paper, explaining that he didn't want his parents to know about the incident either, so blood-stained towels were a no-no. He also said that he couldn't afford anymore bog roll, there was very little left and his brother and father had not made their evening pilgrimage to the loo yet, which was a clean up job of mammoth proportions in itself.

I did as best I could with the materials provided, which let's face it was not going to be much of a job, then returned home to face the music. The babysitter nearly crapped herself when I walked through the door: understandably she thought that because she was looking after us, she would get the blame. She needn't have worried. My parents, having spent many years in my company, knew me rather well at this stage and knew exactly where the blame lay. Thankfully rescue from the wrath of the Ma and Da was at hand in the shape of my sister Elish who, after reassuring me that her Brownie training included first aid, proceeded to dress my arm.

The next morning, having confirmed the babysitter's prediction that I wouldn't die in my sleep, I was summoned to the parental boudoir by means of a, 'Get down here right this minute.' When I entered the room I could feel a sense of relief from my Ma that I didn't resemble Boris Karloff in 'The Mummy': the facial wounds were only superficial. The arm on the other hand, if you'll pardon the expression, was a different matter altogether; it was bandaged from wrist to the oxter with an adhesive surgical tape. 'Let me take a look at that,' says the Ma. 'Who put this on?' she enquired, her expression becoming slightly distressed. 'I did,' said Elish, with a sense of pride. She had followed me into the room, as had the rest of the siblings, probably in the hope that I was going to get a bollocking. 'What did you put on under this tape?' was my

Ma's next question, to which the reply nearly had her in tears.

My highly medically trained sister had put dressing tape straight onto the raw flesh of my arm. The options now were to remove it inch by inch slowly, to try and do as little damage as possible, or rip the thing off quickly so as not to prolong the agony. The latter option was taken and to this day I believe my parents chose the wrong one. I think there was more damage caused by the dressing than from the high-speed collision with the wall. I can also confirm that the crash was less painful and a damn sight less traumatic.

Strange bedfellows.

When I said previously that Fish and myself had little in common, there was one love we did share and that was Rock music. My interest went beyond just listening and going to gigs, remember I was going to be a rock star. Fish, on the other hand was content to increase his record collection and watch from the sidelines. Going to gigs was something we really looked forward to; one that we had eagerly anticipated was to be by Fermanagh band Mamas Boys. We had all their albums and knew the words to all their songs. On the big night Elish, her friend Bronagh and myself met up in Fish's house to consume a couple of bottles of cider and get in the mood. Fish was the only one who was over eighteen at the time, so he purchased the liquor; his mum turned a blind eye to the under-age drinkers under her roof. God bless her.

The Fishers had a rather energetic springer spaniel called Ringo who took great pleasure in jumping all over anyone that came into the house. That night Elish was paranoid about a white pair of trousers she was wearing for the special occasion. She kept screaming at Fish to 'Get the dog down!' whenever it came within a mile of her. Ringo must have felt slightly aggrieved at the suggestion that he was somewhat unclean, but he decided that he would bide his time to make a protest. Just before we were about to leave Elish leaned over the side of the chair to retrieve her coat. She mustn't have been paying enough attention to our canine friend because Ringo was able to sneak up to her, turn himself around and wipe his arse the full length of her shin. There was a skid mark thicker and darker than any that you would find on the starting grid at Donnington Park.

The screams from the owner of the trousers were drowned out by the laughter of those who had been privy to the scene.

The gig, which was at the Ulster Hall, was fantastic. Pat 'The Professor' McManus was on fine form with the old fiddle. On a sad note, as we left for home, dripping in sweat, few of us would have thought that it was going to be the last time that we would see Tommy behind the kit – he would succumb to leukaemia a few years later.

I can't remember how we got back but we did. Where Elish and Bronagh had stopped drinking after the shitty trouser incident, Fish and myself carried on. So while they were sober enough to go back to our house I was not. This meant that Elish would have to tell my Ma and Da that I was over at Fish's house, having a cup of tea, and would probably stay the night there, leaving my bed free for Bronagh, the fine gentleman that I was.

When confronted with the prospect of sharing a single bed with my large, bearded, sweaty friend, for that is what I was informed I would have to do, I nearly changed my mind. But this would have meant me facing the wrath of my Catholic, 'No drink before you're eighteen', parents. I normally sleep in the nude but that night, for fear of our buttocks, or worse, touching in our sleep, I elected to keep my boxers on. After the first few initial embarrassing minutes were over, drink dragged sleep to my weary eyes.

I woke with a breath on the back of my neck; I just ignored it reasoning that Fish had turned around in his sleep. What happened next I couldn't ignore. The breathing quickened and I could feel him licking the back of my ear. 'Pretend you're asleep,' I told myself, 'maybe he'll get bored.' I was wracking my brain to try and remember any time in the past when my long-time friend had shown any signs of homosexuality. I couldn't think of any, in fact, we spent an awful lot of our time discussing the local girls and their attributes. What had brought this on after all this time? Was it similar to the stories you hear about prisoners starved of female company, which we both had been at that time, resorting to a little male entertainment to relieve frustrations? I mean I wouldn't consider myself really ugly but my God, if you were going to experience your first gay tussle wouldn't you want it to be with someone a bit more pleasing on the eye? Better still wouldn't you want it to be with someone with the same sexual proclivities? To my relief the ear licking arousal attempt stopped.

My respite, however, was short lived; to my horror things took a turn for the worse. I could now feel Fish's tongue running along the waistband of my monks, lingering for a second on an inch of arse crack. His beard was tickling to the point of torture. This I'm afraid, was way too much; the forbidden valley was out of bounds to friend or foe. I jumped from the bed shouting, 'What the feck are you playing at?' As I spun round I could just make out, in the gloom, the startled figure of my bedfellow sitting bolt upright rubbing the sleep from his eyes. Just then the cowering figure of the dog emerged from under the bedclothes at the bottom of the bed.

With my nerves in tatters, I decided that whatever my parents could deal out by way of punishment, was nowhere near the torture that my imagination had inflicted on my fragile mind. I went home for a tongue lashing of an altogether different kind and an uncomfortable, sleepless night on the sofa.

We're walking in the air . . .

My parents must have trusted Fish because they didn't bat an eyelid when I suggested that he be the one to teach me to drive. I think my Da was just glad he had been let off the hook, as there had been a few hair- and voice-raising experiences on the odd occasions that he had tried to prepare me for a future behind the wheel. It was winter 1982 and I was seventeen. That year there had been very heavy snowfall, so much in fact, that some of the local kids had made a massive snowman in the middle of the road, not far from our houses. The arctic conditions had curtailed my driving adventures so when the weather started to warm I was glad to see the back of it. Fish and myself could now get back to using up my Da's petrol in the pursuit of girls, especially those residing in the seaside town of Bangor.

My Da had a Datsun Stanza at the time. It was relatively new so it looked quite good, except of course for the L-plates. One night, following the usual unsuccessful attempt to chat up some 'women' at a sea-front car park, we headed back home. As I was driving past Fish's house towards ours, I spotted the snowman, still alive and well and not yet melted. A funny thought entered my mind – wouldn't it be an absolute hoot to drive through him sending a massive puff of snow into the air? 'Wait till you see this,' I said to Fish as I picked up speed and changed direction. I was now on a collision course with Old Frosty. 'What the feck are you doing?' I heard Fish shout and for a moment I was genuinely startled by his obvious panic, but adrenalin blocked sane thoughts from my brain and I stupidly ignored his high-pitched screams.

We hit the browning mass of snow at about 40mph; unfortunately it was no longer of the consistency that it had fallen from the skies – it was now a solid wall of concrete-hard ice. Both of us were thrown forward, resembling those dummies you see doing crash testing. If it hadn't been for the seat belts we would've both gone through the windscreen and would've had to use our faces to slow our progress along the tarmac.

Now at a stop and forgetting to check in the rear view mirror before engaging the handbrake, I looked at Fish, who was as white as a sheet, and said, 'Holy shit, my Da's gonna kill me.' 'Not if I do it first,' was the slightly unprofessional response from my unqualified instructor. I got out to inspect the damage and found that it was worse than I could've possibly imagined. The whole front of the car had caved in – all the ice from the snowman's body was packed solid underneath. The decapitated head, with its carrot nose, coal eyes and twig mouth was sitting heavily in a massive dent on the bonnet.

My Da, for some reason, didn't see the funny side of the story: his new car had been written off after all. In short he went ballistic. I turned to get a slither of support from Fish but he was noticeable by his absence, and you know what, I don't blame him for one second.

Van the Man

One summer's evening I returned from school to be informed by my Da that Van Morrison had been on the phone and that he wanted to meet up in the Culloden Hotel to relive old times. Normally I was greeted with, 'Get your uniform off, peel the spuds and scrape the clinker out of the central heating boiler', not with the news that there had been a world-renowned singer/songwriting genius, who I idolised, on the blower. 'Do you want to come along?' the auld lad asks. 'Can I bring Ken?' I asks. My Da had a massive soft spot for my mate, mainly because he was a genius on the guitar, so he says, 'Yeah, I suppose so.'

Ken wasn't at home when we called so I begged my Da to drive around the town until we found him. Ken was working at the time in the Kinegar, a strange little enclave of Holywood that was separated from the rest of the town by Belfast Lough and the railway track that links Belfast to Bangor. It's sort of like a down-market Monaco, a principality if you like, with a cracking bar that has been called the Kinegar Inn, the Clipper and the Dirty Duck. It is also the sight of the Royal Army Ordnance which is where the British military coordinated its surveillance, repaired Saracen tanks that had been blown up and was the main store for all the paraphernalia needed to keep young men operational and in the sights of snipers and bombers. It was also the place of employment of one Kenneth Heaven. One of his duties, believe it or not, was to check in and out the stocks of body bags that were needed following killings of military personnel. Can you think of a more depressing job?

On his way home Ken would stop outside every fast food joint or restaurant to peruse the menus. The benefits of this, I presume, were twofold. One, it would erase the macabre memory of a day spent bored and surrounded by representations of death and destruction. And secondly it provided him with a ferocious appetite that would see him through the slightly confused culinary delights his mother would have waiting for him. Kay had a very strange and original way with the kitchen. I remember one Christmas day particularly well.

Sid tantalisingly drew the family carving knife back and forward along the steel making sure that there was an even distribution of friction across both sides of the blade rendering it as sharp as a barber's razor. The family, who had celebrated Christmas morning the way Mary and Joseph had hoped their son's birthday would be commemorated (with Tuborg Special and two-litre bottles of Liebfraumilch), licked their lips and held their breaths. The knife made the inch-deep incision like a surgeon delicately slicing through epidermis. The crisp skin crackled, a trickle of succulent juices escaped from the flesh and made its way along the blade, dragging with it the aroma of festive fowl.

A cheer filled the air and plates were thrust in front of the head of the household in a competition to win the first serving. However, the playful chatter and clatter of best Delft was cut short when the knife shuddered and bent after making contact with a solid block of turkey meat. The traditional bird had went straight from freezer to gas mark 10 without a thought of thawing. Drink turned bad inside the family and the spirit of Christmas evaporated. Accusing fingers were pointed and clenched fists shaken. Kay used the mayhem to make her escape to the kitchen where she cracked open another can of German lager and remembered that she didn't really like turkey that much anyway, it was much too tough.

Anyway it was outside the Dragon Palace Chinese restaurant that we spotted him drooling.

'Fancy meeting Van the Man?' I asked through the passenger seat window.

'Ma ballacks,' Ken replied thinking I was joking. He then quickly said, 'Sorry Mr Nancarrow,' realising that he had just sworn in front of my Da.

Once I explained that that we were on our way to the Culloden to meet the genius behind 'Into the Mystic', 'TB Sheets', and 'Jackie Wilson Said', Ken was in the back of the car faster than Ian Paisley after taking a wrong turn onto the Falls Road. Before we set off I asked if he needed to let his mum know that he wouldn't be home for dinner. He shuddered and said that she would leave it for him and he could chip it off the plate for the dog when he got home.

At the reception desk the clerk, who had never seen anybody dressed like Ken and myself in all the years he had worked at the most exclusive hotel in the North, eyed us with suspicion. After a quick phone call to confirm that Mr Morrison was expecting us, and that we weren't gay deranged fans planning to kidnap and have our evil way with the balding, overweight East Belfast love God, we were asked to go to his room.

There was a fight going in room Number 15. It was loud and sounded like all arguments: unpleasant. My Da was close to walking away but I wouldn't let him – we were a mahogany door's width away from meeting a Rock hero. Reluctantly and tentatively my Da knocked on the door. From behind it the fight stopped and then it swung open. Van Morrison's face was red and the little hair he had looked windswept and interesting. He was obviously flustered and said, 'Great to see you Marcus. Could you go to the bar, order yourselves a couple of drinks, use my room number and I'll be with you in a minute, I'm just . . . eh . . . finishing off a letter.' He spoke like an East Belfast docker pretending to be Roy Rodgers while chewing a brick. The door closed and the fight was back on.

My Da was driving; I was under eighteen and wouldn't drink in front of the auld lad so it was left to Ken to partake of Van Morrison's kind hospitality. And oh how he partook. By the time our host had finished his 'correspondence', Ken had gulped down four pints of Guinness and was starting to become very animated. I could see my Da getting a little concerned – he was probably asking himself why had he let me persuade him into bringing Ken along. Van sat down in a beautiful dark brown leather armchair and asked us if we had got ourselves a drink. Ken downed the full pint in his hand in one, wiped the froth from his chops with the sleeve of his denim jacket, dragged his battered cowboy boots (scoring the antique coffee table he had put them up on) and said, 'Oh go on then if yer offering.'

The two old friends relived old times and laughed at the photos my Da had brought along of them in the bands they had played in together. Just a couple of musos enjoying stories and craic, not a millionaire rock star and a man with six kids and a mortgage that left him without a pot to piss in each month. As the conversation went on Van's accent slipped back across the Atlantic and settled somewhere around Cyprus Avenue. He was great company, not the ogre that the press portrayed him as. Don't get me wrong, I had seen some of his interviews and he hadn't done himself any favours, but that night he was a jovial, entertaining gent.

'This guy here is a great guitar player,' my Da said pointing to Ken who was now onto his seventh pint. Ken beamed with pride and offered his services to Van who, for some reason, nearly wet himself laughing. Van then asked Ken if he was a full-time musician. Ken said that at that moment in time he wasn't able to make a living as a guitar player, then touching the side of his nose and winking he said he was making ends meet by working for the British Army. Van, taking note of Ken's shoulder-length hair and attire, lowered his voice to a hush, leaned forward and asked him if he was an undercover agent or something. Slightly confused Ken answered, 'No, I'm a store man at the Ordnance.' There was baffled silence before it was cracked by the throaty laughter of Van Morrison who, in between gasps for air, said, 'A bloody store man! I thought you were in the SAS.'

One of my prized possessions is a photograph taken that night of the four of us laughing. Van is waving to the camera oblivious that Ken is behind him giggling at his bald patch.

Those Holywood nights in those Holywood hills

When I finally turned eighteen I was able to go to the bars with Ken, thus ending our ritual of standing in all weathers at the beach with a carry-out. Every night we would do a pub crawl in search of women. This would prove to be optimistic in the extreme: the town is quite small and we knew nearly every available female, and a few that weren't. Unfortunately they also knew us, which meant luck was rarely on our side.

Visiting every watering hole sounds expensive and excessive but there were only a few licensed establishments in Holywood at that time and we would have only half a pint of lager in each one. To make up for the low levels of alcohol we could purchase, we were usually fortified with, and had our cockles warmed by, my Da's poteen, which was smuggled out of the house in a Lucozade bottle. Why Lucozade? Well it used to be wrapped in orange cellophane, thus disguising the contents within. Genius really when you think about it.

Prior to starting our rounds of the bars we would join a band of gentlemen that drank in the woods of the Holywood Hills. They were no more than vagrants and we fitted in seamlessly. It should've been an indicator of the social circles we were moving in when our illegal Irish moonshine was probably the least potent and toxic of the bottles that were passed around the camp fires of this hardy band of liver-damaged brothers, but we didn't care, we always had the best of craic.

One of the bars we would frequent was called Cicerino's, named after the American owner Peter. One evening while Ken and myself were having a pleasant tête-à-tête with two local loonies, namely, Seamie 'Shambo' Rice and Paddy 'The Web' McMahon, another 'wing nut', Marty 'Johnny Rondo' McGowan ('sixteen tried and sixteen died at the hands of Johnny Rondo') came running in. He was shouting that he needed to get out the back door as he had fallen foul of the law; the cops were hot on his trail. Ken quick as a flash told him that he had seen a film once where a fugitive had stood under the American flag, the result being that the police couldn't arrest him because technically he was on the soil of the good old US of A. Marty ran to the front door where a large Stars and Stripes hung: now safe and immune from the law he awaited the arrival of the authorities.

The chase mustn't have been that high on the list of the sheriff's priorities. Marty was able to order and consume three pints of cider in the interim. However he was not stupid, and to avoid drifting onto Irish soil he engaged the services of one of the waitresses to bring him his drinks. Thank God he hadn't needed to do a piss – I think the barmaids would've drawn the line at bringing him a bucket. When the cops eventually did appear, Marty drew himself up to his full height, raised a finger in the air and declared that they had no jurisdiction over him, he was standing on the land of the free and the brave.

Holywood's very own Johnny Rondo was grabbed by the throat, his arm shoved up his back and then he was dragged screaming outside to a waiting meat wagon where he was given a couple of taps on the head with a truncheon, just to ease him off to sleep mind. He would awaken the next day in the cells, as he had done on numerous occasions, refreshed and ready to start mischief-making again.

After the dust had settled I asked Ken which film had inspired him to give such dangerous advice. He scratched his head and said, 'No, I remember now it wasn't a film, I think it was in the cartoon "Yogi Bear".'

Later that night, or should I say in the early hours of the next day, we were walking home when Ken spotted a huge bag of Brussels sprouts sitting outside Lemon's fruit and veg shop. Never being one to miss an opportunity he decided that it would be a good idea to 'half inch' the mini cabbages. I marvelled at his strength as he tried to lift them onto his shoulder – they must've weighed at least four stone. It took him three attempts: the first two ended with them hitting the floor with a thud. Once he had got his balance he set off on the mile and a half walk home.

It was a sight to behold; he staggered from one side of the street to the other, his knees bent like he was doing some sort of bizarre Russian dance. The sack of sprouts had a very fluid centre of gravity and with each step it changed, dragging the thief here and there. His Dunlop Green Flash trainers started to split due to the strain put upon them by the Herculean efforts of their owner. I only had a further twenty yards or so to go before I turned into a side street and made my own way home. I was almost tempted to go the full distance to Ken's house, the entertainment was that good, but I thought the likelihood of an arrest taking place was pretty much on the cards. I didn't want to be helped off to sleep in the same way poor McGowan had earlier, so I watched my mate and his prize undulate into the distance.

The next day, curious to see if 'Raffles' had been successful in pulling off the crime of the century, I phoned him. His mother answered, but before she called Ken, who was still in bed, she asked me if I knew anything about a massive bag of sprouts that had fallen on her foot, causing a certain amount of pain and a large amount of bruising, due to her daily aspirin. I lied through my teeth telling her I had no knowledge of the offending vegetables. When Ken finally came to the phone he sounded a little groggy. I asked him about the sprouts. For a second he couldn't remember a thing, then it all came flooding back.

He had made it halfway home with his loot and decided that the cover of darkness, as master criminals do, was the order of the day. He climbed the railings of the local grammar school, Sullivan Upper. This took a massive effort: he was ridiculously drunk, carrying half his body weight in turkey complements and the fence was over ten foot tall. The relief he must have felt, on the other side, was short lived when he realised that to get out he had the same height of fence to traverse again. Finally home, the sweat was pouring out of him, and he found that he didn't have a key to get in, a recurring theme in Ken's life. Leaving his ill-gotten gains leaning against the back door, he climbed in through the bathroom window, before retiring for the rest of the morning.

The irony of course is that no one in the Heaven household ate sprouts, they despised them. So there they sat in the back garden until they stunk to high heaven, pardon the pun, which was not that long considering the battering they had taken – let's face it there were less distressed chestnuts during conker season. Eventually the stench, which wafted into the kitchen and made everyone think boiled cabbage was always on the menu, resulted in them being tossed onto Sid's compost heap. Any stray cats that ventured near the garden, when old Darkie was otherwise occupied perched on the TV, soon turned tail and ran when the rotting vegetation assaulted their delicate nasal passages.

The perm

Amazingly, in between all the drunken frivolity and hangovers, we did try to play music and there actually was a line-up, of sorts, of the Pink variety of the Rogues. My schoolmate, Paddy McGrattan, was persuaded to play the drums, but we couldn't coax a bass player to complete the ensemble. We practised in my Ma and Da's front room. To keep the noise down Paddy had to keep a blanket over his kit, making it sound like someone rattling a golf ball around a biscuit tin. We were truly awful, we still had not matured as musicians. Or as people for that matter – the former was not far off, the latter never happened. Paddy went off to join a hotly tipped for the big time band called No Hot Ashes. Ken moved to London, leaving me to roadie for Lawrence McKeown, the drummer in Lado's new band Renegade. I would have to wait patiently for my next opportunity to become a rock star.

I challenge anyone to look back at old photos of themselves and not cringe at least once. I'm in the rather unfortunate position of not being able to look at virtually any of my old snaps without blushing like a schoolgirl. I had committed crimes against fashion that if they had carried the death penalty I would've needed to have been a cat to survive past my twenties.

One such sartorial felony happened when I decided that if I was going to get into a band I needed to get a perm. It didn't even occur to me that maybe it would've been better taking singing lessons, or sitting down and actually practising the guitar. Oh no, I reasoned that any band worth their salt would be falling over themselves to get me in once they saw me with a chemically altered Barnet.

My sister Elish had kindly helped me with a dummy run by putting my hair in rollers for a couple of hours, making sure we were well away from the disapproving eyes of my Da. The results were less than satisfactory, I sort of resembled Farrah Fawcett-Majors without the curves. I pointed out to my untrained sibling hairdresser that my locks didn't look anything like hers, she having had a perm in the recent past. She assured me that when I got the real thing it would look much better. Never trust anyone who doesn't really know what they are talking about.

The girl on the other end of the phone felt the need to remind me that it was a woman's hairdressers that I was calling, not a barbers. Holywood still hadn't really taken to the idea of male grooming as such. Men only went to the barbers when absolutely necessary or in Specky Beard MaCaffery's case when his nasal and ear hairs became the talking point of the kids in the street. The thought of a male asking for a cut and blow dry nearly had the local priest visiting the family home with a little pamphlet about the birds and the bees and the benefits of the Rhythm Method. Eventually the receptionist took my details and booked me in for a permanent wave for Friday lunchtime. I wrote the details down and quickly put them in my pocket in case my Ma or Da saw them. Homosexuality was a sin in the eyes of the Lord you know.

On arrival at, 'Give us a wave, then curl up and dye' (OK I made that up but it was something like that), there was a stunned silence and an adjusting of their skirts from the old ladies with the blue hair sitting at the mirrors. A gum-chewing teenager called Doris led me to a vacant chair at the front window; she sniggered when I told her I wanted a perm. Elish had warned me that it was imperative that I didn't get my hair cut as the new curls would make the length shorten. I was only doing this so as I would look like a Rock God in the vein of David Coverdale, Robert Plant and Joe Elliot (no scrap that last one: his picture on Def Leppard's 'On Through the Night' album sleeve should've served as a warning), so I was keen to keep the length of my mane. Anyway Doris wouldn't listen to my protestations saying that as a trained professional she was bound by her code of conduct to cut away the split ends like a surgeon with a cancerous growth. Having my crowning glory likened to a life-threatening tumour I thought was a little excessive, but I was obviously in the hands of a professional, so cut away.

I had estimated that the whole process shouldn't take any more than half an hour. Three hours later I was still sitting there with a head full of rollers, a plastic bag covering them and the smell of human cells being scorched with substances that don't occur in the natural world. The burning sensation on my scalp was bad but the real pain I was about to feel was that of acute embarrassment.

Right outside the shop was the bus stop that let the pupils from my old school, which I had only recently left, alight for home. At 3.20pm the blue and white Ulster Bus from St Columbanus pulled up, as it always did, right beside the window where I sat. The fifth formers, who had now taken over the mantle of the 'big kids' from my classmates, and myself, couldn't believe their luck. There was one of their archenemies, from recent years, poofing it up big style, right in front of their very eyes.

The screaming and shouting could be easily heard within the hairdressers and the banging on the window nearly gave the old dears heart attacks. I slumped down in the seat hoping to make myself a smaller target for the homophobic chanting. One kid that I had given the odd clip around the ear to, when he deserved it mind, repeatedly walked past the window, his hand bent at the wrist and mincing like he was Larry Grayson at the Mardi Gras. The disturbance was so bad that a passing police car, thankfully, stopped and moved them all on, but not before a few of them left smears on the window planting big smackers of kisses, directed at me, through the glass.

When the rollers were removed I nearly screamed, the reflection in the mirror was that frightening. I looked like someone had skinned a miniature white poodle and placed the pelt on my head. Doris was beaming with pride and held a mirror at the back of my head to confirm to me that it was just as bad as the front.

'My God is it meant to look like that?' I asked.

'I think it looks wonderful,' Doris said starting to get a little defensive.

'I really didn't imagine it looking just so short and wiry,' I said.

'It'll wash down,' she offered as comfort.

'It'll wash down what?' I asked hoping she didn't mean the plughole.

'I mean once you shampoo it a dozen or so times the curls will relax,' she explained. I was far from relaxed and asked to speak to the manager.

Doris stormed off and returned with a heavyset woman with

purple hair munching on a chocolate digestive. 'What seems to be the matter?' she asked.

'This,' I said pointing to the mirror and thinking that it was so obvious that I shouldn't need to be pointing at anything.

The manageress took another mouthful of biscuit and said, 'I think it's a fine effort for a first attempt, well done Doris.' I couldn't believe it: the female version of Sweeny Todd was being publicly praised for disfiguring me on a practice run.

I didn't leave a tip, which earned me a V sign from Doris as I walked past the window, the hood pulled up on my snorkel jacket in case the townsfolk threw things at me. I made a mental note to never go anywhere near the glass at the front of 'Give us a wave, then curl up and dye' because there seemed to be a bad Karma about it.

The family had only just moved from Park Avenue to the top of the next road, Trevor Street, and were now the proud owners of Molly's corner shop. My Da usually finished work a bit earlier on a Friday and would visit the cash and carry on the way home to get provisions. He would bring the stock in through the double doors at the back of our covered yard. Behind one of the doors was a tumble dryer and as he came in I was going through its contents looking for a hat. Only being able to see the back of me he asked, 'Are you not supposed to be in work today?' obviously mistaking me for Elish. When I turned around to show him that he had made an error he dropped a box of pickled onions onto the concrete floor smashing all of the jars.

'Jesus fuck what the fuck have you done to your fuckin' head?' my father shouted, ignoring the broken glass and pungent smell of vinegar.

'I got a perm and I like it,' I said lying through my teeth.

'Get it off,' he said, obviously unaware that perm was short for permanent.

'I can't,' I said while wishing I could. 'It's there for the foreseeable future.'

'We'll see about that,' my Da said as he ran into the store and returned with a packet of disposable razors. I made good my escape through the open back doors, leaving my Ma to calm down the auld lad before I could return home.

A fire in the sky

The shop became a source of many hilarious characters and stories that could fill a book in itself, but there was one incident that illustrates the fact that at that point in my life music was the most important thing to me. My sister Elish forgot that my Da had blocked off the chimney after we had got central heating in. She decided, for some reason, to burn a load of old newspapers in the hearth and effectively set fire to the family home. All the bedrooms had old fireplaces; the walls of the chimney-breasts became virtually untouchable due to the furnace raging in the soot. At first we thought that it would burn itself out and we wouldn't have to worry about informing my Da, who had just returned from work and was settling down in front of the telly with his dinner and wouldn't have been best pleased. But the heat from the walls and the smoke billowing through the floorboards of the upstairs rooms necessitated that we must draw attention to the imminent razing to ground of the family home.

We all trooped downstairs, safety in numbers, and informed the potato-chomping head of the household that his mortgaged-up-to-the-eyeballs bricks and mortar was in danger of bursting into flames. Setting down his knife and fork my Da uttered the words, 'Jesus Christ will I ever get my dinner in peace.'

As my Da always says, when talking about his lovely kids, he has no favourites: he hates us all equally. I too don't have a favourite sibling but I do have a big soft spot for my sister Louise. She has a heart the size of a whale and is generous to a fault. She is also easily hurt and unfortunately this has happened over the years and to my shame by my hand as well. She would do anything for you, so while the rest of the family were running around the house frantically trying to get the tills, accountancy books and all the money from the safe out of the house, I persuaded her that she should help me evacuate my stereo and record collection.

My room was in the attic so trip after trip we ran up and down five flights of stairs, our precious cargo clutched to our chests. It was only when everything was safe outside that Louise was able to return for her stuff while I stood guard over my gear in case it was stolen.

The house thankfully didn't burn down. A part-time fireman owned a garage across the road from our shop and he climbed onto the roof, pouring bucket after bucket of water carefully down the chimney, putting the blaze out and avoiding horrendous damage to the carpets and furniture that would've happened had we called the fire brigade.

CHAPTER TWO

Guilt Edge

The start of a rocky road

When the chance finally arrived of getting myself into a band it unexpectedly came in the shape of one, Marty 'Hedge Belly Bruce' O'Sullivan. Will I first explain his name? Oh all right then, you've twisted my arm. He had a mad, thick, red setter-style, shock of hair, hence the 'Hedge'. He was fond of a pint of Bass Ale, which had gathered around his midriff, hence the 'Belly'. And finally he had a protruding chin, hence the 'Bruce' (from Forsyth fame). This description makes him sound like he could've sat by the hearth in a family home scaring the children away from the fire, but actually, he was quite handsome in a Gene Wilder sort of way, that is, you know he is but don't really know why. Anyway he thought that I looked a bit like Robert Plant – by this time the perm was growing out and I no longer resembled a six-foot Shirley Temple. By his reasoning looking like a rock star meant that you must be able to sing. Amazingly my perm plan had worked.

I had known Marty for a while: we had been partners in crime, in that we used to mitch off Mass together and talk music, along with a skinny bass player called Colin Shiels, more of whom much later. I had no qualms about sneaking out of the Chapel as arthritic fingers and the blocked pipes of the organ were mangling the opening hymn. By this stage in my life I was a confirmed atheist, in fact, I knew from about the age of twelve that there was no God. When I started to question the existence of a divine entity, demanding evidence, my Ma and Da, being devout Catholics, were borderline hysterical at the thought of their eldest turning his back on the Church.

Believe me I have no problem with anybody believing in a god, no matter what flavour it is, Catholic, Protestant, Muslim, Jew, I just demand the respect not to believe; it's not much to ask really. My philosophy is that everyone is equal until they prove by their words or actions that they are not. Let me explain. I will accept anyone I'm introduced to on face value, a clean slate, however if they turn out to be a bigot, racist, homophobe, a male chauvinist or man hater, then the slate starts to fill quite quickly and I'm afraid there is no duster, the copy book has been blotted. I will not be ignorant or bad mannered towards them because that's not how my Ma and Da brought me up, but the black mark is there forever and I cannot trust someone who has hate in their hearts.

It was not just the existence of God that I had a problem with. I had become very distrustful of the Catholic Church, an organisation that had billions of pounds worth of assets tied up in property, land, art, precious metals and jewels and was still prepared to promote mass reproduction amongst the poorest people on the planet, then sit back and watch them starve to death. I also couldn't see the sense in that, with all this wealth, it was their hard-up parishioners who were expected to dig deep to raise money to support the next famine relief appeal. Don't get me wrong, I'm all for charity and all, but this is similar to the world's banks asking their customers and taxpayers to bail them out after getting into massive debt, paying themselves obscene bonuses, taking wonderful little jollies to Monaco and actually being crap at their jobs by investing badly. But of course this would never happen, it's way too far fetched.

There were also the accusations of child abuse that were being bandied about, although strenuously denied at the time; there was something just not right. As I write, apologies from the Vatican and the Catholic Church in Ireland for the decades of abuse are being issued. I'll draw a veil over this as nausea prevents me from further discussion.

Anyway I spent the time I should've been genuflecting, kneeling, head bowed and kissing the bishop's ring, discussing the sounds that Angus Young was able to get out of such a thin-bodied Gibson SG. It was during these debates that I became aware that there are, contrary to public opinion, many different formats of Rock and Metal, it's not all headbanging noise. Marty was a Thin Lizzy,

Lynyrd Skynyrd nut, Colin a connoisseur of Prog Rock and Kiss. It was a great education and gave me a grounding that saw me, in the same week, buy 'Gimme Back my Bullets' and 'The Lamb Lies Down on Broadway', two great albums that are poles apart, style wise, but linked through marvellous musicianship and songwriting.

What I lost spiritually from bunking off Mass, I gained by enriching my soul with music. I would sit at the Sunday dinner table and when questioned by my parents about what that morning's sermon had been about I always said 'love thy neighbour', which was ironic, in that, with the suspicion and in some cases the downright hatred with which the different 'Christian' faiths viewed each other, I was the only one that seemed to be practising what I preached.

Marty was a bit of a local guitar hero and I felt flattered that he would even consider me. I decided that this was an opportunity too good to miss, even if I did consider myself a guitar player and had never really contemplated singing. Well that's not strictly true. About a year previously, in school, the afore-mentioned Paddy McGrattan had persuaded me to join a band he was in called Bad Reputation. I turned up at the first rehearsal with my guitar and amp to be confronted by two other guitarists. I pulled Paddy aside and said, 'I know Skynyrd have three guitarists but don't you think that this is a bit excessive?'

He said, 'No, you're going to be the singer.'

I laughed and said, 'You must be joking,' to which he replied, 'No, I heard you doing an Elvis impersonation in metalwork.'

Thus I became the vocalist in my first band. We played one gig, in a youth club in Bangor, that was a total shambles; all of the blame must fall at my feet. I didn't realise that instead of singing songs in the key that they were recorded, you could do them in the key that the band were playing, or at least in one that is comfortable for you to sing. Geddy Lee, if he had been dead, would have spun in his grave like a naked break-dancer on the bonnet of a black Morris Minor sitting in the midday sun of Dubai. The shrieking that masqueraded for singing on 'Spirit of the Radio' had dogs cowering like it was bonfire night. Forgive me Mr Lee; all that were present that night and Rush fans the world over, if you can.

Hedge Belly was an only child, his parents were reasonably well off, and he got a Gibson Les Paul Standard Sunburst and a rehearsal studio built onto the back of the house in which to play it – nice. He had a friend called John McKee who was a phenomenal bass player and backing vocalist. I persuaded Paddy to leave No Hot Ashes and join us, which foolishly he did considering the golden future that seemed to be mapped out in front of them.

I got the name of the band after starting a business studies course, which included classes on stocks and shares: a little spelling adjustment and *voila,* we were called Guilt Edge. We went about getting a set together, which included songs by Thin Lizzy, Lynyrd Skynyrd, Free, Gary Moore, Pat Travers and anything Rock. The band was really tight and I was starting to find my feet as a vocalist. I always felt that the overall sound and power of the band could've done with a second guitarist. Marty wouldn't hear of it, he had a bit of an ego and didn't want to share the Guitar God crown with anyone.

Enter Ken Heaven who returned from London after hearing that I had started a band with two of the most sought-after musos in town. He then put the emotional thumbscrews on me, telling me that he had only come back because he knew that, as a team, we two had unfinished business. I was then forced to virtually beg Marty to take him on as, at Ken's insistence, a 'rhythm guitarist'. He was well aware that if I had said second lead player Marty, who knew of Ken's outstanding natural talent, wouldn't even consider it for a minute. It worked, the ego was stroked, and the thought of Ken playing second fiddle to him was too good for Marty to refuse. Hook, line and sinker.

We were shit hot, all the Lizzy stuff sounded wonderful with the harmony guitars. We even started putting in a few of our own songs – although rough around the edges they definitely had potential. Gigs were the next stepping-stones, but we had no problems securing a couple of nights in the Martello, a local bar that catered for live bands. There was however a slight problem. Since Ken had returned from London, he had been using borrowed gear; the guy who he had conned into lending it to him needed it himself for his own gigs. Ken didn't have as much as a set of strings, so on the day of the first gig we went to a music shop in Belfast called Floods, securing a hire purchase deal, a little illegally, I won't go into details, for a Flying V copy made by a company called Kay, a Marshall 100W head and a Marshall four by four speaker cabinet.

The latter had a metal grill on the front, how Rock is that? Ken even persuaded the staff to deliver the equipment to the venue; we couldn't have possibly taken all that stuff back on the bus. Later that night Ken's new gear was sitting on the stage ready for a new era in Rock history to begin.

The place was packed as we walked on stage, which was not really surprising as we had invited everyone we knew, and this provided a party atmosphere from the off. We played a blinder, going down a storm, so much so that we were cheered back on for an encore. Unfortunately we had not expected to do so well so we didn't have any more songs. Ken, who had been shackled to playing rhythm guitar and the odd bit of harmony lead work, suggested we do an improvised version of 'Johnny B Goode'. I could almost see the cogs turning in his head. We all agreed, Marty reluctantly, and hurtled into the song – it was one of the fastest, heaviest versions ever heard.

Ken at last was allowed to let rip on the lead breaks and was sensational. Don't get me wrong, Marty was technically an excellent musician, but this was in an explosive, raw, uncultured, different class. Ken was duck walking, throwing the guitar about his head and playing it with his teeth. The crowd were going mad and Hedge Belly was starting to go a little green around the gills: his guitar partnership with Ken was destined to be short lived. As the last notes were being rung from the neck of Ken's new guitar, he turned, ran at his equally new speaker cabinet and stabbed its metal grill with the headstock. The guitar rebounded; Ken held it high above his head and let the last note hang.

Or should I say that is what Ken intended to happen. Unfortunately the metal grill on the front of the amp was, in fact, only the usual cloth that you would get to protect the speaker cones, sprayed silver. The guitar went straight through, ripping the grill and one of the speakers and breaking its own neck in the process. The effect was spellbinding and the audience went nuts. From my vantage point at the back of the stage I could see Ken's horrified expression as he mouthed the words 'Holy fuck'. He had not had the gear more than three hours and it was damaged beyond repair. In the blink of an eye he swung around to face his audience, spread his arms wide, milking the applause for all he was worth and hid his agony like an old trooper.

Spuds U like, Spuds U don't like

Guilt Edge got the chance to play a prestigious gig supporting Lado Morrow's band Renegade, at a bar called Spuds in Portstewart on the Saturday of the North West 200 motorcycle-racing weekend. We decided to go up the night before; the traffic was notoriously horrendous on the day of the event. Everybody knew we were going to have to bed down in the van, so we all brought sleeping bags, that is except for Ken who turned up with just a pillow claiming that, 'If your head is comfortable, you are comfortable.'

We started drinking in the van which necessitated many piss stops. It also meant that everybody was blootered on arrival, all except for a friend of ours, Marshall Docherty who had, for his sins, volunteered to do the driving, something he must have regretted as the miles rolled by. At the campsite we tumbled out of the van and proceeded to search for some action. It was hardly going to come in the form of the female variety: any self-respecting woman who was not shackled to a biker wouldn't have been seen within ten miles of the place. The best entertainment was to be had around the large bonfires that the different biker gangs had built. We got the acoustic guitars out and gave impromptu performances, one, because it was great fun, the bikers really got into it and two, because we were hoping that we could encourage a few more people to turn up a bit earlier the next night to catch our support slot.

John McKee you could class as one of the quieter ones in the band, however he would sometimes suffer from a metamorphic transformation when he had too much to drink. When pickled he would turn into his alter ego 'Captain Zep', who had an uncanny knack of behaving like he was one of those freaky monkeys in The Wizard of Oz and thinking he could fly. One of his other beliefs was that he was bullet proof, thus making him invincible. This combination would often get him into trouble; however someone else was usually brought on as a substitute to take the beating he so richly deserved. That night, you've guessed it, the good Captain appeared.

Seized by jungle juice and music John took to running around the bonfire, circled by a local motorcycle club. He leapt into the air like a demented Rudolf Nureyev (that's near enough) knocking over gallon flagons of cider and causing bikers to scatter. Some of the

Hells Angels, sorry Chapter Members, were nearly knocked into the fire; beards were singed and due to the combustible nature of their oil-saturated jeans some of them were almost set alight. Precious scrumpy was used to douse their gently smouldering strides.

Punches were thrown, voices were raised, and myself and Ken tried to diffuse the situation by taking a couple of slaps, while Zep did his impersonation of the Sugar Plum Fairy, spun a few times on his toe and collapsed snoring to the ground, oblivious to all hell breaking loose around him. There was a lot of pushing and shoving, as heavy boots danced to the rhythm of violence. Bruises were collected by all those involved in the fracas, that is of course except for our Super Hero, who came out of the whole thing without a scratch and was all the better for a good night's sleep. The next day, much to everyone's relief, Captain Zep was gone and the bikers accepted apologies and agreed to come to the gig, on the guest list of course.

I'm jumping the gun here a wee bit because the night's weirdness didn't end with John's suicide attempt. After his shenanigans had abated we decided to retire to the van to try and get some sleep. There were eight of us to share the small confines of the rented Transit. Paddy, Marshall and Fishy, who I had asked to roadie for us, attempted some shuteye in the front seats, while the floor at the back was to be split between the rest of us. We all got into our sleeping bags, that is except, of course, for Ken who, as I said earlier, only had a pillow for comfort. Sleep came surprisingly easily; probably the drink and concussion had something to do with it. I did, however, wake up at one point in the early hours aware that there was a silhouette of someone crouching on his honkers at the back doors.

As my eyes adjusted I could make out the familiar figure of Ken. I asked him what he was doing. He said it was the only position he could get comfortable in and it was too cold to lie on the metal floor. His explanation seemed plausible enough, for indeed there was a definite nip in the air. 'He should've brought a sleeping bag,' I thought. 'If your head's comfortable you're comfortable,' my arse.

As the sun came up, the usual grunts, groans, farts and yawns that accompany a group of males waking up together filled the air. There was an extra noise which sounded like someone taking part in one of those bizarre Japanese endurance shows, you know the ones, where you have to lift a brick which has been tied round your testicles and scrotum: it was not pleasant. We all turned to see the source of the bowel-loosening din and there was Ken trying to get to his feet. His hours of sleeping in the crouching position had caused his leg muscles to lock in the grip of a spasmodic pain that drained the colour from his face and the tears from his eyes.

As we all watched Ken in fascination, we also became aware that there were big, brown, rust-flecked, drops of water dripping from the ceiling. All our sleeping bags and our clothes were soaking. Ken, who had regained the power of speech, said, rather hastily, that it was because there had been a load of sweaty bodies, all breathing out moisture, and we were inside a big metal box. What did we expect? 'Of course there was going to be condensation,' I thought, 'but this much?' We spent the next few hours trying to let the morning sun and wind dry out our clothes and sleeping bags. Ken used the time trying to get the feeling back into his legs by walking around bent double like someone with an ill-fitting truss who's looking for a dropped contact lens.

We were all very nervous about the show that night; it was one of the gigs of the year. We decided to leave our own songs out and concentrate on the classics in an attempt to get a positive reaction from the still-sober punters. The plan worked and the crowd roared their approval, many saying we were better than the headliners. Renegade were certainly better musicians than us – Lado made me sound like Lemmy with laryngitis. But hey, Level 42 are more gifted than Motorhead musically, but I know who I'd want to see live. As successful as the gig was, there was, one thing that happened during the last few songs that slightly took the shine off. The heat from the crowd, the running around on stage and the lights made those whose clothes were still damp from the night before, start to steam slightly. There was also the rather sickening stench of stale urine. We were all looking at each other and mouthing the words 'What's that feckin' smell?' But we played on regardless and left the stage to slaps on the back and cheering.

During the post-gig drink it started to become apparent that the odour we had smelt on the stage was getting stronger and it seemed to be coming from us. When I say us I really mean all those that had slept in the back of the van, with the exception of Ken, who was not his usual self following a show. I asked, in front of everyone else, why he had escaped smelling like an old people's home. He blushed and explained.

The reason why Ken had spent most of the night sleeping like a contortionist was because he had been caught short and couldn't make it to the side doors of the van to let himself out. Being ever resourceful he improvised by peeing into two empty beer cans. He then gently set them on the floor careful not to spill them, before promptly kicking them over. He then decided, as all good humanitarians would, that sleeping in a pool of piss was not for him, but OK for the rest of us.

Back in Belfast we converged, as we always did, on a fine little eating establishment situated in Shaftsbury Square, imaginatively named Spuds, also the name of the very bar we had just played. We Irish love our potatoes, don't ya know. Lado, coming from Holywood, had cadged a lift with us. He seemed happy enough to share the van with the band that had just blown his off the stage (my opinion), that is until the windows were closed to keep out the chill night air. The smell of sweat and urine mingling with the normal bacteria of the skin, fragrantly filled the decompression chamber-style interior of the Transit. The stench was unbearable for Lado who hadn't had the exposure time that the rest of us had, and therefore had not built up a certain amount of resistance. He begged for the windows to be reopened.

It reminded me of an occasion a few years previously when sport was my thing, a long time before Rock and Roll came along and led me astray. I played football for a team called Holywood Star; we trained in the Palace Barracks army camp. Following one arduous session we were allowed to use the gym and other facilities, which included a sauna. Those that weren't afraid to sit naked together piled in, let's face it this was mostly the Catholics and the Protestants from the estate. The middle class, born-again Christians of the team believed they needed a letter from God to expose their flesh to another man; they avoided the sweatbox saving themselves from eternal damnation.

One of the kids who made use of the sauna was a headcase called Willy Craig, who, after working up a good perspiration, said he was going to get more water for the coals. When he returned he threw the whole contents of the jug onto the heater, causing a mushroom cloud of steam that obscured everything from view. Willy used this to make good his escape. Once outside he persuaded those that had not taken up the offer to sweat their bollocks off to help him keep the door shut by wedging their bodies against it. Inside it became rapidly clear that Willy had not filled the jug with water but had replenished it with piss. The atmosphere, to say the least, was a very unpleasant one; it was so vile that one of the team threw up. Unfortunately for those imprisoned, some of the projectile vomit landed on the coals adding a further fruity aroma to the pungent atmosphere. It later came to light that the poor sod had had apple pop tarts for his tea.

There was a panic that gripped all that were captured and threats were issued through the small reinforced glass window in the door. But our captors held firm. It was hard to see where they got their strength from – their oxygen levels must've been in their boots with them laughing so much. Just when the mixture of sweat, urine and vomit were getting to a stage where suicide would've been sweet relief, the Sergeant, who had been taking us for physical training, walked into the room and gently removed those at the sauna door by laying into them with an immaculately polished hobnail boot. We came piling out of the wooden box naked, sweating and gasping for uncontaminated air. The Christians covered their eyes with one hand and their nostrils with the other.

Anyway, back to Spuds (the eating place not the bar, is this getting confusing?). The place was always packed on weekend nights after the bars had shut. Myself, Lado and Ken joined the queue, which, through previous experience, we knew we were going to be in for some time. As the line of drunks slowly snaked towards the counter there were a few comments from our fellow starvos that someone was giving off a nasty niff. I had completely forgotten that I had absorbed urine through my clothing twenty-four hours previously, but comments such as, 'What the feck's that smell?', 'Has somebody pissed themselves?' and 'Somebody's knickers need wringing out,' brought the experience flooding back. I quickly took a £10 note from my pocket, handed it to Ken telling him that it had to do me until next dole day and asked him to get me the cheapest burger that they had. Knowing that Ken had no money at all, I told him to get himself something as well. I then retreated to the great outdoors for fear that the mob would turn nasty if they found out who 'piss his pants' was.

Thankfully the night air was carried along by a breeze, which filtered through my clothes and saved me from gassing passers by. I was standing outside for what seemed like an eternity. I had to stop myself from looking through the window to check on the boys' progress because every time I did they seemed to be standing in the same place or had moved only an inch or two. Eventually they reached the counter and I saw them place their orders. 'Thank Christ,' I thought, at least it wouldn't be long before I got something to eat, then got home for a shower.

After another short wait I could see Ken being handed over a paper bag, food at last. I then saw Lado pointing towards a girl who was standing at a bench that ran the length of the wall. It was there for people to consume their food from or hang on to if the alcohol took a toll on their balance. There then seemed to be a bit of a confrontation between Lado and the girl behind the counter. I decided to go in to find out what was going on.

It appeared that Lado's burger had been given, by mistake, to the very drunk girl he had been pointing at. The conversation went something like this. 'You gave my burger to someone else and you want me to pay for it?' Lado enquired of the teenage member of staff, who responded by saying, 'She hasn't touched it yet so you can take it off her.' Lado looked around and saw that the girl, it was true, had not touched it, but she had covered it with all manner of condiments, as was the want of cash-strapped students who needed to get as much nourishment, for the least amount of money, to enable them to buy as much drink as possible. Lado then said, 'I can't eat that she's got coleslaw on it.' To which the drunken student, with his burger remember, shouted, 'Oi you cheeky bastard I feckin don't have cold sores.'

All hell broke loose as the thief attacked Lado with the offending burger and a fist or two for good measure. There were a few shouts of 'Kill Him', 'Cut his balls off' and 'Leave the poor girl alone you, you man you,' from a group of feminists who had just been to a talk about life being too short to stuff a mushroom by Shirley Conran. Lado, being a massive Elvis fan, had adopted the manners of the Southern gentleman and would never think of laying a hand on a lady in anger. He took his beating like a good male chauvinist pig, while still trying to remonstrate with the counter staff. A scream of 'There's that fecking smell again!!' prompted me to grab Lado by the arm and drag him outside to the relative safety of the streets of bomb-torn Belfast.

When we got back to the van Ken handed me a burger that was about the size of a ten pence piece. He then proceeded to take out of the bag and place on the seat beside him a chicken burger, a portion of sticky ribs, a piece of fried fish and a portion of cheesy chips. I couldn't believe my eyes. I said, 'Ken what's all that?' to which he answered, 'Well you did say get yourself something.' I was speechless. I remained so the whole way home, where I got into a nice hot shower, woke the whole family up and got an absolute bollocking from my Ma who had picked up my piss-stained, reeking clothes, before I had a chance to put them into the washing machine.

After the inevitable split of Guilt Edge – Marty and Ken were never going to be able to put egos aside – there was of course the division in the camp between those that took Ken's side, namely me, and the others who took Marty's side, everyone else. With no band to play in Ken deserted me again and went back to London.

Can I play with madness?

The ironic thing is that after getting Paddy to leave No Hot Ashes to join me in Guilt Edge I was asked to become the singer in his old band. They seemed like they could go places: they certainly had the songwriting ability, judging by the demos I had been given to learn for my audition. Like a rat blowing up an inflatable life raft I jumped ship. Paddy was left to soldier on with Hedge Belly and John McKee under the moniker of Perfect Strangers. Paddy and myself had been friends since St Columbanus High School. We had shared many experiences – most of them good, some of them incomprehensible. The latter included us being attacked by a gang of skinheads, with us being arrested and accused of GBH.

Paddy's Ma was far from amused when the cops came to pick us up from her house in the middle of the night. The charges were eventually dropped after we had been dragged to the station and the officers saw the battered and bloody faces of the five bone heads and the stick-thin long-haired hippies that were supposed to have, according to the 'victims', attacked them, out of the blue and without provocation. The laugh is that we *were* responsible for the damage – admittedly in self-defence, but responsible nonetheless.

The incident happened as we walked back from a late-night, under-age, drinking session at a local dive. The wastrels were waiting for us in the stairwell of one of the tenement blocks that populated the estate Paddy lived on. They must have rubbed their India ink-tattooed hands with glee when they saw two 'big girls' blouses' skipping along, singing Marillion's 'Grendel'. We had even incorporated time and key changes which was quite a feat considering we had each consumed ten pints of Bass Ale. You should however, never judge a book by its cover, especially one that is concealing a rather sinister surprise within its dust jacket.

As we drew level with the gang they left their shadowy lair and confronted us face-on with jovial greetings of four-letter expletives and threats. We were outnumbered and unarmed, or so I thought. I had always assumed that Paddy had a bit of a club foot or something, the way he leaned over to one side. Little did I know that the weight of a three-foot long, twenty-link steel chain, capable of holding the QE2 at the quayside, was spoiling the line of his biker's jacket. When he reached into his pocket and started to produce his makeshift weapon the relief for me was twofold. One, Paddy was not deformed, well not in any way that was visible with his clothes on and two, now that the thugs had decided to interrupt our Neo-Prog Rock sing-a-long by attempting to kick the shit out of us, we had something that was going to even the odds out a bit.

Like Tommy Cooper producing a string of coloured handkerchiefs from his trousers, there seemed to be no end to the chain. Link after link glistened in the streetlights, and with each one the tables started to turn, the hunted became the hunters. Like all bullies, when faced with a greater threat than they themselves posed, the skinheads ran. A quick couple of flicks of the wrist to reel in the slack and Paddy was after them like Vanessa Feltz with a Luncheon Voucher. I in turn chased after him and cringed at the way each swing of the chain resulted in a sickening thud, followed by girl-like screams, the links creating deep gouges in baldy flesh. The next few weeks would see our poor victims having to reluctantly grow hair to cover the embarrassing evidence that some of Newtownards' finest racist, bigoted, homophobic swine had been beaten to a pulp by a couple of long-haired, Taig fruits.*

Paddy was a mate who had had to put up with some deplorable behaviour on my part; I was young and fuelled by testosterone stupidity. One cringeworthy incident, while we were at school, that springs to mind was when I tried to get off with the love of his life at a party. Thankfully she had impeccable taste and morals and she turned me down like a flea-infested bedspread. Paddy, to his credit, after I had been exposed as a sleaze bag, didn't kill me, even when I offered myself up for a beating. He did, however, stop talking to me for a while. After much begging he eventually did, kind of, forgive me. I was over the moon that we were friends again but that didn't stop me keeping an ear open for the metallic clanking of a chain slipping from its leather housing. I always made sure I was four foot in front of him, just an inch or two out of reach. Years later Paddy went on to marry the girl in question, though I was not invited to the wedding, I can't think why.

As bad as my attempt to change the course of history by acting like a bastard and trying to seduce his future wife was, I think my mercenary behaviour in joining No Hot Ashes hurt Paddy more. You see sometimes being in a band can have as much, if not more, emotional attachment as any relationship. But I just couldn't remain in Guilt Edge with guys that had sacked Ken and anyway the Ashes were a better prospect as far as I was concerned. I said my farewells to Paddy knowing full well that we would never again have the same friendship. Unfortunately the passage of time proved me right.

Before I go on to tell the many tales that occurred during my days with No Hot Ashes, I must give an account of an incident that happened to Paddy and the boys that made the front pages of the *Belfast Telegraph*, the biggest-selling daily newspaper in the North of Ireland. They had taken to doing talent contests, by all accounts doing very well and winning quite a lot of prize money. It was at one of these events that this story takes place.

They were standing in the wings ready to go on, they just had to wait for the act before them to finish. They had already witnessed a

* 'Taig' – an insulting slang term used to describe Northen Irish Catholics.

nun reciting a passage from the New Testament while juggling three bottles of holy water. Then a seventy-year-old man wearing a dress and a mop on his head sang 'On the Good Ship Lollipop'. Next was a ventriloquist, who had forgotten his dummy, so he improvised, using one of his socks: unfortunately when he sat down it was obvious where his partner had come from. Following that a youth played 'Ave Maria' using two recorders, one up each nostril. As he reached the climax he hit a horrendously moist C# when an ill-timed sneeze erupted from his nasal passages travelling the length of the double barrels, escaping through the holes at the end and spraying the first five rows. A fire breather didn't fare much better: he was so afraid of burning himself that he held the flame as far from himself as he could with the punters at the lip of the stage being able to light their fags off it. Finally a man in a balaclava and dark glasses, who apparently had lost a leg in a botched bombing attempt, did a version of the old Rolf Harris hit 'Jake the Peg'. The act only required one fake limb, he now effectively had two, which seemed to confuse him somewhat for he spent the whole song spinning like a whirling dervish on his one good leg. When he finished he was greeted with a stunned silence but rescued himself, and got the best reaction of the night, when he shouted 'Up the RA!!' (IRA).

OK! OK! I admit it, I may have made some of those acts up, you'll just have to guess which ones, but what was to precede the band was no less outlandish. An escapologist, whom Marty would later describe as having 'a little want in him', a local expression to describe someone who is a bonus ball short of the lottery, was introduced by the dinner-suited, ruddy-faced compere.

The first thing the would-be magician asked for was a volunteer from the audience to help tie him up. A local hood, who would nowadays be described as a chav, jumped up onto the stage egged on by his mates and cheap cider. He proceeded to tie the 'Great Nutto's' hands behind his back with blue nylon rope, the type you would tow a car with. The chav was putting a little too much effort and getting a little too much pleasure from his task for the liking of a lot in the crowd. After he had used up the last bit of rope securing a final granny knot, the star of the show instructed him to pull a plastic bag and a roll of gaffa tape out of his pocket. He was then told to put the bag over the artiste's head and tape it in place, but before the pissed-out-of-mind assistant could get on with his task 'Harry Whodunnit' announced, to a now mesmerised audience, that he would escape before he ran out of air. The now sweating tattooed 'Debbie Magee' secured around the neck, again with too much enjoyment, the bag with layer upon layer of industrial adhesive; the escape attempt was on folks.

The stage lights cut through the cigarette smoke illuminating a madman with a Tesco's bag on his head struggling with his restraints. After about a minute he rolled onto the floor and tried to bring the rope in front of him by bringing his knees up and passing his hands under his feet. When this failed, miserably, he struggled back up again, which considering he couldn't use his hands was a feat in itself. He continued for another frantic minute or two to release himself from the nylon tangle. Suddenly he stopped moving, the bag puffed in and out: inhalation was followed by exhalation six times until oxygen was replaced by carbon dioxide and he collapsed.

There was a gasp from the majority of the crowd and cheer from his assistant and his mates. The compere came running on shouting, 'Does anyone know this guy, is this part of the act?' When there was no response he spun round, dropped to his knees, ripped the arse out of his trousers and the bag from the stricken star's head. The victim lay unconscious and blue around the lips. The now purple-faced MC ignored the shooting pains in his own left arm and gave the dying wretch a punch to the chest that could've killed him had he not already been knocking on the Pearly Gates. To everyone's relief the pain of his fractured ribs caused him to gasp and cough his way back towards the light. The boys in the band watched from the side of the stage open mouthed and in a state of hypnotic horror. Marty, his eyes never leaving the heaving body on stage, asked John and Paddy, 'How the feck do we follow that?'

It was difficult to top someone trying to top himself, especially when they could see, just off stage, a crowd of people trying to untie Lazarus and revive him with a damp cloth. The boys, however, gave it their best shot; unfortunately most of the crowd were no longer in the mood for frivolity – they had, after all, just been put through an emotional wringer. A man of limited intelligence had very nearly breathed his last in front of their very eyes; worse still, his suicide attempt meant that the raffle was now going to be half an hour late.

The straw that broke the camel's back however, came when the boys launched into a rather ill thought-out 'Tie your Mother Down' by Queen. Thinking they were taking the piss the crowd voiced their opinion by chucking anything that came to hand.

As bad as being pelted with lit fag butts, empty bottles of stout and one of Jake the Peg's legs was, it was nothing compared to the humiliation of being beaten into second place by a guy whose act seemed to involve trying to kill himself in front of an audience. With the bits of gaffa tape and plastic bag that, even with their best efforts, his aides couldn't remove still round his neck, he collected his prize money. He thanked everyone for their appreciation and concern and gave a special thanks to his assistant who stood up to tumultuous applause shouting, 'Do I get a cut of the dough?' On hearing this, Belfast's worst-ever escapologist clutched the cheque to his chest, faked a faint and collapsed again. He wasn't that stupid after all.

CHAPTER THREE

No Hot Ashes

The attack of the mad axeman

As Paddy went on to weird and wonderful things I hoped to go on to slightly less unorthodox but a no less exciting future, and you know what? I nearly did. No Hot Ashes had a reputation for being one of the only Melodic Rock bands on the scene. This was the type of music that I was most into at the time – Journey, Foreigner, Loverboy, UFO, Mr Mister, Bon Jovi, John Waite etc. – so it looked like this could be a perfect vehicle for me to develop as a songwriter and performer. The band consisted of Davy Irvine on lead guitar, Paul Boyd on bass and Stephen Campbell on drums. One of the first things to happen was that the hierarchy of the band was made apparent. It became obvious that Davy considered himself the boss with his second in command being Paul. I could see that Davy was the main driving force as far as songwriting was concerned and he did, after all, come up with the name, which he incidentally got off the wheelie bins that proliferated the area that he came from. Even though it was obvious whose band it was, I was determined to make an impact. I felt I had a lot to offer.

We rehearsed at the back of Paul's mum and dad's house in a large shed with a PA and a stage at one end. We worked on a set and when it was up to speed the first gig was arranged. It was to be in Comber Orange Hall. My new Protestant bandmates didn't, for a second, consider that there might be a problem with their new, so-called Catholic, lead vocalist making his stage debut at the local bastion to all things Loyalist. My Ma and Da on the other hand, had a different perspective altogether: they had severe reservations about the whole thing. Visions of me being dragged from the building, tied to the nearest lamppost then tarred and feathered filled their daydreams and nightmares. I had a monumental job on my hands to try to quash their fears. Eventually they would capitulate but probably spent the night of the gig reciting decade after decade of the Rosary.

There were a few things that needed sorting out set-wise before I would do the gig. Firstly we needed some more decent Melodic Rock songs, so a couple of Foreigner and Lizzy songs were drafted in. Secondly, God forbid, Chris de Burgh songs needed to be dropped like the fifty pence pieces that my old school mate Marty Hughes used to heat in the metalwork furnace until white hot, toss onto the floor, then wait for some unsuspecting scavenger to happen upon, pick up, scream and spend the rest of the day in A&E. Oh how we laughed.

Before I joined the band Paul had been the lead vocalist; his girl-friend was a big fan of the chart-bothering, big-eyebrowed, Irish Pixie. I really couldn't have handled the embarrassment of singing 'Don't Pay the Ferry Man' to a bunch of Metal-loving mates, who would be turning up en masse for the first outing of the new look Ashes.

On the day of the unveiling we were let into the hall early to set up and sound check. As we were running through a couple of songs I noticed that there were a collection of portraits of past and present Grand Masters of the Orange Lodge hanging from the walls. For a laugh, I told the band that I couldn't perform with papist-hating eyes glaring at me. I jumped from the stage and one by one turned the pictures around so that their gaze was now directed to the off white emulsion on the walls. There was much laughter and merriment until the caretaker, led by his floor brush, entered the hall.

On finding that the images of the much respected sash-wearing alumni had been sacrilegiously disrespected in such a heinous manner, he went ape shit. He threw down his broom in a manner that suggested that if he found the culprit there would be a telling-off of biblical proportions. In such instances I have always found that honesty is the best policy, so I honestly hid in a room at the back of the hall until the rest of the band calmed him down. We resumed sound checking under the even more menacing stare of the reinstated bowler hatted brethren and the purple-faced janitor. They, however, weren't the only ones eyeing me suspiciously – my new bandmates looked like they were having second thoughts about taking on a loony as their lead vocalist.

The Ashes had a guy called Rollo Gillespie who did roadie and lights. He spent the time while we were putting the final touches to the set securing to the floor boards a plank that housed a dozen coloured lights. This delicate operation was carried out by gently coaxing six-inch nails through both layers of wood with the blunt edge of a hatchet. I couldn't help thinking that if Hong Kong Phooey the mild-mannered janitor returned and saw what was happening to the platform from which many a rabble-rousing, pope-hating speech, and the odd prayer, had taken place he would have apoplexy and try to shove the handle of his ever present brush up Rollo's hollo.

The reason why our 'lighting technician' was performing this DIY disaster was that the stage had a very bouncy consistency, which meant that the lights jumped all over the place when as much as a foot was placed on it. Why use gaffa tape when wood-splintering nails would do the job nicely?

There was a massive turnout for the gig, many of whom were in local bands and there to assess the competition. Others that would be casting a critical eye over these 'young whippersnapper' newcomers on the scene were the support act for the night, Thunderchild. They had been going for quite a while and had the unique novelty factors of having a guitar player with only two fingers on his fretting hand and a singer who looked like Bobby Ball. Despite these obvious setbacks they were actually a very good band who would end their set with an excellent, elongated version of 'Shadow Play'. And indeed it was the Rory Gallagher classic that they climaxed with on that particular night.

The guitar player, in a state of orgasmic bliss, got a tad carried away and decided that he would show the so-called main band that he was not easily upstaged. As the final note of the crescendo was being held by his bandmates Thunderchild's guitarist proceeded to try and smash his instrument up. Unfortunately the flexibility of the floorboards meant that instead of the Gibson SG shattering into a million pieces it just bounced around the stage like a basketball.

His embarrassment was quite palpable. In an attempt save face, he put even more effort into his swings, which only caused the six-string to bounce higher and higher, smashing some of the lights on the lip of the stage and sending shards of red-hot coloured glass into the crowd. Shoulders slumped, drenched in sweat and sporting a reddner like a flasher's giblets in July, he was just about to give up when he spotted the hatchet that Rollo had used to secure the now demolished lighting board.

A heavily perspiring guitarist ran off stage and returned brandishing the axe above his head like a mad Comanche on the hunt for a fresh paleface scalp. He grabbed the guitar by the neck, knelt down and took a swing. The hatchet made contact, forcing the SG into the trampoline-like stage. The elasticity of the floorboards caused the poor instrument to catapult past the rabbit-in-the-headlights eyes of its ungrateful owner. I couldn't help but think that for a guitar player with two fingers of his hand already missing this was quite frankly a ludicrously risky thing to do.

Any thought, however, for his own safety and the risk of having to tie his shoelaces with his teeth were ignored as he jumped to his feet and chased the object of his anger around the stage raining down blows. The rest of his band were watching on in disbelief, as the guitar seemed to come to life and made off like a kangaroo being chased by Ted Nugent. The band's bass player stood statue still, dutifully strumming the same note. He hoped the nightmare would finish soon. Unfortunately there was worse to come for him as the fleeing guitar, following one particularly heavy whack, was now heading in his direction.

The escape-attempting instrument shot past the cowboy-booted feet of the bass player whose eyes followed its bid for freedom. A glint of silver brought his vision back to his snakeskin footwear just as the 'mad axe man' brought the hatchet down. The blade's trajectory put it on course for the poor bass player's right foot. Too slow to act, he could only whisper the famous Irish prayer 'Holy fuck!!' as the front of his boot was severed off. There were screams from those in the crowd who thought that the toes were still in the tip, which was now spinning on the boards of the stage. Fortunately the fight or flight mechanism in his brain had kicked in and the normal responses of the eyes dilating, the heart racing and the scrotum shrinking were accompanied by the reflex to curl the toes in moments of absolute bowel-loosening terror.

He had avoided amputation of several of his phalanges by mere millimetres. So fine was the distance that a small section of his sock had been shaved off, revealing his still curled tight pinkies. A fight ensued, the bass player, for some reason, taking exception to a raving lunatic trying to cripple him for life during a failed attempted to up-stage the headlining act. He swung his guitar, whacking the maniac over the head. The irony of course, was that it only took this one act of violence to reduce his bass to matchwood, whereas the fool he had rendered unconscious still had, after nearly five minutes of frenzied attack, a fully intact guitar with barely a scratch on it. Follow that No Hot Ashes.

A pedicure with an axe and a murder attempt are quite frankly difficult to upstage. Even Kiss would have struggled. But we took it in our stride and the gig went really well. There were few mistakes but the musicians in attendance were suitably pissed off that we had not fallen flat on our faces and that we were, in fact, rather good. There was one incident, however, that happened just as we were about to go on stage that could have scuppered the whole gig.

The place was in darkness as an intro tape played, I think it was the 1812 Overture or something as pompous. The absence of light was obviously done for dramatic effect, however it made navigating the leads and effects pedals that lay on the floor rather difficult. I had also, for some reason, borrowed a headband from my sister Elish that had flashing lights which blinked on and off in a chasing motion. As the name suggests this naffest piece of fashion accessory should have been placed around my nut, but I, in a fit of artistic expressionism, decided to put it around my thigh, garter style (don't ask).

As I made my way in the pitch black to the centre of the stage the flashing lights could be clearly seen by the crowd. To them it must have looked like a small UFO or something floating across the stage. Motorhead had the massive Bomber; we had a girls' adornment masquerading as a tiny spaceship, which hovered three foot off the ground.

Without warning the lights stopped moving and then dropped out of sight for a second. Some of the audience, who were on magic mushrooms, looked around for the funny little illuminations, wondering, with concern, what could've happened to the little craft and its occupants? There was a sigh of relief when, from the ground, the twinkling lights reappeared safe and well. The intro tape ended: the stage lights that weren't wrecked by the hatchet wielding mad man burst into life. I stood tall and proud, arms outstretched, the luminous garter around my leg making it blatantly obvious that I had just fallen flat on my arse.

And the bands played on

During the first year that I was in No Hot Ashes I was at Bangor Tech taking a business studies course. I didn't have the slightest interest in business but what I did have an interest in was girls. I was persuaded to enrol by a friend, Lawrence Mawhinney, who assured me that there would be a bountiful supply of beautiful, contraceptive-taking, Protestant members of the opposite sex. Where do I sign up?

I, however, never got to 'play the field' because on the first day I clapped eyes on a black-haired, blue-eyed, Amazonian beauty called Adele. I had quite a job wooing her, she put up a fight befitting of her race. Only joking – she had never been anywhere near Latin America, she was from the rainforests of Dundonald. I think she was a little wary of the long-haired hippy who said he was going to be a rock star. I also think she may have been frightened that my image was in some way an indicator that I was a drug addict or something or maybe she just thought I was an asshole. Eventually I did break her down and we started dating.

While pretending to be a student at Bangor Tech an opportunity arose where I was asked to take part in a battle of the bands competition organised by the Students' Union. One of my classmates was a brilliant character called James who was in a band called Definite Glare. They were a sort of Indie band. When I say sort of, I'm not sure if I mean sort of Indie or sort of a band, they really weren't that good, but I persuaded him to take part as well, mainly for the company and the craic. The Ashes were a little reticent about taking part in the competition, which could be viewed as a step backwards, but there was to be a lot of press coverage so they reluctantly agreed.

The venue was a place called the Co-op Hall, which was just behind the market square in Bangor. There were about five or six bands taking part, as well as ourselves and James's band there was an OTT Metal band called Bloodstone, and a band called 70% Proof who were a weird mix doing Kiss covers but with a punk following. They also had in their ranks a drummer who I would become great friends with many years later. The bands congregated backstage and passed suspicious glances. The very Heavy Metal band were overheard planning how to get an advantage over the competition by putting on a little theatrics. Their idea was to copy a band called W.A.S.P. who would throw raw steak or liver into the crowd. They had a whip-round and a roadie was dispatched off to the nearest butchers.

James's band were, in truth, awful. He was playing guitar, where in reality his main instrument of expertise was the French horn – maybe he should have stuck to that. They were also using a drum machine, which they hadn't used before that night. They were under-rehearsed, scared and quite frankly, with their 'Flock of Seagulls' hair cuts they looked a little gay, which at one of the trendier bars in Belfast wouldn't have been a problem but in front of a packed hall of punks, skinheads and rockers was tantamount to suicide. They were forced off the stage in hail of abuse and V-signs.

The next band up were 70% Proof who were excellent, the punks went mad. Watching Mohawks jumping up and down to 'Detroit Rock City' is a kind of surreal experience, but the lads made a big impression. We had a fight on our hands to beat this lot.

The penultimate band before us was the W.A.S.P. wannabes. They were very average but had, as they thought, an ace up their sleeves in the meat-throwing stunt. We all waited, with mock baited breath, for the moment to arrive, which it did at the end of their final song. The singer bent down at the foot of the drum riser and picked up a brown paper bag, the arse of which was slightly reddened with blood. He carried it to the front of the stage, put his hand in and teased the crowd by removing it a few times empty. When he finally revealed the contents of the bag there was a moment's silence before the whole place erupted in hysterical laughter. Dangling from the singer's raised arm and clenched fist was a half-pound string of beef sausages, all they could afford apparently. The idea was to triumphantly toss the meat into an ecstatic crowd like an offering from the gods. Instead what we witnessed was a visibly furious dickhead chucking one of the ingredients of an Ulster Fry at the heads of those at the front of the stage who had the gall to giggle at his attempt at being a Rock deity.

We had a great crowd with us, we were rehearsed and honestly we were good. We played a blinder and went down a storm with our contingent; we, however, were causing a little bit of concern with the punks, who could see their favourites' title slipping. They decided to take matters into their own hands by doing what punks do best: they gobbed at us. I was always very active on stage; I would do a strange sort of dance, which was kind of like a mixture of Paul Stanley, David Lee Roth, Arthur Mullard and Champion the wonder horse. Some commented that I looked like someone waking from a six-year coma and trying to get out of bed. It really didn't look as good as I thought it did. As bad as it was however, it did have the advantage of making me a difficult target to hit.

Davy and Paul didn't move much on stage at all, so I decided for badness to dance in front of the punks goading them, doing 'come on' gestures encouraging even more phlegm. As the spittle left the punks' mouths it disappeared in the stage lights, giving me plenty of time to get out of the way; unfortunately my statuesque colleagues were rooted to the spot. The greeners came back into view and peppered them like the ceiling of a TB ward. Being spat on has to be one of the most disgusting and degrading things any human being can do to another, but what followed made being soaked with tobacco-stained saliva feel like being showered with champagne in comparison.

Seeing as they couldn't quite hit the object of their hatred, namely me, with bacteria-loaded body fluids, the bondage-trousered hordes pelted me with the sausages that they themselves had been attacked with earlier. Oh the utter humiliation, but to add total insult to injury they then proceeded to chuck a burning bag of fine quality sniffing glue at me. Thankfully it missed, but made a rather nasty mess of Stephen's drum kit. I got slightly annoyed, lifted a cymbal stand, entered the crowd and needed a police escort out of the building. The result of the competition was a draw between 70% Proof and us, probably the fairest and may I say safest result for the town centre of Bangor.

Great balls of fire

Somehow, and don't ask me how because I can't remember, we were booked to play a gig in a place called Newtownstewart in Scotland. It was to take place on the day of the final exam of my business studies course. The band and crew, who now counted among their number Fishy – well, you need your mates around you don't you? – travelled on ahead to set up while I went through the motions of putting pen to paper. The exam was immaterial; it would make no difference to my grades as I had already failed by not handing in the course work. As futile as this sounds I did it for the benefit of my parents, whom I hoped wouldn't realise that I had spent the past two years mitching off for romantic walks along the beach in Helens Bay.

Can't remember much about the test but I do remember afterwards being driven at high speed, by my Da, to Larne to catch the last ferry that would get me to Scotland in time for the gig. I made it by the skin of my teeth. Being on my own and a tad lonely, I decided to share the journey with a couple of pints of beer – this, I reasoned, would ward off seasickness by bamboozling the inner ear. With great pride and a certain amount of scientific fortitude I can announce that it worked: I didn't vomit once. I think there should be a clinical trial set up to ascertain the validity of my hypothesis.

'You should see the size of this place,' Dougie, one of our roadies, said as he picked me up from the ferry terminal at Stranraer. 'It's absolutely massive,' he went on. He then explained that we were to play in an equestrian centre, the stage being made up of two articulated lorries backed onto each other. This sounded good to me; they must be expecting a big crowd.

They were indeed hoping for a large turnout and that is what they got. There were at least five hundred in attendance. Unfortunately they didn't look like a crowd that would appreciate a bunch of long-haired loons blasting out Heavy Metal. They looked more like they were waiting for a barn dance and of course that's exactly what they were there for. The guy who booked us, on seeing the makeup of the crowd, was getting a little twitchy. He started slipping in suggestions about playing a few numbers for the older members of the audience. What exactly he thought we were going to play was a mystery. I couldn't really see us rattling off 'Lay the Blanket on the Ground' or

'Drop Kick me Jesus through the Goal Posts of Life.' In saying that, it was not beyond the talents of Paul and Davy: they both had a healthy, Ards Peninsula, taste for all things Roly Daniels. I certainly didn't, so we just decided that we would do what we normally do and hope that we weren't all dragged off to the local witch-dunking stool.

To hide the fact that the stage was two lorries it was draped with camouflage that stretched down to the sawdust-covered floor. This kept the wheels and so on out of sight; it also meant that when the lights were off you couldn't see beyond the netting, which was great for storing drum cases and other band paraphernalia leaving the stage uncluttered.

The changing rooms were Portakabins that were situated outside the riding arena about fifty yards away. The lighting tech for this gig was a guy called Vinty; he was a very funny guy with a thirst that demanded regular quenching. Early on in the day he had started drinking and had no intention of stopping anytime soon. When show time arrived he was well lubricated and just as the intro music was about to start he called a 'time out', revealing that he needed an emergency evacuation of his bowels. With the dressing rooms being so far away and reasoning that horses are not known for their toiletry etiquette, he decided that he would climb under the stage to add his own droppings to the sawdust. The house lights were off in preparation for our grand entrance, so he squatted down happy in the knowledge that his ablutions were hidden from the public's gaze.

It seemed like an eternity standing there on the stage in the pitch black waiting for Vinty to finish his alcohol-enhanced doings. The person in charge of the house lights must've thought that the wait was just a little too long; he flicked a switch flooding the whole place with blinding light. Everyone was blinking and trying to focus, but one little boy's eyes adjusted quicker than everyone else's. He reached round for his mother's comforting hand and pointing said, 'Look mum, there's a man under that lorry doing a loadie!' Vinty, who was crouching down facing away from the front of the stage, turned his head to witness 500 people staring through the netting at him mid-strain. The house lights, mercifully, were shut down rapidly when it was realised that there were numerous decency laws being violated by a drunken red-haired Irish man.

We launched into the first song with most of the audience think-ing that Vinty's guest appearance was some disgusting part of the show, and who could blame them? It was 1985 and the gutter press were implicating Heavy Metal as the cause of all the world's ills. The media fingers were being pointed at the pseudomasochistic buffoon-ery of W.A.S.P. and their 'Animal Fuck like a Beast' tomfoolery as the reason for the decline of Western civilization and family values. As silly as the cod horror of Blackie Lawless and his mates was, it was no more offensive or dangerous than a Hammer Horror movie.

The failed burglar, Ozzy Osbourne, was also, at the time, being portrayed as the son of Satan. Admittedly he wasn't doing himself any favours by filling his 'Diary of a madman' with daily entries of biting the heads off defenceless animals. So Vinty announcing our arrival on stage with a Richard III could quite easily have been seen as just another Heavy Metal outrage by the villagers.

Surprisingly the gig was not a complete disaster. Admittedly there were people leaving in their droves, praying and covering their ears, but a younger crowd of around two hundred and fifty stayed and really got into what we were doing. Realising that we may have grasped victory from the jaws of defeat we really started to enjoy ourselves. And why wouldn't we? We were being paid a fortune, we were on foreign soil, therefore technically we were on tour, and we had been supplied with a rider that consisted of mainly beer. We charged into the last song of the night ready to go out on a high with all the lighting, volume and explosions we could muster: we had our tails up.

Fishy had had problems getting a licence to bring our usual quota of pyrotechnics. This was due to the very strict laws in Northern Ireland that prevented the sale of anything with gunpowder as an ingredient. This was supposed to prevent the IRA from making bombs – well, that worked, didn't it folks? It also meant that for decades kids in the province were deprived of having fireworks at home on Hallowe'en night. Years later when the ban was lifted the little angels celebrated by buying copious amounts of rockets and Catherine wheels, sticking them through pensioners' letterboxes and tying them to the tails of cats and dogs. The authorities reacted by outlawing them again. This time however, they decided that it wouldn't be a total ban; instead you could only purchase them if you were over eighteen, thus creating another black market for the para-militaries to exploit. It just became a little harder to inconvenience old people by sending a rocket up their hallways and keeping them out of their beds while the fire brigade put their houses out.

Anyway Fishy got around these laws by making his own pyros with gunpowder from the cartridges of a legally held shotgun. He also developed contraptions for the detonation of these potentially lethal bombs, which I think, were cobbled together from beer cans, batteries and insulating wires. Let's just say that health and safety would've had a field day if they had been tipped off about the deadly explosive nature of our visual effects. We, I'm afraid, didn't give a flying fig if anyone was maimed or worse, as long as we looked good. Oh, the vanity of the wannabe rockstar.

The home-made flash bombs were used at strategic moments in the set to increase the drama and to heighten the visual experience. For safety reasons, and I mean our safety here, the band knew where and when they were going to be set off. One of these moments came right at the end of the set as we went into the last chorus of the last song.

With the rider consisting of four stale ham baps and copious amounts of McEwen's lager, young Fishy looked after his waistline by ignoring the buffet and instead consuming vast quantities of the tartan-themed gut rot. For some reason his senses were now slightly impaired. With bleary eyes and a brain struggling with the effects of intoxication he positioned the last and most explosive pyro wrongly at the base of the vocal monitor.

Being an Iron Maiden fan I always enjoyed a foot on the monitor moment or two throughout the set and of course, at the very second that Fishy pushed the detonator my genitals were situated directly above the incendiary device. The blast knocked me off my feet, sending me four feet into the air. The impact and pain, when I finally came down, caused me to writhe in agony around the floor. I didn't, however, remain in the prone position for long. On discovering that my PVC trousers were smouldering into a melting mess and sticking to the rapidly vanishing hairs on my thighs and scrotum, I jumped up, and in an attempt to extinguish the forest fire raging twixt my loins, I ran around the stage whacking myself with an open hand between the legs. The ferocity of the blows caused a few of the male members of the audience to come over all faint. It would take weeks before all the little black balls were carefully picked from my own little black balls.

I'm sure you'll agree it was not the best way to begin or end a gig: defecation and castration are never easy on the eye, even as part of a Rock and Roll show. Alice Cooper gets away with this sort of thing because everyone knows it's fake: ours was unnervingly real, but the crowd lapped it up. After the gig the police escorted us, for some reason that escapes me, to our accommodation for the night. We had been told it was to be a caravan on a site about five miles away in Newtownstewart village. There were ten of us in total so we were expecting quite a large mobile home affair. What we were presented with was a two-berth rust bucket with a flat tyre.

As we stood, sweating, knackered and speechless, the promoter made good his escape, leaving the superstars of the night to fight over the two beds available. Davy was too drunk to care about the sleeping arrangements, but he did put in a dazzling display of stuntmanship when he opened the door of the caravan to walk out. Not realising that it was split level, he went head first over the bottom half. As inebriated as he was he still had the presence of mind to save his guitar-playing hands by breaking the fall with his face. The impact would, at least, help get him to sleep but it would hinder his modelling career, which had not got off to the best start due to his lack of height and not being that good looking. Some of us, the ones that weren't lucky or quick enough to share a bed with the caravan's fleas, slept in the front seats of the van. I on the other hand, decided that I would get my head down in Dougie's Datsun Sunny: for a six-footer this was a bit of a contortionist's act, but at least I would get some peace.

It was a cloudless night and the temperature dropped quite dramatically. The chill even woke me, which was surprising given the amount of drink I had had. Having been left the keys to the car, I started the engine and turned on the heater, just to warm up. While I was bringing my core temperature back to a normal 37 degrees C, I turned on the radio and listened to a little late-night highland flinging. I awoke the next morning to the news being read by someone with a Scottish accent. I raised my weary head and went to look for sustenance and company. The former was in short supply, the latter plentiful, as nobody had been able to sleep due to the cold and flea bites. I however, had slept like a baby.

We were all starving, so it was decided that Dougie should drive the short distance into the village and pick up whatever food he could. I volunteered to accompany him seeing as I was the only one feeling as fresh as daisy. We jumped into his car and Dougie turned the ignition. There was not a sound. He tried it again and again nothing. He looked at the petrol gauge and was faced with a flat needle. 'That's funny,' he said, 'I filled it up yesterday. It must have a leak.' I began to realise that I must have fallen asleep with the engine running all night. I stood silent as Dougie rolled around in the muck under the car looking for a non-existent puddle of petrol.

With no leak evident a flat battery was suspected. After a few attempts to push-start the car, a couple of which I took part in myself, knowing full well that there was not a hope in hell of it starting, we gave up and took the van into the village.

There was only one shop open: it was one of those quaint establishments that sold everything, from tins of beans to Wellington boots, from tin foil to maggots for fishing. There was an elderly couple behind the counter who pointed in the general direction of the items we requested. There seemed to be no rhyme nor reason to their displaying system – the toothpaste was beside the super glue, which was beside the haemorrhoid cream. A slight miscalculation, while filling your shopping basket, could result in a life-threatening accident.

We got chatting to the rather grumpy owners, or should I say the female of the duo, though it was hard to tell seeing as both of them were wearing skirts and both had substantial facial hair of the ginger variety. They were complaining about a lack of sleep – or should I say the lady was as the man was talking like a ventriloquist. He seemed to be having trouble with his dentures, which appeared to be stuck together. The old dear complained that they had been kept awake due to the deafening volume of a band which must have been playing in the pub next door. We didn't have the balls to tell them that the racket that had kept them from their well-earned rest was us, and we had been five miles away. The lady said that it wouldn't have been so bad but since she had applied her Preparation H, over a week ago, she had been suffering dreadful constipation. We made a hasty retreat, but a rustic old fella who was complaining that his Airfix model of a Harrier Jump Jet kept falling apart and smelt of spearmint, momentarily blocked our exit. We side-stepped him and rejoined the band for breakfast before heading back across the shuck.

Stephen Magee

Soon after we returned from the land of the haggis I found out and was amazed that, by some miracle, I had passed my exams, gaining an ONC in business studies. It transpires that my lack of course work meant that I couldn't gain the OND, a more academically prestigious award, but I didn't care. Adele passed with flying colours, naturally, and was about to enroll on a degree course in England; we would have to kiss via British Telecom for the foreseeable future. I would remain in Belfast and try to help No Hot Ashes to world domination.

Up to this point we had never really had a manager as such. There had been one well-intentioned guy called Jonathon who owned a record shop, but he was just too nice. Enter Stephen Magee, a friend of sorts, who approached me about representing the band. When I say a friend of sorts, I mean that he was more of an acquaintance; he used to frequent my Ma's shop and entertain me with tales of Rock and Roll excess while trying to shoplift. I was not easily distracted however, and knew what was going on all the time. Stephen being Stephen you could forgive the rogue anything and when you asked him to pay for the items in his pockets, he always did.

So how did Stephen end up managing a pretty successful band from this situation? Well we had just recorded a new demo tape and when he came into the shop one day I let him have a copy. He left, and roughly in the time it took to walk to his house, which was just around the corner, listen to the tape and return, he was back declaring that he was the new manager of No Hot Ashes. I laughed – but not nearly as much as the rest of the band did when I told them the good news. But Stephen was determined and one by one he won everyone over, and after all isn't that what a good manager is supposed to be about?

Stephen's first name was dropped and he became known simply as Magee. He used to walk around with what would now be called a manbag; he thought he was setting a new fashion trend with what was just a girl's canvas school satchel. I'm sure the style icons of today would get away with it, but 80s Belfast was not quite ready for such a bold expression of sartorial eloquence. It would often get him into heated discussions with bone-headed Nazi scumbags that, on many occasions, would result in him getting a good hiding. The bag was only one instance of how Magee expressed his individuality and lack of fear; he was brave and principled to the point of madness, and this endeared him to me immensely.

Magee shared a flat just off Shaftsbury Square, the entertainment epicentre of Belfast, with a loveable eccentric loon called Eric, who would go off to places like India and take photographs of steam trains. While he was off on his travels, which was very regularly, the flat became party central for the Rock fraternity and many a memorable evening of frivolity occurred there. At one of these social gatherings the Ashes drummer Stephen Campbell was trying to get off with this 'well to do' girl who had as much interest in Metal as Linda McCartney had in pork chops. She said she loved classical music. Stephen saw an opportunity to impress when he remembered a record he had come across in Eric's collection. He proudly announced that his favorite composer was Chopping. 'Who?' the out of place Daddy's girl asked, wishing she had taken up the invitation to go to the golf club with Quentin Stelfox, the leader of the Young Conservatives (Ulster branch). 'Chopping, Chopping!' our stereo-typical drummer shouted while miming the motion of Rufus T. Roughcut taking an axe to a tree. He then went to the pile of albums and returned with Piano Concerto No. 1 in E minor by Chopin.

Magee considered himself a bit of a ladies' man; he had the gift of the gab and looked like a cross between Jimmy Rabbit, the charac-ter in 'The Commitments', and Richard E. Grant in 'Withnail and I'. His brother Arty, another fine human being, reminded me lately that a friend of theirs used to call him 'Jimmy the Weed' from the Thin Lizzy song 'Johnny the Fox'. And you know, that was just about perfect: he was tall and skinny as a rake with an air of mischief and menace thrown in. I could see why women would easily fall for him; bad girls like bad boys and good girls like bad boys more.

One night he had invited a young lady he had been seeing for a while back to the flat for a little light supper and a bottle of red wine. There was only one problem: I was staying in Eric's room while he was away. Magee announced, 'I have the feeling that I may get lucky tonight young Nancarrow,' which he had not been up to this point. 'So I would appreciate you making yourself scarce this evening,' he went on. Being just around the corner from the best watering holes in the city, I needed no further encouragement. I made my way to Lavery's Gin Palace and met up with some of the creatures of the night that frequent its legendary back bar.

I stayed for as long as I thought it would take Magee to complete his despicable mission and luckily this coincided with chucking-out time. On my return the would-be lovers were still sitting at the table, the lights dimmed, candles burning, a hint of incense in the air and the romantic sounds of 'The Who Live at Leeds' gently blasting from the stereo speakers.

'Back so soon?' the slightly annoyed Lothario asked.

'Don't worry I shall be retiring to my room,' I replied. And off to my solitary confinement I trooped.

I was awoken a couple of hours later by the stomach-churning screams of a woman. I jumped out of bed and to my horror realised that the wailing was coming from Magee's room. 'My God, he's beating her up,' I thought. But that would've been totally out of character. 'Everything OK?' I shouted through the door, knowing fine well rightly that it bloody well was not. There then came a hysterical request for me to enter, which I did with great trepidation. What greeted me was a vision that still haunts me to this very day.

There standing in the smoke-filled room, was the naked, holocaust victim-type figure of Magee beating the equally naked but certainly better nourished body of his date for the evening, with a pillow. What was even more disturbing was that I thought I could smell mulled wine wafting in the air; Christmas would never be the same. To my disgust Magee appeared to be in a semi-excited state, if ya catch my drift, causing me to divert my eyes, but no matter where I looked I found no solace.

'What's going on?' I shouted over the sobs of the young lady. 'Just help me get her out,' Magee squealed. Being very careful not to touch anything that would get me arrested I got the victim under the arms, while Valentino lifted her legs and we carried her out of the room. Even though I was now choking I was actually quite glad of the smoke; it partially obstructed the nauseating sight that befell my eyes. We dispatched our burden onto the sofa, quickly covering her with a throw and then we rushed back into room to deal with the cause of the smoke.

When calm was restored I demanded an explanation from Magee. What I was told still makes me chuckle. It transpires that the happy couple had retired to the boudoir with their wine and a candle to ensure the mood was relaxed. At some point during the proceedings the candle was kicked over onto the quilt, setting it alight. When Magee finally realised what was going on – he originally mistook the screaming from his conquest as squeals of pleasure – he resourcefully threw the remainder of their drinks onto the flames, hence the smell of mulled wine. He then tried to further extinguish the fire by beating it with the pillow. It was of course at this point that I entered the room to help remove the paralysed with fear wretch. You know, I never saw her again, and unsurprisingly neither did Magee.

The Ashes played a gig in the depths of mid-Ulster one cold winter's night. It was in a bar in Ballymena that was run by para-militaries, a fact that if we had known before we arrived we probably wouldn't have done it. Although in saying that, if we were to refuse to play gigs that had paramilitary involvement we wouldn't have had a great selection to choose from, such was the state of affairs in Northern Ireland.

We were shown into a back room that had a stage at one end and we set up our substantial amount of amplifying gear, lights and pyrotechnics. We then went to the closed upstairs lounge, which was to be our changing room for the night. On the floor was disco equip-ment; Paul pointed out that we could purchase a similar amplifier and speakers and make much-needed bigger monitors. This was quite literally music to my ears as I was having difficulty hearing myself above the deafening volume we played at. Magee took note and said he would see if the finances would stretch.

The gig was an unmitigated disaster. We had somehow been booked for the Country and Western night and there was nearly a riot after we finished the very first song. Imagine the scene, there we were dressed in the latest women's fashion and there was the clientele looking like the cast from the gunfight at the OK Corral. There were Stetsons, fringed jackets, chaps and guns, some of which were fired into the air, as the locals got restless. The words 'There'll be lynchin' in the old town tonight' came to mind.

The bar manager came running to the stage and politely screamed, 'Fuck off you bunch of poofy bastards!' We didn't need to be homophobicly insulted twice; we left the stage post-haste to the strains of 'Elijah was a Wooden Indian' the old Charlie Pride song, which had been hastily shoved onto the sound system. And oh, how the townsfolk danced: they were a-whoopin' and a-hollerin', their spurs cutting large furrows in the ground just as some of their ploughs had done earlier that day.

All joking aside, we really did fear for our lives: the people who ran the bar were not the sort of people you pissed off, especially as some of us were from the other side of the political divide, namely myself and our now drunk manager. It was Magee's job to get the money we thought we so richly deserved for the excellent song we had played. He went off in an attempt to prise the money from the local intelligentsia and we got changed – we didn't want our silly clothes causing any further offence to Jesse James and his gang of square-dancing civil servants.

On his return Magee said the management had refused to pay us because the Buffalo Bills and Minnie Hahas had demanded their money back. However, he did say that to compensate they had said we could take the amplifier and speakers from the disco, as they were broken and were going to be thrown out anyway. We didn't argue, we were more than ready to leave; Fishy and Dougie had got the gear into the van in the quickest time ever. We walked past the manager and his Johnny 'Mad Dog' Adair lookalike bar staff, and with a wave we thanked them for not killing us and for the broken gear they so generously paid us with. They totally blanked us.

When we got to the van Magee, who could hardly stand at this point, said he had changed his mind, he wasn't going until we got paid properly. Everyone told him to 'wise up' but he was insistent. He needed someone to go with him as backup; everyone refused except me. We returned to the bar to be greeted with, 'And what the fuck do you two ladies want now?' from our jovial host. Magee explained that we had no petrol to get us home: we would have to stay parked in the grounds of his delightful little hostelry overnight, which might just attract the attention of the local constabulary. Thick-neck thought this over. He didn't want any cops sniffing around his whiter than white establishment: they might just turn up an arms cache or drugs consignment mistakenly left by a customer or someone (ahem!!).

From the till the irate manager took out a wad of notes, handed it to Magee, then whispered, 'Take this and take your band of fruits out of here, but remember this, there are an awful lot of accidents on the roads around these parts at this time of the year.' I could feel my blood run cold. I turned to make my escape and as I reached the door I couldn't believe my ears when I heard Magee over-egg the pudding by saying, 'It was a pleasure doing business with you.' The reply, 'Fuck off,' was the last thing I heard as we left the premises.

We jumped into the van, Magee held up his fist full of notes and shouted, 'Result!!' Everyone cheered as we drove off. A short distance along the icy, winding roads I relayed the tale of what happened back at the bar and the manager's road safety warning. There was a nervous silence and to a man everybody looked out the back window of the van. Magee then says, 'I suppose this is a bad time to tell you that they didn't give us the amplifier and speakers – we've just stolen them.' Every car that approached us for the rest of the journey was greeted with breaths held.

What a marvellous night for a moonshine

Magee got a job doing PR for a local charity called Physically Handicapped and Able Bodied (PHAB). On their flag days we would help raise funds by shaking tins in the streets of Belfast; Magee hoped that this would get us some positive media coverage, which it did. It was following one such day that we decided to meet up with Ken in Holywood for a drink. He had just started going out with a blonde-haired beauty called Elaine. It was a coincidence that we had just done our bit for the physically and mentally disabled seeing as she must have had impairments of her own. I mean, who would go out with Ken Heaven unless they were blind, deaf and minus the senses of taste and smell? The poor girl at least had her looks to fall back on.

We met up with them in Cicerino's and had a fine evening of drink and craic – it was so good that the night was in danger of ending too soon when last orders were called. It was decided, not by me I hasten to add, that to elongate the proceedings we should go back to Magee's house and on the way I was to stop off at my house and sneak a bottle of my Da's poteen. The auld lad had a collection of Irish Moonshine that he kept above the store door of the shop, I know not where he got it officer honestly I don't. I had had a few drinks myself at this stage but I still thought it was a bad idea, for death at the hands of your father is not an ideal way to go and this would have been the result if I had been caught. We argued for a while and I lost, and I was sent on my mission with a further request to get a couple of bottles of Coke as a mixer.

I tiptoed through the house like an elephant with a flea up its ass, but I did make it to the store door, amazingly, without waking the whole house. It was here that I came upon a problem, you see there were many different bottles, all opened, all looking the same but with different amounts in them.

The Craythure (pronounced crater), as it is known, can be made from anything with sugar: potatoes (traditional), apples, brandy balls and even jam. In the interests of mental and physical health you really shouldn't combine them. However I couldn't take a bottle with a lot in it as it would be missed, so I broke this cardinal rule and lifted a bottle from the far left of the shelf that was about a third full. I then topped it up with a small amount from each of the other bottles. Safely back out on the street I made my way round the corner to chez Magee. When I got to the door I suddenly remembered that the bottle I had lifted was sitting away from the others for a reason: it was white spirit that my Da used for cleaning his paintbrushes.

The door opened and a cheering Magee snatched the bottle of paint thinners and illegal whiskey from my hands. 'Get the glasses!' he shouted.

'Wait,' I screamed, 'I've accidentally mixed a bottle of white spirit with the poteen.'

'Sure you have,' the now salivating Magee laughed.

'No seriously, I have,' I said.

This seemed to bring him to his senses and he asked if I was certain. I told him I couldn't be 100% sure but I thought so. He stroked his chin for a moment and then ran upstairs, returning with his bleary-eyed brother.

'Sniff this,' Magee says holding the open bottle under his confused sibling's nose. After a couple of inhalations he was then asked 'can you smell white spirit?'

'No, now can I go back to bed?' was the reply.

'Ha ha!' Magee shouts. 'That's it settled, it's just poteen.'

'How do you know?' I asked.

A triumphant Magee replied, 'Young David here does a bit of painting and decorating, and surely he would know the smell of white spirit.'

His logic floored me, but it seemed to be enough for the rest of the company, who sat down to a paraffin derivative and once-distilled hooch concoction, mixed with Coke. Tasty. I politely declined.

Around 2pm next day I got a phone call from Ken who called me a bastard. He had tried to make his way home after consuming the toxic cocktail but was somewhat hindered by a loss of his peripheral vision. He could just see through a pinprick of light, which was only possible when he got down on all fours. He said that every car that passed tooted their horns and shouted obscenities. Worse still, Elaine had accompanied him – it was one of their first dates and with her coming from a slightly more privileged background than Ken, God knows what she was thinking as she walked beside him as he crawled along the road. With his shock of long black hair it must have looked like Penelope Keith in 'To The Manor Born' walking a denim-clad Afghan hound.

The mile and a half to Ken's house caused havoc to those body parts that were in constant contact with the stony tarmac, and his hands and knees were in tatters by the time he got home. His injuries gave him cause to give me more abuse down the phone; he claimed that the damage would hinder his musical career. I countered that not being able to play the guitar very well would be a bigger hindrance; again he called me a bastard and hung up.

A couple of hours later I got another phone call. This time it was Magee asking me to call round to his house ASAP. On arrival I found him lying on his back on the floor.

'What's up?' I asked.

'What's up? What's up?' he screams. 'I'll tell you what the feck's up.' It transpires that he had been able to make it into work that morning, but was feeling a tad fragile. While sitting at his desk, he decided to put his head down and get 40 winks. On waking, four hours later, he found that the muscles in his back had seized up: he couldn't move. He started calling for help but unfortunately this was late arriving: he had locked the door of his office to enable him to get his well-earned kip.

It was a good, agonising, half hour before a maintenance man could be found to remove the door. But the ultimate humiliation, Magee said, was that he had to be carried to a waiting cab, on the displaced door, by the physically disabled staff that worked with him. I nearly wet myself laughing which made Magee start laughing, which only made the pain worse, which made me laugh and so on. There was one further twist to this tale; all who consumed the elixir of death were constipated for about two weeks, which I also got the blame for.

Stand and deliver – your money or your life

We played a fund-raising gig for PHAB in an East Belfast hotel called the Earlswood. Magee had asked a number of other local bands to bolster the bill; the response was so good that it had to be turned into an all-day event. We, of course, as it was our gig, were to headline. It turned out to be a cracking day with a really good turnout for all the bands, which was satisfying as the proceedings kicked off at the hangover-nursing hour of twelve noon on a Saturday. This is not the time of day that most self-respecting Rock and Roll animals see normally, but to the credit of Belfast's metalheads, from both sides of the community, they turned up in their bloodshot-eyed droves.

By the time we were to hit the stage the place was packed, the punters suitably refreshed. One guy was so refreshed that he congratulated Fishy, who was manning the lighting console at the side of the stage, on being a brilliant keyboard player.

At the end of our set a friend of ours, Big Stevie Wright, jumped up onto the stage and lifted me onto his shoulders, à la Angus Young. Stevie got the 'big' part of his name for being big, funnily enough. He must have weighed twenty stone and stood six feet tall. With me being roughly about the same height and with the ceiling of the stage just ten feet from the floor there wasn't any clearance.

To avoid hitting my head I had to lean forward; unfortunately it now looked like I was sniffing Stevie's hair. As gay as this appeared, it worked, that is until the big lad decided to jump up and down, ramming my head into the roof. I tried to alert him to the possible brain damage he was causing, by slapping him on the crown with my fist. Unfortunately he took this as a sign of encouragement, jumping all the higher. If that was not bad enough his neck was a little on the thick side – it was hard to tell where it finished and his head began. My strides were tight, offering no protection for my 'Jackson Pollocks'.

My testicles lifted off Big Stevie's neck with each ascent and came crashing down with each descent. Considering I was actually supposed to be singing at this point it made for a very interesting listening experience. The noise was sort of like a mixture of Paul Robeson ('Old Man River') as I went up and Tiny Tim ('Tiptoe Through the Tulips') as I came down. Added to this was the percussive effect of my head being pounded and my teeth being cracked by the mic. Personally I think I was years ahead of my time by inventing rap/Metal/opera crossover. I even threw in a beat box for good measure.

There was major bruising to my inner thighs, head and lips but worst of all my testicles had swollen up to the size of grapes. These injuries, however, were the least of my worries when members of the local paramilitaries approached us after the gig. The two 'war heroes' with their bum fluff moustaches confronted Magee and myself in the changing room. They declared that it would be in our best interests if we could find it within our hearts to donate 25% of the proceeds to help them in their cause of keeping the Protestant North of Ireland part of the British Isles, by primarily shooting people. In reality, judging by the rat-like appearance and limited vocabulary, mostly swear words with no more than four letters, the likelihood was that the money would have been used to buy cheap cider and Benson & Hedges. But there was still a risk that it would be used to purchase bullets that would end up embedded in the heads of Catholic taxi drivers, as was the gut-churning fashion of the times.

As far as we could remember the gig had not been set up to enable the murder of anyone so we politely refused the thugs' kind invita-

tion. 'Rodent boys' didn't take this too kindly and dragged themselves up to their full 5 foot 4 heights issuing a direct threat of
physical violence if we didn't hand over the cash. Magee's gentlemanly demeanour was starting to slip, his face was turning red, and
he himself stood up, dwarfing the latter-day Robin Hoods. He then
said, 'The bands that took part in this event were from both sides of
the political divide, they did it to raise money for people less fortunate than themselves from both sides of the political divide, so take
your hatred and fuck off into the night!!' This went down like a
Bhangra band at a National Front convention. Slaps were exchanged
and throats were grabbed, the end result being that two short-arsed
men left the changing room quicker than they came in.

Magee was purple with anger: he ranted and raged for about ten
minutes until there was a knock on the door. There was an uneasy
silence. Had the wee shits come back with a gun? Probably not, I
mean would they have knocked on the door if they had intended
shooting us? From their previous show of manners I thought not.

'Who is it?' I asked.

'It's me, Jim, the manager, can I have a chat?' A sheepish proprietor entered the room avoiding any eye contact. He then proceeded
to tell us that he had just had a committee meeting with his security
team and the upshot was that he was to advise us that we needed to
shut up and pay up. He apologised and left the room; I think he was
genuinely embarrassed.

The band had our own meeting and to our shame we concluded
that it was probably a good idea to avoid future auditions by ensuring that the musicians we already had were not killed. Magee
reluctantly agreed but was absolutely adamant that it was not going
to be a quarter of the takings but a small token gesture. £50 was
literally ripped from the wad of notes in Magee's hand. It was given
to Jim as we left, he thanked us with a knowing nod and wished us
luck. Thankfully we didn't need it.

Plastic fantastic

It was decided that the way forward was to independently release a
single in an attempt to try and get record company interest. The

labels were nearly all based in London and with it being the height of the 'Troubles' they were as likely to come to Belfast, as you were to see Keith Richards at A.A.

Magee put the PR machine in top gear and went about raising the funds that would be necessary to produce the seven-inch piece of plastic that would propel us to the top of the charts. With his gift of the gab he was able to persuade many people to make a healthy investment in the guaranteed future of Belfast's leading purveyors of all things Wimp Metal. What they received back however, was a critically ill return.

I can't really remember much about the recording process, but I do remember thinking that the guys doing the engineering and producing were more familiar with Irish folk music, which didn't bode well. One of them also had a very keen interest in extremely strong foreign porn and would spend the time when he was supposed to be listening to the band, flicking through dog-eared magazines depicting heavily mustachioed German men and women loving each other with grimaces on their faces. The results, in retrospect, were less than impressive, especially my vocal performance, which was truly awful: Mutt Lange couldn't have made me sound good in those days.

We of course, at the time, thought that the recording sounded bloody marvellous, it would be a hit and we were going to be millionaires. Final mix done, we all climbed into Davy's Mini Cooper with all the talk being of limousines and champagne. I cracked open what I hoped would be my last, twenty-four for a fiver, can of 'Top Brass' lager. When we were stars I would be able to afford something a little more refined, perhaps Harp, Tennent's or heaven forbid the liquid gold of Heineken – yes, from now on it was only the best for me.

I had to put my decadent tastes on hold for a while. The pressing of the single, which was being carried out in England, dragged on. It took so long in fact, that most people had forgotten about it. Worse still, there were mumblings from those liberated from their cash to finance the thing, that maybe it didn't exist at all and that the whole thing was a scam. When it finally arrived it looked very impressive but sounded less so. Regardless of the quality we now had to sell it in enough quantities to recoup the initial outlay and to try to prick the interest of the labels by proving that we could shift units.

All opportunities were taken to flog it; stalls were set up at gigs, adverts taken out in the local press. Even my Ma and Da's corner shop had a box of them sitting on the counter ready for the next customer to be bullied into purchasing a Heavy Metal single with their 'Pretty Polly' support hosiery. There were elderly customers who bought a copy with the only rationale being that 'Our Eamon's on it.' Most didn't even have a record player. As the years passed and they passed away themselves, relatives would scratch their heads wondering why their 86-year-old aunt had taken to buying numerous copies of the same record by a poodle-haired Rock band. None of them would contest that part of the will.

The charts in Northern Ireland, at that time, were based on sales reported from the big record store, 'Caroline Music'. Everyone we knew was dispatched to their nearest branch and ordered to buy, buy, buy!! By some miracle and a little creative accountancy, the single went top ten in the Caroline Music hot 100. Well in one store anyway. I remember going into that shop and staring at the bank of singles on the wall and there at number 8 or 9 was 'She Drives me Crazy', just behind Roland Rat's version of 'Love Me Tender'. I was famous at last, just not as famous as a stuffed rodent with a man's hand up its arse, who sounded like an even more congested Bob Dylan.

Joking aside, we were getting quite well known. Magee was beside himself with glee when one Saturday afternoon I was stopped outside Belfast City Hall by two very attractive young ladies and asked to sign their freshly purchased singles. Magee stood beside me beaming with pride. I, on the other hand, turned crimson as the punks and skinheads, who regularly congregated in the grounds of the old Victorian building, jeered and called me a pretty boy poof. I could handle the verbal abuse but I couldn't help feeling degraded, like I was a piece of meat for these teenage girls to lust and letch over. Could they not see beyond the good looks, the thick luxuriant hair and the thin wiry muscular frame, that there was a human being with feelings and philosophies on all manner of life's questions? Stuff that – I loved every second of it, I could ride this train forever, I mean my looks would never fade, would they?

There is nothing quite like hearing yourself on the radio for the first time. I was driving back from dropping Adele, who was home on holiday, off at her mum and dad's house in Dundonald, just cruising over the Craigantlet Hills listening to a late-night show on 'Downtown Radio' called 'Flavell Unravels'. Jackie was an old blues/jazz head so I was quite surprised when I heard the opening keyboard intro to the A side of the single. I was even more surprised when he announced that he liked it so much he was going to play it again, and again and again. By the time I made it home he had spun 'She Drives me Crazy' four times back to back and the B side 'Don't Drag my Name Around' twice. I sat outside my Ma and Da's house listening, with a rosy glow inside, until old Jackie got bored or capitulated to the listeners' phone calls of complaint. A great moment that still lives on in the memory.

A summer trip

We all used to frequent a bar in Holywood called the Gallery; it was a great wee pub, which had a rather eclectic jukebox. There was everything from folk to Rock and Roll, from Country and Western to Richard Clayderman. There was also a copy of our single that we had conned the owner into putting in. One Twelfth of July the band, crew and selected hangers-on all met up there for a few swift ones before returning to my Ma and Da's house for a party. They had made the rather foolhardy decision to go on holiday leaving their teenage kids in charge of the house and shop.

Whilst consuming a couple of pints of Holstein we gathered together our spare change and charged up the jukebox to play the single twenty times in a row. We hoped it would generate a bit of interest from the locals and drown out the noise of the local 'kick the Pope' band marching up and down the High Street just outside. After about ten spins of the disc an old soak at the bar threw his hands in the air, and not knowing who we were, shouted, 'If I hear that fecking song one more time I'm gonna feckin kill myself, I mean it, I'm gonna paint myself green, white and gold and throw myself in front of that fecking band outside!' Jesus, I know it wasn't the best single ever released but it wasn't that bad, some people just have no taste.

We headed back to the house for our traditional Twelfth of July multi-denominational party. Any excuse for a session would do, a day off is, after all, a day off, even if it does celebrate one side of the community killing members of the other side in a muddy field four centuries ago. On the way we stopped off at the Chinese takeaway in order to get something with which to line our stomachs.

As I was ordering from the orange plastic menu board on the wall, the lettering started to move. Being a lifelong sufferer of migraine headaches, I just thought I was having the usual visual disturbances that herald the beginning of one of the most nauseating, debilitating afflictions that anyone can suffer from.

Migraines have on occasions made my life misery; there were periods when I would get one per day for months on end. It takes three days to get over one so I was never really recovered before I had the next one. I must admit that the lack of sleep, constant pain, nausea and puberty caused the black clouds of depression to rain down their drops of self-loathing. I had some very dark days as a teenager.

People who have never suffered from migraines don't understand – maybe it's the word 'headache' that gives them the opportunity to scoff and insinuate that you are swinging the lead. I'm not a vindictive person but I wish that all those people who think that they can be sorted out with an aspirin could have one just to experience the misery. Only the one mind; you wouldn't wish this curse on your worst enemy.

Anyway I digress, we collected the meals, me knowing that mine would remain untouched due to the impending illness. At least I could content myself that the food wouldn't go to waste: the human eating machine that is Ken Heaven would polish it off after he had had his own of course.

Back in the house I told Adele that I was having a migraine, I made my excuses and retired to my darkened bedroom to await the blinding pain behind my eyes to travel across my head, down my neck and eventually settle into my back muscles. Painkillers, quiet and absence of light were, at the time, the only way I could deal with my affliction; however in later years, and to remain employable, I would have to just ignore the symptoms, hide the misery and get on with it – not easy. I fell into a doze filled with horrendous nightmares.

I woke with a jump, glad to be released from the images that had crammed my sleeping head. After breathing a sigh of relief I suddenly realised that, far from the visions fading, they were getting more vivid with my eyes open. In the dim light I could see the posters on my walls rippling: Mick Jagger, David Coverdale, Angus Young and Elvis were making like they were trying to escape their two-dimensional state and join the party. Blinking, I rubbed my eyes and tried to focus. I thought I could hear noises. It sounded like Mick was asking me if I was 'avin' a gooood tyme'. Coverdale was shouting 'Ere's a song for ya' and Angus's guitar was wailing while he headbanged like a good 'un.

Even Lado Morrow, who was now living in Dublin, made a guest appearance, sitting in an armchair facing the bed and screaming like he used to when singing Deep Purple's 'Child in Time'. I pulled the covers over my head and begged for the madness to stop. Then out of the swirling vortex of damnation came a voice that normally sounded like a Belfast bum with nodes on his vocal chords – now, however, it was so comforting it sounded like the lilt of Maureen O'Hara mixed with the saccharine sweetness of a praying Daniel O'Donnell.

'Eamon, are you coming down? It's getting late, Adele's away home and the house is packed.' I slowly pulled back the quilt and there standing in the doorway was St Kenneth of Heaven.

'Are you real?' I enquired.

'What?' he asked.

I said, 'Jagger, Angus, Cov, Elvis and Big Lado were here just a minute ago. They were screaming and dancing to some sort of cacophonous mix of "Highway to Hell", "Midnight Rambler", "Ready and willing" and for feck's sake "American Trilogy". I'm not feeling that great mate, I'm really not.'

Thank goodness for friends. On seeing the distress I was in Ken jumped into action. He quietly closed the door, leaving me to whatever madness had gripped me with the comforting words, 'Jesus Christ he's finally flipped, he won't be needing that Sweet and Sour I suppose?'

Indeed I really did think that I had finally flipped; I genuinely believed that I was having some sort of mental breakdown. And as if to confirm my summations, Satan's house band started to play again.

I jumped out of the bed and tried to remonstrate with the very unwelcome rock stars; they were having none of it and started laughing at me, their faces and bodies melting and mingling like something Salvador Dali would knock up. Let me tell you there is no more frightening sight than that of David Coverdale with a massive quiff, rubbery lips and wearing a schoolboy's crotch-hugging shorts. I was that convinced that I had succumbed to a mental illness that I contemplated throwing myself out of the skylight window in the hope that the pavement, three floors below, would bring some peace of mind.

I kid you not, I really was considering suicide: the visions and noises were so frightening that I thought that if I had to spend the rest of my life in this state then it would be a life better cut short. I opened the window and pulled over the armchair, which thankfully Lado had vacated. I stood on it and pulled myself up using the window ledges. As my head met the cool night air a wave of nausea came over me and I threw up onto the roof tiles.

The retching went on for about ten minutes; most of the time there was nothing to come up which was agony on my abdominal muscles. With the pain, however, came a kind of epiphany, a realisation that I didn't want to die; there was a snapping back to reality, of sorts, that allowed me to step away from the armchair, thus avoiding a rather unsightly mess for the milkman to find on the doorstep the next day. Don't get me wrong, there were still visions and noises but they were less vivid and I somehow knew they would pass. I climbed into bed and held on to my pillow like a rodeo rider who knows the consequences of letting go are worse than the pain of holding on. I finally fell asleep.

The next day things had returned, more or less, to normal. When I say normal I did find that for the next few days, every now and then, I would see things moving out of the corner of my eye, but when I turned to look at them there was nothing and, eventually they went forever. There was one thing that was definitely out of the ordinary the morning after the worst night of my life that I must report.

When I entered the living room I was greeted by a poteen-drenched mess, in the form of Magee prostrate on the carpet. He was blubbering and begging forgiveness for attempting to eat a cooked chicken that had been in the fridge. He slurred that he had dropped it on the floor after taking a couple of bites out of it. He had then attempted to retrieve it, but the state he was in he had to give up after three goes. I went berserk thinking that it must have been roasted in preparation of my Ma and Da's return that very day. I ran into the kitchen to inspect the carnage but instead of the carcass of a ravaged bird I found a large lump of dough that my sister Louise had made for biscuits, lying on the ground with two huge teeth marks in it.

Around Christmas time that same year, I was in the Gallery again and I bumped into a guy who I had not seen for some time. I must admit he wasn't somebody I would normally pass the time of day with, but there are occasions when you are put in a social setting where you are forced to converse. He said the last time we had been talking was on the 'Glorious Twelfth'. I said I couldn't really recall. He said, with a big ugly smirk on his mug, that he wasn't surprised. I asked him what he was going on about. He just asked me if I had had a good time that day. I was just about to say that I couldn't remember that far back, when the whole nightmare of the wall-crawling visions returned and I said, 'Actually, no, I had a terrible time, I was sick as a dog.'

'That's a shame,' he says, 'that was a good bit of gear I wasted on you then.'

'What do you mean?' I asked, the penny starting to drop.

He said, 'You're obviously into your Rock music so I popped a wee acid tab into your pint to get you off your face. Let's just call it a gift.'

I really felt like stringing this little piece of shit up by his balls, he had literally nearly killed me. Unfortunately, as with many things in our wonderful province, he was a very dangerous person who would have made my life and my family's hell if I had laid a finger on him. To my shame I let the smug little bastard off.

Have a drink on me

No Hot Ashes got the chance to support one of my all-time favourite singers, Steve Marriot. He was playing with his band 'Packet of Three' at the La Mon House Hotel, the scene of what has been described as, one of the worst atrocities of the Troubles. In 1978 the

IRA attached a bomb containing a napalm-type concoction of petrol and sugar to an outside window of the hotel, killing twelve people and horrendously burning many more. The perpetrators used the excuse that they had tried to phone through a warning from a public phone box but it had been vandalised. Imagine trying to blame the carnage on a couple of kids who had wrecked the phone. Here's a thought: if they don't want to hurt anybody they should try not sticking bombs outside packed bars, that would probably work.

For years to come the name La Mon was synonymous with the barbarism that had taken place there. In an attempt to change the image of the place the management had decided to put on Rock nights. We had headlined many a triumphant gig there so we were looking forward to playing it again with a Rock legend of the caliber of Steve Marriot. With Jerry Shirley on the drums, and I think it was Jim Leverton on the bass, they were exactly what a power trio should be: powerful, tight and wonderful.

The Ashes at the time had taken to dressing like colour-blind girls. Bon Jovi had set new highs in poncing. They were selling albums by the truckload and snogging supermodels so naturally we followed suit. Considering our Rock attire we were a bit dismayed when the place started filling up with Mods. They were there, obviously, wanting to revel in the diminutive singer's 'ace face' past. I think Steve Marriot himself was just as dismayed by the Lambretta-riding turnout. He had left that scene behind many years previously when he had formed the altogether harder edged Humble Pie.

I had always wanted us to take on either a second guitar player or a keyboard player to fill out our live sound. The latter were as scarce as a sash at a First Holy Communion and Davy, who had the usual lead guitarist's aversion to other guitar players, dismissed the former out of hand. Probably the real reason for wanting another guitar player was to get my old mate Ken into the band. Davy's opposition called for a little subterfuge.

I persuaded the band that it would be a cool stage gimmick to build Ken up as one of London's top session men and then get him up for a couple of songs. So it came to pass that Ken would, occasionally, get to play on two of our songs, one of which was called 'Any Answer' and another I can't remember the name of. I hoped that if these went well it might lead to more songs and eventually a permanent place in the band. Unfortunately Davy stood his ground and Ken only made a couple of guest appearances, even though in my humble opinion we sounded bigger and better.

The Steve Marriot support slot was one of the nights that Ken was given his two-song moment of fame. To celebrate and in an attempt to help him blend in with the rest of the band I lent Ken some of my stage gear. He was given a pair of black and red tiger stripe trousers, a Japanese Rising Sun T-shirt and my Ma's white denim jacket, which I must point out she was unaware of. Being a Quo fan and therefore a jeans and T-shirt wearer, Ken protested about having to dress like a cross between Jane Fonda and Kendo Nagasaki, until I informed him that if he didn't wear them he wouldn't be allowed to get up on stage as he would look ridiculous beside the rest of us.

For a joke and probably in an attempt at reverse psychology, I had brought along one of my Uncle Charlie's butchers' hats, which he had been wearing that very day when I visited him at his shop. My plan was that when I told Ken to put it on he would give in to the other gear as long as he didn't have to wear the hat. It seemed to work for he did indeed voice his concerns about dressing like Barbie, but he did take the clothes to the band's changing room while we headed for the stage and our Heavy Metal showdown with a hall packed to the gills with Rock-hating Mods.

It was not our best gig ever; there were Christians that got an easier ride from the lions in the Colosseum. We were slaughtered. The abuse was relentless, each song being met with booing and shouts of, 'Feck off you poofy bastards.' I have always been a great believer in the philosophical idiom that when the going gets tough the tough give it back as good as they are getting. I started hurling back the abuse, which I thoroughly enjoyed; the rest of the band didn't, as the atmosphere was becoming one of restrained violence. 'Time for a ballad to relax the mood,' I thought, which meant it was also the time for Ken to make his entrance.

Up he walked, resplendent in my migraine-inducing clobber, topped off with the butcher's hat on his head. I couldn't believe it – Ken was going to step out in front of a crowd baying for blood wearing a nylon titfer so flimsy that, when the light shone through it, you could see his head and a couple of pieces of mince meat that had stuck in the grooves of the plastic latticework. I was nearly wetting myself laughing. The rest of the band were not: they thought he was taking the piss and was going to reduce the anti-war lyrics of 'Any Answer' to a joke.

I pulled myself together; at this point, it looked like I was going to get a beating from the Mods and my own band. I told the crowd that the next song had a very important anti-violence message and that it featured guest guitarist Ken Heaven, one of London's most respected session men. This was greeted with disinterested silence, that is until just before the first chord was about to be struck, when a voice from the dark shouted, 'Hey mate, give us a half pound of tripe and a couple of pigs' trotters will ye?' The poignant words of the song lost to the deafening laughter of a victorious enemy. Thank you and good night.

Thankfully we were able to get backstage before we could be set upon. Steve Marriot didn't fare any better really: the crowd wanted to hear his back catalogue from the Small Faces days, he wanted to play the Blues Rock he was famous for at the time. I think he was as glad as we were to leave the stage. When we all got back to the VIP area, which was really just the residents' bar, Ken was not going to miss the opportunity to converse with one of his heroes.

He struck up a conversation with Mr Marriot about the ethical/sociological implications of white men playing the Blues. It was all very cerebral and Ken thought he was giving a good account of himself, but he couldn't help but notice that Steve's gaze kept drifting up towards his head. When I say his head it was more like what was on it. Marriot probably thought, 'Why am I conversing with an obvious lunatic who thinks it's cool to decorate his hat with little bits of raw meat?'

Myself and Magee, assuming that the headlining band were getting free drink, decided that we should be able to partake of the refreshments – after all we earned it with such a spectacular perform-ance. Each time we went to the bar, which was often, we just pointed in the direction of Steve Marriot *et al.* and gave a knowing nod to the barman. Hey presto – free whiskeys, vodka, beer, we even, in a fit of generosity, sent over three bottles of vintage champagne to the headliners which they accepted with huge grins and the thumbs-up sign.

As we watched the local news the next day I couldn't help but feel partly responsible when Steve Marriot and his band were arrested trying to board the ferry at Larne Harbour. They apparently had done a runner from the hotel after refusing to pay what they considered to be a massively excessive bar bill. The drinks apparently weren't free after all.

You can always hear the king call

The day that Phil Lynott died, 4th January 1986, was a dark day for the world of music; it was also a dark day for me. We had just got Christmas over with when Fish called to our front door to tell me the devastating news that Philip Parris Lynott had died. At first I didn't believe him, even though I knew the singer had been rushed into hospital late on Christmas Day. I had been a lifelong Thin Lizzy fan; I had all their albums and had seen them in concert more times than I could remember, so this news was a very big blow to me.

When faced with the realisation that Phil really had passed away, from complications of drug and alcohol abuse, what could a poor boy do but go out and get very drunk in an attempt to numb the pain and because it seemed like an absurdly romantic thing to do.

Fish and myself went to the Seaside Tavern on the shore of Belfast Lough, or Old Keaky Bay as it was known, due to the open sewerage that ran straight into it. The upstairs lounge was a haven for Holywood's Rock fraternity; we were allowed to make compilation tapes and play them over the sound system. That night, of course, there was a massive amount of Lizzy tracks played. There wasn't a dry eye in the house, that is except for one ex-fan and a member of the RUC who had taken umbrage at the 'Smash H Block' reference on the back of the 'China Town' album. He called the great man a Fenian nigger; he was ignored and was lucky to leave with all his teeth. He shall remain nameless.

In those days the bars closed at 11pm, which was distastefully early when you consider that we were honouring the memory of one the greatest party animals of all time. In response to the Draconian licensing laws my mate Fish persuaded me to go back to my Ma and Da's house, the plan being to stick on the 'Live and Dangerous' video and have a few more drinks as a mark of respect. In the tired and emotional state we were in, more drink was exactly what we didn't need.

When we got back no one was up so we fired up the video player; we couldn't have the volume too loud for obvious reasons. I was dispatched to find refreshments of the alcoholic variety. All I could find was a bottle of gin, a drink I had never consumed. I had watched my Ma and Da sip what looked like large thirst-quenching glasses mixed with tonic and ice, a slice of lemon dancing as the bubbles skipped on and around it. This would do nicely, and I'm sure old Phil must've partaken of one or two in his day.

I must admit that the visual experience of a G and T was a lot better than the taste. I found it quite disgusting, very sweet, with a smell like cheap perfume. But needs must and all that, so we sat and drank large measures and sang, quietly, along to 'The Boys are Back in Town,' and 'Dancing in the Moonlight', and a tear was shed when 'Still in Love with You' was aired.

About 3am I could hear a movement from upstairs. I turned to Fish and said, 'Hide the glass.' I knew that the parents wouldn't be best pleased that I had quaffed their weekend tipple. We then heard the footsteps on the stairs; I turned the volume down as the boys were just launching into 'Baby Drives me Crazy'. We braced ourselves for the bollocking that was bound to happen; we had obviously woken up one of the elders with our drunken singing in the early hours.

The door opened and there stood my father resplendent in his white vest and Y-fronts: the upside-down letter of the alphabet was slightly gaping open, revealing way too much family flesh for a friend, even a close one. I was horrified and even more so when I realised that the head of the household had his eyes closed, I assume to lessen the pain from the glare of the light when it was turned on. He was groping around with his hand on the wall looking for the switch. When he found it there was a confused look came upon his face as he realised that it was already down. He then started to slowly open his sleep-engorged peepers to be greeted with 'Alright there' from his eldest and his mate. A crimson colour rose from his neck to his face as he walked past us on his way to the kitchen for a glass of water.

Now that my Da was thankfully out of sight Fish and myself both tried to suppress hysterical laughter. We obviously weren't that successful for, 'I can hear you Mr Fisher,' came wafting from next door. My role model in life, after dispatching his thirst, walked past us, not even passing a glance in our direction. He made his way to the door. To my relief the Y had been adjusted and the man satchel was once more secured under the flimsy, slightly frayed material of a gentleman's brief.

'Goodnight,' said Fish.

'Piss off,' said my Da.

I knew then that Fish would forever see my father in a different light; I also knew that forever more, my Da would never enter another room in the middle of the night without checking the light switch.

After Fish had finally gone home I retired to bed. Still very drunk, I decided that it would be a good time to check out the headphones that he had lent me. They were the type that made you look like Princess Leah from 'Star Wars', the ones that covered half of each side of your head. I put 'Black Rose' the album on and selected the song of the same name. With the headphones in place I turned the volume up to full blast. I then tried to climb into bed, which was a struggle as the long curly lead kept getting caught under my feet. Eventually I settled down, but just as I was about to close my eyes the door flew open and there he was again, looking like an advert for Persil.

My Da was shouting something, which I obviously couldn't hear due to the Celtic Rock rattling around my head. As I took the headphones off I realised that the volume, if anything, was getting louder. In a panic I glanced down and followed the path of the lead along the floor, and there lying on the carpet was the jack. I must've pulled it out when I had been crawling into bed.

The thumping strains of Gary Moore's best-ever lead break was entertaining the household, the neighbours and most of the surrounding area. Like the 'everyone remembers what they were doing when they heard that JFK had died', phenomenon, the residents of Trevor Street will always remember what they were doing the night they heard that Phil Lynott had died, which was leaping from their sleep at 4 in the morning.

The next day, in an attempt to minimise the effects of the horrendous hangover I was brewing, I decided that Adele, who was back from college for Christmas, Fish, his girlfriend and myself should go for a pub lunch. The Seaside Tavern, the scene of the previous night's wake, was chosen. After one pint the room was spinning; cold sweats were breaking on me. Adele, who eyed me suspiciously, advised that I should excuse myself and get a breath of fresh air, or maybe the smell of drink seeping from every pore meant that if I left the room *she* might get a breath of fresh air.

I ignored the advice and stayed on. I even made it to lunchtime and I ordered a full Ulster fry in an attempt to try and soak up some of the booze. Each greasy mouth full slipped down the old oesophagus like I was trying to swallow a brick. When I'd finished lining my stomach and adding a fur vest to my arteries I was overcome with a nausea that started around my feet and rapidly worked its way up to my throat. Quickly I covered my mouth with my hand and excused myself by kicking my chair out of the way and charging from the room knocking anyone in my path for six.

In the toilets I did an impersonation of Karen Carpenter and brought my breakfast back up. This, as everyone knows, is a horrible experience at the best of times but added to the mix of double sausage, bacon, double egg, potato bread, soda bread, mushrooms, white pudding and beans (I left out the black pudding, ironically in case it made me sick), was the pungent aroma of the Beefeaters tipple. Each retch brought the horrible taste and smell of what I can only describe as Old Spice after-shave, this in turn brought on another retch and so the whole process was repeated again and again. To this very day I can barely be in the same room as someone drinking gin; it takes all my resolve to go to the bar and purchase it if someone in my company requests it as part of a round. The day Phil Lynott died broke my heart and scarred me for life. I can't help but think that excess was responsible for both.

Ashes to Ashes

The Ashes played many gigs over the three years I spent with them; we had many triumphant nights at Joe Toomey's Rock Night at the Labour Club in Waring Street Belfast. The place used to be so packed that when the crowd started bouncing up and down there was the chance that the floor would collapse. There were also gigs in England, which we did as part of a tour to promote the single, one of which was in a bar called the Red Admiral situated in the middle of a housing estate in Hume South, Manchester. How the hell we got this gig I can only assume was through the brothers Magee, Stephen and his sibling Arthur who lived there and was a member of the pretty successful Indie band Fallover 24.

The estate was one of the most run-down depressingly violent places I have ever set foot in, which is saying something for someone from Belfast. The members of the band and crew had to take it in turns to sleep in the van to protect the gear as the local junkies had tried to break into it while we had stopped to ask for directions. The Red Admiral was no more than a glorified workingmen's club with the patrons smoking dope and drinking pints of mild and bitter. They had never seen the likes of us before and I think we only escaped being stabbed by the sheer fact that they thought we must've had balls the size of coconuts to get up and assault their senses with lights, pyros and 5,000 watts of Heavy Metal bullshit.

All things considered I had a brilliant time while I was with the Ashes, but as the old saying goes, all good things must come to an end. I was sad to leave such a talented band: Davy was an exceptional guitar player with a sense of melody second to none, and he was also able to write a mean tune. Paul was a great bass player but his real talent was his ability to nail down vocal harmonies and Stephen was as flash a drummer as you could get.

As far as things running their course went it was the same for Adele and myself. Her move to London had put a strain on the relationship, absence had not made the heart grow fonder on her part, and we subsequently split up, or I was dropped should I say. I was heartbroken and feeling sorry for myself. I drove everyone mad by repeatedly playing over and over again John Waite's 1983 hit, 'Missing You'. In an attempt to prophylactically prevent the crushing weight of depression settling on me, pastures new felt necessary for me to cope.

There was, however, one final gig booked before I parted ways with the band. The event was called School Aid. It was around the time of Live Aid, and everyone was holding concerts for every conceivable charity or cause. I've got to admit that I haven't got a clue as to the reason for this gig. I do however, remember the reason for another event we took part in – it was called 'Self Aid' it was to raise the profile of those people who were trying to set up their own businesses and bring down the massive unemployment figures on the Island of Ireland.

Seeing as we had self-financed, sort of, and produced the single, we were asked to take part in a radio interview to be held at the Radio Ulster studios in Belfast. It was usually Davy and myself that did any press interviews, but for some reason Stephen Campbell was asked to join me for the show. I really don't know how this happened as everyone was well aware that our drummer, like all drummers, could be vague at the best of times.

Caron Keating showed us into the studio. A guy called Jackie Hamilton, who was a member of the band The Moon Dogs, did the interview I think: the passage of time has left greasy fingerprints on the once crystal clarity of my memory. We were to be questioned in between two of the acts that were playing live in Dublin, one of which was Rory Gallagher; the event was playing on TV screens in the studio. While we waited Jackie asked us our names and told me that I would be given the first question, Stephen the second; there would only be time for the two. We waited for Rory to finish and then the interview began.

I was asked how we had gone about raising the money to finance the single. I waxed lyrical about playing as many gigs as we could, the proceeds of which were put aside. I also told Jackie that we had received sponsorship from some businesses that Magee had coaxed into parting with their hard-earned cash. That was me finished, thank God. The interviewer then turned to Stephen and started to ask him his question.

Relieved to be finished, I turned to take in the view of a beautiful Miss Keating laughing and giggling on the other side of the studio glass. She really was a natural beauty, who my mate Johnny Bramley would later bombard with flowers and cards each Valentine's Day, when they worked together at the Beeb in London. He never got as much as a peck on the cheek. It's very sad to think of her family's loss following her death at the tender age of 41, but that was many, not enough, years in the future; that day in Belfast she had made me lose concentration by simply being herself.

I could hear the question being delivered to Stephen but it was really only a noise in the background as my attention strayed. When Jackie finished he nodded towards Stephen for his response, but instead of calling him by his name he used mine. Any sane person would've just answered the question himself but as I pointed out Stephen was a drummer; he hit things with sticks to make loud noises. He simply swung round in his chair and motioned, with raised eyebrows, for me to talk.

I didn't have the first notion as to what the question was. I shrugged my shoulders and raised my hands in a soundless attempt to kick Stephen's arse into gear. He, to my horror, just looked blankly back at me. There was an obvious gap in the conversation: the radio broadcaster's worst nightmare, dead air, had become a reality. Our interviewer, wide-eyed and panicking, made rolling signs with his hands to hurry me up. I started to splutter, stutter and cough my way through a load of bollocks that I could tell from the baffled faces in no way corresponded with what had been asked.

The question, I later found out, had related to those who found themselves in the seemingly hopeless position of being unemployed and who perceived themselves as worthless to their families and society in general. Stephen was asked if he could offer any suggestions as to what could be done for these poor unfortunate souls. Now that I was to answer the question and still thinking they were talking about the single my answer went something like this. I said that I thought it was not a good idea to send them to England, as we had had personal experience of many of them being sent back cracked and broken. I then added that it would be much better to ship them off to France or somewhere where you would have them returned in wooden boxes, dyed in whatever colour you preferred, but I pointed out as a traditionalist I preferred mine jet black and shiny as possible with funny little inscriptions around their holes.

Through the studio glass I could see Caron Keating and her friends wetting themselves laughing at the garbage that was coming out of the speakers behind them. At home my Da switched off the tape recorder that he had proudly set up to capture his eldest son's interview on the BBC. He shook his head and poured himself a large Bacardi, finally convinced that I had succumbed to the lure of heroin or some other drug that infested the world of strange men in tight trousers and perms.

I don't know how my contribution to Self Aid helped, in fact, I have a suspicion that it probably caused many people to decide that staying on the dole was preferable to trying to find employment elsewhere. I also don't know or remember if there was a positive outcome from the School Aid gig but I do remember that it was a humdinger of a night.

With it being an under-age event there was no alcohol, so we had to smuggle in our usual quota, hidden in Stephen's bass drums. Unfortunately nobody had told Fishy of the contraband, so when he dragged the cases onto the stage and opened them the contents spilled out onto the floor. A stage invasion by thirsty schoolkids ensued; they thought it had been done as some sort of rebellious act. The teachers, who were doing security, on seeing what was happening, invaded themselves in an attempt to save their charges from the evils of drink. Small boys were seen being led by the ear to the back of the stage while they frantically guzzled on the contents of a frothing can of Budweiser. The organisers were less than happy. Magee was over the moon.

As we waited for our headlining spot there were a selection of bands that were made up of pupils from the school. Unfortunately for them a very large crowd of Ashes fans had assembled for my farewell gig and as was the disgusting fashion of the time they showed their appreciation of these young impressionable musicians by gobbing at them and hurling abuse. Some of the kids were so scared they would never lift an instrument again. The organisers were less than happy. Magee was over the moon.

When we finally got up to play, the crowd went nuts and there was another invasion halfway through the first number. Two of those who dodged the outstretched hands of the security, for reasons only known to themselves, were my sister Elish and her mate Bronagh. Fish took his job as roadie/lighting tech/security man very seriously, but he had reservations about tackling anyone bigger than himself, so he decided that the band could fend off the stampeding Neanderthals themselves, and he would make sure that we were saved from my sister and her four-foot-two friend. He grabbed both of them and tossed them off the stage. On witnessing scenes that resembled World War One cannon fodder climbing over the trenches and also the sight of two young ladies being thrown onto their heads from the assembly hall stage, the organisers were less than happy. Magee was over the moon.

I pleaded for calm and eventually the crowd settled down. A certain amount of normality restored, the show went on. As we neared the end of the set, realisation started to set in that this would be the last time I would play with the boys and I felt a twinge of sadness. The nostalgia however was short lived – out of the corner of my eye I saw Magee walking towards me and behind him, standing in the wings, were the rather burley shapes of about six RUC men. I put my mouth up to Magee's ear and asked him what the problem was. He said, 'Don't worry, they're just here to make sure that there's no trouble after the gig.' I went back to singing the last song and then a crowd-demanding encore. Again from the corner of my eye I could see Magee wrestling with a couple of the cops who appeared to be trying to get onto the stage.

We finished my last-ever song with No Hot Ashes to a brilliant response and another storming of the stage: however this time it was not by the Ashes fans, but by the police. Sensing that there was more to this than what Magee had told me, I asked him the real reason for the boys in green's appearance. He told me that there had been a telephoned bomb threat to the nearby Europa hotel, and he had been asked to go on stage and get us to stop. I was also to be instructed to tell everyone, over the mic, to vacate the building; of course Magee, seeing the headlines in the next day's paper, ignored the police pleas. My last gig with the Ashes could've quite literally ended with a bang. Fearing for the lives of their pupils the organisers were less than happy. Magee was, you've guessed it, over the moon.

CHAPTER FOUR

Nellie Dean

Ahoooooo – the werewolves of London

Ken and Elaine had been in the Big Smoke for about a year when I decided to up sticks. They said I should get my ass over there as they were living in a palatial hotel in Paddington where I wouldn't have a problem getting a room of my own. Sounded good to me. With Ken being a great guitar player and close personal friend I would already have the beginnings of a Rock and Roll machine capable of trampling the opposition – how could we fail?

I increased my hours at C&C, the soft drinks factory I worked in when I was not a rock star. Many night shifts later I had about £4000 to get me to the banks of Old Father Thames. I also hoped that this princely sum would keep me going for the first few months that I was there or until I got myself sorted out.

I wished my family a fond farewell and with their laughter ringing in my ears I walked through the shop for what would turn out to be the last time, although I was unaware of that at that juncture. My sister Louise was serving behind the counter. As I left she was crying – like I said, I have no favourites, but there will always be a soft spot in my heart for her.

My old Mucker Ken greeted me at Heathrow Airport; we had a drink at the bar while I waited for my baggage, start as you mean to go on I say. I was so excited about being in the Rock and Roll capital of the world and couldn't wait to get started. Ken however was not as raring to go as myself; he had had to drag himself from his sick bed to meet me. He was suffering from a terrible affliction the likes of which man had never suffered before. It would in years to come be known as the common cold. His illness, he told me, made him incapable of activities of daily living and meant he had to spend the daylight hours in bed with hot whiskeys. Furthermore he had to spend the night-time hours in a quiet corner of a local hostelry with more hot whiskeys – his fear, you see, was that he would become disassociated from the outside world if he spent all his time in bed.

The terrible news of Ken's terminal illness couldn't dampen my excitement as we caught the tube to the mystical land of Lancaster Gate. 'What will my new room look like?' 'Will I have a view of Marble Arch from the window?' 'Does it have an en-suite?' 'Would a Jacuzzi be too much to ask?' These questions tripped off my tongue like a small child going on a surprise journey. Ken kept the delicious anticipation going by repeating, 'Just wait and see.'

I did wait and see and found that I was sharing a room with Ken and Elaine. There was only one double bed, but there was a nice damp-free spot on the dirty carpet where I could rest my weary bones. It was so small that even Ronnie Corbett would've felt cramped. The en-suite shower was a sink and the temperature was regulated by a refreshing November wind blowing merrily through a hole in the window. When I clapped eyes on the dump I was expected to live in I nearly had a heart attack.

On seeing my distress, my lying dirt-bag of an ex-best friend said, 'Don't worry, when I'm well enough to wander the streets I'll find us alternative accommodation more in keeping with our standing in life.' God knows what that meant – a park bench in Siberia would've been a considerable improvement on what we had at present. Also with the state Ken was in and with the air-conditioning system blowing hail, sleet and snow through the ventilation hole in the glass, I doubted that he would ever walk the streets again, and if he did it would be with his new best friend Pneumonia for company.

It took Ken about two weeks to recover from the deadly illness he had acquired. In the meantime I was left to my own devices with the remit to discover the sights, smells and sounds of the capital. Elaine accompanied me on many of my fact-finding missions while the patient healed himself into a stupor. One morning after a rather heavy night in Paddington we decided to get a cooked breakfast from a greasy spoon just around the corner from our accommodation. The place was run by a load of Greek guys who, according to Elaine, did a mean hangover-curing fry-up. So that's just what I ordered, the large one. I settled back with a cup of tea and awaited my meal.

From my vantage point at the very back of the place I spotted a tramp looking through the window. I said, 'I bet he picks on me.'

'Why?' Elaine enquired.

I told her that I was the type of person that when sitting quietly on the bus, the loony who has just got on will always sit beside me and insist on telling me his life story, that or threaten me with death.

She laughed, insisting that I was paranoid. 'He would have to walk the full length of the café to get to you, and he's more likely to pick on someone closer to the door,' she reasoned. Wrong.

Just as my fry was set down in front of me he entered the building, weaving his way from table to table. I looked around in desperation in the hope that one of the staff would intercept him before he reached us. Unfortunately they all seemed oblivious to him, or maybe they were ignoring him deliberately.

Anyway it didn't really matter why the staff let the tramp reach our table, perhaps he had stabbed one of them before or something, but that's what he did. I just knew he was going to take out his anger at a failed Tory 'care in the community' system and his many nights spent freezing in damp doorways, on me. He stood still for a second. I thought he was going to turn and walk away, but he was only steadying himself before he collapsed face first into my untouched cooked breakfast. Quick as a flash he straightened up and looked at me with a huge grin on his face. The smile however was not the only thing that adorned his gob – a sausage hung from his mouth like one of WC Fields' cigars; his beard was festooned with baked beans and egg. He turned and left as if nothing had happened.

I sat motionless, unable to quite make sense of it all. No one took this bizarre occurrence under their notice, they just carried on doing what they were doing – well, that is except for Elaine who was pissing herself laughing. I looked around and caught the eye of the manager. With a bamboozled expression on my face I beckoned him over. I said, 'Look, I don't mean to be a nuisance but someone has just stuck their face into my food and made off with a sausage and a selection of side portions captured in his beard. Is there any chance that I can have a fresh one please?'

'Was it a member of staff?' asked the manager.

Astonished by the question I answered, 'No, he was a tramp off the street.'

To which he said, 'If he was not a member of staff you will have to pay again.'

I couldn't believe my ears. I said 'Look, you let him into your establishment; therefore it is your responsibility.'

He then asked, 'How do I know that this is not a set-up to get free food?'

I said, 'Do you really think that I would ask a tramp to follow me into a café, get him to deliberately dive into my breakfast, just to get another breakfast, to replace one that I had not even touched?' It just didn't make sense.

He came back, 'How do I know that you didn't touch it? And anyway he could've been a friend of yours that has now made off with a free breakfast.'

I said, 'Don't be stupid, do I look like someone who hangs around with tramps?' Then remembering my hungover state I said, 'Forget that, anyway what did you mean asking me if it was one of the staff?'

He explained that if the complaint had been about one of his employees he would refund or replace the meal.

I was getting angry and I said, 'Is there a member of your staff that would like to stick their face into my breakfast?' and he said, 'Of course not.' I said, 'What about if I were to push it into your face, would I get my meal?'

We were asked to leave as his hairy mates came sauntering from behind the counter.

When Ken had made his full recovery, I was keen on getting the band together. Ken on the other hand, having missed out on the jollifications around the West End, decided that I should help the poor landlords of Soho and Covent Garden by giving them the remainder of the funds I had left. The Nellie Dean, The Ship, The Intrepid Fox, The Coal Hole, The Punch and Judy, The St Moritz and many more watering holes were all better off to the tune of four grand by the time the coffers were gone. We had a ball and I don't regret a shekel spent. I was now penniless but still dying to get rocking the city; anyway superstardom and the riches that go with it could only be just around the corner.

Ken had been playing in a band called 'Stone the Giant' with an old friend of ours from Holywood, Michael Smiley, later to become an excellent comedian and actor. They were a weird bunch whose interest in performing music was in direct correlation to their interest in smoking dope. The rhythm guitar player was an Aussie called Danny who was also the manager of the hellhole of a B&B we were residing in.

Danny stored the band's gear, after gigs, in a room on the ground floor of Fawlty Towers. When Ken went down to retrieve his guitar and amp he was told that it wasn't there. Danny couldn't remember it being loaded into the van following the last gig, which had taken place many weeks previously. Ken was devastated, I even more so. I had given up my job, my band, moved away from home, I had spent all the money I had saved and now I was to form a band with a guitarist who didn't even have a guitar or amp. Things were not looking good; superstardom had moved on around the corner, out of sight and was boarding the Number 8 bus, destination Skid Row. At least I knew how to steal sausages when I ended up homeless.

We were a band with no instruments; it was like a jockey without a horse. Thanks to Ken encouraging me to rid myself of all my savings on drink and fast food – Taco Bell anyone? – we also had no means of reversing the situation. Elaine's parents were contacted, money was begged for, gear was bought and we were ready to begin. I make it sound easy but in reality it was far from it, it is just too painful and not that funny to impart.

The living arrangements were not ideal. Ken and Elaine were still going through the 'getting to know you' euphoria of new romance. Therefore I would have to go for a jog every time they felt the urge to display their lust for each other. It was the fittest I had ever been in my life, the dirty dogs. To give the happy couple the privacy they so richly deserved and to prevent me from a severe case of jogger's nipple or a heart attack, we decided that a change in our accommodation was needed. We signed up to a letting agency that promised us the world.

Dollis Hill or bust

We carried all our possessions in black plastic sacks on the tube from Lancaster Gate to Dollis Hill station. We resembled the bag people that lived on the streets outside the Embankment Station, apart from the infested facial hair, a dog on a bit of string, the stale smell of urine and the spitting. On arrival at our new accommodation we were struck by the dreadful state of the exterior: the garden was so overgrown that it appeared that there was no path.

I found a discarded bamboo that must've been used in a previous century as a growing strut for the massive oak tree that grew in the centre of the garden. Using the stick I poked through the undergrowth looking for a solid surface on which to walk. I hoped that I wouldn't tread on the remains of the Victorian postman who had gone missing shortly after the last time the grass had been cut.

After traversing the jungle we rapped on the mouldy front door. After a wait of about two minutes and repeated knocking, it opened and we were greeted by a six-foot-four dreadlocked Rastafarian smoking a soggy big joint the size of a kitchen roll. 'Welcome man,' he said as he offered us the wet end of his ganja log. When we refused he viewed us with a suspicious yellow eye – in his opinion we had offended the part of his religion that dictated you must always have cannabis in the bloodstream at all times. We had made an enemy already and we hadn't even crossed the doorstep.

The three of us had been given keys to the locks of our bedrooms. Ken and Elaine used theirs and the door opened, I used mine and it remained closed. I thought that I could hear someone in the room. I knocked on the door – there was no answer but there was definitely a shuffling noise that sounded like someone dragging something along the floor. I had handed over a very substantial amount of the taxpayer's money to get this room so I was not just going to walk away. I banged on the door with a clenched fist repeatedly until the door flew open with a violent jerk.

There standing in the doorway was a five-foot skeleton with a red crew cut and a mass of freckles: there were so many, in fact, that if a few more had been added he could've lived in India as a national without turning a head, although bright ginger hair might have been a bit of a giveaway. 'What the fuck do you want?' was the delightful greeting I received, delivered in a high-pitched nasally Dublin brogue. When I pointed out that the room he was occupying was bought and paid for by me and therefore mine, he said, 'Take it up with that gab shite Hondros,' referring to the Greek half of our dodgy letting agents. And with that he slammed the door in my face. 'What a charming little gentleman that was,' I thought to myself as I banged the door and informed him that he had until the start of the next week to be out or I would evict him myself.

When I joined Ken and Elaine in their 'new' room I was just about to enter into a rant about the encounter with the leprechaun from hell, when I was knocked off my stride by the vision that greeted me. In a room that should've only had a double bed there were crammed in ten single mattresses, all of which were lying on the floor. Each one had upon it a multi-stained sheet. I didn't want to hazard a guess as to the nature of the individual messes but a bacteriology laboratory would've been kept busy for a year from one square inch of any of the disgusting rags. On closer inspection you could actually see the imprint and body shape of the long-term inhabitants. We had, it appeared, uncovered North West London's answer to the Turin Shroud.

Elaine refused to touch the offending items; she left the room in floods of tears. Ken and myself piled the mattresses one on top of each other, discovering skid mark-encrusted underwear everywhere. We picked out the two least stained mattresses for the lucky couple to share; there would be no loving that night I hazarded a guess.

I was relegated to a horrible smelly sofa in the living room; luckily I had a quilt and a sleeping bag with which to protect my skin from the menagerie of microscopic wildlife that made the fabric undulate as they marched up and down looking for delicious skin cells. The bugs were not the only things I had to share the living room with; the guy who had answered the door to us was sitting in an armchair watching the communal TV. On his lap sat his teenage, white, bespectacled girlfriend, the pair of them covered with a blanket. The air in the room became denser and denser with each Caribbean herbal cigarette he lit. Both of them sucked huge cough-inducing quantities of smoke into their lungs as they passed the lit joint between themselves. I must admit that they were very sociable in that with each draw I was offered a whack; not being a smoker and being anti-drugs I declined.

After a while the room was filled with the fragrant swirls of class B narcotics and I must admit that I was feeling no pain, in fact, I would say that there was a certain mellow euphoria settling upon me. With the pleasant calm, however, came a certain giddiness and the uncontrollable urge to laugh; this became even harder to suppress when the couple decided that I had obviously left the room and began to get jiggy with each other.

I was now in the rather embarrassing situation of not wanting to alert the mating pair to my presence, by getting up to leave, and also not really wanting to be there in the first place. I have never even liked being the company of a couple snogging let alone bearing witness to a giant dreadlocked Adonis having his wicked way with what looked like a rag doll.

With my reason, unintentionally, slightly narcoticly impaired, I decided that it would be a good idea to roll onto the floor and crawl to the door. This proved to be rather difficult due to the rubbery nature of my legs, both of which promptly gave way resulting in me wriggling on the floor like a drugged worm. As I neared the door the ridiculousness of the situation hit me like a ton of bricks and I started to convulse with laughter. I turned round to witness the two lovers, in mid-coital bliss, realise that I was still with them. Their eyes were wide with disbelief, their pupils like saucers, and I could see them attempting to make sense of the vision in front of them. To their credit they didn't miss a stroke as I scrambled to my feet and ran out the door.

With nowhere else to go I sat on the foot of the stairs and covered my ears with my hands in an attempt to block out the squeals of stoned delight coming from the living room. Again the situation caused me to burst into fits of laughter, which literally had the tears rolling down my cheeks. After the happy couple had finished they retired to their bedroom, which I think is where they should've been in the first place. They stepped past me, visibly limping, without an apology or explanation. It was as if they had been taking up the front room, and keeping me from my sleep, by doing something as inno-cent as playing a game of tiddlywinks, instead of trying out every position on every page of *The Joy of Sex*.

With the room now free of illegal substances and multi-cultural copulating, I resumed my infestation attempt on the sofa. Sleep didn't come easy: I was suddenly overcome with a hunger that wouldn't have been out of place during the Potato Famine. I needed food ASAP; the only problem was that we hadn't brought any with us and we hadn't had the chance to buy any. Irrationally I thought I would die if I didn't fill the chasm in my gut. Desperation set in.

Seeing as the knackered lovers should, or should I say must, be unconscious following their anaesthetised exertions, I decided that I would raid their provisions and make myself a feast: it was the least they could do after making me a captive spectator to their exchanging of body fluids.

In the boggin' kitchen I opened the fridge to find it empty, rancid and broken. Panicking, I tried to calm myself by saying, 'Don't worry old flower, there must be something in here somewhere.' With a shaky hand I opened every cupboard door in the whole place, but the only things I found were a variety box of instant soup, a tub of curry powder and a bag of rice – obviously the sexual gymnasts upstairs didn't need that much sustenance to keep their fornicating energies up. I was despondent, then suddenly out of the blue a culinary miracle happened: the germ of a recipe started to formulate in my brain.

Munchie chicken curry with boiled rice.

Take one packet of out of date chicken instant soup and empty the contents into a cracked stained mug.

Add one level teaspoonful of Madras curry powder.

Remove as much as you can, without the aid of washing up liquid, the caked-on residue of God knows what, from the bottom of a handleless blackened saucepan.

Pour into the saucepan a pint and a half of brown water straight from the tap and bring to the boil using the only working ring on the hob.

After removing the saucepan from the hob using a stained dishcloth that is still smouldering from coming into contact with the bright red ring, fill the mug with boiling water.

Mix the fragrant substance using the blunt end of a butter knife.

Add to the remaining water in the saucepan two handfuls of rice and return to the slightly sparking hob ring.

Boil the rice until *al dente* then drain using the lid of the teapot.

Empty the rice into a breakfast cereal bowl and then cover with the concoction in the mug.

Season to taste.

Warning: It is probably best before you start this recipe that you check that the rice you are using is not of the pudding variety, which on this occasion I didn't.

Following my meal, which tasted something like Ambrosia Creamed Rice mixed with the dust off the floor of an Indian restaurant, I returned to my bed for the night. Even though I was feeling slightly queasy – every burp had me reliving the whole horror of what I had just ingested – I did eventually fall into a restless sleep.

With it being early spring the sun rose at around 5am, the first rays forcing their way through the cracks in the nicotine-heavy curtains, barely taking the gloom off the room. I have always been an early riser and I found myself lying in the dull light with my hands behind my head thinking that my Ma would have been as proud as punch had she known that her son was spending his time in London watching drugged loonies having sex and consuming food that you wouldn't feed a stray dog.

Just as the shame was reaching its peak I heard the door behind me start to creak open. I slightly turned my head just enough to see who was coming in. I was praying to God, Allah, Buddha and Haile Selassie (now that I was a pot smoker man) that it was not the 'Marijuana Two' coming back for an encore. I was finding it hard enough to keep last night's gastronomic delight down without having to witness them sweating, grunting and writhing again. When I finally made out who was entering I found myself wishing that it had been the smelly funsters after all.

A squat, short-arsed man carrying a hammer was tiptoeing his way into the room. For a second I held my breath hoping that he wouldn't be able to see me and would think that I was not there. He, however, just kept coming closer and closer until he was standing above my head. He raised the hammer shoulder high and was just about to bring it down when I jumped up from the sofa and screamed, 'What the fuck are you at?' Funny enough this seemed to scare the shite out of him; he had just joined my club.

He turned and made a bolt for the door, which was quite good seeing as the only tool he had available was the hammer he had attempted to brain me with. Joking aside, I was furious, I jumped forward and grabbed him from behind around the neck while knocking the weapon from his grip and repeated my question.

'Nuttin' nuttin',' he shouted, 'I'm just on me way to work.'

'My arse,' I said. 'You were just about to smash my skull open you wee bastard.'

'I wasn't, I wasn't, I was just looking for me work boots,' he protested.

'Is that right?' I said, pointing to the cement-covered heavy-duty footwear he had on. 'I want you out of my room by tonight or I'll make a trip to the police station, I'm sure they'll be interested in what has been going on in this shithole.'

'Deal, deal,' he said and was off like a greyhound chasing a rabbit with a tin of Pedigree Chum on its head.

When I told Ken and Elaine about my rude awakening it was decided that there was no way that we were going to spend one more night in a pit that was even less appealing than the house in the 'Amityville Horror'. We made a short trip to Harlesden and the offices of D and T Hondros, letting agents to the desperate. We basically told them that we wanted somewhere there and then or we would be going to the DHSS and telling them about the condition of the accommodation that they were providing for the poor dole victims of North West London.

Hondros himself, seeing the milk drying up form his social security cash cow, threw us the keys to a property he hadn't seen yet himself. He told us that if we weren't happy with it he would find us something else. We took the keys to a house in Leigh Gardens, Kensal Rise and were over the moon to open the door to a beautiful four-bedroom semi in pristine condition. Ken phoned Hondros and informed him that 'it would have to do' – we didn't want to sound too keen in case he increased the rent.

E.T. phone home

Before we could move into the new place proper we had to get a deposit and four weeks' rent from the DHSS: this was an experience to say the least. Ken and Elaine secured their deposits quite easily; I on the other hand had to fight tooth and nail, knocking years off my life.

Paddington dole office is a grey soulless building with peeling paintwork and the stench of the body's less fragrant odours. It became, for a few days, my home, as I reduced myself to the status of a social pariah trying to get money I was entitled to. Every cloud has a silver lining however and while I begged for a government handout I met a very beautiful girl called Lisa Roberts there. We got on like a house on fire and I must admit to a little flirting. All the while that I was trying to charm the pants off her I kept thinking that I had seen her somewhere before. And then it came to me.

There had been, before I moved to London, a Heavy Metal programme called ECT, that had some of the lower league bands performing live every Friday night. I loved it but it was a cheap production, sort of a low-budget Mad Max affair that threw up some hilarious moments. One such instance had Bob Catley of Magnum being transported around the studio on a chair attached to a crane while he sang the whole of the first verse of 'On a Story Teller's Night', the camera never leaving him. Unfortunately his mic was not working so for four excruciating minutes he mouthed the words, gesticulating like a Pomp Rock Marcel Marceau, with only the music being heard.

There was also a very interesting vocal interpretation by Shy doing 'Hold on to Your Love', which actually put me off a band that I had previously been a fan of. Then there was Venom, I need say no more. As well as these disasters there were some great moments including Motorhead with Pete Gill on drums and The Grip, the best unsigned band in the world as they called themselves. Other brilliant performances came from Chariot, Mamas Boys, UFO and an outstanding display by Gary Moore and an obviously ailing Phil Lynott. I would sit transfixed to the TV while trying to hear the bands over the hysterical laughter of my Ma and Da as they sat pointing at the 'big girls' blouses' on the screen.

Another thing that kept me glued to the screen one Friday night was a skintight pair of jeans worn by a curvaceous blonde bombshell called Lisa Dominique. They filled the screen and distracted me from the music that she and her band were playing, which in retrospect was probably a blessing. And believe it or not, Lisa Roberts, AKA Dominique, was wearing the very same pair of jeans the day we met in Paddington dole office. I think I recognised the shape of the jeans before I recognised her face; I was young and male, what can I say? Get a copy of the show and then argue with me.

Lisa certainly made the time go a lot quicker as we both queued up to be belittled. We got talking about all things Rock; she happened to mention that she had a new album coming out and that she needed a live band for some gigs she had booked at the Marquee. My ears pricked up: this could be a perfect opportunity to get a foothold into the London music scene. Now all I needed was a guitar player to audition for her band. Where would I get one of those?

I told Lisa that I had the perfect guitarist for her. I added that he was a personal friend of mine with impeccable manners, an excellent work ethic and dedication to his art. I had only just met this poor girl and I was lying through my teeth, but needs must. She seemed very interested so we exchanged telephone numbers as she was leaving. I put hers in my pocket knowing that my call wouldn't be all about Ken – result all round really.

Lisa left me to the mercy of Her Majesty's disinterested civil servants in that municipal dump. As much as the surroundings were depressing and I really didn't want to be there, I had no qualms about making full use of the generous handouts bestowed upon the riffraff by Maggie Thatcher and her mine-closing, criminal government. Don't get me wrong, I wanted to work; I even attended an interview to help me achieve this. After explaining that I was seeking employment within the music business, as a singer or songwriter, the teenage clerk, whose spots outnumbered his O Levels, informed me that he had the very job for me. He set up an interview with a local independent record company. This was, if you'll pardon the pun, music to my ears. 'What a fine city this is,' I thought. You only had to ask for a job as a rock star and it was handed to you on a plate.

I was filled with excitement on the day of the interview. As I sat outside the office waiting to be called all manner of wonderful possibilities filled my head. 'Who would I be writing for? I wondered. I hoped it was in the Rock genre as my Calypso and Barbershop were not exactly up to scratch. The place looked a little run down, but that was independent for you and you have to start somewhere.

On entering the office I was introduced to a couple of elderly gentlemen who didn't look anything like I was expecting. Neither of them resembled Richard Branson; they were more like Arthur from

'On the Buses'. The first guy asked me what experience I had, so I waxed lyrical about my days in No Hot Ashes and how we had released an independent single of our own which we had financed, packaged and distributed ourselves. I thought this would impress them but they looked sort of confused by my ramblings.

The second guy asked if I was OK for working shifts. This seemed like a strange question. I had visions of the old music-hall writers who beavered away in Tin Pan Alley, basically producing music to order. I soldiered on and told them that I did a lot of my songwriting at night or in the early hours of the morning, so no I didn't mind doing shifts. I did point out, however, that my muse couldn't be switched on and off like a light bulb. I needed to be stimulated, I needed to have the old creative juices flowing to be able to prise a piece of art from my inner being. On hearing my second answer I could see that my Reg Varney lookalike interviewers were even more perplexed. One of them then asked if I knew what the job entailed, to which I replied, 'Writing songs.'

My answer was greeted with hysterical laughter; both men could hardly speak. When one of them had gained control of himself, but was still wiping the tears from his eyes, he informed me that I was being interviewed for the job of an assembly line worker putting together cardboard boxes that held records. I was aghast and a little embarrassed, I mean I hadn't come all the way to London to work in a factory; I could have, and had, done that back in Belfast. I also had ten O Levels and an ONC in Business Studies for Christ's sake.

That was the trouble with Maggie's Britain; there was no perception of art. To her and her cronies music obviously means anything to do with the subject regardless of content or quality. Instead of nurturing talent and realising its worth, by providing grants, or as they do in the South of Ireland, allowing artists to be exempt from paying tax, it is looked upon as an excuse to waste time and scrounge. Well if you call someone a dog long enough they will eventually start barking. I fully intended to get all that was owed to me from my years of tax paying and scrounge with the best of them, until I did get something out of music.

The final laugh is that I was offered the bloody job, which of course I turned down. Thank God it was before the days when you would be forced to accept what was offered, again ignoring the fact that, instead of cardboard boxes and paper cuts, you may have something more valuable to contribute to society.

Anyway, back to the dole office. I had been in the queue to be interviewed for my claim for unemployment and housing benefit for three days. There I was every morning at 9am sharp pulling my numbered ticket from the dispenser on the wall and every day I was ignored, as members of what seemed to be two families, one from Dublin, one from Cork came walking in, carrying what looked suspiciously like the same baby. They then proceeded to bang on the Perspex glass and demand an emergency payment for the child in arms, as it was 'fecking starvin'.

This would take ages to arrange and eventually 5pm would roll around and I would walk back to Kensal Rise penniless, unable to afford the bus fare. On the fourth day I was just about to give up hope when an Asian gentleman, from behind the glass, called out my number. I was asked all my personal details and told to wait back at my seat as my claim was being processed; obviously no emergency payment for me and I really was 'fecking starvin'.

While I waited I became aware of an uncomfortable stand-off brewing between the two Irish families. The clerk returned and in a strong Indian accent shouted 'E.T., E.T.' To my horror he was shouting out my first two initials instead of my full names, Eamon and Thomas. There was much laughing from the gathered flotsam, so I sat for a second in the hope that he would see his mistake and call me properly. But oh no, again he shouted, 'Is there an E.T. here?' I feared that I would miss my opportunity to get some funds with which to cure the ache in my belly and to keep a roof above my head, so I mustered up all my courage and stood.

There was a cheer and numerous choruses of, 'Phone home you bum, phone home you bum.' I walked red-faced to my tormentor and sat down. 'Well Mr E.T., I am glad to tell you that your claim has been successful and I will give you your giro once you have signed this acceptance form.' I was almost euphoric as the paper was passed under the glass.

I was halfway through putting my signature on the dotted line when a bottle of Mundies fortified wine smashed above my head: the stand-off had come to its natural drunken conclusion and a fight had broken out. I was showered with glass and foul-smelling sticky liquid. I spun round to see what the feck was going on and when I turned back the protective glass of my booth had been replaced by a metal screen. My clerk was on his toes and out of there, leaving me holding a worthless piece of paper in my blood-speckled hands.

The fight raged on – there were teeth and sovereign rings flying everywhere. The police arrived and investigated the situation by beating people about the head with truncheons. One of the cops asked me to leave. I said that I was going nowhere because I needed to stay to get my cheque. On hearing my accent and seeing the state I was in he assumed that I was one of the protagonists, so he thought it only right to administer justice using the full force of the strong arm of the law, which was attached to a wooden night stick.

Thankfully I dodged the assault and ran out of the building making good my escape, still holding the form that should've meant that it would have been on the bus rather than on foot. I never did get any money from Paddington dole office; I would have to go to another one in Kensal Rise where they were altogether more civilised – the bums drank cider there.

Legend in his own lunchtime

Ken and myself made our way to Lisa's basement flat where he did an audition, which he passed with flying colours, of course. Before we left Lisa happened to mention that her brother Marino was looking for a singer, again the lightbulb above my head came on and I offered my services and again I was successful. Ken and myself decided that while we were ensconced in Lisa and Marino's bands we would also carry out our original plan of putting together a band of our own. We thought it best to keep this from our new employers; we didn't want to appear as mercenary as we actually were.

One very rainy day, the sort of day that only London can throw up, you know the type – cold, wet and very dark – I ventured over to Marino's flat with the intention of us writing songs together. I had just been announced as the new singer of Marino the Band in the hallowed pages of *Kerrang!* no less. The weather is a factor in this tale, as I had to shelter in the doorway of the train station, making me late, a thing I absolutely despise even to this day. Anyway, on arrival at the guitar leg end's door I was greeted with a terse, 'You're late.' I almost found myself starting to make excuses about the weather and had to catch myself on. 'I'm not at school you git,' I thought, next I'll be needing a letter from my Ma saying, 'Sorry young Eamon's late but the dog ate his PE kit.'

On entering the flat I was greeted with the unmistakable smell of joss sticks. Marino's tie-dyed T-shirt and long ringleted hair got the alarm bells ringing. 'I hope he doesn't start telling my fortune or rubbing Ylang Ylang into my ear lobes.' I thought. Thankfully there were no mystic advances and we quickly settled down to work on a song that I had already had the structure for.

I had been led to believe, from the music press, that Marino was a guitar wizard, so I was a little dismayed by his contributions to the writing process, which were far from satisfactory. I wanted a strong verse and chorus; he just wanted something that he could pretend he was Carlos Santana over. I sang the first verse, miraculously made it to the chorus and he then noodled around for half an hour boring the arse off me. The next-door neighbour kept the beat by banging on the wall with what sounded like a hammer. Our hero was oblivious to all this as his sonic chakras took him to a place only the divine can reach. When he reached his last tremulous note, a fret too low I may add, he opened his eyes, let the orgasmic haze disperse and uttered the immortal line, 'Would you like a little pasta?'

At the time we were short of funds and living on cheap soya-based abominations called Bean Feasts. A little bit of Italian cuisine sounded marvellous, so I told Marino that it would be a pleasure to break bread at his table. While he was out preparing the meal I imagined what sort of food a man of the world such as he would be creating. I hoped for a steaming bowl of *al dente* pasta with a light seafood sauce topped with a drizzle of extra virgin olive oil. Hull's answer to Keith Floyd returned from the kitchen a little too quick. 'He must have prepared something earlier,' I thought. I sat down at the table, tucked the tablecloth into my collar, my taste buds flooding my mouth with suggestive juices and was set down a bowl of Heinz Ravioli!

After our sumptuous meal Marino, and I swear this is true, stripped to his tight black briefs and started doing stretching exercises, saying this was to ward off love handles. Where I come from, dear reader, it is not the done thing for men to strip down to what looked like a posing pouch and carry out strenuous physical exercises, and they certainly don't mention anything to do with love handles in front of each other.

The look of horror on my face must've shocked him, for he said I shouldn't worry, I should relax and try to get in touch with my inner self. At this point I must admit it was my outer self I was more worried about being touched. Even though I knew he was straight – I had met his wife – I still felt the need to excuse myself saying that I needed a breath of fresh air. I said that I would be back in half an hour and I would expect him to be fully clothed and ready to work on something other than his figure. I left not caring a jot about the rain, which was falling harder than ever.

On my return I was overjoyed to find that Marino had covered his delightful physique with his astral robes. We resumed work, well no we didn't, he returned to strangling a cat and I returned to a bored stupor. We were due to go to the Marquee that night to watch a band called Jagged Edge. About 7.30pm we headed off, but Marino seemed a little perplexed that I wanted to stop at the pub just before the train station. He said we could get a drink when we got there. I, on the other hand, was desperate to, or at least start to, wash the vision of a semi-naked shaman dancing in front of me from my panic-stricken mind. So I laid the logic on him that it would be at least a fifteen minute journey into Soho and that we would need a drink for the trip. Reluctantly he agreed but he said, 'It must be only one,' as he wanted a clear mind to do business later on. Four pints of Red Stripe later we emerged suitably refreshed and ready to take on any *business* that might come our way.

There was a good crowd at the Marquee that night, with the usual liggers and hangers on – step forward Neil Murray, Gary Barden and Lemmy – geniuses all in my opinion, but let's be honest they would go to the opening of a wound. There were also the Z listers: Marino, me, the guys out of Tigertailz, and members of Rogue Male. We had a few more pints and I must confess I can't really remember much about the band except that they were very good and I conveyed my opinion to them after the gig. They seemed blasé but happy enough with my assessment and I was asked by one of them which band I was in. Here I made my first mistake in telling them that I was in the process of getting a band together myself instead of saying I was in Marino the Band, much to his nibs' annoyance.

Then came my second mistake. I laughed when the guitar player, Mike Gray, said I should concentrate on Marino's band. He was obviously sucking up to the beaming guitar hero standing beside me for some reason. The third mistake came when Mr Gray announced that he thought himself the best guitar player around with Marino a close second. I had never witnessed such big-headed arrogance in my life; this caused even more laughter with me pointing out that Marino's sister's new guitar player, Ken of course, was better than both of them put together.

It all kicked off a little bit, not the way it would have in Belfast but there were a few pushes from the Jagged Edge guitarist; he threw his weight about like he was trying to shake a piece of tissue off his finger. Frightened I was not, but I had the sense not to knock him out – best not scupper getting a gig in the Marquee in the future by getting barred on one of the first times of being there. I was led away by Marino; he was afraid that the scene was getting a little ugly.

Away from the threat of being pushed on the chest, having my nipple tweaked, given a Chinese burn or being punched on the BCG, I told Marino that I expected band members to back each other up in times of trouble. He was slurring his speech and wobbling on his loafers. He said he would've done but he was too drunk, having downed a bottle of brandy before he had left the flat. The half-wit had forgotten that I had been with him all day and there certainly had been no spirits consumed. When I pointed this out to him he said 'Goodnight', and staggered out into the bright lights of Soho. His 'Rock and Roll Gypsy heart' was not so Rock and Roll after all. Bottle of brandy my arse. Mike Gray would later call my new band a comedy act and then go on to make a fortune by playing with that well-known quality super-group Right Said Fred. He also studied Martial Arts – maybe next time, big guy.

The Kensal Rise Kennel

About a month after we had moved into Leigh Gardens, I was lying in bed watching breakfast TV when a news flash came on about a house in Dollis Hill where there had been an IRA arms find. When they went to the outside broadcast the reporter was standing in front of the wreck of a house where I had spent the evening in the pleasant company of the couple that performed cannabis-induced sexual contortions while I sat on the sofa. It was also the place where I had been nearly murdered by a multi-freckled, ginger midget.

It transpires that under the floorboards of one of the bedrooms there had been planted dozens of guns and explosives; no one had been apprehended as the occupant had done a runner a month previously. A cold sweat broke as it dawned on me that if I had stayed in that house then I would've been sitting in that very room when the cops came a-calling. 'Yes officer I know my name is Eamon, the Irish for Edward, and I am well aware that I would be classed as a Belfast Catholic, but I swear I know absolutely nothing about the Armalites and Semtex stashed below my feet.'

Visions of my mother boarding the Larne–Stranraer ferry, a cake with a file in it under her arm, filled my head as I breathed a sigh of relief. At Heathrow a squat, short-arsed man with a brown marker, for filling in the gaps in his freckles, was boarding a plane to Calcutta. To his chest he clutched a bottle of 'Just For Men' black, and 'Speak Bengali in a Day' could just be seen poking out of his back pocket.

When in contact with friends back in Belfast I was regularly informed that Magee's alcohol and drug consumption had spiralled out of control. So when I got a call from him saying that he was coming over for a visit, I must confess I was not that delighted, which is a terrible shame because we had been such good, close friends for a very long time. You see the problem was that now that I had started making connections in the music business and Ken and my songs were really coming along, I just didn't want Magee wrecking what progress I had made, and unfortunately when you deal with addicts destruction comes as part of the territory.

I met him at Kensal Rise station and straightaway I realised how much I'd missed him. We hugged. 'Come on, let's Rock and Roll,' I said.

'Let's,' was his reply.

On the way to the 'Kennel', as our new abode had been christened, there was an off licence conveniently situated and Magee and myself happened upon it. At that time there were – as part of the European Union's initiative of subsistence farming – butter mountains, grain silos, wine lakes and beer reservoirs. To drain the latter, there was a cheeky little number called Euro Breu (*sic*) produced. It came in an electric blue can with a prancing horse logo (trying to raise the brand with a Ferrari association perhaps). It was 8.5% proof, stronger than Special Brew but without the sophisticated taste, and only half the price.

The proprietor of the offy was Lebanese and great craic. As Magee and myself entered he exclaimed 'Welcome my friend, how I can help you today?'

'Twenty-four of your finest Euro Buck,' as we childishly called it, I requested.

'My friend an excellent choice if I may say so,' he responded.

'Chilled to perfection as usual?' I enquired.

'Yes indeed, just the way you like them.'

As we left the liquor emporium Magee said, 'He was a lovely guy,' and I had to agree, adding, 'He always has been, but I think he's even more so now that our custom has put two of his kids through school.'

I had been spending a lot of time in the company of Lisa and I have to admit that it was not unpleasant in the slightest. She was beautiful; she had an hourglass figure, most of the sand having drained to the bottom, which in my opinion is nice. She was also far from the sex kitten that she was portrayed as in the press; she was quite shy, in many ways a little innocent. All in all a lovely person, who was not difficult to like. She was engaged to a guy called Michael Machet who, if I remember correctly, was a very high-powered music business attorney who lived in New York and with this in mind I would just like to point out that nothing ever happened between myself and Lisa, OK?

Lisa shared a basement flat with her bass player-drummer Dick Glazebrook (no he didn't play both instruments at once, he wasn't an octopus, he would swap as was needed, a talented guy really). He was a good bit older than Lisa, and I think he was in love with her; this is just my opinion as nothing was ever said. He was a dentist who had his practice in Hammersmith. I think this is correct as I seem to remember the Odeon being close by and thinking 'How cool is that? That's where "Live in the Heart of the City" by Whitesnake was recorded in 1980 – well the first disc, not the second, that was 1978' – stop me, where's my anorak? Anyway he was a lovely, kind, intelligent, gentleman who I had nothing in common with especially from a socioeconomic perspective but we both loved music and therefore got on like a council house on fire.

The evening Magee came to visit I had planned to visit Lisa at the flat, so against my better judgement I invited him along. On the tube journey my guest, who had consumed quite a few Euro Breu and snorted a snowdrift of coke was becoming very loud and animated. He was telling me of his plans to get me back into the Ashes and move the whole operation to London. This was news to me, as far as I was concerned I was more than happy with the way things were going music wise, and the Ashes, who I'm sure had no knowledge of this either, had a new vocalist in the shape of a very talented guy called Tommy Quinn. It wouldn't have been in anyone's interest for Magee's plans to come to fruition. The coke, it seemed was really talking, and logic had long since made its way out the double-glazing.

I could see the panic in Lisa's eyes when she was introduced to Magee; he had ignored her outstretched hand and hugged her like you would an old friend you haven't seen in decades. I looked around and to my relief Dick didn't appear to be in. 'Where's the drink?' Magee asked, laughing.

'I think there's a couple of beers in the fridge,' Lisa responded.

'Well go and get them, serving wench,' Magee giggled.

I should've knocked him out at this point really.

With a beer in his hand Magee seemed to calm down a bit. He sat and listened to some of the new tracks that Lisa was working on. On their completion he calmly said, 'That's all right, but wait till I get the Ashes over here, they'll piss all over that.' I was embarrassed beyond belief: don't get me wrong, I was no big fan of Lisa's music, but manners are manners. She got up and excused herself and went to the bathroom.

'Listen Magee, stop acting like an arse,' I said.

He retorted, 'What are you doing licking up to her for?'

I said, 'You've known me for many years and you of all people know that I don't lick up to anyone, I happen to like her and you also know I hate bullies, as supposedly you do, but that's exactly the way you're coming across so wise the feck up.'

Then I got the Magee smile, he put his arm around my shoulder and apologised. 'Calm down, I'm only taking the piss, now is there any more drink?'

'No there's not, and anyway we'll be leaving soon,' I said.

Lisa was in the kitchen making a coffee and I went in to apologise for my so-called friend's behaviour. I shouldn't have left him on his own, because when I returned to the living room Magee had poured himself a half pint of Dick's sacred eighteen-year-old Scotch, lit up one of his precious Havana cigars and had his feet up on the antique coffee table that caused its owner to have apoplexy if anyone should by chance put a cup on it. Before I could grab Magee by the throat in walked Dick. All I could say was, 'Hi Dick, this is Stephen.'

'Hello there,' said Dick, while his gaze shifted from glass to cigar, from cigar to table and back to the grinning face of Magee. Who greeted a gentleman with, 'Dick, that name must get the odd laugh?'

Luckily there was an escape plan; I had arranged to meet Adele. I had contacted her after finding two tickets to see Bon Jovi at the Hammersmith Odeon that I had bought for her birthday. She said she would love the tickets and suggested we meet up. Basically, if I'm honest, I was trying to get back out with her. I made our excuses and we left the visibly relieved Dick and Lisa to their reinstated tranquility.

The meeting place was a bar called the Oporto and when we arrived Magee went straight to the bogs to powder his nose and came back energised. He had known Adele for many years; we had been going out with each other virtually the whole time I was in the Ashes. He had seen how devastated I had been at our split and as friends do he had taken sides and formed a negative opinion of her. For this reason I had not made him privy to the fact that I was trying to rekindle the romance. As far as he was concerned this was just a meeting of old friends, but in his state I feared that he would become abusive towards her.

I need not have worried because on her arrival Magee was his warm, friendly self – pity he hadn't been that way earlier in the evening. I was relieved at his acceptance of Adele and was further relieved when he, by chance, met up with a music journalist called Carol Clerk from Belfast, who worked for the *Melody Maker*. The band manager side of Magee kicked in; he was unlikely to bother us for the rest of the night.

It was getting late and Adele and I decided it was time to leave, so

I went over to Magee, who was holding court, the way only he could. Carol and her company were hanging on his every word.

'It's time to go,' I said.

'Nonsense, the night is but a pup, and anyway I want to introduce you to Carol here,' Magee replied.

'Hi,' I nodded towards her and she said, 'Stephen has been telling me that he's going to bring the band you sing for over from Belfast. You must give me a call when this happens.'

I was really pissed off at this. I put the record straight and when I was finished Carol appeared keen to hear the stuff Ken and myself were writing. 'At least something positive may come of the evening,' I thought. Magee got me to put my address down on a piece of paper; he was staying on and would follow me later.

My room was a downstairs converted living room with French windows at the back of the house; someone pounding on them rudely awakened me at 4am. This was very perplexing as there was no access to the back garden from the front; you had to go through the house. I opened the curtains and there in the dark I could just make out the figure of Magee.

'Let me in,' he pleaded.

'I can't, I haven't got the key,' I said. 'How did you get round there in the first place?' I enquired through the glass.

'I climbed over the garage,' he shouted back.

'Why?' I asked.

'Because there was no answer at the front,' he explained.

'Well you'll have to go back the way you came,' I said.

Magee knocked over the bins, which he was using as a step, waking half the neighbourhood. I opened the front door; the light from the hall illuminated a clearly drunk and drugged mess. As disturbing as was the intoxicated state he was in, it was less alarming than discovering that he was covered in blood which was trickling from a nasty gash on his forehead. At first I thought he had fallen off the garage, which wouldn't have been surprising the state he was in, but the blood looked like it was drying up and was not gushing, the way you would expect from such a wound. 'What happened to you?' I asked.

'That bitch Carol Clerk smashed a glass over my head,' was his reply.'

It seems that they had gone to the St Moritz nightclub and while there they had gotten into an argument, which resulted in the injury. I can't confirm that this is actually what happened, as I was not there but I must confess that if he had been behaving the way he had earlier in the day I wouldn't have blamed her – in fact, I think he got away quite leniently. I had had enough and knowing that he was not going to bleed to death, I gave him a quilt and showed him to the sofa and said we would talk about it in the morning. I switched off the light and returned to my room.

But coke was still circulating in the toxic soup of Magee's blood. He barged through the bedroom door ready to repeat the story he had just told me, a classic cocaine trait. On seeing that Adele was with me he said, 'What the fuck is she doing here?' I returned him to his bed with a little more force than you really should when dealing with an injured man, but I think I can safely say that if my patience was a tissue you could've blown your nose through it.

The next morning around 3pm Nosferatu rose and boy did he look shit, not only from his injuries but also from the substance abuse. Can I point out at this stage that I am certainly no shrinking violet when it comes to partying, but I never did narcotics, not from a moral standpoint, freedom of choice and all that, but just through total fear of what they can do to you and those around you. When I saw Magee that day I felt no need to change my mind. I sat down with him and told him that in the 24-hour period that he had been with me he had done irreparable damage to my social, love and professional life. For once he didn't bullshit me, he just told me that he would never drink or take drugs again. I took the tube with him to Heathrow in silence, not believing a word of what he had said. We didn't embrace as he went to board the plane.

Oh Danny boy the pipes the pipes are frozen

1987 was one of the worst winters I can ever remember; the snow was thigh deep in some places. It was so cold that the water pipes froze in the house, depriving us of water with which to wash, cook and, worst of all, a means to flush the toilet. This last problem was compounded when there was the need to dispose of solids. We came upon the solution, when the need arose, to go around the corner to a pub and make use of their facilities.

Adele was living in Woolwich at the time and after the sorry incident with Magee was probably reluctant to return to Leigh Gardens any time soon. Which was unfortunate because, apart from Magee's display of social idiocy, Adele and myself had got on like the split had never happened. I bit the bullet, chanced my arm and asked her over. To my delight she said yes, just as long as Magee had gone – he had, so she said she would be over on Sunday.

I spent the morning tidying the house, with special emphasis on my downstairs bedroom. I was ever the optimist. However trying to create an atmosphere conducive to romance was difficult with a blocked toilet and the resulting smells. About half an hour before Adele's ETA I got hopped up and made the wintry journey to the pub. I had held off going, even though the urge had come upon me a couple of hours earlier, so it was with a certain amount of urgency that I skipped along.

On reaching the bar door I sighed a sigh of relief and started to relax. To my horror it was locked – I had forgotten about the damned Sunday licensing hours. All of sudden my now relaxed bowel decided that enough was enough and that it no longer wanted to retain its contents; it went into spasm. I turned on my heels; with buttocks clenched so tight that you couldn't have passed a Rizla between them I started to run. It was the kind of straight-legged jog employed by those poor individuals who have conditions that necessitate wearing callipers, or goose-stepping Nazis in a hurry.

At our front door I was beside myself with panic: the lack of water had also curtailed our laundry and I was wearing the only pair of monks that could be passed off as clean. The fact that I had on more layers than an onion, due to the weather, meant that just dropping the strides was a no-no. I was stripping as I headed for the privacy of my room, and on entering I frantically looked around for inspiration.

My paper of choice was and still is the *Independent* and at the time it was still a broadsheet. On seeing a discarded edition I came upon the idea of spreading it out on the ground and doing my worst. I toyed with the idea, to cut down on the smell, of going out to the garden but quickly rejected this due to the fear of nether region frostbite and also the great possibility of pissing off even more the already demented next door neighbours. I would just have to do it, Sweet Mother of Jesus, on the floor of my room.

Adele arrived to find the front door ajar. She pushed it open and announced her arrival with, 'Hi, anybody home?' Still squatting above the paper I kept quiet; maybe she would go away. Like Magnus Magnusson used to say, 'I've started so I'll finish.' This was not a job that could be interrupted, I mean it's not like smoking a cigarette round the back of the bike sheds when the teacher comes, you can hardly nick it and put it behind your ear for later. My room door started to edge open and Adele's head peered around it. She witnessed her recently dropped boyfriend making like Mr Whippy and curling one out onto the floor. For a minute she just stood speechless, then she asked, 'What are you doing?' To which I replied, 'What does it look like I'm doing?' She just shrugged and said, 'I really wouldn't like to hazard a guess.' I then asked her if she wouldn't mind leaving the room while I cleaned up – a gentleman has his standards you know.

By some sort of miracle Adele moved into the Kensal Rise Kennel with me. We had a ball. We had not, before this, had the opportunity to spend this much quality time together and we made good use of it. This couldn't really have got much better: we were sharing a house with Ken and Elaine, the craic was ninety and for some reason I can't remember being short of money, which I'm sure we were. I was on the dole – sorry, training to be a rock star – and Adele was working, as part of her degree, in a travel agents in the centre of London, which didn't pay much. But we were never hungry or short of a drink. Then again there was no mortgage and no kids, so what little we had could be wasted on ourselves – the luxury of being financially and emotionally carefree.

Now that we had a comfortable home it was a great excuse for friends from home to visit. One such guest was our old Bangor Tech friend James. Remember him? He was the guy I had persuaded to take part in the battle of the bands competition where the sausages and glue were thrown from the crowd. He had secured an audition as a French horn player for the Royal Air Force band. There are hundreds of people each year who try to get this prestigious gig, the standard is set very high, so for James to have got this far was impressive in itself. Anyway he asked us if it was OK if he stayed with us while he was over in London. The guy's a gem so we were only too pleased to oblige.

The day before James's audition he arrived at the Kennel and we proceeded to introduce him to the joys of the mighty Euro Breu on which he got right royally pissed. We then took him to the San Moritz where we danced the night away to the sounds of Hanoi Rocks doing 'Don't You Ever Leave Me Baby': a class song that still conjures up wonderful memories even today. The upshot is that James turned up late for the audition the next morning smelling of drink and unshaven. He failed miserably. Crestfallen and deflated he returned back to the bosom of the hallions that had effectively scuppered any chance he had of wearing the grey uniform and touring the world. When I answered the front door to him it was obvious by his face that he had flunked. He was handed a can of E. Breu and he reconvened the consumption of its syrupy contents.

A phone call had been promised to his parents after the audition, to let them know the good news. They were very straight-laced, religious, lovely people who I know were very wary of our friendship: don't get me wrong, nothing was ever said and they were always very welcoming of me, but I just knew that their Christian Protestant background didn't legislate for their son and heir hanging around with a Metal maniac.

James had done very well for himself, considering that we had laughed and drunk our way through two years of college, wasting time and the taxpayer's money. But what we lost in academia we gained in friendship, life experience and love. He had secured a job in Shorts, the world-famous airplane manufacturer, and was set up for life, even if he hadn't got into the Air Force. Even so his family would have loved for him to have joined an institution that numbered among its ranks members of the royal family. Imagine his parents' surprise when their clearly drunk son phoned to inform them that he had failed the chance of a lifetime, but reassured them saying that he didn't care because he was going to quit his job and stay on in London as the keyboard player in mine and Ken's band. I must point out that this was something we had not even discussed. I know for a fact that his parents never ever used profanities but in this instance they made an exception.

With the receiver held away from his reddening ear James made mouthing motions with his hand to Ken and myself in a blasé display of rebellion. He had thrown off the shackles of conformity and joined the ranks of the Rock and Roll great unwashed. I could see the giddy look in his eye of experiences new, and all the while the barrage of shouting was coming from Bangor County Down via the earpiece of the phone.

Even I was visualising the new-look band with all the possibilities that a keyboard player would offer us. A group called FM were my band of choice at the time. They had a sound that was based on fluffy keyboard noodlings, and we could sound just like them, I thought. I raised my beer to offer encouragement, or as AC/DC would scream, 'For Those About to Rock We Salute You'. James held up his thumb in response, just as the shouting finished on the other end of the line. Defiantly he returned the phone to his ear, puffed out his chest and said, 'I'll see you tomorrow mummy.'

There's an old mill by the stream, Nellie Dean

Ken and myself had somehow persuaded Stephen Campbell, the old No Hot Ashes drummer, to come over from Belfast and play with us. There was spare room in the house so it made sense that he move in. We also got him the drummer's job in Lisa's band to fill the time until we got a bass player in. Then came that fateful Friday night.

We were religiously listening to the Tommy Vance Rock show when an advert came on. A bass player, called Eugene Scribes, wanted to form a Rock band. Perfect, it was just what we needed and to top it all Tommy had said that he lived in Kensal Rise; he must be just round the corner. I phoned the show and got his number. When I rang it a girl answered and started to snigger when I asked to speak to Eugene. A voice came to the phone that sounded a little too educated for my liking. 'Beggars can't be choosers,' I thought. 'Hi, I'm calling about the advert you placed on the Friday Rock Show looking for a band,' I said.

'Well actually I didn't want it to go out on that slot, I don't really like that type of music,' was the response.

'What!' I thought. 'He doesn't like Rock music? What sort of a moron have I happened upon here?'

I'm a patient man and I have also made it my lifelong work to educate those less fortunate than myself when it comes to taste in music. 'That's OK, we'll convert you,' I said to Eugene.

'I'm not sure I want converting,' was his reply.

'We'll call round and help you with your gear tomorrow and we'll have a jam at our house,' I said ignoring his previous remark. I felt like a missionary who has just told a Polynesian that his life of free love with the beautiful local women was a sin and celibacy was the way forward.

Eugene responded in exactly the same way that that islander would. 'Mmmm . . . I'm *really* not sure about this.'

Following the directions that we were given, myself and Stephen arrived at Eugene's front door. When he answered I was immediately taken by how tall and square he was. I don't mean he had four equal sides; he was just a little uncool. He had short hair (that could grow, no problem) he was wearing baggy jeans and a jumper (Carnaby St, no problem) and he spoke with a very posh English accent (a week in Ken's company should sort that out, no problem). For some reason he seemed to be squinting at our attire. I assume that the sun was shining in his eyes, I mean how could he possibly find fault with holey skintight jeans tucked into cowboy boots, bandanas and fringed jackets. 'Where's your gear?' I enquired?

'You don't want me to dress like that do you?' he asked.

I disregarded his cheek and said, 'No, your bass and amp.'

'Oh, thank God for that,' he quipped. Then pointing, he said, 'It's behind the door here.' Sitting on the hall floor was a guitar case with a Fender Precision sticker on it, a Trace Elliot four by four speaker cabinet and Trace Elliot head. This was very expensive equipment and I felt a satisfied glow rising; he must have a bit of money behind him. The Milky Bars would be on him I thought, especially after that remark about our threads.

'I'd help you into the car with the gear but I have a bad back,' Eugene said.

'What car?' we replied.

'You don't have a car? Then how are you going to get all this stuff to your house?' he asked.

'We'll carry it,' I said.

'How far away do you live?' he asked.

'About half a mile,' I answered. Stephen and myself took a handle each of the speaker cab. What Eugene must have thought as he snailed along behind two long-haired oafs carrying a very heavy amp and speaker cabinet through the streets of Kensal Rise is anybody's guess. He must've been further embarrassed when Stephen requested a smoke break every hundred yards or so, and would sit on the amp in the middle of the street sweating and puff away. I'm sure Eugene was praying he wouldn't be seen by anyone he knew.

Our new bass player, although he didn't know that at the time, was introduced to Ken. Surprisingly he stayed and we began the long process of moulding him into a four-string Rock Demon. The Kennel was a modest three-bedroom semi-detached, by which I mean it was no sprawling mansion. The living room was adequate for a family with 2.5 children to sit in and watch *Emmerdale* over a Pot Noodle. What it was not adequate for was a full drum kit, PA system, guitar amp and bass rig – however that is what was crammed into it.

We started jamming and the neighbours were subjected to a full-on Rock band that were not quite familiar with their songs yet and kept stopping and starting. It was with a sense of pride that we realised that next door's residents were banging on the walls, shouting words of encouragement; you just don't get community spirit like that any more.

Eugene was shown the chords to 'Heartbreak City', the first song we had written, he picked them up really quickly and it was noted that he had a slightly unorthodox style of playing. It was a bit similar to Phil Lynott. This was a pleasant surprise, as we were all Thin Lizzy nuts. It was also a surprise for him – he had never really listened to the Irish Rock legends. Fate I think.

The afternoon wore on, we showed Eugene more songs, and it started to become clear that Little Lord Fauntleroy was starting to let loose a little. When we wrapped up I asked him if he had enjoyed himself, and he said he had. 'Good,' I said, 'because we are having a party tonight and young fella ma lad you are invited. Bring some refreshments for fear that your throat may become parched and as is traditional bring more than you can consume yourself, for there may be those poor souls that are in need of a drink but are not in a financial position to purchase it.' (Us, need you ask.) I told you I'd get my own back concerning that crack he made about our clothes.

That night Eugene came back to the house to be met by an assortment of reprobates milling around the house in various states of inebriation. The craic was great and the music was an eclectic mix of what Andy Kershaw would call world music: we had everything from AC/DC to ZZ Top, well you have to cater for all tastes after all. The stereo was linked through the PA system so people in Harlesden, three miles away, could enjoy the vibes man.

One of the guests was Dick Glazebrook from Lisa's band. He looked a little out of place – even though he would be a frequent visitor to the Rock haunts of London he was not really prepared for the frivolity that was taking place and certainly not from such an early part of the evening.

At that time in the Rock world a form of Metal was starting to dominate: Thrash was massive. Bands like Metallica, Megadeth and Slayer were the big players, but my personal favourites were Anthrax; they were a bunch of Bermuda-short wearing madmen who even then were mixing Rock and Rap. Dick was a blues/jazz man who hated this new breed of mayhem, describing it as 'ruddy noise'. I could see his nose turn up as ' Madhouse' from the 'Spreading the Disease' album shook the foundations.

Eugene, not knowing anything about Heavy Metal at all, was also looking slightly uncomfortable. With him and Dick experiencing a certain amount of social exclusion I saw an opportunity to bring two public schoolboys together, not in the biblical sense may I add, and have a little laugh as well. I persuaded Eugene to approach Dick and gave him an opening line to break the ice.

'Hi, my name is Eugene I just thought I would introduce myself. Eamon has just told me that you are the bass player in Anthrax.'

'No I bloody well am not,' said Dick as he stormed off. Eugene just stood for a second, hand still outstretched, and then he started laughing. I think it was at this point that I knew we had really found our man.

It was a cracking party, however the evening didn't end on a high for everyone. At the rather early hour of 2am I decided that I had had enough so I announced that I was going to bed. Knowing that Adele always went to the kitchen to get a drink of water before retiring for the night, I thought it would be an absolute hoot to climb into the cupboard below the sink and jump out when she did so. I waited until I knew everyone had left the kitchen, wrapped a sheet around my naked waist and crawled head first into the small cramped cupboard where we stored the vegetables.

Adele must have been having a ball because she resisted the temptation to join her drunk boyfriend in bed and continued to party. Back under the sink I waited patiently until I fell asleep. Shortly afterwards my makeshift Mahatma Gandhi attire slipped loose and I accidentally nudged the door open with my naked backside. One of our female guests, after going to the fridge for a drink, returned to the living room horrified and hysterical. She told Adele that there was a pervert baring all in the kitchen. Adele said to Eugene, 'Go and get Eamon out of bed. He'll deal with him.'

Eugene was slightly confused to find that my room was empty and retuned to the party with the news that I had gone. A posse was gathered amongst the male guests. As they entered the kitchen they were greeted with a big bare arse filling the frame of the cupboard and a set of giblets blowing in the breeze created by the draught from under the back door. Luckily I woke just in time to prevent a kicking. For Eugene the drunken exposure of my man bits mustn't have been that traumatic an incident because he stayed on in the band. However it was a few days before Adele spoke to me again.

It was many months before Eugene revealed his true identity; he was in fact, called Xan Phillips. Why he gave us an alias I can only assume was so that we couldn't trace him if things didn't work out. Ken, being quick on the uptake, called him Eugene for the next year or so. You know sometimes even after all these years when thinking of those early days I still remember him as Eugene. Anyway Xan became the heartbeat of Nellie Dean, which was the name we chose for our ensemble, after the pub in Soho we frequented the most. He had to carry the lunacy of Ken and myself on his shoulders as well as the debts we incurred. One such fiscal backache was a PA system, which Xan got out on hire purchase with our encouragement. We only used it once or twice; he would be paying it off for years.

He was also once persuaded to release his grip on the band's last £20 by Ken, to put on a horse that he claimed was a cert because it was trained in a swimming pool. It inevitably finished last. If only the track had been waterlogged, it probably would've given Mark Spitz a run for his money. But despite all these mishaps we all hit it off and I presume that if Xan thinks about it really, really hard he would admit that even he benefited from getting involved with us.

Gone Fishing

Shortly before I moved to London myself and Fish had a major falling out. When I say *we* did, what I really mean is that our girl-friends did and of course we stupidly took their sides and thus a long and funny relationship was knackered. Stephen Campbell, however, remained good friends with him and invited him over for a holiday. Due to the bad feeling between us I was a bit apprehensive about seeing Fish again. I had also heard, from home, that he was quite ill and had lost a lot of weight, so when he arrived on the doorstep of the Kennel, I nearly died when I saw him.

My old mate had lost about three stone; it was the kind of weight loss that you know is not through good diet and exercise, the skin tells its own tale. But as bad as he looked physically, it was his new perm that scared me more. It's a hell of a shock, when you are waiting to see an old familiar face, and what you are met with is a weird mix of Deidre from 'Coronation Street' and Brian May. Anyway despite his Frankenstein's monster makeover, it was great to see him and we went straight back to the way we were before the lovers' tiff.

I think he stayed for about a week in June 1987, and boy what a week it was. Ken and Stephen were playing the Marquee with Lisa Dominique and Stephen had persuaded her to let Fish roadie for the night. Lisa's crowd, how shall I put this, consisted of balding perverts with thick national health glasses. Towards the end of the gig a few of the 'Dr Crippin' lookalikes jumped up on to the stage to get a slobbery kiss from the object of their desires. Fish took great pleasure in throwing them off the stage once they had left their genetic fingerprint on the side of her face. I thought that it would be very funny if I got up on stage, make like I was going to kiss Lisa, duck past her and give Ken a big smacker on the lips. So that's just what I did.

There were astonished looks on the faces of the crowd, who couldn't believe I had passed up the chance of a letch with Lisa. Ken was pissing himself laughing. I turned round to see what Fish's reaction was but before I could catch his eye I felt an arm around my neck and I was hurled from the stage. As I lay on the sticky floor of the Wardour Street sweatbox, I could just make out the retreating figure of Fish rubbing his hands following a job well done. After the show, when quizzed as to why he had manhandled me in such a manner, Fish explained that professionals couldn't show favouritism. I think the roar of the greasepaint, the smell of the crowd, and a certain Ms Dominique's assets had gone to his head.

A couple of nights later we were on the guest list, thanks to Lisa, to see a little-known band from America play their first gig in the UK, which just happened to be at the Marquee again. It had been arranged before Fish had arrived so we couldn't get him in. This would've meant that he would have been left on his own in a strange city. So like a true friend I let him take my place. What a mug.

I stayed in the Ship and had a few pints before going across Wardour Street to the San Moritiz to await everyone's return. When they finally arrived I asked Fish what he had thought of the band. He said that they were a bad version of AC/DC, and that the skinny wee singer was actually sitting over in the corner of the club. I looked over to where he was pointing to see a sweaty, red-haired man, wearing a cowboy hat, no shirt and towel around his shoulders. He looked like a grumpy little shit and I couldn't help wondering that if he ever made it big would that cheer him up? Axl Rose and his most dangerous band in the world became the biggest thing on the planet. Axl never did cheer up.

I don't know why but for many years I had been carrying around in my head a yearning to become a nurse, and I don't mean I wanted to dress like one or anything dodgy like that, I really thought that I could somehow be good at it. With this in mind I decided that it was my duty, now that we were mates again, to cure Fish. I did a bit of research (none) and decided that Crohn's disease was curable by large amounts of Euro Breu and Chinese curries. I put my regimen into operation, much to Fish's objections: he feared for his life.

We had a few setbacks, which had a knock-on effect on our supply of toilet rolls, but by God I was not going to lose my first patient. I pushed on, using the maxim that 'If it doesn't kill you it will make you stronger.' When he returned to Holywood he was a changed man; even his mother couldn't believe his improvement and right up to the present day he is fit and healthy. This is obviously a good thing for him and as a friend, a good thing for me as well.

Footnote: do not under any circumstances view the above as a cure for any illnesses; in fact it may be a cause of a few.

Ride like the wind

October 15th 1987 started like any other day at the Kensal Rise Kennel; that is quite late. Elaine and Adele had gone to work to sweat blood for some hard-earned cash leaving myself and Ken preparing to take on the Rock world by staying in bed and waiting for stardom to come a knocking at the door. At this point we thought that sheer talent was enough and that hard work was something those less gifted than ourselves did. The problem with this philosophical stand is that in actual fact we were not as talented as we thought we were and that hard work might have helped us bring our strengths to the fore and disguise our weaknesses. Youthful arrogance has a delusional myopic effect on the testosterone-fuelled brain of would-be Rock heroes, and we were happy with our shortsightedness.

Around late afternoon we noticed the wind getting up a bit, then it started to rain. We were used to inclement weather; we came from Ireland where the only difference between summer and winter is that the rain in summer is slightly warmer. At around 5.45pm I would walk round to the bus stop at the Italian Deli and meet Adele as she returned from slavery, happy in the knowledge that she had worked her fingers to the bone to enable her artist of a boyfriend the space to create a big fat nothing all day. As we walked back the wind was really starting to make an impression, and the tree-lined streets became a swirling vortex of autumnal leaves.

On arrival at the house the usual sight of the front door lying ajar greeted us. Ken had returned late one night without his key and gently eased it open by putting his size 9s through it, busting the lock. Security-wise it meant that someone nearly always had to be in the house. If we were all going out the last person to leave put the chain on and, due to the back door key being lost, climbed out the kitchen window. It also meant that that person had to scramble over the garage to gain access to the street. As gentlemen we never let the girls do this job – well, almost never.

Why did we not get the door fixed? I hear you ask. Well we were renting and on a point of principle we felt that our hard-earned housing benefit should facilitate our landlord the necessary funds to fix it as part of our contract. Unfortunately said landlord had been arrested and was sewing mailbags at the pleasure of Elizabeth II. The reason he fell foul of the law was something to do with false claims for housing benefit – something I'm sure we had nothing to do with. Anyway the fact that we were not going to waste good dole money on securing the house and its contents meant that the door was nearly always open – false economy at its finest – 'Come on in Mr Thief and take what ever expensive guitars and amps you want as I'm sure we would never miss them and your need is obviously greater than ours.'

The wind got even stronger. We nearly had to cancel our traditional trip to the off licence, but as I said the Irish are a hardy race as far as weather (and thirst) are concerned. Ignoring the now falling branches and debris from the trees Ken and myself commenced our quest in search of Thunderbird and Night Train Express. These cheeky little numbers were advertised as Californian party wines. I haven't been to many soirées in Beverly Hills but I can almost guarantee you that Jack Nicholson and Meryl Streep are not sitting around their pools, their little pinkies in the air, sipping these gut-rot-inducing concoctions. Never mind the people of Hollywood California, the people of Holywood County Down Northern Ireland, where they would drink almost anything, would turn their noses up at them. That is, of course, with the exception of Ken and myself. We ex-pats of the White City council housing estate found them palatable (just), cheap and best of all they did the job.

Returning with our precious cargo we noticed that the wind had transformed into a gale. We hurried along, pulling our short denim jackets tight. Great gusts of icy wind rushed through the holes in our jeans, made their way upwards past the family jewels and gave rise to the sensation of needing to pee with alarming urgency. On arrival we fought each other to be the first to avail of the bog. Ken won and I spent a couple of agonising minutes as he made splashing sounds and sighed great sighs of relief. When we were both bladder deflated we retired to the lounge and cracked open a bottle of Thunderbird, savouring its pear flavoured contents: we could almost feel the San Fernando sun beating down on us.

By the time we retired to bed the gales had turned into a hurricane and the front door was straining at its chain. A short while later the weakest link lived up to its name and separated from its comrades leaving the door to smash against the inside wall, bounce back and smash again. The noise was horrendous. I jumped out of bed and ran to the gaping hole that had all manner of things blowing through it. I looked around for something heavy enough to stop the door from blowing open again.

Big Xan had left his very expensive speaker cabinet in our care knowing that it would be in safe hands. It made a marvellous doorstop but because of the step it didn't sit flush: there was a gap of about two inches that allowed the door to bang repeatedly off it. Xan had only used the Trace Elliot a couple of times; after that night it looked like it had just come off a world tour with The Who.

One of the most disconcerting things about the whole night, apart from the actual fear of death, which tragically did happen to some poor souls, was the repeated bombardment of the French windows of my room by fruit. With it being autumn the pear and apple trees at the back of the house were heavy with their seasonal bounty and although reluctant to give them up until ready they had no choice but to let the full force of the storm carry them in all directions including the back of the house. The bins had fallen early on and their contents were being tossed all over the place. There was a temptation to try to minimise the damage by going out and putting the refuse receptacles into the garage but I had a terrible feeling that my parents may not have been able to live down the shame that their eldest had survived the Troubles only to meet his death at the hands of a stray Granny Smith or Cox's Pippin.

In the morning the winds had abated and we could survey the damage to the local area. There were chimneys and walls down, some cars had been crushed by falling tress, and in short the place was a mess. Our house was unscathed, not a roof tile was missing, and even if it had been the landlord, on his release, would have had to get the damage fixed, not us. I couldn't help feel for those poor people who were paying a mortgage on a place that was their pride and joy. They were soon to be told that an 'act of God' would mean that some bastard insurance companies would try to wriggle out of paying them or if they were to stump up it would be years before they settled. Heaven forbid that you missed a payment to them, you would soon get a nasty letter reminding you that your oversight was inconveniencing their poor shareholders from making another million or two; rant over.

Christmas in hell

The first Christmas at the Kennel Adele and myself decided to return home to good old 'Norn Iron' for some home cooking and bomb scares. Ken and Elaine, with it being their first Yuletide together, stayed on and had the added benefit of being flush with cash due to a mix-up at the dole office. Ken was the grateful recipient of someone else's £500 which he intended to spend on a Christmas dinner, lingerie and alcohol, just as the Baby Jesus had intended.

With the turkey in the oven and the underwear in place the festive couple settled down for a few relaxing Euro Breu before the Morcambe and Wise show, the Queen's speech and dinner. As the cans went down so did the urgency for food; the fowl was turned down to gas mark 2. The tipsy couple then decided to take the Christmas spirit upstairs if you know what I mean. A short detour to the bathroom allowed Ken to demonstrate, for some reason only known to himself, his Mohammed Ali 'dope-a-rope' technique, encouraging his partner to attempt to hit him as hard as she could.

The drunken playful blows rained down. Ken did a marvellous job of weaving, dodging, bobbing and protecting his rib cage with his elbows. Ali would have been proud. He egged Elaine on with blood-boiling encouragement, using phrases such as, 'My granny could do better than that' and 'Would you like to sit down for a while and catch your breath?' The love of his life, fuelled by 8.4% alcohol and rage, increased her efforts by using her feet in a slight flaunting of the Queensberry rules. When this failed to deliver the desired injuries she improvised.

We returned from Belfast rested and basking in the afterglow of a family Christmas to be met by Ken sporting a broken nose, split lip and two black eyes. We also had to do a balancing act each time we went to sit on the toilet, the seat having been Elaine's weapon of choice to inflict the injuries. God bless us, one and all.

A year later I got the chance of getting home for Christmas with Paul Brown, Elaine's brother and my good friend Johnny Bramley (later the editor of the programme 'Grandstand' and a Bafta award-winner none the less, the talented git). Adele had already flown back and I would meet up with her on my return. The three of us traveled from London to Liverpool through the night to catch the ferry. Once on board we sought a quiet spot to try to catch up on the sleep we had missed.

There was a lounge that was empty with long bench-like seats around the wall. We each choose a comfortable spot, stretched out and started to doze. What we didn't know was that the area was actually the ship's disco and while we were sleeping it had filled with hundreds of children from the roughest estates in Northern Ireland. They had been on a cross-community initiative to Alton Towers and were now full of delirious excitement, fizzy drinks and E numbers.

I am a light sleeper and woke with the hubbub of voices. When I opened my eyes it looked like there were thousands of boys, with upper lips covered in snotters, sliding on their knees around the tiny dance floor. Johnny and Paul slept on, that is until the DJ cranked out the first tune of the day making Johnny leap out of his skin. I had bought a drink and was sitting watching the scene unfold. I nearly wet myself as Johnny rubbed his eyes trying to make sense of the mayhem that was his waking vision. Paul slept on, that is until one of the little dears decided that he was taking up too much space and emptied a full ashtray into his exposed right ear. Paul jumped awake and fell off the seat, fag buts and ash filling the air. Johnny and myself could hardly speak we were laughing that much.

Paul was furious. He sprang to his feet and came running over to us. 'Where the feck did these wee bastards come from?' he yelled over the sound of 'When Will I be Famous,' by Bros blasting from the disco speakers. We couldn't answer due to hysterics. 'Right,' he said. 'That's it,' and he went to run off.

'Where are you going?' I managed to ask him.

'I'm going to get a black plastic bag.'

'You're not going to clear up the mess are you?' I said.

'No, I'm going to put the wee bastard that dumped the contents of the ashtray onto my head into it and throw the fecker overboard; they won't miss one of the shits.' For a second I really thought he meant it, and who could've blamed him? He spent the rest of the trip, which was many hours, standing on the deck, in the freezing cold. Being a non-smoker the smell from his head was making him sick. His travelling companions toasted him from the window of the bar.

No sleep till Hammersmith

Even though I now knew Xan's real name I was still intrigued as to the origins of his alias. He told me that he had got the name from the Irish composer Michael Balfe whose headstone is in the graveyard close to his Kensal Green home. I still couldn't see the connection so I pushed him further. Xan said that Michael had been a great traveller and had composed many classical pieces using London and Paris as inspiration. Again I was still at a loss. He went on that whilst in Paris Michael had socialised with the great and the good within the world of the arts. Eventually I said 'Please Xan, where is all this going?'

'Isn't it obvious?' he asked.

'No,' I said.

Xan sighed. 'Michael Balfe was a close personal friend of the famous French playwright Eugene Scribe. Does that answer your question?'

Jesus H Christ I'm sorry I asked. I would never get those ten minutes back again.

Anyway it got me thinking that the graveyard in question, which was also the resting place of Isambard Kingdom Brunel, might make a good venue for some photos. Boy do I wish I could get my hands on those pictures now. From memory, I wore a ripped to the navel T-shirt with the sleeves cut off, and a pair of patched jeans that were way too tight and showed off my ever-expanding beer gut. Ken had on Elaine's blue leather trousers that left you in no doubt that he was not a member of the Tribe of David. Stephen Campbell was wearing a black Arthur-Daly type titfer and a pair of candy-striped Jane Fonda workout trousers that, again, were so tight that a good cough could've put him back in time to when his 'Ulster Halls' hadn't dropped. Xan I think was wearing a pair of tight black jeans and a matching leather biker's jacket. In retrospect and with the passage of time he was the only cool looking one among us and yet we thought him a geek.

The reason for the photo was to enter a battle of the bands competition to be held at the Riverside Studios in Hammersmith. A biography, demo ('Heartbreak City', recorded in Xan's house with Steve Smith of the Vapours fame producing) and that awful snap were submitted and by some miracle (or was it the £5 note stuck to the tape?) we were accepted. We rehearsed in our house for a while longer but felt that the neighbours deserved a break.

We looked up the Yellow Pages for a studio to practise in. There was one in the near vicinity; it was called the BBMC and was located in Harlesden, a short bus journey away. A slot was booked for the start of the following week. On arrival you couldn't help but notice that we were the only white faces in the building. We were greeted cordially enough but there was still an air of suspicion that you couldn't ignore.

With our gear set up we launched into the first song. In the three and half minutes it took to complete, there were about ten incidences of Rastafarians with large spliffs and cans of Red Stripe coming in uninvited, pointing at us, belly laughing and then leaving. This, as you can imagine, was a little off-putting, especially as it continued throughout the day with the same people reappearing, bringing with them new faces and laughing their heads off. Some of them were in such hysterics that they needed to virtually kneel on the floor. Maybe it was the ganja, maybe it was the ridiculous clothes we were wearing or maybe it was the non-laid-back racket we were making that caused the hilarity. I suspect a combination of all three.

When the ridicule was over we went to the reception to book ourselves another session. It was only then that we saw the notice above the counter which read, 'Welcome to the Brent Black Music

Co-Operative'. The girl taking the reservation said we were the only white band to rehearse there in the whole time the place had been opened; we were the topic of conversation everywhere and that the gut-busting laughter was because they couldn't believe we had the guts to turn up. We being there had nothing to do with bravery, just stupidity. We hadn't even thought to find out what the initials stood for.

For many months we rehearsed at the BBMC. We were accepted because they realised that there was not a racist bone in any of our bodies and we, through our consumption of Red Stripe from the studio tuck shop, could hold our own, man. We were so at home that at the annual Christmas party we were asked to play. Unfortunately, due to circumstances beyond our control, which I will get on to, we couldn't, but we attended and it was a brilliant night.

A week before the big gig, there came a rapping on the Kennel front door at 5am dragging me from my night's slumber. There standing in the porch light was a ruddy-faced gentleman, and behind him a lorry for transporting horses was idling. Leigh Gardens was neither wide enough nor affluent enough to cater for a vehicle of the equestrian variety. 'I'm here to pick up Stephen Campbell's stuff,' said the driver.

'What stuff?' I asked.

'All of it,' he replied.

Thinking he must be a debt collector or something, I thought 'I'll sort this out.'

'Stevie Stevie!!' I shouted up the stairs. No answer, so I ran up and pushed open his door.

Our drummer's room was bare – not a possession was left; the bastard had done a runner. I descended the stairs feeling gutted that a friend had not had the balls to tell us he was leaving. 'OK, you can take it all,' I said pointing to the drum kit sitting in the hall.

'I can't lift that, I have a bad back,' said the removal man, who was turning out to be as useful as a horsehair vest at a dermatitis sufferers' support group meeting.

I really felt the urge to say 'Feck it, it can stay there, I'm not going to move it'. But for some reason, probably a long friendship or maybe because deep down I still really liked the guy, I lifted Stephen's whole seven-piece kit, plus a coffin-type wooden box that held all the metal stands and weighed an absolute ton. The lorry backfired its way down the street waking everyone within a five-mile radius and left me with the realisation that we would have to cancel our first gig and first break.

The bird-rousing rays of morning sunshine brought with them the dawning that the Nellies had suffered a major blow, and that I hadn't got Ken out of bed to help me with the drum kit. I would never learn. I phoned Xan and gave him the bad news. To his credit and with what would turn out to be an unwavering belief in the power of positive thinking, he said it would be sorted out.

By chance we were going to see Def Leppard at the Hammersmith Odeon that very night. While the support band, who I think were Tesla, were playing, we visited the notoriously crowded balcony bar. On seeing the throngs of metalheads Big Xan saw an opportunity for problem solving. He stood tall, which is very tall, and shouted above the assembled masses, 'Are there any drummers here?' A voice answered in the affirmative and a hand was raised in the air.

Tony Lawless, a cross between King William of Orange and Lawrence Llewellyn Bowen, made himself known. Regardless of known ability he was told to be at the BBMC the next day at 12 noon. We entered the auditorium as the first chords of 'Stage Fright' rang out; we might have just survived a fright of our own.

At the appointed time Tony appeared, a little bleary of the eye and a lot ruffled around his shirt cuffs, but he was ready to rock. We were to play three songs for the competition so it was down to business, time was of the essence. The first thing we noticed about our new drummer was that he was not that great at playing his instrument of choice. His timing was bad, he seemed to mix the bass drum beat with the snare for no apparent reason, and he had a fixation with Tommy Lee from Motley Crue, which meant a lot of stick twirling. But we were desperate and as I've said the clock was ticking. To Tony's credit he learnt the basics of the songs very quickly and was sent home with demo tapes to listen to. The next day he had them down pat, in his own unorthodox way.

By the end of the week the songs sounded really good. We had got used to Tony's mad-as-a-box-of-frogs style of playing; there was a hint of confidence returning. On the night of the competition we pulled in all our favours and dragged along as many friends and relatives as we could for vocal support. I think we went on third or fourth; we were the only Metal band competing amongst a lot of Indie and pop bands. Also on the bill was a band that modelled themselves on Level 42 and who seemed to be very friendly with the judges.

Thanks to our rent-a-crowd and the fact that we played an excellent set, with only a couple of mistakes, we went down a storm, better than anyone else the whole night in fact. When battle was done the result was read out and surprise surprise, the wannabe Level 42ers won, with us coming second.

Boos (not booze) rang out as even those who were there to support other bands saw a travesty of justice. The chief judge, on hearing the crowd's derision, had to explain, from the stage, the decision, saying that the winners were superior musicians and that their songs were better. With hindsight he was probably right, but it gave us an excuse to claim victimisation. We thought at the time and still do now that the music business does not give the Rock and Metal genres the credit that they deserve.

We may have been runners up, but we scored a moral victory that night. It also gave us the excuse to celebrate, which we did back at the Kennel, where we reflected on how we had faced adversity and come out triumphant. This gang mentality would last amongst the Nellies, band members and friends, until the very end.

Out of the doghouse

Soon after the Riverside miscarriage of justice we were looking for new accommodation; the owner reclaimed the Kensal Rise Kennel. He had finally started asking questions, like why he hadn't received any rent for about a year. We had paid the landlord but he had been incarcerated and seen fit not to pass the funds over to the owner, who was to say the least a little miffed. I really had to admire his patience, but enough was enough and he finally decided that he didn't want us in his property any more, and who could blame him?

It was a good thing we left when we did, because due to a leak from the toilet, which had been there since we moved in, the bathroom decided it didn't like its position in the architecture of the house and collapsed through the rotten floorboards into the kitchen below, nearly killing the owner as he sat having his breakfast. This was only found out when Ken went back to retrieve mail, which he hoped would contain a dole cheque or two. The owner invited him in to survey the mess made by the toilet, bath and wash hand basin. He was then chased down the street, which must've been a sight and a half as Ken is at least six foot tall and the owner was a five foot four Indian man whose English was just good enough for him to hurl obscenities and the mail at Ken as he fled for his life.

Tony informed Adele and me that there was a spare room in his house; we jumped at the opportunity, moving in with him, his girl-friend and a vegetarian Goth who I think was called Julie. We found out very quickly that we were not compatible with our new house-mates. Tony and his girlfriend were constantly fighting or having sex; both were noisy and equally unpleasant. Julie used to take an age in the bathroom and left a rather silage-type aroma in the air after using it. Let this serve as a warning against the practice of surviving on lentils, which was her sole diet. It meant she didn't need face paint to give her that consumptive pallor that the Goths so love. She also seemed to have very little energy and what she did have she must've stored to help her through her toilet manoeuvres, for when she was finished she looked positively exhausted and in need of a lie down afterwards. That's my bit of health promotion over; my consultancy bill will be in the post.

There was one advantage to our new premises; it was just round the corner from the Rock Mecca the Ruskin Arms. I set about getting known there by spending most of my time propping up its bar. This sounds like an excuse to drink all day but was actually a cunning plan to get a gig. I reasoned that if I were to spend all my money there the owner would be obliged to book us. Adele was uncon-vinced by this strategy and eyed me with a certain amount of suspicion when I would roll home at dinner time smelling of Toby Bitter, £1.00 a pint, and doing a passable impersonation of an exuberant Oliver Reid. But she was wrong and I proved it. After spending close on £400 of much-needed dole money on beer, I secured a Friday night gig. We would be paid £40, a fair return on my outlay. I did mention my business studies qualification didn't I?

It was shortly before the gig that we decided that we needed to add a second guitarist to give us the Thin Lizzy sound we craved. An advert was put onto the wall of Allbang and Strumit, a music shop on Denmark Street, and low and behold we got a reply from a Dublin-born guitarist called Noel O'Rielly. This would be perfect, we thought: he was Irish and he said that his favourite band was Thin Lizzy. Noel was drafted in just in time to play the first Ruskin Arms gig.

The Ruskin Arms, East Ham, was the spiritual home of the one and only Iron Maiden. With us living just around the corner in Sherrard Road it was hoped that it would become a home fixture for Nellie Dean as well. We invited as many people as possible to attend the first gig. We arrived early to get a good sound check and set up. We had been to many gigs there before and knew that we needed as big a PA as we could afford, so thousands of watts of deafening gear was hired.

Dark and dirty with the smell of beer, smoke and numerous body fluids lingering in the air, the Ruskin was just the sort of place we loved. If we played our cards right we could use it as a stepping-stone to superstardom just like Maiden had done before, but we would have to impress. A long sound check was the order of the day to ensure that our strengths, twin lead guitar, vocal harmonies and powerful well-crafted catchy songs would come to the fore. We worked through the afternoon and as gig time approached the first 'Billy Bunters' appeared with the last rays of daylight. The room started to get darker, and with the arrival of nightfall came the horrible realisation that there was no house lighting rig.

The room started to fill up nicely and so did our trunks. What the hell would we do? It was too late to hire lights. Even we were not insane enough to play a whole gig in total darkness, or could we? And then a light bulb came on; quite literally, for there hanging from the middle of the ceiling was a nicotine-stained lampshade, and in it was a 40 watt bulb, also coated from years' worth of Jamaican woodbines being smoked under it. A cunning plan was afoot.

I was dispatched back to Sherrard Road to get the longest piece of string I could find. On my triumphant return I was greeted with cheers from the band when I produced a tatty ball of twine from my pocket. Noel stood on a chair and Tony sat on his shoulders; the bulb was given a quick wipe with the front of a jumper and the string was tied around the sticky shade.

There is a very large knowledgeable crowd that frequents the Ruskin, they didn't suffer fools gladly, so the sight of the night's entertainment doing a circus-balancing act in the middle of the floor must have puzzled a few of them. The string was pulled taut towards the stage and positioned in such a way that it shone a weak ray of light on stage centre; this could only be achieved by tying the end of the string to the bottom of the bass drum. It was dim, in more ways than one, but by the God of Thunder it might just work.

We took to the stage in full Metal gear, you know the type: leopardskin trousers, Japanese design T-shirts and for good measure bandanas tied around some foreheads. We, my friend, looked hot to trot. The first song kicked in at sickening volume scaring the bejasus out of most of the crowd, who hadn't seen us coming on due to the light being so bad. We were determined to give value for money – it being free to get in should've maybe worried us, but it didn't, we were in our element, this is what we were put on this planet for, to entertain, bleed for our public and die if needs be.

A death unfortunately nearly happened. In the poor visibility I tried to run to the far side of the stage for a pose with Ken and was nearly decapitated by the throat-level piece of string which promptly snapped and sent the light into a sickening spinning motion above the heads of the crowd. The song ended with me on my back holding my jugular and a deafening silence from the crowd who were squinting in the direction of the stage not quite knowing what they had just witnessed.

Tony left Nellie Dean shortly after the first Ruskin Arms gig; he thought he was too good for us. As laughable as this seems, it made it quite uncomfortable to live in the same house, especially as myself and Adele committed the terrible crimes of washing our clothes too often and would turn the central heating on to thaw the ice on the inside of the windows. It also meant that the Nellies were drummerless again, but not for long.

Noel, who had only been with us a matter of weeks, informed us that he had a friend who was also from Dublin and happened to be a drummer. One audition later and it was discovered that John 'JJ' Jameson was a brilliant addition to the band. There was one snag however – he didn't drink. This, as stupid as it sounds, could've been a major stumbling block. If you have ever had the misfortune of being perfectly sober and in the company of a group of drunken buffoons you will know what a horrible experience this can be. We were permanently that group of drunken buffoons, but for some reason JJ just fitted like Biff Byford into his satin strides, snugly. He didn't even seem to mind our fondness for inebriated highjinks.

Even though Tony had left the band of his own free will, he started to show signs of jealousy following the arrival of JJ, making the atmosphere even worse in the house. Thank Christ for *Kerrang!* magazine. One day while leafing through the pages of the then monthly Metal bible, I came upon an advert in the classifieds section seeking a couple to help run a Rock bar.

The interview

The cockney accent on the other end of the phone told me his name was Steve and that we should come to his bar, the Flying Scud, the following Tuesday at 10am, just before opening time. When we arrived Steve greeted us with handshakes and the offer of a drink. I liked him already. He asked me if I had any experience of the bar business and I told him I had many, many years around the trade. I wasn't lying, as such, I had spent hundreds, nay thousands, of hours at the counters of the bars of Holywood, Belfast and now London – just none on the side where the business took place.

Steve then asked Adele if she had ever served drinks. Before she could answer I chipped in that her family owned bars back in Ireland and that she could pull a pint before she could talk. Adele's eyes narrowed until they were virtually closed but she did leave enough of a gap to send me daggers. She had never worked in a bar in her life. My thinking was that it would be my love of music that would swing the job, how hard could it be to run a bar anyway? What a twit.

As part of my charm offensive I told Steve all about the Nellies, knowing that this must impress him. Steve revealed that he had been in a band himself called Cock Sparrer. I had heard of them and was a bit surprised. Steve had long hair and wore the regulation rocker clobber of the time – fringed leather jacket, jeans and cowboy boots. From memory I seemed to recall that his old band were a skinhead

Oi group that had a right-wing following. This was a bit disconcerting; I hated racism nearly as much as I hated bigotry. Just when I was about to have second thoughts I suddenly recognised the album Steve was playing on the bar stereo.

It had been nagging me the whole time that I had been sitting there lying through my teeth. It was one of those occasions where you know something, but you just can't put your finger on it, that old 'It's on the tip of my tongue' scenario. Then out of the blue it's there and you can't understand why you didn't recognise it in the first place.

Living Colour were a fantastic band that had the backing of Mick Jagger; he had even produced their demos for their first record. The album was called 'Vivid' and that is what was playing on the turntable. Why would someone who was in a supposedly racist band be playing the songs of a black Rock band? The answer was simple: he wasn't racist.

I did quiz Steve on the perception of Cock Sparrer. He explained that the band's image and in particular a song called 'England Belongs to Me' had, wrongly, attracted a right-wing following, which they had been trying to shake off ever since. While he was telling me all this I couldn't help thinking that if I wrote a song called 'Ireland Belongs to Me' it would be sung every St Patrick's Day with hand on heart and a tear in the eye for the auld turf. There would never be the suggestion that it was remotely racist. I was beginning to realise that even seeing yourself as English could be perceived as right wing which is wrong: being proud of where you come from does not mean you hate everyone else.

Steve told us that Cock Sparrer invented a form of music called Street Punk and that they had been playing this sort of music long before Malcolm McLaren had hijacked it and left it terminally ill, a hypodermic needle hanging from its arm. They were working-class kids from the East End who watched West Ham United and wrote about life on the streets and terraces. I was warming to Steve: he was a nice guy, and honest. We left the bar and I thought even if we don't get the job I'll be back for a pint, I liked the vibe.

Two days later I was delighted to be informed that we had been successful and that we were going to help run a new Rock club that Steve was going to open on the Bethnal Green Road. This was the start of a long working relationship and friendship. And you know what? In all the years I've known Steve Bruce I never heard him utter a racist word. Fact.

There was one slight hitch before we took up the challenge of running the club. Steve wanted Adele to do a couple of shifts in the Flying Scud. To give her a little support and also because I had been threatened with physical violence if I didn't, I went along. I decided that there is safety in numbers so I invited Big Xan along for the show.

Adele looked like a vegetarian in a sausage factory behind the bar. Steve, I think, was starting to get a little suspicious. As a test he asked her to pour a pint of Guinness. This shouldn't have been a problem for an Irish Coleen who had been brought up hanging on to her father's coattails behind the counter of their many public houses.

It looked like three foot of snow on a piece of coal, the head of the pint was that big. Repeated pouring only increased the froth and decreased the amount of stout in the glass. It also meant that Steve was watching his profits slowly flowing down the drain. It suddenly occurred to me that I had never seen Adele so red in the face and sweating; it actually wasn't that unattractive. But any thoughts of love were banished from my head when she threw me a glance that could've killed a charging rhino. Steve finally put her out of her misery when he shouted, 'For fuck's sake stop!'

'She's never worked in a bar before has she?' Steve asked. I waited a minute before I answered; this was to assess the situation in my head and also to give Xan the opportunity to extract himself from this most embarrassing of situations by going to the bogs.

'Stuff it,' I thought, just tell the truth. 'No, she has never worked in a bar before, but she is beautiful is she not?' I said.

Steve just laughed and said, 'Yes she is.'

And that was that. Xan returned from the toilets, there was no blood spilt; so he ordered a round of Wild Turkeys. I later found myself soaking wet, fully clothed, boots and all, climbing into bed beside Adele, after trying to sober up by getting into a bath full of cold water. How was I to know that the sipping whiskey we had been throwing down our necks was 101% proof? It was not one of Adele's better nights and I think if I look deep down into my soul I should accept a small part of the blame.

Bastards

Ken and Elaine went and got themselves up the duff and moved into a house of a friend of Elaine's brother called Pete. He turned out to be a git of massive proportions. Living with a sadistic asshole, Elaine being pregnant and having no regular source of income, Ken was beginning to feel the pressure, which manifested itself in the form of panic attacks.

Thames Mead is where Pete had decided to live and it does not surprise me, you are where you live, it is a hellhole of a place, similar to Milton Keynes but without the concrete cows and without the class. This sort of environment has its own stressors. Ken had started to experience chest pains, shortness of breath and palpitations at moments of anxiety. His gigs with Lisa had become headaches due to a hate campaign against him conducted, mainly, by her brother Marino.

I had recently parted company with Marino's band following a gig in Bogeys Cardiff where I stole the show after he had bored the arse of the crowd with an hour of instrumental waffling. Don't get me wrong, I was not great, I was just sweet relief. Marino was becoming aware that there was very little interest in a second-rate Santana – hell there wasn't even interest in the real thing at the time – so he decided that he would tag onto his altogether more marketable sister, but she already had Ken in the band. Do you see where this is going?

Ken longed for the day that the Nellies would start gigging on a more regular basis and he could bail out of the Lisa Dominique Band, but at that time it was his only source of money. A decision on his future in the band however, was about to be made for him.

They were booked to play in a place called Edwards Number 8 in Birmingham. Ken caught the train to King's Cross Station from where he was supposed to make his way to Lisa's flat, and there he would board the band's van to Brum. However, in the station the thought of another night of dirty looks and bad Rock and Roll brought on sweaty palms, dizziness, tightness in the throat and heavy breathing. It was sort of like the first time Ken and Elaine had made love minus the screaming, scratching, crying and biting. Apparently Elaine had been quite enthusiastic as well.

Ken had tried many cures for his anxious episodes, like breathing into a paper bag, counting to ten, visualising a white sheet blowing on a clothesline and putting his head between his knees. All but the last intervention had failed in the past but even Ken had the wit to not attempt a manoeuvre with such scope for misinterpretation, especially on one of the busiest public transport concourses in Europe. The sight of a long-haired man with his head between his own legs while thousands of men, women and children walked past may have been a wee bit too much for the British Transport Police.

A couple of pints have been the cure-all of many an Irishman. The hair of the dog has saved many from the horrors of a hangover, sobriety or reality. The medicinal value of alcohol has been written into Irish folklore: a hot Powers, it is believed, can cure everything – the common cold, terminal flatulence and baldness. So with this in mind Ken made his way it to the station bar and ordered a pint of iron-rich Guinness.

The perfect accompaniment to a glass of the black stuff is good company and Ken happened upon a fellow traveller from the Emerald Isle who would provide a quantity of craic and a distraction from the causes of Ken's stress. The conversation was that good that Ken lost track of time as well as the number of units of alcohol he had consumed.

At Lisa's flat the shit was in mid-air heading towards the revolving blades. She was fuming that she would have to travel in the van with the rest of the band while her fiancé and his Ferrari, her usual mode of transport, would wait behind hoping that Ken would eventually turn up. Back in King's Cross Ken asked his new best buddy what time it was. He nearly choked on his sixth pint when he found out that he was nearly two hours late. He rushed from platform to platform changing underground line numerous times until he found himself just around the corner from the rendezvous point. To his relief he spotted the red sports car outside the flat, but his heart sank when there was no sign of the van. Michael Machet was furious and could only muster a 'Get in the fuckin' car,' as a greeting. Ken slurred an apology and climbed into the low-set bucket seat, putting even more pressure on his stout-engorged bladder.

The dull ache of dissention made way to the excruciating agony of imminent rupture as Ken's kidneys transformed Guinness to urine, which was then deposited via the ureters in to his already full to the brim bladder. Ken was brave to the point of heroism; he held on, not wanting to infuriate his millionaire American chauffeur any more than he had to. He thought of things that he hoped would distract him, but everything that entered his head morphed into the crystal clear waterfall at Glenariff in the Glens of Antrim. He had visited the local beauty spot as a lad with Ian Paisley's church, not because he believed in the 'Pope is the anti-Christ' doctrine of the lovable old cuddly teddy bear of a pulpit-pounding Reverend, but because they had promised him a pencil and sharpener if he did.

With the vision of the waters breaking on the rocks below in his mind's eye, Ken valiantly held on and held on. Sweat broke on his brow and a nausea came over him. But he wouldn't give in and provide Marino and his cronies with more ammunition to fire at him. He summoned up the courage that had seen thousands of Irishmen win many battles all over the world for everyone but themselves. His resolve, he thought, was beyond criticism.

Three minutes after getting into the high performance penis extension, Ken asked his driver to find him a toilet; they hadn't even made it to the bottom of the street. The atmosphere could've been cut with a rolling pin as they pulled into a service station that, due to its urban setting, didn't offer lavatory facilities. Ken begged the snotty shop assistant to let him use their bog. There were regulatory rules cited and protocols recited as to why this was not going to happen. A clenched fist and a threat of physical violence from Ken ensured it would.

After a draining of Volga Dam proportions Ken dusted himself down and purchased a bag of Walkers pickled onion. As he walked towards the apoplectic face of his co-traveller he scoffed the crisps; he didn't want to offend him with the smell of his acidic snack. He looked down into the plastic bag trying to get the last few crumbs out and took his eye off the ball.

The journey was back under way. They were on a race against time; the gig was less than three hours away; they had two and a half hours' travelling time to go; it was going to be tight. There was not a word passed between driver and passenger as the miles rolled by. The sun went down and the air began to take on a chill. A flick of a switch and the aircon changed to heater. As the inside of the car warmed there was a definite fragrance in the air that was not pleasant. After more than an hour the first words that cracked the silence came with an American twang, 'Wha tha faks that smell?' Ken felt a twisting in his guts as he looked down at his feet; there edging over the tread of his boots was the unmistakable sight of dog shit.

Ken had never been aware that the carpet of some Ferraris was white – how would he? He had been brought up dodging fares on Ulster buses. The luxury car in which he was sitting now looked like it had been fitted out with the streaky fur of a Siberian tiger. The financially pampered owner, who would never know the joy of waiting in the hall for a giro to fall through the letter box, treated this setback as almost life-threatening. Birmingham's Spaghetti Junction, never the most welcoming of structures, was like Eldorado to Ken.

Ken played a blinder, as always he stole the show. This in itself was becoming tiresome for Lisa and was highlighted afterwards by her less talented brother. Ken's sacking was not unexpected, he had not covered himself in glory as far as behaviour was concerned, but he was still the most talented member, by a mile, to play in the Lisa Dominique Band. Ken Heaven's gift, like that of all geniuses, needs to be accepted with the flaws of its owner. It should therefore be remembered in Rock history that people of less artistic depth sacked one of the fastest, most fluent guitarists on earth, because of canine faeces in the fibres of a status symbol that has to adhere to the speed limit. His job done, Marino joined Lisa's band the next day.

The following week's editions of the Metal press carried two news items: the first announced that Lisa Dominique had parted company with her Irish Guitarist Ken Heaven due to alcohol problems; the other said that Marino the Band had parted company with his Irish lead vocalist Eamon Nancarrow due to alcohol problems. I only have five words to say: 'Rock and feckin' Roll baby.'

Ken was now without any source of income and the baby was on its way. It is at times like this that the milk of human kindness flows freely and you are reliant on that part of mankind that separates us from the vermin and roaches. Pete threw them out of his shitty apartment in their hour of need. He even held onto a copy of *Where Have all the Bullets Gone*, signed by Spike Milligan, in lew of payment of rent.

Before I go on I must tell the story of how we got the book signed by the ex-Goon. He was doing an autograph session in Covent Garden, and being huge Milligan fans we decided to go down in an attempt to meet the great man. We soon realised that the only way that this was going to happen was if we had a copy of the book, so we scraped up enough money between us and bought one. We joined the queue and waited our turn, as we drew close we could see that Spike was not making much contact with those who had been awaiting his signature. Knowing his history of manic depression we feared that he wouldn't converse with us. When it was our turn he never looked up, he just said 'Who do you want this made out to?'

Ken said, 'Can you say it's for Big Bad Kenny?'

On hearing his accent Spike lifted his head, and with a big smile, looked Ken in the eye and asked, 'Who are you on the run from?' Priceless.

Keeping that book with its inscription was a dirty move by a small man who knew the value of the book was not a monetary one. Ken never saw it again. Pete went on to work in a bank or something, so he's still robbing people; he obviously had a talent for it. Anyway after the eviction Ken and Elaine arrived on our doorstep, in East Ham in a taxi; we had not moved into the bar yet. All their stuff that Pete didn't want was wrapped up in black plastic bags.

Tony, his sparring partner and Elvira were not best pleased and basically told us that if Mary and Joseph moved in we would all be moving out. Elaine's parents were contacted and informed of the imminent arrival: not the best way I suppose, to be told you're going to be grandparents. Anyway Granny and Granda basically told Elaine's brother Paul, that because there was no room at the inn, his house in Loughton was to become the stable.

The Stick

The Stick of Rock was situated at 143 Bethnal Green Road, virtually on the corner of Brick Lane. Before it opened and while it was being renovated Adele and myself moved into a massive flat on the first floor. Steve, the proud new owner, and myself did some of the work including painting the walls and varnishing the floors and bar. A slight mishap occurred while doing the latter.

A plasterer Steve knew from the Flying Scud was asked to fill in a hole left by the removal of a skylight at the far end of the bar. For the life of me I can't remember the name of the guy commissioned to undertake the task, but he was Irish and with that came the inevitable thirst. To keep up with his dry mouth syndrome he was actually paid in pints of lager, surely a recipe for disaster you would think.

The bar counter ran the length of the place and must have been about thirty foot long which meant that varnishing it was quite a long laborious job, especially as it took many applications. The grand opening day was fast approaching, time was of the essence, so we were delighted to finally put the last coat on the bar. All that was needed now was to let it dry. Our plasterer was nearing completion of his task as well so things were running on time, just. Lunchtime had arrived and tools were downed along with some liquid nourishment by our tradesman from the Emerald Isle. Steve and myself retired upstairs to our respective flats.

While I was digesting my meal and getting some well-earned rest, work recommenced on the ceiling downstairs. I closed my eyes and tried to catch a few minutes' kip. I was rudely wakened by a crash, which sounded like it came from the bar. Initially I ignored it thinking something had fallen over, but then came the voice lilting up the stairs. 'Eamon, Eamon come down quick there's been a wee bit of an accident.' I took the steps four at a time and when I got to the door I was greeted by a scene of total carnage.

'What happened?' I shouted.

'I was leaning over trying to fill in the last wee bit and the ladder slipped. I feared for my life so I grabbed at the last bit of the hole to prevent my fall and, well, you can see what happened,' was his response.

And yes, I could see what had happened and I didn't like it one tiny bit, for there lying on the floor and all over the still-wet bar was most of the ceiling.

'You'd better tell Steve,' Handy Andy says.

Knowing Steve's temper I said, 'I think you'd better fecking tell him actually.'

And him also knowing Steve's temper said, 'Feck off,' and he did exactly that – he ran out the door.

When I finally plucked up the courage to get Steve down I was privileged to witness one of the dickiest fits the world has ever seen. I think more damage was done by it than by what had caused it. 'Where is he? I'll fucking kill him,' he kept screaming as he kicked debris all over the place. 'Probably halfway to the ferry,' I thought, but kept it to myself, as silence, in this instance, was the best policy, you see I didn't want to be barred from a place that hadn't even opened and certainly not from a bar that I was supposed to manage.

When Steve finally calmed down, which only took about four hours, work got back under way. Unbelievably we actually did make the date for the opening night; mind you this was only by the skin of our teeth. It was a brilliant evening, the place was packed and the drink flew. The band chosen for this historic occasion, would you believe were called Paddy Goes to Holyhead, I kid you not.

In the bar trade sometimes you have to converse with people that you wouldn't pee on if they were on fire. There are also those that once you have made their acquaintance you know will be friends for life. One such individual was a guy called Ian 'Inky' Worland. From the second we met in the Flying Scud I knew we were kindred spirits. Inky had a ferocious appetite for all things Heavy Metal. He drank like a fish, smoked like a train, drugged like an addicted pharmacist, rocked like a wooden horse on runners and rolled like the stone outside Jesus' tomb: in short he was a mutha.

One of the first things Inky did when we were acquainted was point out that I was losing my hair. Normally this would have resulted in a smack in the mouth, but on noticing that his own locks were thinning as quickly as my own, I realised that we would be able to share the agony of male pattern baldness. How unfair, we agreed, was it that Rock Gods like ourselves could lose our pride and joy, like leaves on an autumnal tree, when there were skinheads with full heads of hair that took great pleasure in shaving theirs down to the wood. Like the old saying goes, 'Youth is wasted on the young.' Hair, I'm afraid, is wasted on a bonehead.

Inky and I became great mates and were amazed to find out that we had consecutive membership numbers in the Diamond Head fan club: we were destined to meet. He quickly became a fixture at all the Nellie Dean gigs and would travel with us when we were on tour, even working his holidays around it. His wife, I thought at the time, must be very understanding or have the patience of a saint.

For a while after the Stick opened Steve, his wife Ness and their newborn baby Samantha lived on at the Flying Scud, but eventually they had to move into the new place. Steve needed to get all his furniture and stuff shifted. This was a delicate job that required trained personnel, those with years of experience in removals; old East End houses posed many problems with their numerous floors and narrow staircases. So ignoring the lesson from the ceiling incident Steve decided to employ a couple of his regulars and myself. Our combined experience, in such matters, added up to exactly zero and had disaster written all over it.

The two selected for this challenge were Inky and Colin Bow. The latter was a gem of a guy who had the maddest 'fro ever seen on a white man; he also wore the thickest glasses I have ever seen. He was, I was told, encouraged by the Fire Service not to walk in the woods in summer time in case sunlight passing through them caused parched gorse to catch ablaze (just kidding folks). Thank goodness Colin's mane held properties similar to Samson's; he was as strong as an ox – at least one of us was.

The Flying Scud had a very narrow staircase from the first floor to the bar below so everything could be got to the kitchen but no further. This, as you can imagine, posed a slight problem. The solution was to remove the window in the kitchen and lower everything, on ropes, down to Steve in the street below. Initially everything went well: a three-piece suite, fridge and massive TV were all successfully dispatched. Then came a rather large and heavy wardrobe. The rope was tied around it and we braced ourselves. Colin took up the anchorman position as if he were in a tug of war team. The wardrobe was positioned on the ledge and eased over.

The three of us took the strain but Inky and myself started slipping in water that had spilt out of the fridge we had lowered earlier and both of us fell on our arses, leaving Colin on his own. He started hurtling towards the hole in the wall, his feet skidding on the wet floor. About two foot from the window he stopped dead in his tracks and for a split second I marvelled at his strength. 'How,' I thought, 'can one man hold on to something that had the three of us busting a gut?' A crash brought the answer. We ran to the window and looked over the edge. There, swinging from the end of the rope, was the small top door of the wardrobe; the rest of it was spread all over the Hackney Road. Steve was as white as a sheet as the expensive piece of furniture had missed him by mere inches.

Another lesson learnt you would think, but oh no, the mess was cleared up and thrown into the back of Steve's ancient blue Transit van, and another attempt at emptying the house was under way. Steve had moved into the Stick of Rock about a week before, leaving the Scud without electricity, hence the reason why the fridge had water in it. So when a large freezer came to be moved we weren't going to get caught like that again, oh no, we were too smart for that by Jove. I opened the door of the appliance to check for melted ice.

There was a pool of water there but there also something else, something slightly more concerning: an object in a plastic bag was floating around and from it emitted a smell so rancid that it could have singed the nasal hairs of Old Nick himself. It was so bad it caused a mad dash to the window by everyone. Life and limb was risked as we tried to fill our lungs with untainted fresh air. 'What the hell was that?' Inky screamed as he tried to stop himself from gagging. Then it came to Steve. Before he had moved he had forgotten to remove, from the freezer, a bag of tripe that he fed Bruce his German Shepherd. I turned to my new boss and having nearly been dragged to my death by a runaway wardrobe and then gassed by the rotten lining of a sheep's stomach, I inquired, 'Is it too early to hand in my notice?'

Hell's bells

I loved working at the Stick of Rock. Don't get me wrong, there were some bad times – especially when we couldn't get people to come to see the less established bands. This obviously meant that the takings were down and balancing the books became a problem. I particularly felt guilty about this because I booked the bands and therefore it was my fault if things became tight and don't forget that this was not just Steve's business, it was also his family's home. But thankfully this was not a regular occurrence and the good times well outnumbered the bad.

One of the jobs I hated though was getting the beer delivery in the morning because the brewery couldn't be specific about the time and with London being a twenty-four-hour city it could happen at 3, 4, or 5 o'clock in the morning, which was not good if you had had a busy night. One evening before one of these deliveries was due we had a particularly hot and spicy Mexican meal.

When the door was rapped at 6am I jumped out of bed and ran downstairs to open the trapdoors that led to the cellar. When all the barrels had been dropped down, the deliveryman came in to have his docket signed. He had sneaked up behind me without me seeing him. Thinking I was on my own and with the previous evening's meal dancing the lambada in my gastrointestinal tract I was relieved to let rip with a gaseous exchange that rippled the very fabric of my tracksuit bottoms. As I turned round I was embarrassed to see the drayman standing there and even more so when he said 'Chilli last night?'

'Jesus, I'm sorry mate, I didn't see you standing there. If I had known I would've held on, it's stinking isn't it?' I said.

He just looked at me in disgust and said, 'I meant it was chilly last night.'

There were very few people living around the pub, which was a blessing as the volume the bands played at would've seen a local residents' committee taking up an armed struggle. What there were lots of, were leather shops, all of which had burglar alarms that could be set off by the No. 8 bus that went past every twenty minutes. This became very annoying; the key holders never returned to switch them off at night and would wait until they returned to work the next morning. If one went off at the weekend you could have 48 hours of it merrily ringing away.

As I mentioned before Steve had a bit of a temper, and this was very evident on a Sunday night after the bar had shut. Adele and myself had just settled into a cuddle when the good old No. 8 drove past setting off an alarm. The next thing I know there is a knocking at my door; on the other side stood Steve with a hammer in his hand. 'Right, let's sort this out once and for all,' he said. For a second I thought he was challenging me to a fight (were the takings that bad?) but quickly I realised the alarm was going to get it big style.

'I'll be with you in a minute,' I said, returning to the room to put some clothes on.

Adele was less than ecstatic by the scenario that was unfolding and said she wouldn't be bailing me out if I was arrested. I laughed a nervous laugh because I actually think she meant it. 'Don't worry,' I said, 'I'll be alright.'

'Oh I'm not worried,' she said, 'just letting you know what will happen if things get out of hand again.' I think her patience, like my hair, was starting to wear thin.

When I got downstairs Steve had a set of ladders ready to go. 'Jesus, he is serious this time,' I thought. Across the road we ran and set the steps against the wall. Up went Steve with hammer at the ready and started to whack the living daylights out of the deafening security device. When I say deafening I mean I didn't realise how loud these things were close up. Another thing that I didn't know was that they are not connected to the mains and work by a battery, so when the thing was eventually knocked off the wall it lay ringing and a rattling in the middle of the Bethnal Green Road. Steve descended with a look of grim determination on his face and unsuccessfully tried to stop the noise by raining down repeated blows on his defiant nemesis.

Back in bed Adele could hear the whole sorry assault taking place, each pound with the hammer making her jump. Then something strange started to happen. The volume of the alarm seemed to get louder, she could have sworn that the noise was coming from the bar below. She laughed, 'They wouldn't be that stupid would they?'

We had, for some inexplicable reason, started to draw attention from passers-by and the vehicles that use one of the busiest thoroughfares in the city. Steve decided that, to prevent us having our collars felt by the Old Bill, we should carry the alarm over to the bar and deal with it there. As he had the ladder and the hammer I was charged with the job of carrying the clanging quivering mess that lay in a bed of metal fragments and Perspex. On lifting it I found that the vibrations travelled through my hands, wrists, arms, shoulders and neck, and found a resting place rattling my fillings around my head. My teeth were actually chattering like I was standing naked in a bucket of iced water with an ice-lolly between my buttocks (this, I would like to point out, is an assumption as I swear I have never tried this).

When I finally got to the bar I gratefully dropped my burden on the floor and proceeded to pour myself a large Wild Turkey to calm my nerves. However, I could hardly drink the bourbon as my hands were shaking that much, but I persevered and eventually succeeded by setting the glass on the bar, gripping it with my teeth and then tipping my head back. My mother would have been proud.

As the alcohol hit my empty stomach I felt its effect almost instantly and boy was I glad of it, because the sight of Steve stripped to the waist, from the top down may I add, chasing the alarm around the floor, each welt from the hammer sending it spinning across the painstakingly varnished floor, was not one you would want to experience sober.

Eventually, with sweat leaking from every pore, his long grey hair a sopping mess, Steve stood triumphant in silence. He had won, his victory complete. There, lying in the middle of the bar, was his defeated opponent, a pile of wires and twisted casing. The floor, which had taken many hours of labour on our knees with paint brushes to get its glorious lustre, now resembled the body of Rory Gallagher's old Stratocaster. We congratulated each other, and to the vanquished their spoils, we toasted our success with another drink before we took the stairs to bed, content in the knowledge that the night's work had been a good one. Just then another No. 8 passed and we heard the sound of an alarm going off.

Twisted sisters

Nepotism is a horrible thing. It is the blight of the upper classes and politicians of all colours. 'Jobs for the boys,' has always been the battle-cry of exclusive organisations such as the Freemasons, Orange Order, Irish National Foresters and the Ancient Order of Hibernians. Throughout history many have missed out on employment opportunities that they were best qualified for, the job to be given to a buck toothed inbred son of a civil servant or to someone with the right or left handshake. I have always despised the insidious nature of the social elite; I wonder how many job interviews Princes Willy and Harry have been to? With all this in mind I took great pleasure, as soon as I got my feet under the Stick of Rock table, in employing my sisters Elish and Roisin as bar staff. Keep it in the family, don't ya know!

The 'skin and blisters' were a breath of fresh air. Don't get me wrong – we had some brilliant barmaids who would complete a perfect night of mayhem with dance routines, behind the bar, to songs such as David Lee Roth's 'California Girls' and 'Copperhead Road' by Steve Earle, but my sisters have a sense of humour that is second to none. Within hours they had given nicknames to a lot of the regular customers, most of which were not that complimentary, but they were so funny that no one seemed to mind.

Elish even used Steve's fury at the amount of tissue paper that the women seemed to use in the toilets to concoct a hilarious ruse. She cobbled together letter-headed paper with Tower Hamlets Borough Council across the top. She then sent it to Steve, claiming that it came from one of their researchers and that she had carried out an undercover study on his premises. The result of the bogus audit found that for the number of customers using the Ladies there was very little toilet paper being used. Steve was instructed that, from a health and safety and infection control perspective, he should order everyone entering the bogs to use more toilet paper.

Steve was furious, brandishing the correspondence in his hand like a Heavy Metal Neville Chamberlain and regaling his tale of woe to anyone who would listen. Eventually he decided that he would write back to this 'bureaucratic bitch' and give her what for. The signature was so bad at the bottom of the letter that he asked a number of customers if they could decipher it. Only one was successful and when the name Ms Choccy Whizzpipe was read out Steve just said 'Elish'.

The owner and boss of the Stick of Rock was not spared from my other sister's humour either. One evening while Steve was stocking up and before the bar had opened Roisin had, for reasons best known to herself, dressed up as a pregnant bag lady. She even went as far as blacking out a couple of teeth and hanging a homeless sign around her neck. I let her out the front door and then went into the bar to watch the fun unfurl. When the knock arrived Steve, thinking it was the band for the night, jumped up and ran to welcome them.

'Hello darling, remember me?' said the toothless hag while

Marcus, Eamon and Molly Nancarrow.
It's all Bill Wyman's fault.

Three rock stars and Van Morrison.
L–R: Marcus Nancarrow, Van Morrison, Ken Heaven,
Eamon Nancarrow

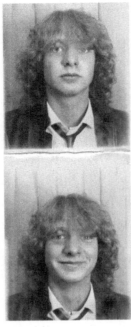

That perm relaxing
after six months.

Eamon Nancarrow;
before the explosion.

No Hot Ashes.
Stephen Campbell, David Irvine, Eamon Nancarrow, Paul Boyd

No Hot Ashes supporting Steve Marriott. Ken Heaven on lead guitar
and butcher's hat, mince meat just out of shot.

David Irvine and
Eamon Nancarrow
wearing their
girlfriends' clothes.

Stephen Magee.
My friend (RIP).

Nellie Dean MK I.
Xan Phillips, Stephen Campbell, Eamon Nancarrow, Ken Heaven.

Dave Shack and Brendan
'Beckly' Kelly
Moments before Ken sets fire to
Brendan's hair and Dave splits
his shorts.

Ken Heaven. His shirt wasn't the only thing shredded.

Nellie Dean MK V – L–R: John Jameson, Xan Phillips,
Eamon Nancarrow, Ken Heaven, Dave Bigwood.

Eamon Nancarrow and Ian 'Inky'
Worland. City Slickers

Señorita Nancarrow

From *Metal Forces* magazine's
feature on the Stick of Rock.
Steve Bruce and Eamon
Nancarrow (The Guvnors)

Nellie Dean MK VII.
Clive Hellier, Xan Phillips, Eamon Nancarrow, Ken Heaven,
Gary Baker (RIP)

Strictly No Ballroom MK I.
Mixi McMillan, Roger Davidson, Eamonn Keyes, Eamon Nancarrow,
Colin Shiels

Harry Heaven.
Wearing that wig

Paul Kane (Strictly No Ballroom MK II).
The Saviour

shaking a potato in a saucepan (don't ask). She then added, 'I hope you're going to make an honest woman of me?' Steve was speechless; this was the last thing in the world he was expecting. He stood for a second bug eyed and open-mouthed, and then did what any man would have in a similar situation when presented with an opportunity to accept his responsibilities. He screamed and slammed the door in her face. To Steve's credit he took these two incidents and many more with great humour and incredibly he became very fond of my sisters.

No Travellers

When I first moved to London I couldn't help but be struck by how many bars restricted travelling salesmen from entering their premises. Every bar had a sign on the door stating 'No Travellers'. An old family friend, Paddy Cashman, who was a rep for Bulmer's Cider, need not have moved his family to the capital for they would've starved from lack of sales. I was later told that the signs didn't refer to those hardy souls that run their Ford Mondeos into the ground in the quest for the next big sale. My Da had been in a band called the Travellers and by all accounts they could kick up a drunken storm with the best of them, but I'm sure their reputation had not spread as far as London. So who were these mysterious people that were far from welcome?

It was not until I started working in the Stick of Rock that I was surprised to find out that the Travellers were in fact the Travelling Community of Ireland. I don't know why I was surprised – it was not that long ago that bars, B&Bs, hotels etc., had signs saying 'No blacks, no dogs and no Irish' (notice we were last on the list behind the dogs). I'm sure now political correctness would ensure that such racial exclusion (I'm not including the dogs in this mind) wouldn't be tolerated, but at the time nobody batted an eyelid.

I would consider myself a very broadminded person and certainly would never see myself as racist in any way but the tales I'm about to tell you are ones that caused me to scratch my humanist head and question some of my tolerance levels. These are true, from my perspective, and are told as they happened. It will be up to the reader to make his or her mind up as to whether there is bias or not.

The Stick of Rock certainly didn't have a 'No Travellers' sign on the door; it just never seemed to come up as a concern. Then one quiet Monday night, when I was in the bar on my own and not a regular punter had arrived yet, the door opened and in walked two massive ginger-haired men wearing Aran sweaters, shiny trousers, white socks and black slip-on shoes. One of them approached the bar while the other took a seat at a large group of tables and chairs that sat just behind the pool table.

'Two pints of your finest stout,' was the order spoken in an Irish brogue that was so strong I nearly didn't understand it myself. If a massive finger, which was attached to a hand the size of a Parma ham, hadn't been pointing at the beverage requested, the two gentlemen might have received two pounds of finest sprouts. While I was pouring the black stuff the door opened again and in walked two more red-haired giants. Before I knew it there were about thirty men and women making themselves comfortable. I had been caught off-guard and they now stormed the bar shouting orders like their lives depended on it.

One of the orders was a case of Coke, a case of Fanta and a box of cheese and onion crisps. All, as was requested, had to be left in their cases; a woman carried all these items, by herself, out the door. The brewery that supplied us with our mixers demanded that the empties be returned, so I shouldn't have let her leave the premises, but I couldn't go after her or I would've left the bar unattended.

Colin Bow arrived, as he always did, at exactly 7.45pm and greeted me with, 'There's a van out there with dozens of kids in it and a woman is throwing crates of soft drinks and crisps into the back.' I put my finger to my lips to keep him from saying any more; I didn't want him disrespecting the gentle folk of the road and their parenting skills.

The noise from the corner was getting proportionately louder with the amount of drink consumed. I felt, as the first fight started, which incidentally was between two of the women – the hair and Claddagh earrings were everywhere – that it might be a good idea to get Steve down as back-up in case things got out of hand. After a quick phone call he appeared and said, 'Holy shit what did you let them in here for?'

'They caught me unawares,' I replied, feeling like a right twit.

'Phone the boys,' Steve said. I got the contact book out and called a selection of friends and regulars that we knew could handle themselves; they dropped everything and made their way to our aid.

We were still outnumbered, when the lads all arrived, but at least if it all kicked off we could put up some sort of a fight, and the rowdy crowd in the corner, on seeing the motley crew of biker types that had assembled, were not looking quite as confident or as menacing as they had done.

The plan was to turn the PA up and blast out some good old-fashioned Metal tunes, I think it was the Turbo album by Judas Priest, in an attempt to disrupt their conversation and therefore, it was hoped, encourage them to move on. One of their representatives approached the bar. He was massive and had hair sprouting from every visible orifice. I'm sure the ones that were not visible were the same, but I hoped it was something that would never be confirmed to me either verbally or visually. He told Steve to turn the music down as they were trying to do business and couldn't hear themselves think. Steve replied by pointing out that it was Rock bar they were in and that if they wanted to stay they would have to put up with the now deafening, even for us, racket.

The red-headed monster was not a happy man and responded by threatening to wreck the bar if his requests were not met. Steve basically told him that if he tried to carry out his threats, we would have to resort to a bit of fisticuffs and they would suffer as a consequence. Steve stood tall and confident as he spoke, which was difficult as he is only about 5ft 5 inches from the heel of his Cuban cowboy boot to the top of his grey mullet. I couldn't help but marvel at his balls – by that I mean his nerve: he was wearing a long T-shirt and I couldn't see his Royal Alberts even if I had wanted to, which I didn't, phew is that clear? Steve would later tell me that he nearly blemished his briefs but to his credit it didn't show. However if he had followed through the smell might have helped in emptying the bar – I know I would have been one of the first to vacate the premises. The top man returned to the throng and imparted Steve's words.

A delegation approached us and said that if we turned down the music and served them a last drink they would leave peacefully and not return; they obviously realised that this was not their type of bar. Steve agreed, turned down the music and asked the order. The chief then asked for, I kid you not, 150 pints of Guinness. Steve couldn't believe his ears; we only ever ordered a couple of barrels a week; it wasn't exactly the most popular drink in the East End. 'Wise up, I'm not going to serve you 150 pints. I don't think we even have 150 pints left anyway.'

'Ah, come on,' the big fella says, 'it's only five pints each.'

Steve came up with an ultimatum. 'I'll tell you what, I'll serve you all the Guinness we have left in this last barrel and then you leave.'

Fionn McCool smiled, spat on his right hand, and held it out for Steve to shake, which, reluctantly he did.

Fifty pints of Ireland's finest later and the gang were ready to go. As they left one of the women, in a last act of defiance, put her cigarette out on the pool table burning a small hole. Steve had to be restrained by a few of us while they trooped out, in a torrent of foul language (I think) and V-signs. I reasoned that a slightly damaged baize was the least of our worries and that we should cut our losses. I also think that Steve was secretly relieved that we had held him back; he looked like he was straining at the leash but it didn't feel like he was if you know what I mean. Don't get me wrong, Steve could handle himself: I once witnessed him take on all the members of a band called Horse (London) with a baseball bat, for insulting our regulars and for doing drugs in the changing room. This however, was a very different kettle of Irish livestock we were dealing with, not some poncy bunch of mummy's boys who thought they were Guns and Roses.

When we were sure that the travellers had really left Steve shouted, 'Drinks are on the house!' A few people fainted as this was a phrase that was only used on the rarest of occasions, a cheer filled the air and there was much back-slapping. When we totted up the cost of the repair of the pool table and the free drinks we were still quids in. There had been liver-crushing amounts of Guinness consumed and the tills were full. I would, however, not recommend this as a way of getting rich quick, that is unless you find the constant threat of physical violence appealing.

When the last of our posse had left myself and Steve checked the place over, as we always did, before retiring. My job was to check the toilets, oh the heady heights of management, usually to make sure that nobody had fallen asleep in one of the cubicles. The Gents was fine, apart from the usual gentlemanly deposits and splashes, but when I went into the Ladies I was greeted by the sight of one of the wash hand basins ripped from the wall and lying smashed on the floor. 'There goes the profits,' I thought. When Steve saw it I'm sure he wished he had put more of an effort into trying to escape our earlier restraining grip. He looked like he could kill, and you know what? With the expression on his face, this time I fancied his chances, well, against the men at least.

I couldn't say that all travelling folk behave in the way described and I'm sure there are those that will take exception to what I have written but these are facts witnessed by all those present. You can't tar everyone with the same brush. We had a doorman at the Stick in the early days before we realised that we didn't need one. His name was Tony Quinn he was a member of the Travelling Community and a prizefighter who would take on opponents, in drained swimming pools, until one of them was unconscious, something I wouldn't agree with on principle, but that was his choice and he made good money at it. What he also was was one of the funniest, most honest, decent people I have ever met and I'm proud to say for the short time I knew him, a friend.

A quick story about Tony that still makes me laugh. At the time that he worked for us one of the favourite artists of the DJs was David Lee Roth. They would play his high-kicking videos all the time, one of which, 'Yankee Rose', had Diamond Dave doing a split kick in the air and touching his toes. We egged Tony into attempting the same stunt by basically telling him that he couldn't do it.

The 'Mighty Quinn' was not a man to spurn a challenge: he leapt into the air and expertly executed the move, to much cheering from the punters. He triumphantly threw his arms wide open and bowed to his adoring fans. In the process of doing so he split his trousers right up the crack of his arse. The jump had left his strides intact but the celebration had ripped them asunder. He spent the rest of the night wearing my Day-Glo Bermuda shorts, his dress shirt, dickey bow, white socks and slip-on black shoes; he must've been the least threatening bouncer to have ever manned a door.

The confrontation with the travellers, as uncomfortable as it was, needs to be put into perspective. I have had even worse run-ins with so called City gents with their Armani suits, filofaxes and mobile phones. They think because they've had a few expensive bottles of imported lager and have disgustingly big salaries, that they can treat barmaids like dirt, well let's just say that they left the Stick knowing that they can't.

There was also a very nasty incident when a right-wing, Nazi scumbag told me that he thought that the UVF and the UDA were doing a marvellous job in keeping Britain pure. He didn't even take the time to find out which side of the political/religious divide I supposedly came from. I had to let him know that I was opposed to violence based on hatred, bigotry and racism, by contradicting myself and calmly giving a couple of slaps when he got a little naughty with his fists. I'm not proud of this, but you just can't help yourself sometimes. A white supremacist who wasn't that supreme was given a good lesson by a bog-trotting Paddy.

Thankfully trouble at the Stick was very rare. In fact, apart from the incidents I have imparted, I can't think of any more. Most nights were cause for the celebration of life, craic, good company, beer and Rock and Roll. One such time was the night Conor Francis Heaven was born. Ken came down in order to wet his newborn's head. The drink was flying and everyone was in great spirits.

I have never smoked as much as a cigarette in my life, but Ken insisted that I smoke a cigar, as is traditional on such occasions. I refused until his barracking and the drink convinced me that this was a good idea. The vomit I cleaned up from the men's toilets that night was my own for a change.

I'm no Billy Shakespeare

Tuesday nights the doors were closed at the Stick of Rock. It was less expensive to not open than to have staff working and electricity being used with only the most hardened of alcos venturing out. This worked to the advantage of Nellie Dean: we had a ready-made rehearsal studio with its own stage, bar and pool table at our disposal, for no cost. We would spend the time that we were not standing around with drinks and cues in our hands honing our new songs.

The writing process always went like this. I would come up with the melodies, lyrics and a basic structure, worked out on the acoustic guitar. I would then bring it to the rest of the band for them to work their musical magic. That's why all Nellie's songs were credited to the band because even though I would come up with most of the ideas they were exactly that – ideas – until the boys had their input, especially Ken.

As much as it would appear from what I have explained before that the Nellies were purely in existence as an excuse to have a good time, we really did take the music seriously. It was a passion of ours; we were proud and protective of our songs. With this in mind I would like to give a flavour of what we were about musically and lyrically.

Before we start let me point out that I don't and never have considered myself a great lyricist or writer. I'm certainly no Christy Moore, Paul Brady, Van Morrison, John Waite or Lemmy for that matter. Many of my songs are lazy rhyming couplets that fit into a theme: as David Coverdale once said, 'I'm no Billy Shakespeare.' I'm also not one of those 'artists' that come out with the classic phrase, 'Let the listener decide what the lyrics mean.' Mine could be under-stood by a four-year-old, which is handy because some people believe that that is my mental age anyway. What follows is a selection of some of the Nellies' greatest misses and the reasons behind them.

The songs

Title – Homeward bound
Sample lyric – 'You think you've got me in the palm of your hand, what makes you think that babe I don't understand. I'm packin' up, I'm movin' out, I'm out of here, couldn't stand your whinging babe don't cut no shit round here.'

Analysis philosophis – All about being in a relationship with someone who drags you down with their negativity. I have tried to always keep people like this at arm's length. Being an atheist I don't believe that life is a rehearsal; therefore you should try to have as much positivity around you as you can. This song was a brilliant one to play live and a firm favourite with the punters.

Title – Making a living
Sample lyric – 'Happiness in a credit card won't make the problems go away, makes me mad to see you work so hard, you get tireder every day.'

Analysis philosophis – A song written for someone who was living to work, not working to live. It was written during the recession of the 1980s. The Nellies would sit in the Stick of Rock, with the City of London visible above the brothel across the road. None of us owned houses and basically we were living to play music. However, others at the time were throwing themselves off the ledges of the Stock Exchange – it was kind of bizarre really. If only they had sat back, cracked open a brew and Rock and Rolled maybe it would have all seemed a little less important; it's only money after all. Easy for me to say I suppose. Great song this with a chorus catchier than scabies. Also contains a word that doesn't exist – 'tireder' anyone?

Title – Out of touch
Sample lyric – 'If only she could change her point of view, he'd change his clothes, his hair and she'd love him too.'

Analysis philosophis – Song about people who change to please someone they fancy. This never works, be yourself. It was written with a guy called Lee Powis and I think it is a great song.

Title – The Ballad of Cactus Breeks
Sample lyric – 'Pick up a bottle, catch the night train, and ride down to Cactus Breeks' (Irish slang for soiling one's trousers i.e. kacked his breeks).

Analysis philosophis – When I was in No Hot Ashes I went about buying the regulation stage gear of the time. One of these said items was a black and white pair of leopardskin print trousers, which Ken would borrow from time to time. On one of these occasions he returned them to me in a plastic bag; I needed them for a gig the next day so I just emptied them into the basket for the next wash.

When I returned from college the next day my Ma sat me down, and with great concern asked me how I was feeling and was there anything I needed to discuss with her. I was totally confused and asked why I was being given the third degree. It transpired that Ken, who as we know enjoys the odd pint of Guinness, thought he had a touch of wind, but it was a little more serious than that. He followed through, leaving a black sticky deposit in my breeks, thus the interrogation from the old dear. She thought I had been incontinent, the colour of the sample making her think that there may have been a bleed involved as well. I was slightly miffed to say the least and when I asked Ken why he hadn't washed my trousers before returning them he said, 'I couldn't give that to my Ma to wash.' It was obviously all right for my Ma to come into contact with the offending items.

The worst song I think we ever wrote, the chorus is atrocious, an instance of the story being way better than the song.

Title – Last time
Sample lyric – 'You left me standin' lost in pain, fists clenched tightly I swore never again.'

Analysis philosophis – You split up with someone, it breaks your heart so much that you decide that it's going to be the last time you get hurt. Then you see a face in the crowd and off you go again. The harmony lead work at the start is so tasteful that it provides the perfect aperitif for the chorus.

Title – Breaking all the rules
Sample lyric – 'Cards on the table, hearts fighting pound for pound, you can win if you're able but you've got to go the last round.'

Analysis philosophis – Forbidden love can sometimes be the best kind, breaking the rules can be worth it.

Title – Danielle
Sample lyric – 'When you look in new-born eyes, hear genetic fingerprint of cries that only sound unique to those who care.'

Analysis philosophis – My good friend John Doherty, his wife Noelle and their new baby girl Danielle came to visit us at the Stick of Rock one day. Adele and myself were babysitting Steve Bruce's daughter Samantha so we put the two kids into the bedroom for a wee snooze.

After a while one of them started crying and I asked which one it was. Noelle said it was Danielle. I couldn't tell the difference between the two kids crying but the mum who loved her could. This is one of my favorite songs, I even mention Ken's son Conor Francis in the lyrics. It is a warning to kids not to grow up too quick and to enjoy being kids and not to waste it.

Title – Holding out for the night time
Sample lyric – 'If you wanna live for the moment, be like us and just go for it.'

Analysis philosophis – Written about the film *The Lost Boys*, no real story just a stupid song about having a good time at night. Features Pete Franklin of Chariot fame on backing vocals. Also on the choruses we brought all the punters from the Stick of Rock down to the studio for a shout-along and a drink at £100 per hour studio time.

Title – Love speaks
Sample lyric – 'Like that song your memory hangs in the air, brightens up my day but proves that you're not there.'

Analysis philosophis – Written about a time when a girl I was going out with used to pop into my head when the Police song 'Every Little Thing She Does is Magic' came on the radio.

Title – If I
Sample lyric – 'You wrote the script now you want me to play the part, but real life's not acting and acting's not real from the start.'

Analysis philosophis – For people who play psychological head games in relationships.

Title – Heartbreak City
Sample lyric – 'The Renegade he once said, Chinatown do not go down.'

Analysis philosophis – Obviously a tribute to Phil Lynott. It was also written about being in one of the biggest of cities surrounded by friends but being totally lonely because the person you want to be with isn't there. A song that was recorded very cheaply and there is no copy available but again a live favourite. Correction: Big Xan recently unearthed a studio version and it's actually pretty good.

Title – Strange situation
Sample lyric – 'You say you read a holy book and you live by its rules, what about the ones that don't suit you, oh you hypocrites, you fools.'

Analysis philosophis – A song for all those people that justify killing by using religion as an excuse, assholes.

The lunatic in charge of the asylum

The Stick of Rock was only half a mile away from Liverpool Street and therefore not far from the City of London and the Stock Exchange. Around 1990 a full renovation was to take place there, part of which was installing large metal structures that required welding. With these procedures comes the risk of fire from a stray spark and therefore to prevent the economy of the Western World grinding to a halt, a fire watchman of the highest quality was needed. Someone so fastidious, that the protection of this ancient financial institution would become an obsession. Where could such an individual be found? Step forward Ken Heaven, protector of the world's fiscal operations from fire, and guitar player with Nellie Dean.

Ken took his position as a Chief Fire Officer very seriously; how he got the job in the first place is a mystery. Every afternoon at lunchtime he would tell anyone who would listen just how important his job was, while propping up the bar of the Stick of Rock. The hour allocated for the consumption of his afternoon meal must have been flexitime as he was able to fit in six games of pool and down four or five pints before returning. On one exceptionally long lunch break I asked him, 'Should you not be going back to work?' He thought about it for a second and clicked his fingers as if he'd just remembered this himself. Instead of getting his coat he left the pool table, went outside, shaded the sun from his eyes with his hand and looked above the brothel (sorry massage parlour), directly across the street, and in the general direction of Liverpool Street. He returned to the bar, chalked his cue and announced 'No smoke,' while taking his next shot.

While Ken was doing his Fireman Sam impersonation he had a birthday. Elaine worked at an exclusive Covent Garden boutique called Casa Fina and from there she purchased a beautiful Christian Dior coat as a present for the love of her life.

The great day fell on a Sunday and Ken decided to spend a pleasant afternoon at the Stick of Rock, while Elaine, who was an excellent cook, prepared a delicious meal in celebration of the day that the world benefited from the arrival of her life partner.

We had just got Budweiser in on draft and Ken asked if it was strong – he wanted to keep a clearish head for his birthday dinner. Not knowing the strength I assumed it was the same as the other lagers we sold and told him this. He ordered a pint of the double-chilled nectar not knowing that it was, in fact, much stronger than anything on offer at that time. It went down so well that he treated himself to a few more pints and was treated, by those in attendance, to a few more.

The time flew and the phone rang. I answered it; it was Elaine asking if Ken had left yet. I shouted over to Ken at the pool table that Elaine wanted to speak to him. 'Tell her I'm leaving right this minute,' as he potted the 8 ball. I relayed his response and hung up. Ken racked up the balls for another, winner stays on, game.

The time flew and the phone rang again. Ken shouted, 'If that's Elaine tell her I've left.'

I said, 'I'll do it once Ken and that's all.' And to my shame this I did.

The time flew, and the phone rang again. I said, 'You can answer it this time, Kenny boy.' He let it ring until it stopped. I can only assume that Elaine didn't ring back thinking that the bar had closed for the afternoon as was the licensing law of the time for Sundays. We, however, were having our 'stuff the law' traditional Sunday afternoon lock-in.

The time flew and it was time to open the doors to the evening's trade. Elaine had stopped ringing and was probably keeping the dinner warm by scraping it onto the fire. Ken waited for official closing time before *he* finally flew.

After the doors were closed at 10pm on a Sunday the party really began and another after-hours session would start. That night however, a knock came to the door. 'It's the Cops!!' somebody shouted. The lights were switched off, the music turned down and the punters were shooshed quiet. I opened the door fully expecting to be greeted by the men in blue, but oh no, there he stood in all his drunken glory, birthday boy himself. 'You let me leave without my coat ya balloon ye,' he slurred. 'She'll kill me if I don't come home with it.' I got him his coat and he wandered down the street towards Bethnal Green tube station to the sounds of illegal drinking kicking back into gear.

Nellie Dean were rehearsing the next night and Ken arrived late, as he always did, but tonight he looked a little bruised around the chops. 'What happened to you?' I asked. 'Did you get a slap for missing dinner?'

'No, it was much worse than that,' was Ken's reply.

Ken then explained that he had got the train to Leytonstone where he was to change for Hainault. This part of the Central Line is over ground so he sat on a bench to get some fresh air as he was feeling a little queasy, and dozed off. When he woke he discovered to his horror that he had puked all over Christian Dior's finest creation. Panic set in and he decided to throw the soiled garment over the fence where it landed in the middle of the bus terminal.

Buses started to roll over his present. This sight caused guilt to raise its nagging head, each one causing torment in his far from innocent mind, until it was too much and with alcohol-induced agility he climbed the fence to retrieve the gift so lovingly bought for him.

When he was finally in possession of the coat he tried to climb back over the fence cutting himself in the process thus adding another body fluid to the stains on the coat: only a few more to go and he would have a full house, and in his state there was a good possibility that he would be collecting first prize in his self-induced X-rated game of bingo. He was just in time to get the last train home.

Ken woke to the sound of Elaine screaming and raining down blows about his head and vital organs. 'What the feck happened to your coat?' she bellowed. Ken was a little confused, having been awakened in such a discourteous manner, and at first didn't know what she was going on about. With his one good eye he looked in the direction that his partner was pointing and there at the bottom of the sofa, which had been his choice of bed for the night, was the object in question covered in vomit, blood and tyre tracks. It all came flooding back in sweat-inducing Technicolor. Ken sat up, rubbed his hands up and down his abdomen, as if inspecting himself and said, 'Darlin' I think I was run over last night while trying to get home for dinner.'

Three lions? Not on my shirt mate.

Having played many successful and not so successful gigs around London we had built up quite a sizeable following, especially at the Stick of Rock, which was fast becoming a cracking little venue (being the entertainments manager had the perk of me being able to book us on a regular basis, which I did of course). We decided to dip our collective toes into the Rock and Roll pools that lay outside the capital. One such place we hoped we could establish a foot hold was Godalming, an affluent picturesque little place in Surrey quite close to Guildford, Xan's home town. There is nothing like returning to old pastures and putting on a triumphant performance for those locals that laughed when you said you were going to be a rock star. This was nothing like that.

Steve had decided to close the Stick for the night and put on a coach, thus transporting the clientele of his bar to another one to support us. We had travelled down earlier in the day to set up our gear and get a sound check under our belts. On arrival at the bar, which was called The Three Lions, we were shown, by the landlord, to an alcove that was to be the stage for the evening. I think he nearly had a fit when he saw the amount of equipment that we were going to use.

'You're not going to be very loud are you?' asked the owner. 'Its just we have the residents to think of,' he went on.

'Don't worry, you'll hardly know we're here,' I lied. We deliberately did the sound check at about a tenth of the volume we would be playing at later, a trick we had used many times in the past. Even though the PA was working at a fraction of its usual power our host asked us to turn it down a bit; he was assured that when our coachload arrived they would soak up most of the sound. He accepted this answer but there was definitely a look in his eyes that suggested that he had begun to realise that letting the local hippy and his band of circus freaks loose in his precious establishment was a bad idea – how right he was.

As gig time approached, the bar, which must have only held about fifty people on a good night, was decidedly empty. Xan's beautiul sister Abi was there and a few of her old school friends, if memory serves. The landlord was looking a little unsettled; it appeared that he had put on extra staff to deal with a coachload that had been promised and was conspicuous by its absence. What we were unaware of was that the driver of said coach had got lost and there were sixty Nellie Dean fans driving around Surrey, drunk, listening to 'If You Want Blood' by AC/DC on the stereo and having such a good time that if they made the gig it was an added bonus to a good night out.

The passengers on the coach may not have been missing us but we were missing them terribly; without them the night looked as if it was going to turn into a total disaster. 10.30pm arrived and we were supposed to start playing. We held out for another fifteen minutes but were forced on by a now slightly miffed licensee. I turned to the boys and said, 'Let's go for it,' and we took to the stage, which wasn't really a stage, we were playing on the floor.

I no more wanted to gig that night than I wanted to kiss Bernard Manning, not just because there were very few people in attendance – we had at times played to nobody – but because I was worried for the safety of Adele, my sisters and all my friends who for all I knew were wrapped around a tree. Mobile phones in those days were the possession of the very rich; you also would've needed another coach to drive along behind with one on board – they were the size of a small detached bungalow. In short without contact we could only wait and hope that everyone was OK.

We started as we meant to go on, that is at our normal volume. I remember seeing the bar staff standing with their backs to us. They looked like they were reaching up to bottles on shelves to either clean them or do a stock check or something; I thought, how rude is that? I then realised that they were in fact, trying to stop them falling to the floor. The vibrations we were creating were making the spirits bounce to the edge of their perch. The crescendo of the first song brought the manager scurrying across the bar to beg us to turn down. I said, 'Of course we will,' and of course didn't; this made him even more animated and I think he went looking for something to hit me with.

From where I stood on the stage I could see out the fire door. I had a good view of the car park. To my total relief, three songs in, the coach drove in. Because those stumbling from it could hear us playing they disembarked cheering and dancing to the tune we were banging out. They also spotted us through the glass of the door and thought that this must be the entrance to the bar. Like a Heavy Metal conga they snaked to the locked door and I spent an embarrassing minute or two pointing and mouthing the words telling them to go round the side of the building to get in.

When the penny finally dropped they invaded the pub, still singing and dancing and scaring the bejasus out of the boss, who was now close to a nervous breakdown. Thirsty travellers invaded the bar; those not ordering drinks piled into the area where we were playing and proceeded to kick up a storm. I was never so glad to see a bunch of drunken lunatics in my life.

As the set wore on the landlord's mood was changing; the place was jumping, he was selling more drink than he would've done in a whole week; he even seemed to be smiling. All that was going to change. As I said before we were on the same level as the crowd, so effectively we were looking straight into their faces. The bar had a lot of hunting memorabilia on the walls, a piece of which was an old horn, the type that you would see the army playing the last post on. In a fit of pique I jumped up onto a chair and went to lift it down off the bracket it was sitting on. Unfortunately, unknown to me, it was attached to the wall with screws, probably to prevent some idiot from doing exactly what I was trying to do.

One good tug later and to my delight the cornet came free; a large amount of the plaster also came free, which was not to the landlord's delight. 'Oh well,' I thought 'there's nothing I can do about that now.' So I did what I intended to in the first place, which was to blow out a raspberry-type note for comic effect, oh what a laugh I was.

I placed the instrument to my lips, and blew with all the force I could muster. The result was that the first couple of rows of the people that had travelled many miles to see us were showered with a thick dense cloud of fluff and skin cells. The dust had accumulated in the horn for the fifteen years that it had been on the wall. I couldn't believe it; not only had I wrecked the wall and the chances of ever playing there again but I had probably infected our friends and family with every disease known to man.

We ended the song and the set not to rapturous applause, but to our nearest and dearest coughing, spluttering and trying to shake the microorganisms out of their hair. I apologised to all those contaminated, but my best sincere sorry was saved for the gutted landlord, who I fear wasn't taking me seriously. Unknown to me, in the process of spring-cleaning his prized hunting horn I had covered my lips with a decade and a half's nicotine residue. I looked like I had freshly applied black lipstick to make my apologies. We never played there again.

Stoned

I have been a massive Stones fan all my life, since before birth in fact, so I was delighted when Adele presented me with tickets to see them twice at Wembley Stadium on the Steele Wheels and the Urban Jungle tour. If memory serves these tours merged into one for some reason, I think it was because one show of the Steele Wheels tour was cancelled and rescheduled for the Urban Jungle tour a few months later. Therefore we saw them on two different tours but only a short time apart. Does this make sense? I could be wrong here but I think I'm not, waffling again.

The day of the first gig started with great excitement. We all met up in the, closed for the day, Stick of Rock and had a few liveners. There was the usual motley crew of reprobates in attendance including Inky, his wife Paula, a beautiful Indian girl called Jay, her posh husband Chris, Steve, Ness, Paul Taylor, our Elish, and many more. Great company one and all. We set off for Wembley Stadium, the scene of many a historic event, including that memorable cheat-fest in 1966.

Inky had been consuming for many years about fifteen pints of Strongbow cider a day; he would also add in the odd pharmaceutical enhancer just to keep the level of craic from dipping. Even though I didn't approve of his drug taking I had been on many of the most enjoyable experiences of my life in his unequalled company and to this day value his friendship like I cherish the love of my family. Anyway that day we had all been partying with enthusiasm and as the Twin Towers of Wembley Way came into view, there was a surge of adrenalin. The roar of the crowd within the huge concrete walls rose in accordance with the music blasting from the PA; the hairs were starting to stand.

Halfway along the hallowed concourse Inky started to experience crushing chest pain. Considering he had had his usual quota of cider plus a litre of Black Label Smirnoff and his usual forty cigarettes, this probably was not unexpected. He proceeded to collapse into the road clutching his chest; his face resembled the colour of a clinker from a coal-fired central heating boiler. We all stood around in horror, looking at each other, hoping that one of us would take the initiative. I decided that urgent action was needed so I knelt down beside him, straightened out his legs, raised his head, parted his lips and then poured in a splash of my Jack Daniel's. This didn't have the desired effect I had hoped for. Inky started to choke and splutter something about me trying to kill him. Gratitude, eh?

The spectre of death hovered above the prostrate forlorn figure of one of the most decent human beings ever created. A call went out for someone to get the St Johns Ambulance Brigade. I sat down and my mind wandered to an old TV programme with Peter Purves, of 'Blue Peter' fame, I think it was called 'Kick Start', which involved young children risking life and limb on motorbikes. Of course the inevitable happened; one of the kids fell off his bike crushing his vitals on the handlebars. Two rotund members of the St Johns Wort Brigade came to the rescue by falling down the ditch, where the writhing child lay, injuring themselves but breaking part of their fall by landing on the kid. I didn't hold out much hope for Inky, who as far as I was concerned lay dying in the gutter.

A guitar tuned to open G cranked out the first chords of 'Start Me Up' – the Stones were kicking off. Some of the girls were crying, everyone was looking down at the stricken body of our comrade, it was not looking good. Chris stepped forward – it looked like he had something to say to Inky, maybe it would be the last words he would ever hear, it needed to be something profound. Chris brought his mouth level with Inky's ear and in an accent that sounded like a posher Hugh Grant he said, 'I think you should maybe reduce the salt in your diet.' Even with the seriousness of the situation being blatantly obvious I nearly pissed myself laughing.

Finally the traffic warden-attired ambulance personnel arrived, carrying a slightly stained and frayed stretcher. After a quick once-over they decided that it would be a good idea for Inky to be rushed to the nearest A&E department post-haste. We waved him goodbye for what could've possibly been the last time, then ran as fast as we could into the stadium lest we miss another note of the Stones.

The Jack the Rippers

I swear this is true: before I started work in the Stick of Rock I had never seen a stripper. In fact, the only females I had seen naked, in the flesh, were my sisters when we were kids sharing a bath together and those poor unfortunates who had consented to be one of my girl-friends. Steve had hinted that he might try to boost the daytime trade by putting on a couple of 'Jack the Rippers', primarily for the workmen who were renovating the Stock Exchange, but as far as I was aware no final decision had been made. I can't say I was shedding a tear because I knew that if my Ma had found out that I was going to be hosting a Revue Bar, à la Paul Raymond, she would've been on the first flight over to 'Sodom and Gomorrah' and dragging me out by the ear like an errant schoolboy.

It was somewhat of a surprise when one day, during the first few months of opening, two girls entered the bar and asked me where they could get changed. I assumed they were new barmaids – we had been looking for new starts and I knew we had advertised, but not having much to do with staffing I just thought Steve had hired them and forgotten to tell me. I pointed them to a small changing room where the bands got ready to play; it was no more than a hallway that led to the beer cellar.

While I waited for our new staff to return, I served the first few customers and discovered that we had run out of one of the draft beers. Needing to change the barrel and therefore needing access to the cellar, I knocked on the 'dressing room' door enquiring if it was OK to come in and if they were decent. I opened the door, after getting the all-clear, to find that no, they were not decent, in fact they were far from fecking decent.

Both new 'barmaids' had nothing on but gold lamé G-strings and a couple of tassels with which to cover their nipples, one of which had not been Blu-tacked, or whatever it was they used, into position yet. Don't get me wrong, they were not unpleasant on the eye, far from it, but I was not used to the sight of that amount of feminine flesh during daylight hours. That is unless I had paid for a meal with a good bottle of wine and done a fair amount of begging. I asked them what they were doing, but I already knew the answer; one of them laughed and said they were there to polish our brasses.

I phoned Steve upstairs and told him about the naked women in the dusty hallway. I also informed him that we were out of Budweiser. Like a modern-day Marie Antoinette he shouted, 'Let them drink Skol.' He dropped the receiver and took the stairs six at a time. He, it transpires, had arranged with a 'talent' agency for the strippers to start, but had not been given an exact date. He was therefore as surprised as me by the arrival of the goose-pimpled ones. The afternoon DJ was John Morris who was duly supplied, by the girls, with the records that they would dance to. The show, I'm afraid, was on.

We had a small afternoon trade, a few regulars and even fewer workmen, who would come in and kick their dirty cement-covered boots against the bar, messing up my freshly washed floors. The regulars were there for the music and craic, the workmen for the beer and food, which was supplied by an American friend of ours called Quinn, who would later go on to open a restaurant in L.A. with Christopher Lloyd from 'Back to the Future' fame. None of those assembled were prepared for the sight that was about to befall their eyes.

As the first act got under way there was an overwhelming atmosphere of embarrassment from all concerned. I had never seen so many people looking at my clean floors before; I would've taken it as a compliment under normal circumstances. Some of the workmen who had positioned themselves at the front of the stage were happily tucking into their burger, chips and sticky barbecue ribs (a special of Quinn's), when the first young lady started removing the little clothes she had on. I don't know about you but there is something slightly unsavoury about exposed pubic hair in the presence of food, especially when it is attached to someone who is performing the splits while doing a handstand.

Maybe they lost their appetites, maybe they were warming to the spectacle, or maybe they just couldn't believe their eyes, but the labourers' food was forgotten about. Their gaze was now transfixed on the action that was, due to their seating arrangements, taking place inches away from their noses. All manner of nooks and crannies were on display – let's be honest this sort of thing doesn't happen round your Ma's house over dinner, thank God, but if it did it would be like a train wreck – scary but hard to take your eyes off the carnage.

As I said before we were not exactly prepared for the day's turn of events, which meant that there were certain protocols and practices that would have been normally in place for such an exhibition. One was that we should've cleared the floor of the stage of cigarette butts, dust, spilt beer and bits of wood from the previous night's drummer's sticks. The first few dances ended embarrassingly with the girls covered in the filters and fag ash from twenty Park Drive. There were splinters embedded in areas that would never have happened to a carpenter, unless of course he was a naturist. The ladies refused to continue until the stage was cleaned and splinters removed. Steve being the boss was not going to do it, so I was dispatched with mop and bucket to swab the decks. I must point out that the girls removed the splinters themselves. I carried out my duties red-faced as those in attendance shouted for me to 'Get 'em off big fella'.

Another thing that we didn't do, which was required by law we found out later, was to black out the windows. This was, I assume, to avoid offending those on their way to Tesco's for a pint of milk, with the gyrations of naked, writhing women. For us this was not really a problem; the windows were actually above head height, so unless Michael Jordon or someone wearing stilts happened to be walking by no one could see in. With the circus and the Chicago Bulls not being in town we assumed we were pretty much safe. Or so we thought.

While one of the acts was in full X-rated flow, the No. 8 bus got snarled up in traffic congestion just outside the bar. The whole top deck was turned into a viewing gallery for a naked gymnastics display. There were horrified grannies, mothers with small children and a bunch of delighted schoolboys. We looked forward to the letter from the council.

I don't know how much these girls were being paid but they obviously needed to supplement their income by coming around after a 'dance' with a pint glass and asking the punters to show their fiscal appreciation by throwing some money into 'the pot'. Being a member of the staff I was spared the humiliating act of putting my hand in my pocket and fumbling around for the amount of loose change that the performance dictated. I mean how the hell do you work that one out? What makes one dance better than another? I think I'll just leave it there as a discussion on this matter could, quite frankly, become disgusting.

Colin Bow was in attendance on that fateful day and each time the glass came around he would pick up the payphone, situated at the end of the bar and pretend he was on a call. Maybe it was because he didn't want the embarrassment of the previously mentioned calculations or he was just tight, I don't know, but his actions didn't go unnoticed by the artistes. One of the girls was rather heavy in the chest department and slightly intimidating. I'm not sure if it was her pendulous mammary glands that made her so, but let's just say they didn't help: in fact, there was an air of oxygen-depleting menace about her and them.

Anyway, one of her dances involved the use of a whip (did I mention the menace?) and when she was finished taking the varnish off the floors and the eyebrows from the lads in the front rows she left the stage, pint glass and whip in hand. Her patience with Colin's attempts at squirming out of paying had worn as thin as her underwear. As he stood with his back to her, receiver to his ear, she let her displeasure be known by giving him a few licks of the lash around his buttock area.

Maybe she had put a little too much effort and pleasure into her strokes, because the cracks of the whip were accompanied by the hair-raising screams of poor Colin, who, in this instance, was not pretending to be on the phone but was, in fact, calling his mum to tell her he was going to be late for lunch. His squeals nearly caused his poor mother to have a few strokes of her own.

I must admit that I was not exactly comfortable with the whole stripper thing – maybe it was my upbringing, or maybe I just saw it as exploitative for both the girls (obviously) and the men who left the premises as frustrated as they had entered and very much lighter in the pockets. Don't get me wrong, there is a certain amount of freedom of choice involved, after all the girls don't really have to do it – the local Hospital, St Barts, was always looking for care assistants. The dancers I spoke to were, on the whole (I know, I know!!), really nice, purporting that they enjoyed what they did. The men had freely made the decision to be liberated from their cash by their loins. It was hard to see who benefited from all of this except for the mafia-type agencies who ran the operation. The girls were not driving Jags, but then again they weren't driving old bangers like the aforementioned care assistants.

Afternoon strippers are very prominent in the East End. It's nearly part of the culture: there are a lot of bars with blacked-out windows, the strains of Motley Crue's 'Girls Girls Girls' escaping through the heavy closed doors. I was not from around those parts and I didn't own the pub, I was just an employee at the end of the day, so I really didn't have a say. This sounds like a cop-out and believe me, I know it does.

What I can say is that I was not disappointed when Steve decided that for the outlay the profits were minimal. So after only a couple of weeks of all shapes, colours, sizes and ping pong balls (don't ask!) the Stick of Rock 'Strip Joint' closed, thankfully just days before my Da showed up on a business trip to London. How the hell could I have explained to my parents the depths of depravity, in their view, that their Catholic-educated son had stooped to? There would've been no rationalising me standing behind the bar serving pints to men, with their backs to the stage, who pretended they were not interested in the flesh on display but had their eyes glued to the show in the mirror.

The dynamic dough bags

Paul Taylor was one of the most welcome of customers at the Stick. He looked like a biker outlaw. He had the full-sleeve tattoos on both

Michelangelo sculpted arms and a renegade gold front tooth. His choice of transport was a custom Harley-Davidson Chopper and he made his living in the statistically lethal profession of motorcycle couriering. He gave off the air of a mean badass but he also had movie star good looks. As a wimpy little wannabe rocker I was in awe of him.

The truth is that even though Paul could handle himself, if the need arose, he was also one of the nicest, most gentle, decent human beings you could ever meet; all these factors meant that he was an easy choice when it came to the Nellies getting a driver. Paul I think loved us, he was a cockney working-class geeza with a heart made of the same precious metal as his gnasher. We could make him laugh easily and he knew he was amongst friends. Friends become family sometimes and this was true of Paul Taylor, a brother in arms.

Being the entertainments manager of the Stick meant that I could pull a 'fly one' when conversing with other venue promoters. I would start by asking them if they could recommend any of the bands that played their place, knowing full well that they would ask the same thing, thus giving me the opportunity to put forward the Nellies without ever disclosing that I was in the band. One such scam led to us playing a salubrious little fleapit called Bogies in Cardiff. It was supposed to be named after Humphrey Bogart but I have my suspicions that it was given its moniker after nasal material.

We had played it a few times and gone down really well. To get the benefit of the kudos and adulation afterwards we would stay late which would necessitate us staying over. There was a great wee B&B that didn't mind when at 8am we ordered the full breakfast and a round of pints; we always looked forward to staying there. But on one occasion we had a gig on the Sunday night in the Marquee, where we had started headlining, so we decided to head back to London after the show.

A carryout was purchased from the gig money and we hit the road in the Transit with Paul Taylor driving. Around 4am we were all feeling a little peckish but the money had been depleted, due to the drink, which was now finished. Ken was volunteered to go into a motorway service station and spend what little funds we had left on as much grub as possible. He returned with two packets of crisps, a packet of ham, a loaf of bread, a tub of margarine and a quality read from the top shelf called, and I swear this is true, *Dynamic Dough Bags.*

Back on the road again the promise of a ham and crisp sandwich lifted our spirits. There was a problem however – we had nothing to spread the margarine with. Paul came upon a solution when he found a child's ruler in the glove compartment; it was a little dusty but by God it would do the trick. I sat in the passenger seat with the loaf on one side and an open bag of crisps on the other. I proceeded to spread the margarine, using the ruler, on each slice, hygienically resting the bread on the leg of my jeans. The gastronomic delights, which only resembled sandwiches in name, were passed around and scoffed with not a word of complaint.

When the Nellies got Noel into the band we also inherited his friend Brendan Kelly as a sound engineer. He was great at what he did so I got him a job behind the eighteen-track mixing desk in the Stick of Rock as well. Brendan was full-on all the time, he never shut his mouth. At sound checks it was a blessing when the bands started blasting out music because it drowned out his twitterings. Adele sort of took him under her wing, making sure that he was fed and clothed; then again she always did have a soft spot for the strays in the street. Brendan even used to call her his Mammy, she was that attentive of him.

I got on great with Brendan and I had no problems with him staying in our flat every weekend, except, that is, when he had been working on the building sites and had neglected to wash for a week. On one such occasion Adele, after I had complained about the stench emanating from his ever-present trainers, used all her powers of diplomacy to get him to take a bath. I could have kissed her as he dandered off to the bathroom with his towel over his shoulder.

I could hear his nasally, whiney voice above the splashing of the water as he sang songs about dirty old Dublin. 'At least,' I thought 'we will be spared the waft of body odour, sweat, cigarettes and beer this weekend.' Imagine my horror when Brendan exited the bathroom, hair wet, face shaved and glowing from the scrubbing it took, but still wearing the same dirty clothes and trainers.

Anyway, back to the van travelling from Bogies and in the direction of London. Brendan had taken a very keen interest in the high-class literature that Ken had squandered our hard-earned money on. Ken was perusing the pages and coming out with things like, 'My God, who would've believed it,' and 'Never in all my life,' while Brendan kept saying, 'Give someone else a look' and, 'It was our money as well you know.' Ken however insisted that everyone who wanted to would get an eyeful after he had finished, while keeping the forbidden sights close to his chest.

After about half an hour Ken reached the last page of the magazine. Shaking his head and muttering, 'Dear, dear, dear,' he closed it and threw it straight out the window. There was a stunned silence. It landed on the windscreen of a car travelling behind, open on the centrefold. The family within, who were obviously going on holiday judging by the suitcases on the roof, looked horrified, their field of vision filled with what looked like an overly explicit anatomy and physiology book. Back in the van an incensed Brendan screamed, 'What the feck did you do that for!!!' Ken calmly turned to him and said, 'I couldn't have forgiven myself if I had exposed your virgin, Catholic eyes to the visions I have just witnessed. Your soul would've surely gone to hell, I just couldn't live with that.'

Emerald

The Nellies somehow managed to persuade *Kerrang!* and *Metal Forces* journalist Dave Shack to accompany us on the road for a tour of Ireland. I think his association with promoting unsigned bands on the *Metal Forces*-sponsored Friday night slot in the Stick of Rock helped. We hoped it would be a way of getting publicity and maybe a feature article in the magazine. I don't think Dave was quite prepared for the depravation and lunacy of life on the road with one of the hardest working, hardest drinking and most stupid bands never to be signed.

A native of the Yorkshire city of Leeds, Dave is a supporter of his hometown team. Being a lifelong follower of the Elland Road crowd this endeared him to me immediately. LUFC were in the old second division when we met and we would discuss their plight, contenting ourselves that such a big club could never stoop so low again. How wrong we were. Sure we were to enjoy the thrill of them winning the First Division Championship (1992) and revel in a Champions

League semi-final (2001) but as I write this they are languishing in league one (the old third division). At least they couldn't possibly drop any lower. Oh shut up Eamon, you're tempting fate again.

Dave was a lovely guy who had an unquenchable passion for Rock and Metal; his articles and reviews were genuine and untainted by record company schmooze. I was becoming increasingly distrustful of the music business; I had seen favourable album reviews secured by the handing over of a small bag of what looked like baking powder. Dave was a breath of fresh air, a diamond in the corporate rough. As down to earth as he was I'm sure, however, he was used to a certain amount of music business comfort and pampering whilst on assignments – well, he could forget all that nonsense as far as the Nellies were concerned. We were the basic of basic.

We all set off to catch the ferry in Stranraer in a Toyota Hiace van, all our gear and baggage piled in around us. We had bought a massive carryout that was to do us until we reached Scotland; it just about got us to Watford. By the time we were aboard the boat we had developed a wicked thirst so we made good use of the bar facilities. As the drink went down the merriment increased and what does a hard rocking band do when they are on tour and drunk? Yes, that's right, we settled down for a pub quiz.

People get their nicknames for all manner of reasons. With the passage of time those reasons fade, but in many cases the name remains. With Brendan Kelly, who had taken leave from doing the sound at the Stick of Rock to go on the road with us, I can remember the exact origin and details of how he acquired his moniker.

There were hundreds of people on the ship, all of varying age groups and intelligence levels and all of them decided that they were going to pit their wits against each other on the battlefield that is 'Trivial Pursuit'. There were prizes up for grabs including bottles of spirits; this caused a girding of the loins in the Nellie Dean camp; the alcohol made it serious.

We had amongst us quite a gathering of the intelligentsia – after all we had a renowned journalist in the form of Dave Shack. We also had an ex-public schoolboy, Big Xan Philips, and then there were the rest of us – at least I could read and write a bit. We surmised, for some reason, that one of us should at least come away with something. After much head scratching, eraser nibbling, crossing out and rewriting we all sat with bated breath as the results were to be read out. For a laugh the compere, who was as camp as a field full of tents, said he was going to read out the name of the person who had finished rock bottom and who had, in fact, scored 'nul points'.

The name 'Beckly' was announced. We all looked around at the faces of the old-age pensioners, children and those who were obviously dimwitted judging by the thick foreheads and joined eyebrows. Who could it be? We all waited for the hand to go up but none did. Just as we were about to give up hope of being able to publicly ridicule a fool, the compere looked at the grubby answer form that he held in his hand and said, 'Sorry, I misread the name, the writing's that bad, it's actually B. Kelly.' With the sound of the hysterical laughter ringing in his ears Brendan went up to receive his prize, a tiny teddy bear that had Velcro hands enabling it to catch little felt balls. He would forever more be known as Beckly. He was also the only one of us who won a prize.

We were to use Ken and my parents' houses for our accommodation and bases for the tour. After each gig we would go back to Holywood to the bosom of our families, thus saving on hotel bills. Dave Shack, being the veteran of many a tour with bands such as Iron Maiden, Def Leppard etc., must've had a chuckle to himself when he discovered that the Rock and Roll animal that is Nellie Dean returned to their mummy's for chicken sandwiches and a wee cup of tea before beddie byes. Our families, however, are not like other peoples'. This became apparent when on our arrival my Da offered everyone an Irish coffee. Everyone accepted of course, it would have been rude not to.

Instead of whiskey my Da uses poteen to liven up his coffees, so after the consumption of a couple of these Molotov cocktails everyone decided that it would be a good idea to visit the local playing fields for a drunken game of football and piggy back fights using acoustic guitars as swords. The next day Xan, who has a chronic back problem, could hardly walk, and the English members of the entourage including Mr Shack had hangovers that Ozzy Osborne couldn't have inflicted.

Knock, knock knockin' on the Heavens' door

As usual Paul Taylor had taken leave of his day job of trying to kill himself delivering parcels on a motorbike and was doing the van driving. He was also staying with Ken's family, which had the potential to be just as interesting and/or borderline dangerous. In a bout of localisation Ken and myself had warned the boys that if they were out and about in the town to watch out for certain undesirables of the paramilitary variety. I won't mention names, I still enjoy my family with their kneecaps where they should be, so I'll make one up, let's see, OK we told them to avoid the Smith family like the plague.

Ken's Mum, Kay, was fond of a drink or two as is the norm in Ireland. However she would often start a little earlier than most and this was indeed the case when she asked Paul to take her to the shops to stock up on provisions with which to feed and water the band and crew. Standing at the checkout of Stewarts Supermarket, Mrs Heaven got talking to someone in the queue. Paul, who had come in from the van to do the donkey work, stood patiently by the filled bags at the end of the conveyer belt and asked if they were all for carrying out. Kay was not really listening and just nodded and waved a confirming hand.

Paul put all the bags into a trolley and transported them to the van then went back to gently ease Kay away from her sociable gossiping. On their return to the house Kay started to realise, while filling the cupboards, that she couldn't remember buying some of the items. For example there were tins of Whiskas: the Heavens didn't have a cat. Later that night there was a heavy-handed metallic knock on the glass of the Heavens' front door. Somebody needed to answer such a knock.

The Nellies had been sampling the best pints of Guinness in Ireland in the best bar in Ireland, Ned's – or The Maypole Bar to give it its full title. Paul, knowing that he was going to have to drive later, had elected to erase any temptation by staying in the Heaven household. Kay and her husband, Sid, were caressing a glass of warmed to perfection QC wine while watching the TV, when the door was rapped. Being otherwise indisposed Kay called for Paul to greet their unexpected guests. As the door swung open two thugs with gold sovereign rings and orthodontist-avoiding teeth confronted him. 'We're the Smiths and you've nicked our Ma's shopping.'

Paul Taylor was good with his fists and in all the years I've known him he has never shown fear in any confrontational situations that we got ourselves into. However, after the warnings we had given him about the undesirables now standing in front of him, there was a loosening of his bowels and a buckling of the knees. 'Hang on mate, I didn't steal anything,' he spluttered in his cockney accent.

'If that's the case, you English bastard, how come you were spotted walking off with our groceries?' said the one with the facial scars doing his bit for the Anglo-Irish agreement.

Then the one with the more pronounced turn in his eye said, 'Our Tiddles is fucking starving.'

'Kay, Kay there's someone at the door for you!' Paul shouted.

Ken's Ma led two morons into her kitchen and basically told them to take what they thought was theirs, which they did, while also removing the stuff that was not. This act of thievery left the band and Heaven family with no means of sustenance. When Ken and his brothers returned from Ned's and found out about the liberation of the contents of their larder the situation was reversed, by a quick visit to the Smith household and the administration of a whack to the odd head. The result was a couple of black eyes, a missing tooth, which should've been removed anyway to avoid over-crowding, and a turf war that rumbles on to this day. Usually in Northern Ireland such feuds are over drugs or arms – however this one was over, amongst other things, six pot noodles, a packet of fig rolls and three cans of pilchard-flavoured cat food.

Hair today, gone tomorrow

Beckly had the hairiest ears ever known to man; they looked like they had a covering of underfelt. It became a bone of contention with Ken, who took great exception to these fruit bat-like monstrosities. He would often bring them up in conversation especially when he was indulging in one of his favourite pastimes, taking the piss out of our poor sound engineer. One drunken evening, after a few of my Da's illegal Irish coffees, it was decided that we would diversify the bands career portfolio by taking up a bit of beauty therapy. We persuaded Beckly to relieve himself of some excess weight by ridding himself the offending fuzz. We came upon the genius idea that we would emulate waxing by cutting out the wax and using a suitable substitute.

Gaffa tape folks, is the musician's friend. It secures leads to floors, fixes broken speaker cabinets and on one occasion even held the crotch area of Ken's trousers together, thus preventing him from arrest. It is so effective in its ability to secure things for good, that if Harland and Wolffe had used it, instead of rivets, the *Titanic* would now be a floating hotel docked in Belfast Lough instead of sitting at the bottom of the Atlantic. It would also have saved us from that horrible song by that Canadian woman with the big snozzle. Anyway the point I'm trying to make is that it is possibly not the best substance to use when you want to remove body hair, but we didn't care.

Two strips of gaffa were carefully secured to Beckly's ears while he was pinned to the carpet of my Ma and Da's living room. When a suitable time had elapsed, roughly half an hour or the time it takes to consume two cans of beer, they were ripped off. The hair was successfully removed; what were also nearly removed were the victim's ears. Beckly's screams filled the air and nearly gave my Ma, who was out in the kitchen making sandwiches, a heart attack. As bad as our disfiguring attempt was, it paled into insignificance when an allergic reaction to the glue, which we had not factored in to our pre-op assessment, occurred.

Beckly's lugs started swelling and continued to do so until they looked like two calf's kidneys. This is not a good look and the living room mirror bore witness to this, much to Beckly's horror. Ken flicking them didn't really help, funny enough, but it did make everyone laugh which is always a good thing.

The ears were so engorged that there were beads of interstitial fluid trickling down them; the skin was so tight that they were nearly translucent with tiny blood vessels quite visible. The pain must have been excruciating but Beckly hid his discomfort well, diverting everyone's attention by crying like a baby. As the days went by the ears eventually returned to their normal size and were as smooth as a billiard ball. You would think that he would've been delighted with the result, but he never once thanked us for our sterling job.

Beckly was a man with little to say but he had a very elongated way of saying it. His monologues could last for hours with there being no end in sight. If there was actually a climax to his ramblings it was rarely funny but always unfathomable. On a night off from gigging we were all sitting in my Ma and Da's house when he decided he would regale everyone, including my parents, with one of his tales of wonderment. His heavy Dublin brogue and speed of delivery made what was coming out of his mouth almost unintelligible. My Ma and Da sat in open-mouthed amazement at the rantings of the funny little foreigner with wiry hair that resembled a very dry tumbleweed.

On and on the story went, while Ken sat on the armchair beside him, waiting patiently to have his say. He tried a couple of times to interrupt by butting in. However Beckly kept him from saying his piece by holding up a hand and saying, 'Howld yer whisht.' As you can imagine this started to get on Ken's nerves. After another failed attempt to get a word in, he removed a cigarette lighter from his pocket, spun the little plastic wheel, ignited the fuel and set the flame to the storyteller's hair.

The tinder-type nature of Beckly's locks provided a very combustible material, and tongues of fire licked towards the ceiling. At first my Ma couldn't quite believe what was happening: there in front of her was someone with his hair on fire who was obviously oblivious to the whole thing – he just carried on talking. She tried to alert him by saying, 'Jesus Brendan, your head's on fire.' He just held up his hand to silence her, he didn't want to be prevented from reaching the conclusion of his tale.

My Ma panicked. The risks were now two-fold: one, the rapidly decreasing volume of Beckly's hair meant that he was in serious risk of roasting his scalp; and two, the flames were licking around the curtains behind his head which meant that her home was in danger of burning to the ground. There was also the noxious smell of burning hair and the thick acrid smoke that was starting to fill the room to contend with. She jumped to her feet and shouted, 'Fer God's sake Brendan, shut your mouth – your head's on fire.'

A look of puzzlement came over Beckly's face, then suddenly the realisation that indeed his napper was alight. Ken, on seeing that the joke, as was usually the case, had gone a bit far, rained down blows upon the smouldering mess that was once Beckly's crowning glory in a brutal attempt at extinguishing the inferno. Beckly, thinking that Ken was attacking him, retaliated by throwing punches of his own. My parents, in the blink of an eye, had had a convivial evening of chat and merriment reduced to an arson attempt on a human being and an all-out punch-up. My Da made a mental note to never let his eldest son's deranged friends stay under his roof again.

Even when he was in the relative safety of London Beckly was never really that safe. While doing sound at the Stick of Rock he would bolster his income by working during the week as a labourer on building sites. One Friday he finished, as was usual, at lunchtime. He decided, as it was such a good day, that he would visit Hyde Park in the company of the *Sun* newspaper and a few cans of cheap lager, both of which were an indicator of his levels of taste.

After a couple of libations and finding he was unable to get beyond Trixie on page three, the little Dubliner started to feel a little fatigued; he stretched out on the grass for a bit of rest and recuperation and promptly fell into an alcohol-induced coma. He awoke two hours later horrendously sunburnt, with his eyelids taking a particularly savage blistering.

When he arrived at the bar to do his shift, I answered the door to him. He resembled a zombie; his arms were outstretched as he groped around in front of him, his field of vision diminished to two tiny slits. I helped him upstairs where I gave him some Sudocrem to apply to his inflamed eyelids; he took it and went to the bathroom to administer. While he was there the doorbell rang. I looked out the window and saw that the band for the evening had arrived. I alerted Beckly to this, and he shouted back that he would let them in.

When it was time for me to go down to get the bar ready for opening, I was confronted by one of the funniest sights I have ever seen. Beckly was standing at the mixing desk shouting instructions to the band, with what looked like thick white eyeshadow on. He had applied two big thick scoops of the cream to his eyelids without even attempting to rub it in. The suspicious looks from the band members were priceless, it looked like they were taking orders from a transvestite roofer. God only knows what they thought when he answered the door to them.

Beckly, from what I have told you so far, would appear to be, at best, unfortunate and at worst, picked upon. He was, however, more than capable of dishing it out as well as receiving it. A case in point occurred when we held a party in the upstairs bar of the Nellie Dean. The fashion of the time, which we all wore, was brightly coloured Bermuda shorts, à la Anthrax. Ken had a particularly garish pair of green and purple ones that he wore for this most auspicious of occasions. As I have stated earlier Ken avoided wearing underwear. This fact didn't help him when, as he was returning from the bar, his hands full with three pints of lager, Beckly decided to sneak up behind him and pull his shorts down.

Ken stood for a couple of seconds right in the middle of the room with his shorts warming his ankles. All eyes, like a train wreck, were upon him. His brain tried to weigh up the pros and cons of the actions available to him. He could keep hold of the pints, waddle to the nearest table, and deposit them there before adjusting his attire or he could drop the drinks on the floor and quickly wrestle his waving member back under cover. Let's face it the latter wasn't going to happen – alcohol was too precious to this man – and the former, with the nearest table being twenty feet away, would've stretched the laws of respectability to their very limits. Then in a moment of inspiration came upon him a solution of eureka-type proportions.

Slowly crouching down to his hunkers, whilst trying to keep the contents of the glasses in the glasses, Ken set the drinks on the floor, and hey presto, shorts retrieved. While attempting this tricky manoeuvre the people in front of him bore witness to a man dragging his penis and scrotum on the ash- and beer-stained carpet, while those behind got a full, cheek-parted, view of his anus. All in all it was not a spectacle for the weak of stomach or frayed of nerve. Beckly stood pissing himself laughing as he licked a finger and drew in the air the figures 1 and 0.

Skullduggery

Back in Belfast we had been booked to play a place called Vicos, which was situated in Belfast City centre. The guy responsible had promised that everything would be taken care of; all we needed to do was to turn up with our guitars, amps and drum kit. Unfortunately when we arrived at the venue there was no sign of a PA and the so-called promoter was uncontactable. We were basically up the creek without a paddle.

Despondency set in: it was too late to try and hire a PA so it looked like we were going to have to cancel the gig, something we had never done before. There was also the added embarrassment of having invited hundreds of family and friends along for what was seen as a homecoming gig.

When the chips are down you always hope that there will be someone who will step up to the plate and save the day. I have to say that when faced with similar situations Big Xan has always come up trumps, and on this occasion he was not going to let his unbeaten run come to an end.

Without telling anyone Xan and a friend of ours from Belfast, Colin Shiels, went to a bar called The Beaten Docket. To say the place was rough would be an understatement: missing teeth, scars and broken noses seemed to be the only dress code. It was late on a Saturday evening and the place was packed with punters drowning the sorrows of another anger-inducing day backing the wrong gee gees. Xan has a very refined, gentle, educated English accent so when he shouted at the top of his voice 'Can I have your attention please?' he may as well have yelled, 'Look over here, I'm a poofy English git with more money than you and I think someone should shoot me!' The place fell into a stunned silence. Colin had to fight the compulsion to drop to his knees in prayer.

Thinking that the crowd were giving him the chance to speak, instead of them being rendered speechless at the sheer nerve of a Brit coming into their bar and interrupting their alcohol poisoning, Xan said, 'Thank you, I was just wondering if any of you fellows would have a PA system, I'm in a band and we seem to be in a bit of a predicament.' The only sound that could be heard was the rustle of hands reaching into pockets for knuckle dusters and flick knives. Just as all hell was about break loose a voice from the bar shouted, 'Oi mate, we have a PA.' Sitting at the bar were two long-haired locals with big grins on their faces and thumbs in the air. Xan to the rescue again.

The gig was an absolute triumph with the crowd going nuts from start to finish, which was very satisfying, and to think it might never have happened thanks to the promoter's cock-up. Still, anyone can make a mistake, or can they? It transpires that the same guy had booked an old nemesis of Ken's, Lisa Dominique, to play in another venue in town called the Rosetta, the same night. Ticket sales had not been good and fearing that he wouldn't have a crowd for the altogether more expensive Rock siren it was decided that a touch of sabotage would be the order of the day.

The PA was cancelled and we were to be left stranded. He hoped that when we couldn't play, the disgruntled punters would make their way across town and swell the numbers at the Rosetta. But he was not prepared for the fortitude that is the Nellie spirit and as you already know we survived and triumphed. Which cannot be said for a deflated Lisa Dominique Band who, it was reported to us later by the support band, Switchblade Serenade, died a death in front of a small crowd that wanted Metal. Funnily enough if they had stuck to their original Pop Rock direction, instead of letting Marino jazz infuse all over the place, then they would've stood a better chance.

Iron Maiden City

Derry/Londonderry is a place steeped in history and culture; it is also the birthplace of the Undertones, one of the greatest bands to ever knock a three-chord classic together. It is a very strange city, in that it must be one of only a few places in the world where half the inhabitants call it one name and the other half a different one and ne'er the twain shall meet. The Nationalists and Loyalists have been fighting each other for centuries over this issue and seem more than happy with the situation. There has not been one inch of compromise from either side and why should there be? It keeps Friday and Saturday nights interesting – after all who wants to go home after the pubs close when a pitched battle in the streets can round the night off just nicely? With this situation in mind we made our way across the country to the Maiden City, a little concerned for the English and Southern Irish members of the contingent; after all we didn't know if the bar was Catholic, Protestant or – heaven forbid – mixed.

The place was called the Rendezvous; it was on one of the steepest streets I have ever been on. It was so bad that we had to go looking for something to stick under the wheels of the van to prevent it rolling into the Foyle River. Luckily there had been a riot just before we had arrived and we were able to pick out two bricks from all the rest of the debris and broken glass on the street.

Inside the bar was dark, dismal and smelling of stout. As we were setting up one of the local Metalheads got talking to us. He was very sociable, giving us directions to the best chip shops etc. He also hung around us making a nuisance of himself and cadging drinks. To be honest we thought he was a bit slow or was perhaps the local idiot, so out of the goodness of our collective hearts we tolerated and humoured him.

As gig time approached the place started filling up with Rock fans. This could turn out to be a good night, we thought, and it was. That is apart from a rather funny incident, which occurred right at the start of the show. Our new 'best friend' was standing at the front of the stage waiting patiently for us to come on. When we did he raised his arms in the air and cheered – it looked like he had been a lifelong fan. He waited until we were halfway through 'Somebody', the first song of the night, before he realised that we were not a Thrash Metal band as he had hoped. He voiced his disapproval at having to listen to music with melody by removing the ice from the drink which we had given him, and pelting us with it. For good measure as he stormed off he gave us the finger and shouted, 'Fruity bastards.' I guess we weren't friends anymore.

We were treated like conquering heroes after a cracking gig, and there were a fair few female fans wanting to show their appreciation, which was nice. One particularly beautiful girl took a shine to Dave Shack, and why would she not? He was a good-looking fella with a fine turn of phrase. They were getting on famously and it looked like our journalist friend was going to get the scoop of a lifetime. Then of course that human wrecking ball that is Ken Heaven had to spoil the fun.

Ken thought it would be a great laugh to tell Dave that the object of his desires was a Mata Hari type temptress who was under the employ of the IRA. He convinced him that she was setting a honey trap for an unsuspecting Englishman, the result being a bullet in the back of the head, once she had got him away from the protection of his friends. How funny was that? Dave nearly freaked out; he kept saying, 'She told me she was a model.'

Ken explained, 'Of course she did, she wasn't going to tell you the truth was she? It would've kinda defeated the purpose of her mission.'

When Dave returned to the bar it was blatantly obvious he was trying to keep the beauty as far away from him as possible. The poor girl looked totally dejected and was actually seen shedding a tear on the shoulder of a friend. Dave turned to Ken and asked, 'Are you sure about this?' Ken replied that he had it on good authority that it was true; he concluded by saying that she was obviously very good at what she was doing the way that she was able to turn on the tears.

The Glenshane Pass links Derry to Belfast and runs through the Sperrin Mountains. It has been the scene of many horrific incidents linked to the so-called 'Troubles'. On days when the weather is fine the views are spectacular, but in bad weather and during the night it can be one of the bleakest, scariest places on earth. As we snaked along the winding roads Paul could see an orange light revolving in the road. Everybody was asleep apart from Noel who had decided to keep the driver company. After having their heads filled with the stories Ken and myself had told them, about shootings and murders, the two boys thought that they were being held up or hijacked. 'What will we do?' Paul asked the Southern Irish guitarist.

'Drive feckin' through,' Noel shouted. I was snoring in the front seat beside him but the commotion dragged me awake.

As my eyes adjusted to dim light within the van, I suddenly sat bolt upright. Seeing the illumination up ahead and I shrieked, 'Stop the feckin van!' Paul slammed on the brakes, going into a massive skid, stopping only feet away from the now non-revolving light. Not being from the Province the lads were not aware that the UDR would stop on-coming cars, to search, by using a hand-held orange torch. There were many instances of people who had driven through the road blocks not knowing what they were, and been shot. The excuse for the deaths, given by the authorities, was that the army had thought they were terrorists.

Everybody in the back of the van was thrown forward and rudely awakened. They all struggled back into their seats and peered into the darkness. Inky, who had only flown over that day to join us after getting the all clear following his suspected heart attack at the Stones gig, looked at JJ and said, 'There's something on your forehead'.

JJ replied, 'That's funny, there's something on your forehead as well.'

Inky and JJ looked like they had converted to Hinduism and were sporting bindis. When Inky tried to remove his the dot transferred from his head to the back of his hand. The realisation started to set in that the spots were not symbols of a religious conversion but were the beams from the telescopic sights of high-velocity rifles. This news was probably not that welcome to Inky who had been told by his GP to avoid stressful situations. The threat of having his head blown off his shoulders was probably the sort of thing that the doctor was referring too. Inky turned grey.

Two military uniformed people pointing guns approached the driver's window. One was six foot four, the other four foot six. They banged heavily on the glass. Paul wound down the window, his hands shaking.

'What the fuck were you trying to do – kill me?' asked the lanky one.

'No no, officer,' Paul sputtered, wrongly addressing the guy as a policeman. 'We're not from around these parts, we just didn't know what was going on,' he explained.

'Where are you from?' asked the dwarf, who happened to be a woman.

Ken, who was now fully awake and ready for mischief, shouted, 'I'm from Holywood County Down,' immediately making a liar out of Paul.

The pixie with the helmet looked suspiciously at our driver, who tried to clarify things by saying, 'Some of us are from here, but they were all asleep and the ones that aren't from here were awake, including me.'

The midget then sarcastically said, 'Seeing as you were driving I'd like to think you were fucking awake.'

Ken had had enough. He couldn't believe that visitors to his homeland were being spoken to in such a manner and being made to feel threatened. He dragged himself forward in his chair until he was looking through the gap in the front seats directly at GI Jane. 'Are you standing in a hole?' he asked.

'What the fuck is that supposed to mean?' she responded aggressively.

'It's just that I have an Action Man that's taller than you. And another thing – your lower jaw seems to stay still when you're talking, while the top of your head seems to be doing all the work. Is there a name for this medical condition?' He then concluded his request to be shot by asking, 'Why don't you go out and catch some terrorists?' – a question that the UDR truly hated as it was a phrase used in a popular TV advert of the time and thrown at them by every smartarse that they stopped.

Cold stares were thrown at Ken as we all stood in the icy rain, our gear being taken apart. When nothing was found we were left to put everything back together and back into the van. Noel had a fractious relationship with Ken at the best of times, again a guitarist thing, but was usually able to keep his anger in check. However, on this occasion, probably due to his near-death experience, he just let rip. He called Ken all the stupid bastards of the day. Ken responded accordingly and only the quick intervention of the rest of the band diverted a fistfight. We would soon be looking for another guitarist.

The next day, with nerves still on edge, we sat in the living room of my Ma and Da's house reading the Sunday papers. Dave Shack looked up from the *Sunday World* in his hands and just said one word, 'Bastard.' There, in her full glory, on the front page, was a photograph of the girl from the previous night's gig – she was described as one of Ireland's top models. We returned back to London the next day and Dave wrote a two-page article for *Metal Forces* magazine about the trip called 'Five go mad in Ireland.'

Changes, I'm going through changes

One of the most colourful characters that I had the good fortune to encounter, through music, was a guy called Alex. He was a Scottish Russian Jew; this eclectic mix must've contributed to his personality for he was a weird and wonderful individual, and a privilege to know.

It all began one Sunday afternoon when the market was on in Brick Lane. Alex had been doing a bit of bargain hunting and entered the Stick of Rock laden down with bags. He also had with him an attractive young lady who I would never see again; this would be a thing that would be repeated with great regularity in the time I knew Alex. He would introduce me to his companion and that would be the last time you'd see her. I would eventually find out the reason why, but that was many years in the future.

After ordering a drink Alex enquired as to what type of bands we put on. He was told that it was exclusively Rock bands and he said that that was a pity as he was representing a gay dance/trance singer who he was booking gigs for. I told him that this was not the venue for him, his client would probably not leave the building alive. It had nothing to do with his sexuality, after all we all loved Queen and Judas Priest – even though Rob Halford had not 'come out' at that time, nobody was in any doubt as to his preferences, the leather cap and bull whip were a bit of a giveaway – it was just that dance music was despised by all who frequented the Stick.

Finding out that Alex was involved in the music business pricked my curiosity. I told him that I was in a band and asked if he would like a copy of our latest demo, which featured, 'I'm Making a Living out of Loving You' and 'Heartbreak City'. He said he would love to hear it, then put it in his pocket. He went on to tell me that he was Paul Weller's accountant. I was not a massive fan of the ex-Jam man's music, I'm still not, but he was a big name and association with him couldn't hurt in our attempts at superstardom. So I told Alex that I had all Mr Weller's records, which was a total lie. Anyway he finished his drink and bid me a fond farewell. As I watched him go I had a feeling that I would never see him, again, he was probably another one of those bullshitters who were all too common in the music business.

About fifteen minutes after he walked out of the Stick, Alex returned with a big grin on his face. 'I want to manage your band,' he announced. 'The songs are absolutely brilliant,' he went on. To say I was taken aback would be an understatement. Apparently he had put the tape on as he was driving home and after it was finished he just had to turn the car around and come back to the bar, to offer his services. I explained that I would have to speak to the rest of the band and arrange a meeting with him. 'As soon as possible,' he said and he was off again, leaving me his business card.

The boys in the band couldn't believe what I was telling them. Things like this just didn't happen to us. The music biz people had thus far ignored us, we just weren't trendy. A meeting was conducted with Alex, we were promised the earth, and he became the first and last manager of Nellie Dean.

One of the first things we told our new manager was that we needed a piece of vinyl out. He arranged for us to get recording time at Soho Studios, situated on Wardour Street, incidentally just around the corner from the bar that gave us our name, the best pub in London, the Nellie Dean. In retrospect the bar may have been just a little too close as the temptation to down tools and a few pints was way too much for a load of young men with thirsts that could cast shadows. With studio time costing £100 per hour Alex encountered his first taste of us wasting money; he should've bailed out there and then. However he didn't and the resulting piece of plastic was the very expensive 'Is this Face Free?' EP.

We took the whole recording process so seriously that we invited about twenty of our closest friends to sing backing vocals on 'Holding Out for the Night Time.' Those asked along included Inky, Steve Bruce, Pete Franklin (from Chariot), Colin Bow and Lee Powis. Only Pete and Lee could actually sing but it was a great laugh, which maybe hinted at one of the reasons why we were never taken that seriously in the music business – we never took anything that seriously ourselves.

Our next chore for Alex was to sack Noel. Even though he had played really well on the EP, he and Ken just were not gelling, especially after the Irish tour where Ken had nearly got us all shot. We were too cowardly to do the dirty deed ourselves. Alex phoned Noel and gave him the news. Noel took it with great grace, saying that if he ever saw any of us again he would 'fucking kill us'. The threat of murder meant that when Noel came to the Stick to pick up his gear I would have to face his wrath. I had asked Ken to be there as back-up; he had told me that he was having a pedicure. 'Likely story,' I thought – he didn't even have a cat.

Noel arrived with a friend, which didn't bode well. He didn't even say hello as he aggressively pushed open the door. After getting his stuff from the cellar he went into an absolute humdinger of a rant demanding to be told what he had done to be kicked out of our 'shitty wee band'. I was not going to have the boys spoken about like that. I didn't care if he was fit to be tied and his mate was looking for a fight, the Nellies were my life. I looked him in the eye and mustered up all my courage and heard myself say, 'Ken didn't want you in the band, it was all his fault. I fought your corner but I was outnumbered.'

One of the bands that played at the Stick had a very good-looking rhythm guitarist. I did the decent thing and stole him to take Noel's place. Dave Bigwood could handle enough lead work to play harmony lead breaks without posing too much of a threat to Ken. He could also sing great backing vocals, which would save us from Ken and Xan's attempts, which were bordering on the excruciating. Dave would be perfect, we thought. He then went and broke his arm by falling off a motorbike, necessitating him doing the first few gigs of his Nellie Dean career standing at the side of the stage singing only backing vocals.

It was every Rock band's dream to get a write-up or review in *Kerrang!* magazine. So it was with bated breath that we awaited the review of the EP. I had every single copy of the magazine since the very first one with Angus Young on the cover. As a kid in Holywood it was not that easy to get a copy – the local newsagents didn't really have an eclectic mix of literature; the closest thing to a Heavy Metal publication they got was *Farrier's Monthly*. I would have to catch the bus into Belfast City centre when it was the issue date and hope that there had been no delay on the ferries or I would be returning home empty-handed. *Kerrang!* became my bible. I would read it from cover to cover numerous times and then cut out selected photos to stick on my bedroom wall. I always dreamed of the day that I would appear in its hallowed pages.

The singles at the time were reviewed by quest rock stars: one week it would be the likes of Steven Tyler, the next it would be Sammy Hagar. The week that we were to be assessed it was a guy called Larry Millar, a milkman from New York who played guitar in a garage Metal band called Uncle Sam.

The lead-off track, 'Holding Out for the Night Time', was picked because we thought it highlighted our strengths, good melodies, twin lead guitars, catchy chorus and great pace. We were proud of this song and it was a live favourite, the crowd would sing along with every word. Really it should've been a cert for a good review.

My hands were shaking slightly as I flicked through the pages to get to the singles reviews. Larry Millar was pictured holding up a selection of the records for his critical analysis. I had never heard of his band before so I couldn't hazard a guess as to what he would write. My eyes scanned past the other singles until there it was: 'Is this Face Free?' EP by Nellie Dean.

The review was only one line long but it was an in-depth synopsis of all the hard work and effort we had put into it. It read, 'What the fuck is he so happy about?' That's all, nothing else just, 'What the fuck is he so happy about?' If I could've gotten my hands on Larry Millar, the Heavy Metal milkman, I would've stuck a bottle of gold top in one of his deaf ear holes, the cheeky bastard.

Shortly after the demolition job in *Kerrang!*, it became obvious that the number of gigs I was doing and the fact that Adele had very successfully completed her degree and got a high-powered job for a company called Yugo Tours, meant that neither of us could dedicate the time necessary to help Steve run the Stick of Rock properly. Business had not been great for a while and I think that Steve was only too glad to hear that we would have to move on – he was probably ready to ask us to leave anyway to save on our wages. It was one of the saddest days of my life when I pulled the door behind me for the last time on the mighty Stick.

In the street Adele, Xan and Beckly sat in a van. We had decided that it would be a great idea to move in together. All our possessions sat in the back ready to be transported to a house we had the keys to in Hounslow. Inky was also in the back after offering his services to help in the move. Again I couldn't help but think how understanding his wife was – it would take all weekend to carry out the move – and numerous pints of cider, of course. Two days later Inky returned to the marital home which was now empty of all furniture; his wife of many years had not had the patience or faithfulness we thought she had. She had taken advantage of his absence and had left him for another man. At least Inky still had the hire purchase repayments for all the electrical appliances, without actually having the appliances, and a blocked kitchen sink, which meant he had to do the dishes in the bath, but not always while he was in it I must point out.

Screaming for vengeance

I was chuffed as hell to be considered Conor's godfather, which seems an odd paradox for an atheist, but I believe it to be a title, not a religious requirement. Anyway today I'm proud to say that Conor is a fine talented good-looking young man and he himself has no religious beliefs. I can't take any credit for this as unfortunately I saw so little of him while he was growing up, but I do love the idea of my godson not believing in God. The role however did bring certain responsibilities, one of which was to babysit on the odd occasion. He was a great kid so it was not much of a chore really.

Conor and myself got on famously, he even had a pet name for me, he called me Uncle Lemon Lemon P. Shall I explain? This could be a tricky one, but I will try. He could never really pronounce my name properly, with it coming out as Uncle Lemon, which was fine. However when he was learning the alphabet he would try to say it as quick as possible, which meant that the letters LMNOP ran into each other making it sound like Lemon Lemon P. This used to make him laugh hysterically, and for a short while everybody else as well. Unfortunately for me it just stuck.

This was only one of the thoroughly cute things Conor did, in fact there are too many to list, but one I will mention was that like most kids he became very attached to his blanket. He would sit watching TV with it against his cheek, gently rubbing the label between his forefinger and thumb. It was very adorable but we were all a bit concerned that he would have to stop this practice before he started school, which at that time, was only a few months away. I pitied his mum and dad as this was going to be an exorcism of Linda Blair proportions.

When Conor was about four Ken and Elaine had decided that they would like a romantic weekend. This created one of those opportunities when I would have to take up some of my responsibilities and babysit. Conor was taken by tube all the way across London from Loughton to the Hounslow Hound Pound, as it became known. Ken and the wee lad arrived at the arranged time; in fact I think they were early which was a first as far as Ken was concerned. I invited Dad in for a drink which, to my amazement, he refused, saying he was going to rush on as he wanted to make the most of the weekend.

From the doorstep Ken handed me over Conor and dropped his bag of necessities at my feet. He said that everything that the wee buck needed for the weekend was in there and off he went. I closed the door and realised that the trip across London had been a little too long for the small developing bowel of a toddler. My first job of Conor's visit was to scoop poo out of his underpants.

I prepared myself for a couple of days raking around with someone of my own mental age. Adele, who loved kids, was overjoyed with the opportunity to play mum for a while, so all in all it promised to be a lovely time. Which it was, that is, up until it was time for bed. To our horror we searched the baby bag and found that there was no blanket. I said to Adele, 'Don't worry, he'll probably not notice it missing, what with him being in a strange environment and all that.' Could I have been any more wrong?

We put his jim-jams on, popped him into our bed, pillows tucked in on both sides to stop him rolling out, and gave him a kiss goodnight.

'Where's my blankey?' he asked.

'Your Dad forgot to leave it with us, but don't worry it will be at home for you when you return,' I reasoned with the child. He responded by screaming his feckin' head off.

The wailing went on and on, and nothing we could do could distract or comfort the wee man. It was the sort of hysterical fit that kids have, you know the ones, where their breathing stops, they turn purple, they have a silent open mouth, it seems to last for hours, you will them to breathe and when at long last the gasp finally comes, it is followed by renewed howling, making you long for the silence again. This was not a pleasant way to end the evening, I can tell you that for nothing. Everyone in the house was demented; nerves were being shattered by the experience.

I decided that enough was enough; the kid was panic-stricken, as were we all. I would just have to disturb the two lovebirds and ask them for advice. Ken answered the phone; when he heard the shrieking in the background he started laughing.

When he had settled down he said, 'He's realised he doesn't have his blanket then?'

I said, 'How did you know that?' beginning to put two and two together.

'You didn't expect us to go through cold turkey with him did you?' the baby's loving father asked, laughing again.

'You bastard,' I said, 'he's going ballistic here and there's nothing we can do for him.'

'I know,' said Ken, 'we tried him without it for ten minutes one night and had to give up the screaming was that bad.'

I then asked, in desperation, 'Is there anything you can suggest we do?'

Ken thought for a moment and then said 'Yes there is.'

'Thank Christ,' I thought.

'Get some earplugs,' came the suggestion through gales of laughter, then Ken hung up.

When I told Xan, Brendan and Adele of the ruse that had been played upon us, the air was filled with expletives, the like of which, I thought, a child of Conor's tender age shouldn't have been subjected to. I then decided that with the racket he was making he couldn't hear it anyway, so I joined my housemates in the barrage of foul language and the cursing of one Kenneth Heaven.

We all tried to deal with the situation in different ways. Brendan cracked open a bottle of whiskey and gently eased his senses into a coma. Adele tried to comfort Conor by rocking him back and forward on her knee. I hid in the toilet for periods, pretending I had the runs, but was really doing a bit of rocking back and forward of my own with my hands over my ears and humming to try to block out the noise. Xan, however, being a very practical sort, thought of a solution.

The big lad had a jumper which was his pride and joy, It was one of those long baggy affairs that the punks were fond of, you know the ones, full of holes. He decided that needs must, so he offered it up for the survival of our collective sanities. A pair of scissors were taken to his beloved garment, in an attempt to make it resemble a blankey.

We all held our breaths, except for Brendan that is, who was now blissfully unconscious, as the butchered jumper was presented to the child. The crying stopped, he looked at it, sniffed it and then held it to his cheek. For a split second it looked like it was going to work, and then the squealing erupted again, this time with renewed vigour – the minute's rest obviously must've done Conor the world of good. He drew back his arm and flung the rag, with all the force of an NFL quarterback, hitting Big Xan square in the face. We all looked at each other in despair, and then hunted for the remains of Brendan's bottle of whiskey.

The crying eventually stopped at about six o'clock the next morning when exhaustion finally set in. We slept while Conor slept and when we awoke, Adele, Xan and myself looked like death warmed up. Brendan and Conor, on the other hand, looked like they had enjoyed the sleep of the innocent, which, when you think about it, they had. The next night started out much the same but the crying ended quicker, much to everyone's relief.

When Ken came to collect his son and heir on the Monday morning his welcome was as frosty as a snowman's Royal Alberts. He thanked us for our contribution to the development of his offspring. He was told to 'feck away off'. Conor never needed his blanket again, which was a good thing. Xan would mourn the loss of his jumper for many years to come. Adele would reconsider her love of children but only for a short while. Brendan became dependent on Jameson's to get him off to sleep and I vowed never to have kids. All in all it was a weekend's work of mental torture and anguish that Conor Francis Heaven's parents should be proud of.

The final straw

Adele had finally had enough. I just couldn't wise up, it was part of my makeup. I knew I needed to grow up, I just didn't know how to or want to. I also knew the consequences. The final, final straw came following a gig we did in the Esplanade, Southend. It was a place we had played many times, however this time there was a change with the PA. The guys doing the sound had placed massive bass bin speakers on picnic-style tables at each side of the stage. The gig went very well and as we were doing our encore 'Nellie Dean', I hammed it up, jumping onto one of the tables, which promptly collapsed.

The stupidest thing I could've done was to try to catch the speaker, which took three people to get up there in the first place;

this is, of course, what I tried. I dislocated two fingers, removed half of my right eyebrow and rendered myself unconscious. The fifteen-stone cabinet hit me square on the head as it made its way to the floor.

The blackout must've only lasted a few seconds because when I came round Ken was playing the lead break to the same song. Inky helped pull the ton weight off my legs and I climbed back up on the stage not really knowing what had happened or what was going on. I did realise, however, that I was sweating quite badly; I could feel the perspiration running down my face. I turned to Big Xan, who looked at me in horror and kept pointing at my mug.

I carried on singing the song and as it came to a conclusion I noticed that the white Elvis T-shirt I was wearing was slowly turning crimson. At first I thought it was an effect of the lights. Then I realised that I wasn't perspiring but bleeding quite profusely from the wound where my eyebrow had been. We finished the song and the crowd went crazy, some of them thinking that the injury was deliberate and that the trashing of the gear was a part of the show. We left the stage to frenzied cheering and applause. I then knew how the bruised and battered victorious prizefighter must feel, agony and elation at the same time.

The changing room, as was the norm at these sort of gigs, wasn't a changing room at all but the kitchen; at least it was not the toilets, which was quite common. JJ grabbed a tea towel that was stained and still slightly damp and he applied pressure to the wound to stem the flow of blood. God knows what the rag had been used for but the bacteria living on it, *salmonella*, *listeria*, *campylobacter*, must've been leaping on their little microscopic legs with glee at the new source of nourishment they had found, namely my bloodstream.

After a while, with a bacteraemia underway, the bleeding stopped and a wad of toilet paper and gaffa tape were applied. Directions were found to the nearest A&E dept. I had been drinking and of course wouldn't hear of visiting the hospital. The alcohol helped in its own welcome way, it dulled the screaming pain when I put my gnarled fingers back into place. This attempt at a DIY medical procedure made me feel a wee bit sick. The nausea along with the blood loss gave me the healthy pallor of a corpse. 'Can I go home?' I asked.

As we left in the van one of the sound engineers waved us to stop.

He handed me, through the window, what I thought was a small caterpillar. I soon realised that it wasn't the early developmental stage of a beautiful butterfly but was, in fact, the bit of my eyebrow that had stuck to the totally intact bass bin. Very kind of him I'm sure but I didn't know what I was supposed to do with it. Maybe he thought I was one of those Christians that believe that if you have a piece of your body removed it has to have a proper burial or you would wander through the afterlife without the missing appendage. I couldn't see myself laying to rest the shrivelled-up piece of flesh and hair, not from an atheistic or cosmetic perspective but from a practical one: where would I get a coffin small enough? Anyway, whatever his reasons, the appearance of the bloody little mess resting in my hands did nothing for my already fragile state.

I don't know if I drifted in and out of consciousness or sleep but the next thing I knew I was outside our house in Hounslow. Adele was fast asleep; so still quite delirious I climbed into bed beside her. I was woken by frantic shaking and the shouts of 'Are you alive?!'

I opened my eyes, or should I say I tried to. The make-shift bandage had dislodged and the wound had reopened, the blood congealing to stick my eyelids together. With one of my senses taken out of the equation I was quite literally groping in the dark for some rationality. 'I'm OK, I'm OK!' I shouted as I picked at my superglued eyelashes. When I was finally able to see it became clear that, coming from the background of the Troubles, it must've looked like I had been shot in my sleep, as was the barbaric fashion of the times. The pillows were covered in blood, my face and blond hair were now black.

Not a pretty scene to wake up to. There were also a few other things Adele was waking up to. One, I was not going to wise up any time soon. Two, I was not going to settle down any time soon, and three, she deserved a quality life sometime soon. What she didn't need was a life filled with the excitement of being shackled to a nutcase. Shortly after this event, she moved back to battle-scarred Belfast, to a better life. Who could blame her, she had put up with a lot, and it was probably safer there than with me and my little adventures.

City slickers

Inky and myself were single and getting over the break-up of a long-term marriage and a long-term relationship respectively. We were offered the opportunity to travel somewhere into the stockbroker belt to attend a gig by the new partner of the beautiful Asian girl Jay, who had been at the Stones gig where Inky had tried to spoil the day by dying. The guy she had been with that day, Chris, had been dropped and she was now going out with a Dublin-born guitar player.

We travelled in the back of the band's van and had a few drinks along the way. What we also had was a plan to introduce the local-wealthy tottie to a little bit of Rock and Roll cockney and Irish rough. To accomplish our mission we were dressed in our Metal finery. This included me wearing a pair of the tightest white jeans known to man. They were so snug that I would remove a large amount of my leg hair in the act of pulling them on. If I were lucky enough to be in the company of somebody else when I took them off, I would have to refrain from shaking them out. The mood could quite easily be spoilt trying to clear the air of small suspicious-looking short curly hairs; casting is not the most romantic thing you will ever do.

When we arrived I remember helping the band in with some of their gear and being surprised that they were playing in a church hall. I couldn't help but feel a little smug knowing that I was above all this, having sold out the Stick of Rock on many occasions and headlined the Marquee a few times. I was a rock star compared to these bozos; they were probably going to have to play their set between the tombola and the whist drive. I am surprised I could get my head through the ornate, slightly Masonic-looking front door.

After the sound check we went, with the band, to an off-licence and purchased some refreshments, which we consumed in a field that was adjacent to the hall. I stood for the duration; I didn't want to spoil my chances by getting grass stains on my pristine strides. The conversation was enlightening. The band, apart from Jay's boyfriend, were all from wealthy backgrounds and they talked about the jobs they were expecting to do after 'uni' – that is, of course, if they didn't make it in the music business. Success however was a very real possibility; their daddies didn't mind indulging them in their little hobby by buying them the best of gear and financing studio time. La dee fecking da.

Inky, a dyed-in-the-wool socialist, and I laughed at the absurdity of the paradox between the situations of this band and our own; we both wanted to make it but I think our want was actually closer to a need. Desperation is no guarantee of success of course. They would aspire to be the 'public school boy' Genesis: if it didn't happen so what? We were in danger of becoming 'borstal boys' Rose Tattoo: low down, dirty, honest, hard working/drinking and ultimately broke, never to have a mansion in the South of France, never to be something in the City. Don't get me wrong, as much as I like Genesis (the stuff before the 'I Can't Dance' rubbish), I know who is the real deal when it comes to Rock and Roll.

The band was actually very good, their musicianship was excellent, but I can't remember a single song. As they played we circled the throng who had given up an evening at the polo club to be deafened by these 'punk rockers with their long hair'. The women had that beauty that was the ease of the terminally rich, you know the type: toothy, clean, manicured, and made up to within an inch of their lives. We couldn't fail but touch.

The alcoholic refreshments seemed to be supplied by the local Women's Institute. As well as the choice of Carlsberg lager, Guinness and Strongbow cider on draft I was fully expecting to see a variety of dandelion wines and home-made preserves. The bar was a fold-away table that looked more like something that you would paste wallpaper on. As I approached it I noticed a rather attractive young debutante. She was looking a little bored so I decided that once I had purchased our thirst quenchers I would brighten up her day, with some slurred speech. With a pint of Guinness in a plastic glass (sacrilege) in my hand and with Inky cuddling a pint of Strongbow with ice, I introduced myself to the well-to-do beauty.

She seemed a little aghast that a drunken man, dressed as a woman and speaking in a foreign tongue, was trying to converse with her. She must've thought I was one of them there immigrant types, the ones she had read about in Daddy's *Times*. When I told her I was Irish I could see her look me up and down, from head to toe, like an airport scanner trying to detect a bomb. I was not to be put off, I wasn't some Mick just of the boat, I was a sophisticated gentleman rock star about town. I tried to show her that I was relaxed in my new surrounds by nonchalantly leaning back onto the bar.

It didn't even hold my weight for a second, collapsing immediately, causing me to drop to the floor in front of her. As I hit the ground I crushed my glass, sending a geyser of Guinness into the air. It held, as if in slow motion, for a moment, before descending straight onto my pearl-white jeans.

What happened next is the absolute truth. I lay in a sopping mess with Inky nearly wetting himself laughing. As he was pointing at me a wasp flew out of nowhere and stung him on his extended digit. He then proceeded to jump up and down, trying not to spill his drink, his already swelling finger tucked between his legs. Having not seen the offending insect most people thought he was gleefully rubbing his genitals while performing some sort of perverse dance, his grimace of pain easily being mistaken for ecstasy. The blue rinse barmaids were flapping about appalled with what had just happened and what they were now witnessing.

It took all our powers of persuasion to convince them that I hadn't wrecked the bar deliberately and that Inky was not pleasuring himself, but trying to ease the throbbing pain. We spent the rest of the evening watching the band from the back of the hall. I looked like I had been doubly incontinent; Inky stood with his finger in the air as if pointing up to heaven, with one of those ice cubes that looks like a glass thimble on the end of it. We didn't touch for any wealthy tottie.

Dragged out by the Trossachs

To promote the 'Is this Face Free?' EP we embarked on a tour of Scotland called 'Rock you by the Trossachs'. One of the gigs was in the picturesque little town of Troon. We had decided to get a bed and breakfast for that night and the next night, when we were playing close by, in a bar called Robbie's in the town of Ayr. When we arrived at the accommodation the owner looked a little concerned by the appearance of his new guests. At this stage of the tour we were looking rougher than we usually did, which was to be honest kinda rough anyway.

I must admit that I can't remember much about the gig in question, which probably means that there were very few people there or we probably didn't go down that well. I only really remember the good ones or the ones where something out of the ordinary happens, like losing an eyebrow or nearly having my genitals blown off. But I do remember what happened after this gig because there were, indeed, events that were out of the ordinary even for us.

Before we returned to the B&B, we decided to sample the local culinary delights of the region by visiting a fast food takeaway. I fancied a little Italian cuisine. After placing my order, I was presented with a deep-fried pizza, I kid you not folks. If you ever decide to commit suicide by rapidly furring up your arteries, here is the recipe for this wonderful gastronomic experience.

1. Take a frozen mushroom and ham pizza; ensuring to leave the plastic type-wrapper on it.
2. Drop it into roasting, hot, bubbling lard; let it fry for about 2 minutes, or until it floats to the surface like a shopping bag discarded in the village pond by the local glue sniffer.
3. When truly done, retrieve the soggy mess with a scoop. Carefully open one end of the packaging, empty the contents from the melting plastic on to a bed of chips, making sure to leave half the cheese and toppings stuck to the still-sizzling container.
4. Consume with a can of chilled to perfection Tennent's Super, or if you have to drive in the next week or so, a bottle of Irn Bru should suffice.

And why not, if you can handle anything more after this sound kicking of your gastrointestinal tract, round the whole meal off with a deep-fried Mars Bar, which was also on the board of fare at Cafè Coronary By-Pass.

It was the early hours of the morning when we finally returned to our digs and we carried on as if the gig was still going on, that is we were loud and drunken. At this juncture I must point out that, in retrospect, I feel sorry for JJ. As a non-drinker it must have been like hell on earth sometimes, especially when he was tired, needing to rest and we were only warming up. We found the need for sleep a requirement that could wait till the next morning. I think now I would be more considerate, maybe that's old age, but then I couldn't really have given a flying fart, we lived for the day and would deal with the hangover when it inevitably came.

The party raged on till the dawn, I think we may have invited a few punters from the gig along, who weren't paying guests at the accommodation, to help us welcome in the new day. To his credit, patience or maybe it was just cold-blooded fear the landlord didn't throw us out, which he was quite within his rights to do, and the next morning we were still residents.

We couldn't afford the breakfast part of bed and breakfast; all we had for sustenance was tea and coffee, the hot water being supplied by a small kettle that sat on a little table in the hall. We were to take turns in the communal bathroom. Some and not others used the shower, but to save blushes I won't name names. When it was my turn I did shower, honest. After drying myself with a towel that was still damp and had not really had the chance to dry in the last week, I commenced the brushing of my teeth.

A frantic banging on the door and the screaming voice of Beckly stopped my oral hygiene in its tracks. He was shouting that if he didn't get in right away there was good chance that he was going to pebble dash his under garments. Knowing that I was going to have to share the same van as him for the next few hours I opened the door to ensure that I and the other artistes wouldn't have to make the journey with our heads out the window.

Beckly was, in fact, one of the ones who wouldn't have availed of the showering facilities; therefore the chance to eliminate the added odour of a bowel mishap was something, if you'll pardon the pun, not to be sniffed at. He rushed in, I rushed out, still brushing my teeth, I didn't want to be privy to the gruntings and strainings that were sure to follow. I too didn't want to lose last night's sumptuous meal from an altogether different orifice.

I left the smallest room in the house, still scrubbing my gnashers. Beckly spent more time practising his abolitions than I had antici-pated and as the time went on the amount of toothpaste in my mouth gradually got to the point that I looked like I was foaming like a rabid dog. It was also making me gag. In a bit of a panic I looked around for something in which to deposit the mass of spearmint foam. Sitting on the low windowsill at the front door was a large yucca plant. Desperation caused me to spit the contents of my mouth onto the soil of the pot.

JJ was mortified, not only because it was a disgusting thing to do but also because it was visibly obvious, to any of the other guests who came into the hall, that something horrible had occurred with the hapless cactus and the finger of blame could only really point in one direction – and that, I'm afraid, was at us. He decided that action needed to be taken to prevent an ugly scene occurring, but with him being a drummer sometimes logic took second place to action. He lifted the kettle and poured the contents onto the foam in an attempt to dissolve it. Unfortunately it had just been boiled; he was successful in dispersing the white gunk, but the plant pot now looked like someone had peed in it and of course this was the moment that the landlord entered the hall. His eyes were immediately drawn to the billowing steam that was emanating from his rapidly dying desert flora; he was also aware that our drummer was standing with his back to him, peering in slightly puzzled by his handiwork.

Turning round, JJ's eyes met with the horrified gaze of a man at the end of his tether. Realising that it looked like he had just urinated in the hall, JJ tried to explain himself. 'It's not what you think,' he said. 'I've just poured the kettle into it,' he went on. The landlord looked appalled. Was this mad Irishman admitting to him that he had poured boiling water over a defenceless plant? Blowing up buildings and shooting people was not enough, now they were taking the war to the heart of British society by attacking their love of all things horticultural. JJ, sensing that his explanation didn't have the desired effect, mumbled something about not trying to hurt the plant; he was, instead trying to wash away the toothpaste. The landlord couldn't believe his ears: was this guy on mind-bending drugs or something? Did he think that the plant was from the 'little shop of horrors' and needed its teeth cleaned? Enough was enough; he just turned and walked away, not saying a word.

The rooms had to be empty by 1pm so that cleaning could take place. We had decided to leave our bags, go and do the next gig and return for a night's sleep afterwards. At least that was the plan; the landlord had other ideas. As we were packing the van he came running out and said the rooms had been, mysteriously, double booked and that he would have to ask us to leave. We had been thrown out of another B&B and another night sleeping in the van with all the smells that six heathens could muster up, lay in front of us. This time, however, it was the only teetotal member of the band who had caused it, or at least that is what we were going to let him believe for as long as we could get away with it.

The accommodation that we had just been bucked out of faced the Town Hall, which, if memory serves, backed onto the seafront and was situated in the middle of a green. Our van was parked right up against one of its walls. Dave Bigwood, who had not availed of the bathroom before we were thrown out, decided he was going to use it as a toilet in broad daylight. Xan was not amused and even less so when, just as our rhythm guitarist had finished, a police car pulled up.

Two cops got out and put their hats on, which, I was once told, usually means official business. We all feared for the worst and we frankly didn't have a legal leg to stand on, or a pot to piss in.

'You boys aren't from around these parts?' one of Ayrshire's finest asked.

'No,' someone muttered, 'we're from London.'

'Were you here last night around 10pm?' was the next enquire.

'Yeah, but we were on stage at that time,' I said.

The cop then told us that there had been a stabbing outside a fish and chip shop (thankfully not the same health hazard we had frequented) and the guy they thought had done it had long hair. They then asked us if we would like to help by taking part in an identity parade.

Ken asked, 'How much?'

The cop said, '£15 each,' and we said, 'Too right.' Thirst and hunger can make you do funny things you know.

Only five of us were required so myself, Ken, Xan, Paul Taylor and Dave were elected as we had the longest hair, which seemed to be an important part of the investigations. We were shown into a room that had a mirror running the full length of one of the walls, which we were to face. We were also told to say nothing and to follow any instructions that came from behind the reflective glass. A door opened at the side of the room and a guy was brought in. He had a big thick woolly jumper on, dirty jeans, work boots and hair that barely touched his collar. He looked like he had just stepped off a trawler, which he probably had, and we looked like we were ready to go on stage, which we really were.

A voice came from the distance and said, 'Can you face the glass Mr Dick?' In the reflection I could see everybody looking at each other with suppressed laughter. Did they really call him Mr Dick? I didn't know at the time but apparently it is a fairly common name north of Hadrian's Wall. In fact Fish, the ex-Marillion man, is called Derek Dick. Nevertheless it was worth a chuckle at the expense of a guy who it looked like was being done up like one of the kippers he normally caught.

We were told that we must keep our faces straight or we wouldn't get paid; this took the nonsense right out of us. A voice from behind the screens then said that we might be asked to turn to the side and that we should do this on the command of an anonymous person. A lady's voice then asked the suspect to turn to the right, addressing him by the unique number which lay at his feet. Another lady did the same thing and then a man's voice did the same thing again. The witnesses were then asked by one of the cops to pick who they thought was the person who wielded the knife and they all said number 4. I could see all our gazes look to the reflection at the reversed numbers on the ground. There was a collective gasp as we realised that everyone had picked Paul Taylor: probably the full-sleeve tattoos on both arms and the gold front tooth didn't help. Paul looked genuinely surprised and a little worried.

Mr Dick was led away and we were asked to go into an office. Paul thought he was going to be arrested but it was soon explained that the trawlerman was a well-known hood in the town and that the cops were not surprised that the locals hadn't wanted to risk a stabbing of their own by picking him. We collected our thirty pieces of silver and got out of Troon ASAP before we could be involved in any further incidents.

The tour was sponsored by Tennent's lager. A dangerous combination really, Nellie Dean being endorsed by a brewery, and this was to be proven on many occasions, including the next gig in Ayr where afterwards, as was our wont and duty, we had a few beverages to lubricate tired throats with the bar manager, who seemed a little worse for wear even before we started our after-hours lock-in. The bar actually appears in one of our videos and features us drinking champagne in celebration of Dave's birthday. Anyway, as the night wore on our drunken host asked us where we were staying the night. With money being tight and having being thrown out of our B&B we told him we were going to sleep in the van. 'Nonsense,' he slurred 'there is accommodation above the very bar where we are standing.' He knew for a fact, even though he only managed the bar side of the business, that there was a four-bedded room available. With his hand on his heart and tear in his eye he announced that it would be an honour and a privilege to have a fine body of minstrel drunks like ourselves stay on the premises.

There were, however, two problems that we were made aware of before we made our decision to take up the kind offer. One, the land-lady must never know we stayed there, we must be up and away by the time she raised her curler-ensconced noggin from her pillow. And two, there were eight of us for the four beds. Thank God for the sweet delusional fog that copious amounts of alcohol brings, because en masse our collective brains weighed up the problems and came to the decision that there were no problems.

The now staggering manager led us to a side door that opened to a set of stairs. In we trooped, doing a 'follow my leader' up and down numerous stairs and landings and round many corners. We kept the silence as only nine paralytic, half deaf morons can. How the landlady wasn't woken by the stumbling, laughing, farting and general mayhem is beyond me but awake, she didn't. Eventually we found ourselves at the door of our place of recuperation. The bar manager bid us a fond farewell, put his finger to his lips, made a shooshing sound and promptly fell backwards down the stairs into the dark and out of sight forever.

It was a tiny very old-fashioned room with a wash hand basin in the corner. Like church mice, quietly we entered and then loudly started a fight over who would get the beds. Rank was pulled and it was decided that the musicians would have the beds and the road crew would sleep on the floor. Ahh! I hear you say, were there not five members in Nellie Dean? Yes indeed there were and as we all know five into four does not go. There was no way that two of us would bunk up, heaven forbid that two heterosexual Metal Gods share the same bed no matter how tired and emotional they are (sorry Mr Halford). So being the illustrious singer and leader of the band rank was pulled again and it was decided that I would join the road crew on the floor.

I was beyond caring where I laid my head at this point; exhaustion had set in and I would've slept on the crawling coat of a Charing Cross Station homeless person. I stripped off, pulled a hearth rug over me and awaited the land of nod to come over the horizon. Then it started: that dull ache in the bladder, not painful but enough to wave nod away. I thought, I'll ignore it and it will pass, but in my heart of hearts I knew that that wonderful amber friend I had partied with for all those hours before had decided that the night was young and he wanted to renew our acquaintance. Did I see a toilet on the way up the stairs? I just couldn't recall, and even if I had I would've had to get dressed again and that would eat into sleepy time so I decided to avail of what facilities were on hand.

The room was now in total darkness but I knew roughly where the position of the sink was so clothes were not a necessity. I made my way gingerly across the floor, praying I wouldn't tread on any of my long-time comrades for fear that they would think that in my undressed state I was in need of a little love cuddle. I made it safely to my destination and in the short space of time between realising that I needed the toilet and my arrival at the sink the dull ache had turned into a screaming pain that had me nearly bent double. I got myself into position, but being hunched over I unsuccessfully tried to empty my football-sized bladder. I mustered up all my strength and straightened up just enough to relieve myself. Thank the Baby Jesus the elimination began and the waves of relief flooded over me like the rains on the drought-devastated Savannah.

My bliss was short lived. The landlady must have woken up and decided to investigate the nocturnal clatter that had eventually dragged her from her unconscious state. As I was peeing in the sink the door opened and a shaft of light moved slowly across the room resting on my naked pert, in my opinion and it is my story, buttocks. In a panic I heard the words 'Do you mind?' tumble from my lips and I then heard the startled response from our hostess. In a delightful Scottish lilt she said, 'Sorry hen.' I didn't know whether to take the fact that she thought that I was a woman as a compliment or a slight. If it was the slender figure, long luxuriant hair or the tight buttocks then fine, but if it was the glimpse of my front view in the mirror she was referring to, then holy shit that was an ego deflator if there ever was one. The door gently closed to the sound of suppressed hysterical laughter from those that were still awake.

Daylight brought with it the realisation that we had to vacate the premises before the Peeping Tom landlady returned. Unfortunately no one could remember the way out of the labyrinth-style premises, not even teetotal JJ. It was an almost 'Hello Cleveland'-style scenario as we passed the room we had vacated many minutes earlier.

Eventually we arrived at the side door where the adventure had begun those oh so few hours ago. We were like children coming to the exit of a stately home maze, thankful to be there but still giddy with the excitement of the ordeal. Outside we tumbled and ran to the parked van, we all piled in and Paul hastily started the engine to make good our escape. But as we moved off, out of the back windscreen came the sight of the diminutive figure of the landlady waving what looked like the bill in her hand.

Like schoolchildren we shouted with glee as we took off. Ha ha, I thought, we had made it. A free night sleeping on a cold floor with a dirty old rug for comfort had been gained for nothing. We rounded the corner and our cheers suddenly stopped as concrete bollards in the middle of the road confronted us. The language that filled the air would've made a Belfast Dock worker raise the back of his hand to his forehead and take a deep breath to steady himself lest he should faint. There was only one thing to do – we must reverse in the direction of the advancing old lady who had not given up the chase; she knew fine well that we would be trapped.

And so it happened. We, a hard rockin' bunch of macho men, nearly ran over a pensioner who had to dive out of the way of a two-ton van. All this just to save a few quid. I can feel my cheeks going slightly pink at the thought of it, even after all these years.

In case you are worrying, don't. The octogenarian wasn't badly injured; she was able to jump to her feet and resumed the chase hurling a few obscenities of her own. Thankfully for us her age-gnarled lower limbs couldn't get up to the 40mph required to catch us. The tour could continue.

There was a final twist to this tale. As I mentioned earlier Tennent's Brewery sponsored us, which meant at the end of each gig the promoter of the respective venues presented us with a cheque from them. After we had successfully escaped the clutches of the frail old dear we were discussing the night's adventures when we realised that nobody had picked up the payment due to various levels of intoxication. It suddenly dawned on us that the senior citizen hadn't been chasing us waving a bill but was actually trying to pay us.

The cheques from Tennent's had posed problems from the off. The main reason for this was that we thought we were going to be paid in cash and therefore after the first gig we were broke and unable to finance making it to the next one. The answer was a simple one: we would make Alex drive all the way from London to Glasgow to cash the cheque. False economy or what?

As funny and as stupid as this was, it was nowhere near as hilarious as when Alex arrived, for he had developed mumps on the way up and his neck, or should I say necks, had almost trebled in size. He got out of the car and was bombarded with sympathy as everyone wet themselves laughing and comments like, 'Are you storing nuts for the winter?' abounded. But the frivolity suddenly stopped when I pointed out that mumps was highly contagious and very serious in men in the nether regions area. The swelling we could deal with, but the thought of the excruciating pain and the chances of becoming sterile were too much to comprehend.

Suddenly Alex had outstayed his welcome and we all ran for cover. I made it to the front of the van with Beckly climbing in beside me. It was at this moment that he turned to me – lowering his voice so as to not be overheard and bringing his face close to mine he whispered, 'My throat and neck have been getting sorer over the last couple of days.' I don't know if it was the smell of his 'roll your own' breath or the horrific news that he may be also diseased that caused me to jump across the driver's seat and out the door, but I found myself on the footpath never the less. I stood there for a second wondering if climbing back into the van and strangling Beckly to death would be worth the risk of contracting the nutcracker bug. I came to the conclusion that as pleasurable as delivering physical pain to a close friend would be, my future family was more important and I backed away with a bandana covering my mouth.

We got Alex to pass the money through a hairline crack made by rolling down the car window a fraction. It was so tight he nearly needed to pass it through note by note. It was then announced that Alex would have to drive Beckly back to London with him thus widening the infection control cordon by hundreds of miles. Alex reluctantly agreed and later told me that it was the longest journey of his life; not only was he feeling terrible but, as we already know, Beckly does not shut his mouth. He talked the whole way back in that unintelligible Dublin brogue. Alex went on to say that he would have hated to experience the journey if Beckly hadn't had a sore throat.

Whole lotta Rosie

Seeing as we were a Fionn McCool stone's throw away from Ireland, we booked a gig in the Rosetta Bar, also known as the Rosie, as a means of financial remuneration and because, what the hell, it was always good to get home to see the folks. When we set foot on the hallowed turf of the Emerald Isle it was party time. Well, it would've been had the RUC not taken exception to me writing 'Rock Star' on the security form, where it asked for my occupation.

The document had to be filled in by everyone visiting the North by sea or air. I often wondered how many people wrote the word 'terrorist' when asked what their job was. I mean hundreds of people had been interrogated for days on end, without sleep, at Castlereagh RUC Station without spilling the beans; I really didn't think that the 'Border fox' would fall for this cunning little trap.

My attempt at mirth resulted in the cops taking everything out of the van, including all the musical equipment, and dismantling it. Dave Bigwood considered himself a Rastafarian – being white and English didn't seem to put him off, he even went as far as sporting dreadlocks. For the life of me I don't know why we ever got him in the band. Don't get me wrong, he was a great guy and a good guitar player but he was so out of tune with the rest of us as far as humour etc. was concerned. I think the huge amount of dope he smoked put him on a different plane to us and it was this habit that nearly got us into a serious amount of trouble at the quayside in Belfast.

Dave had been warned to leave his stash at home; Ken and myself knew that the Harbour Police would be waiting for us, and that they would take great delight, as they always did, in searching the long-haired hippies. While our gear was being ransacked I couldn't help but notice that Dave was turning very pale around the gills. I sidled up to him and whispered, 'You haven't any dope on you do you?' He just nodded with a look of absolute panic on his face.

Each of us was frisked one by one. When they got to Dave I held my breath. If he was caught 'smuggling drugs', as it would be viewed, he would be arrested on the spot and the tour would be off. The officer ran his hands across Dave's shoulders, along his arms, down his body, down the outside of his legs and then up the inside. Just as he got to the pocket area of his jeans he hesitated for a second. I felt sick to my stomach. I breathed a sigh of relief and Dave nearly passed out when the cop said, 'All right, you can go now.'

We were left to put the gear back together again and pack it all back into the van. As we drove towards Belfast City Centre I called Dave all the stupid feckers of the day. He just gave me that glazed smile of his and produced a lump of Lebanese Black the size of a chicken's egg; he then proceeded to roll a joint.

'How the feck did he miss that?' I asked.

Dave giggled and said 'I think he thought it was my left nut,' and carried on rolling.

The Rosetta gig was an absolute triumph; Xan even to this day says it was our best ever gig. Being on the road and playing every night meant that we were as tight as underwear after Christmas. I had asked my old mate Stephen Magee to help us out with promoting the gig; he had just set up his own PR Company called Positive Touch. I think he was reluctant to take us on as he was trying to distance himself from the Rock and Roll lifestyle, but he agreed from a business perspective to take on the job. I didn't really have much contact with him apart from phone calls.

One of the first things Magee did was get us sponsorship from a local pizzeria called 'Pizza the Action'. The deal was that they would pay for promotional photos of us to be taken and we would be supplied with all the Italian food we could eat. They in return would be able to put up large advertising banners at the gig promoting their restaurant.

The photo shoot took place in Ormeau Park in Belfast. The photographer was an old friend of ours, Geoff Lennon. He was a super-fit guy and a top tri-athlete who loved his Rock music. Most of his assignments were for the *Belfast Telegraph* and covered all the usual bombings, shootings and knee-cappings as well as local nonsense like whist drives, fun runs and cake sales, so Geoff jumped at the chance to hang out with a few mates and be a Rock snapper for the day.

We had a brilliant time full of craic and slagging. Geoff kept us in check, because he needed to, but he did it so naturally and with good humour that we didn't even notice. The Nellies had Johnny Bramley paint the backs of our leather jackets with the band's logo. The design had a biker-type 'rocker' at the bottom with 'Belfast, London, and Dublin' on it. We were all pretty proud of these and it became a source of amusement as to how we were going to get the artwork into the photographs. They were draped over chairs, hung nonchalantly over shoulders and there were even pictures of us taken from behind with us looking backwards. This last position we thought was cool, but actually made us look like we had neck injuries.

Geoff did a great job and I felt he would have made a brilliant music business photographer. Unfortunately he never got the opportunity – not long after this session Geoff lost his long battle with leukaemia. What a shitty world this is sometimes, a decent guy with a family who caused nobody a button of harm, taken while some of the vilest human beings on the planet waltz through life destroying other people's lives with nothing ever happening to them. The phrase 'just not fair' does not suffice.

The Rosetta had been the scene of many a cracker gig for me, whether it was with No Hot Ashes or with Nellie Dean, but the one we played that night was exceptional. The place went mental and I think the fact that many were in possession of the new EP meant that they were familiar with a lot of the songs. Dave Bigwood had never been in a band that had gone down so well and commented that he actually felt like a rock star. Afterwards the changing room was packed with well-wishers, hangers-on and family members. Magee had organised that we get five fourteen-inch pizzas delivered after we were finished. Right on cue, there was a knock on the door at the back of the room that led to the fire escape and in walked a guy with the grub.

The boxes were thrown open and everyone told to tuck in. With the number of people present there wouldn't be a lot to go around but at least there was something to eat. Just then there was another knock on the door and in walked the delivery guy again with another five pizzas. The more the merrier; there were a lot of hungry mouths to feed. Unfortunately the pizzas just kept on coming: somehow the order had been taken down wrong and fifty pizzas were actually sent.

It worked out that each person there was in possession of two fourteen-inch multi-topped pizzas. There are few people alive who could consume that amount of cheese and dough – even Ken. What ensued was a food fight that nearly got us barred from the venue for life. I didn't realise that melted cheese was that hard to get out of soft furnishings. The next morning Beckly, who had returned to the fold after his neck and testicles had resumed their normal size and colour, both small and black, was distressed to find a mushroom in his underwear. Unfortunately for him it was not the only fungal growth to settle in around those regions that trip.

The tour continued and ended at the Solid Rock Café in Glasgow, where there was a massive bust up between JJ and Ken. Our lead guitarist claimed, after a fight over a rollie, that Beckly was a Bog Man; in fact, he went further saying he was the missing link between man and ape. JJ took exception to his best friend being implicated in Ken's evolutionary theory. I'm afraid I have never heard of a more bizzare way for a band to split up, but that's effectively what happened to that line-up of Nellie Dean.

Nellie Dean Mark 7, would you believe?

Exit JJ, and shortly after that we would be looking for a new guitarist again. Dave had become more and more spiritual and out there; I'm afraid I just can't be having that. When you are invited round to your guitar player's house for his girlfriend to show you your astral charts you know it's time to get yourself out of there. Enter Gary Baker on the drum stool. He was the brother of a business acquaintance of Alex's, and had not played for a few years. We should've known that if Alex was involved that there must be some sort of an angle.

We got our new drummer through a gentleman's agreement that saw Alex getting office space in D&R Autos, a car repairers, conveniently two doors away from his house. We in return took the owner's brother Gary on – who needs auditions anyway? Luckily for us he could thump the tubs as good as anyone once he had got a few rehearsals under his belt. He brought a more aggressive style to the sound; he wasn't better than JJ, he just had a different approach. What he also brought to the band was a friend of his called Clive Hellier who was a great rhythm guitar player and an excellent vocalist. Now that we were back to being a five-piece it was game on again.

Nomis

When Alex found out that I had an ONC in business studies he asked me to work for him at Nomis Studios, the home of the Paul Weller Empire and situated near Earls Court. Most of the time I spent on my own; I would go in after office hours and go through the touring receipts etc. and then fill in the ledgers. When I was required to work normal hours I met loads of celebs including Seal, Roger Taylor, Brian May and of course Paul Weller and his band. I don't think Paul ever really knew what I was doing there, and I don't think he ever asked.

The restaurant at the studio at times was a who's who of the music business. One day when I was queuing up to get a bit of lunch, I got talking to the girl beside me. I casually informed her that I was in the next big Rock band and that she should watch out for our name.

I bummed and blowed for the whole time that we were waiting to get served and as I turned to go to my table I asked, 'What are you up to?'

In lovely Scottish accent she said, 'Ach, I do a wee bit of singing,' and I said 'I must watch out for you.'

When I returned to our table Alex asked, 'What were you and Barbara Dickson talking about?'

I said 'Who?' Alex said, 'That girl you were boring to death is a world-renowned vocalist.'

I said, 'I thought she looked a bit familiar, which band is she in?'
Alex just shook his head and changed the subject.

Later that night I was watching TV in Gary's house, the Des
O'Connor show was on, and there warbling along for all she was
worth, doing something from the West End musical she was in, was
the girl from the queue. She was all right I suppose, but she could've
done with an Eddie Van Halen beside her just to liven things up a bit.

I loved it at Nomis; when you walked in through the front door
there was a Fender shop. I would drool at the Telecasters, Quo's
weapon of choice, hanging in the window. Donal Gallagher, Rory's
brother and manager, had an office in the building and I would often
see the Strat-playing, checked shirt-wearing, genius and one of my
all-time heroes around the place. Sadly he was not in great shape at
the time and to my total regret I never introduced myself. I think I
was star-struck.

The last time I saw Rory was at a special night that was put on by
the Fender shop to celebrate the 40th anniversary of the Telecaster.
The event took place in one of the larger rehearsal rooms that had a
stage. There must have been about thirty people there tops, two of
which were Alex and myself. The special guests were none other than
James Burton, who was playing his world-famous paisley Tele, and
his band. I couldn't believe my luck standing there in the company of
Rory Gallagher with Elvis's guitar player showing off his chops, no
more than ten feet away, it was literally like he was playing in my
front room.

Cliff Richard was also in attendance, standing right beside me. I
am not much of a fan of his, except for 'Devil Woman' of course, but
after we had a good long conversation about the 'King of Rock and
Roll' he went to the complimentary drinks table and the God-
bothering British Elvis returned with a bottle of mineral water for
himself and a Rolling Rock for me – how cool was that?

Shakin' Stevens, would you believe, was also there, and he got
up to sing a few tunes. It was surreal watching an Elvis imperson-
ator singing with the great man's guitarist, but great fun. Everybody
tried to coax Rory to get up and play; he refused and part of me
regrets this. I would've loved to have seen him rattle out 'Bullfrog
Blues' on James Burton's Tele, but he was in a very bad way, he was
drinking pints of white wine. I think I prefer to have the memory

of a young blues man from Cork laying waste to a packed Ulster Hall. I never saw him again and when he died in 1995 I couldn't help but think back to that wonderful/sad night in West London.

Over the period of Christmas at Nomis there was a party nearly every night with everybody who rehearsed or had an office there trying to outdo each other as far as drink and food were concerned. As you can imagine we all availed of the hospitality with great enthusiasm. Paul Weller's party was an absolute hoot and I just had to invite our Roisin along. I introduced her to Paul and I could see from his face that he was asking himself, 'What exactly does this guy do for me?' But he was too much of a gentleman to say anything. When she met John Weller, Paul's father and manager, they hit it off like a house on fire, and by the end of the evening she had persuaded him to book gigs in Belfast. Roisin ended up calling him 'hucklebuck head' due to his grey quiff, which was a little bit uncomfortable: John's an ex-boxer and even at his age he was not somebody to mess with, but he took it in great humour, much to my relief.

Spandau Ballet have always been a guilty secret of mine so I was over the moon to get talking to front man Tony Hadley that night. Xan takes great pleasure in reminding me that I spent a good portion of the evening trying to persuade him that his next solo album should follow a more Rock-orientated direction. Being a closet fan of the 'Parade' album I analysed that his voice could quite easily handle the crossover from Pop to Rock: after all, 'Through the Barricades' is nothing if not an AOR classic. Amazingly, or maybe it was just manners, he seemed to be taking in everything I was saying and agreeing. I even offered to help him write some of the songs. A short while later he did release a Rock album with disastrous consequences. I'm not sure if it was that conversation that prompted his decision but if he had taken up my offer things might have been different; the songs on the record were just not good enough.

I think I'm turning Japanese

Being involved with Alex and Nomis meant that I had the opportunity to get in free to many gigs, attend album launch parties and promotional events. I must admit that if I had no interest in the band, album or artist involved I sometimes forgot what the shindig was in aid of. Alex would shake his head in disbelief when I was introduced to the host man or woman of the moment and I would ask them what they were doing there. A case in point was a party thrown for the launch of the first UK single by Charles and Eddie. When I was presented to these multi-platinum selling soul singers, not having a clue who they were, I asked them if they had heard the single that we were all there to celebrate.

Eddie asked 'Would I lie to you baby?'

I said, 'You can if you like, I haven't heard it either.' I didn't realise that he was referring to the title of their chart-topping song.

'We're on the guest list for a gig by a very famous Japanese singer/songwriter,' Alex informed me one evening. He told me the artist's name, which I immediately forgot.

The next question I asked, on such occasions, was always, 'How many?', meaning how far could I spread my good fortune – I was generous like that. I was told that I could have as many as I liked, so I phoned everyone. It was 1990 and the start of the Gulf War. Xan was starting to get work as a videotape news editor so he couldn't make it. Ken was under house arrest; Elaine was getting slightly weary of me taking him out and forgetting to bring him home. So it was left to me, Inky, his friend Tony and two lovely girls we knew called Debbie and Lisa to take up the kind offer of free drink and food.

The place was packed with beautiful Japanese girls, there was hardly a male in sight, and therefore no competition if the offer of a little Far Eastern affection were to present itself; things were looking good. We were invited backstage to meet the man responsible for the fine turnout. I had this impression of the Japanese people being small in stature and the people filling the auditorium bore out that stereotype, but when I was faced with the star of the show, I found it hard to hide my shock: he was about 6ft 4", with a spiked bouffant of at least another 4–5 inches standing, making him look like he was nearly 7ft tall. I suddenly found out why so many of London's Nipponese female population had turned out – and it wasn't for a chance encounter with a skinny, pale, balding little Irishman. Things were no longer looking as good as they had been.

The gig was sponsored by a beer called Sapporo. It comes in a silver tin, is very tasty and on the night in question was free to those on the guest list. We had a few and enjoyed an excellent show. The 'giant' was a very talented guy, a great singer and guitar player. With his good looks and striking appearance I could see why he was so popular with the ladies but I couldn't help but feel that perhaps he was being marketed as a 'boy band' type thing and that his talents were being ignored somewhat. With the response he got I'm sure he didn't really care; it was bordering on the fanatical.

The after-show party had free food, served by chefs in those hats that resemble pearl white, atomic bomb mushroom clouds. All the staff involved in the refreshments were wearing black T-shirts with the word Hotel printed on the front. I said to Alex that I wouldn't fancy being a guest where they had come from; there would be no one around to look after you.

'What do you mean?' he asked.

I explained that if you wanted room service you would have to go and get it yourself.

He looked even more puzzled and said, 'I don't understand'.

I thought, how difficult is this, but I kept my patience and said, 'Look, the hotel that all these people work in must have no staff left to look after their guests, there's hundreds of them here seeing to our needs.'

Alex explained that they hadn't come from a hotel. They were from the local Japanese restaurants and community.

I asked, 'Then why are they all wearing shirts with the word hotel on it?'

Alex once again was left virtually speechless, but he did muster up enough vocabulary to inform me that the guy that we had spent the best part of two hours watching and whose hospitality we were now helping ourselves to was called Hotei. It was his name that was plastered all over the place.

The embarrassment did not end there. You have to remember that this was the best part of twenty years ago and let's just say that Japanese cuisine was not high on the list of choices when it came to the British palate. Unlike today, where there are noodle bars, pasta bars and Lebanese restaurants on every street corner in Soho, it wasn't unheard of for someone to enter a Cantonese takeaway and order a sausage supper, then boast to everyone in work the next day that they had had a Chinese the previous night. In the light of this, then, it wasn't surprising that we found the food and the presentation a little unfamiliar.

The guests queued in an orderly line to be presented with raw fish, wafer-thin cuts of meat and cold rice that appeared to be wrapped in what I thought was a cabbage leaf but was of course seaweed. Feeling a little peckish and game to try anything new, Inky and myself joined the others waiting to be served. When it was our turn and not being fluent in the language of the Land of the Rising Sun, we found it difficult to make ourselves understood.

The chef was painstakingly slicing slithers of duck and placing them, with the precision of a fine artist, on to a decorative plate. Inky was trying to tell him that he wanted the lobster, which was presented on a bed of ice and was surrounded with carrots and radishes cut into the shape of roses. The chef didn't seem to understand him and carried on slicing and dicing like a magician. Inky took to pointing at the large crustacean in an attempt to clarify things and again he was ignored. So, good-naturedly, and in all the years I have known him he has never behaved in any other way, Inky reached across and ripped off one of the claws and held it out as a means of telling the chef that this was what he wanted.

What happened next will forever live on in my memory; the chef threw off his hat and then threw a wobbly. He started screaming at Inky then tried to attack him with the chopper-type knife that he had been using with such grace only seconds earlier. Inky made a vain attempt at an explanation while trying to defend himself from the flashing blade that was whizzing just millimeters from his nose, with the claw that had caused the ugly scene in the first place. The chef's colleagues, who were probably thinking that a decapitation was not the best way to promote Japanese culture in London, jumped upon him. Sensing that there might be a diplomatic incident in the offing I pulled our cultural attaché away from the mêlée and dragged him back to Alex, who having witnessed the whole thing, was making apologies and edging towards the door. Outside Alex had a fit, saying that this would be the last time he was ever going to invite us to anything again. I wonder what his problem was?

Not all things in small packages are good

Alex soon broke his promise and invited me to a party that was being thrown by the Grammy-nominated sound track composer Barry Kirsch. I had met him a few times at Weller's office and found him to be a very talented, softly spoken gentleman with an uncanny resemblance to Jeremy Beadle, except for the little hand, which let's face it was a good thing for a man who writes music on the piano. I was told there would be plenty of free drink so I mulled the offer over for about a second and then phoned Ken and Inky.

We all met up at Nomis studios where we acquainted ourselves with the contents of John Weller's globe-shaped drinks cabinet. Alex was unaware that we were helping ourselves to the rather expensive brandy and whiskey; he thought that I was showing my partners in crime the gold and platinum discs on the wall. On returning to Alex's office I could see that he was slightly miffed by our giddy drunkenness.

'Were you drinking John's booze?' he asked.

'Of course not,' I said.

'I fuckin hope not,' he said.

I think he was afraid that Kenny Wheeler, Weller's head of security, would kill him, which would not have been that good for him really. Anyway we were feeling no pain when we got into Alex's new sports car, a Mazda if memory serves. I was in the passenger seat; Ken and Inky were crushed into the tiny seats in the back.

The venue was Barry's rather plush apartment in a very wealthy looking part of London, possibly Kensington. I remember there being a baby grand piano being used as a launching pad for some nose candy by some of the guests, but not the host I hasten to add who I think would've been horrified if he had known. Not being drug users, well not Ken and myself anyway, we made good use of the liquid refreshments. Feeling out of place we sort of kept ourselves to ourselves. There were a lot of weird people there, who probably thought we were even weirder.

One of the guests I did know was the singer Alex had been managing that fateful day when he walked into the Stick of Rock for the first time. He was a slightly portly, shaven-headed wee man who could go camping without a tent. His over the top mincing would've made Boy George blush, but he was great company and I liked him. We struck up a conversation and I found it funny that he thought the company was a little too 'out there', even for him.

As the night progressed and the beer went down I enquired as to where the bog was. I was pointed in the direction of the hall. The toilet door was closed so I waited a while before knocking. There was no answer so I walked in to find a girl sitting on the throne.

'I'm sorry, I did knock,' I said. Totally embarrassed, I turned to leave.

'Come in and make yourself at home,' she said.

'I beg your pardon?' I asked, not knowing what she was going on about.

'You can go over there,' she said pointing to the sink, 'and I can watch you.'

Where I come from this is not the sort of thing you hear every day and I'm glad, nay delighted for that. Being slightly out of my depth and a little tongue-tied I couldn't believe it when I heard myself say, 'Actually it's a number two I want to do.'

To which she replied, 'All the better.'

I'm sorry, but this is not my idea of romance, and besides I hardly knew the host, who I'm sure if he found himself hoking my waste products from the plug hole of his porcelain sink wouldn't have been best pleased.

Quite frankly the whole situation made me feel nauseated and a little dirty. I thanked the weirdo for her kind offer and went to vacate the room. As a passing shot I informed her that there was a lock on the door and that as a matter of respect for herself, she should maybe use it, to which she eloquently called me a 'fuckin' freak'.

Ken and Inky couldn't believe their ears when I told them about my bathroom romance. Alex, who was sitting in one of those weird seats that you would've seen in the sixties, you know the ones, made of wicker and that hang from the ceiling, looked slightly too interested in the story for my liking. He asked where the toilets were.

'Jesus, Alex, catch a grip of yourself,' I said.

'No seriously, I really do need to go,' he said, not too convincingly. He then unsteadily moved to the edge of the seat and went to push up.

The chair and its occupant came crashing to the floor leaving a massive hole in the ceiling. Alex was always very conscious about his weight and so the embarrassment of all eyes being upon him and the not-too-pleased stare of the owner of the apartment and host prompted him to call an early end to the evening. Thankfully we 'squares' found ourselves walking down the corridor towards the exit without saying goodbye to anybody and without Alex using the toilet, which he mustn't have really needed to do that badly after all.

On the way back to the car I spotted what looked like a postbag lying on the path. There had been, at that time, a lot of postmen robbed in the capital and I said, jokingly, that it might have been dropped by a crim and it could be full of used notes.

'Pick it up,' said Alex, whose love of money was renowned.

I did what he asked and back in the car gave it to Ken to open. He had a good rummage and then said, 'What the feck is this?' holding up a small blue bundle.

'Unwrap it,' I said, which he did.

A scream filled the air that any B movie actress would've been proud of. Ken threw the package into the front of the car; it landed in Alex's lap.

'What is it?' our driver was shouting hysterically, while driving at 70mph.

'It's a Thora,' Ken shouted.

'What?!!' Alex was now screaming.

'It's a Thora Hird, a turd,' Ken repeated.

I looked over and yes, indeed, it was what Ken had said it was but I knew that already from the smell that was filling the small cramped confines of the car.

'Take it away,' Alex begged me.

'I feckin' will not,' I said. I had never seen an incontinence pad before, otherwise I would've stopped Ken from opening it in the first place, but I'm glad, in a way, he did or I would've missed the sight of Alex driving with one hand, whilst trying to open the window with the other and swallowing hard to stop himself from gagging. He eventually gathered up the steaming mess, careful not to have any of it drop onto his pristine upholstery, and he threw it out into the night. There was a huge sigh of relief from all of us. Now that the air was turning back to normal we did the only thing that a fright of that nature would dictate, we pissed ourselves laughing, well all except the poor driver who looked visibly shaken and I think glad that this particular night was nearly over.

Right that does it, I'm off to Italy

Heartbreak is a funny thing, it can render you into a state similar to that of the walking dead; as a gormless zombie you prefer the night-time. The solace of the dark gives you the opportunity to avoid all social contact. Then in the next breath, especially with the young, virile male, you find it provides the opportunity for conquests anew. It can be very confusing and exciting all at the same time. After Adele left I was devastated, not enough to change my ways, but devastated all the same. I didn't want to go out or even rehearse. I decided, in a fit of dramatic pique, that I was going to move to Italy and live with my sister Marie for a while. I hadn't asked her of course, I just assumed that there would be no problems.

A leaving do was organised at the Hounslow Hound Pound and it was a night to remember for many reasons. There were the usual suspects in attendance as well as Abi, Xan's sister, and her friend Anna (more of her later). Another guest was a character called Bert from Belfast, who had been in bands around the same time that I had been in No Hot Ashes. He had moved, purely by chance, into the same street as us and had, equally by chance, recently split up with his girlfriend. Bert drowned his 'Heartbreak Hotel' sorrows by quaffing down large quantities of QC wine, a drink I only associated with grannies at Christmas. On the night in question this was indeed his tipple of choice, and it rendered him inebriated very quickly. The evening was only warming up but Bert could be seen dozing on the sofa, his bottle of sipping sherry held at a jaunty angle, dripping slowly onto the carpet.

I had known Bert for many years and always found him fun company, but for some reason, and I'll never know why, he called me Shaunie; it was kind of like the Trigger/Rodney situation in 'Only Fools and Horses'. I could see people who had only met him for the first time and known me for many years, giving each other quizzical looks when he addressed me as Shaunie. They were even more confused when I responded; I had given up telling him my real name.

Anyway the craic went on, getting louder and louder and every-one was in great spirits. Johnny Bramley was, as he always did, videoing the proceedings. I'm glad he did, for on waking the next day I had forgotten most of it. Later that afternoon everyone that stayed over settled down in front of the TV, with a saveloy supper and a few cans of beer; we were only too glad of the chance to remind ourselves of the previous night's highlights.

At one point in the video people were being interviewed by Johnny but their responses were being drowned out by a loud thudding noise. For example he would ask, 'Have you anything ... Thud!! to Eamon before ... Thud!! ... departure?'

Their response, 'Yeah, I'd ... Thud!! ... to say Thud!! ... hope he never Thud!! ... back.'

Those watching looked at each other in puzzlement. 'What the feck was that noise?' someone asked. The camera panned round to reveal the answer.

I must've thought that I could add to the ambience of the evening by dancing along to AC/DC's 'Let There be Rock'. while keeping the beat by banging on the bottom of a large plastic fermenting bucket, used in the production of 'Nellie Brew', our home-made beer. More worryingly however, was that behind me two cops are seen holding Bert, one on each arm. 'What are they doing there?' I asked. Luckily Beckly could remember, which wasn't like him. What he told us would be the stuff of legend and the reason why the neighbours never spoke to us again.

As I said before, Bert was exercising his social skills by falling asleep on the sofa and spilling drink all over the place. I decided that it was probably best if he went to bed. He only lived around the corner so he was led through the living room to the front door and pointed in the right direction. We had a very overgrown garden with tall hedges on both sides, making it invisible to the outside world. As Bert was making his way to the gate, the night breeze must have caused him to lose his footing; nothing to do with litres of fermented grape juice, you understand. He fell through the hedge on the right hand side and ended up lying on next door's lawn. When he had regained his composure, he dusted himself down and decided that it was way too early to go home; he wanted to rejoin the festivities.

Bert's bearings were not what they had once been; he didn't realise that he was now in the wrong garden. He walked back towards what he thought was the party house and let himself in through the porch door, made his way up the hall and entered the living room. He then proceeded to walk into the middle of the room, where he found himself confronted by a family of Sikhs. The women were resplendent, wearing traditional dress, and the men were sporting full beards and wearing turbans. Bert, who was a sartorial vision himself with his spiked peroxide blond hair, tiger skin box jacket and PVC trousers, stood puzzled for a second and then asked 'Where's Shaunie?' The family sat open-mouthed in disbelief for a second, before wrestling him to the ground and calling the police. Hence the Old Bill's guest appearance in our home video. Thankfully they saw the funny side of the whole thing and were later caught on camera dancing with some of the girls, who were now wearing their copper hats. Bert, having found a new lease of energy, joined in the merriment by gently snoring on the sofa in the same key as the music, professional to the end.

One part of that evening I didn't forget was having a romantic tussle with Abi's friend Anna. She was a very attractive girl; I was leaving for Italy soon, so what was the problem? Well the problem was that when I decided to finally contact Marie to let her know that I was going to grace her with my company, she told me that she didn't have permanent accommodation, she was travelling all the time and was effectively living out of a suitcase, therefore there was nowhere for me to move to. I must say I felt just a tad thick, seeing as I had just had a leaving party, wishing a lot of people a fond farewell, many of them getting quite emotional. Furthermore, on finding out that I was not migrating to Italy, and maybe because I phoned her for a date, Anna thought it would be a good idea that we become a couple.

I was just out of a relationship that had left scars and was not remotely interested in going into another one. Unfortunately I don't deal with this sort of situation well, so I kind of went along with it; the fact that she was so good looking and that she was so rich didn't hurt I suppose (socialist idealism left at the bedroom door). Anna would arrive at the Pound, her Gti Golf weighed down with beer and groceries. All these factors maybe prolonged the inevitable split a good bit longer than it should have. That and the fact that I was encouraged by my housemates to keep her calling round, as they were able to benefit from the leftovers. By that I mean the food and drink – we weren't total savages.

I had to at some point act like a man and finish the relationship.

The year-long lease was up on the house and once again, unsurprisingly, the owner didn't want to extend. I mustered up all my courage and like a true gent I moved house without letting Anna know where I was going.

Rocking around the Christmas trees

I moved in, briefly, with Gary, our new drummer, his pregnant wife Ann (who incidentally made a wicked brew) and their delightful son Derek. The eviction also meant that Xan and Beckly needed new abodes. Beckly moved in with some labourer mates and poor Xan had to temporarily go back to his parents in Guildford, causing severe logistical problems as far as the band was concerned. Gary's house was in Chiswick, a delightful area of London that was the residence of many musicians and media stars.

Gary didn't have a job as such, he sort of wheeled and dealed but was never short of a bob or two. His income was no concern of mine, that was his business; all I was interested in was if he could play the drums, which thank goodness he could. He was a powerhouse on the kit, a very muscular guy; he kept himself fit by going to the gym nearly every day, pumping iron. No amount of persuasion could get me to join him. I preferred the 'letting yourself go' look, and God, I was good at it – the beer belly was coming along a treat, it took very little maintenance and the little it did never once caused a sweat.

It was coming up to Christmas. Gary every year would obtain (ahem, ahem!) a couple of hundred trees and sell them at the side of the Hogarth Flyover, which was just at the bottom of his street. From where he got the trees I do not know and as I was finding out, the less I knew the better it would be if I ever found myself giving evidence in a court of law. Being short of cash Gary asked me if I would like to earn a few quid by helping him sell the festive flora. I was due to go back to Holywood for the holiday period, so I jumped at the chance; anyway I'd heard they did a fine Christmas dinner in Wormwood Scrubs.

It was freezing standing by the side of that road waiting for people to pull up in their luxury cars to inspect and hopefully purchase one of our yuletide stock; Gary supplying me with cockle-warming brandies kept some of the chill at bay. As I said before, Chiswick is a very affluent place with a lot of thesps and musos living around there, so I took it upon myself to promote the Nellies to whomever I could, in the hope that they had connections. One such opportunity saw me waxing lyrical to a guy who had risked life and limb crossing the road, on foot, to where I was standing. If you knew the flyover in question you would know that this was quite a dangerous feat. The brandy had loosened the old Blarney muscles. I told him what a great band I was in and that I was only doing this sort of work until I got my big break; he just nodded his head and checked out the trees. He must have been drinking himself, as miraculously he made a purchase. As he was about to leave I told him we were playing in the Stick of Rock the next Saturday and if he wanted I could, in view of him buying one of the already balding pines, arrange for him to be put on the guest list. He then informed me that, as generous as my offer was, it was unlikely that he could make it as he had a gig of his own.

I said, 'Oh, you do a wee bit yourself do you?'

He said, 'Yeah, I'm the singer in the Stranglers.'

What an arse I felt, as I watched Paul Roberts dodge Chelsea tractors, dragging one of our 'half-inched' Norwegian spruces in his wake. I hadn't even given him one of our EPs, which were kept under our makeshift counter for just such an occasion. I couldn't chase after him, as I would've been leaving our precious merchandise to the mercy of millionaire thieves. I also thought that one rock star nearly getting killed on the Hogarth Flyover was quite enough for one day.

One evening, after I had returned from Holywood after the Christmas break, I was sitting watching TV with Gary and his family when the phone rang. I lifted the receiver; I knew it was unlikely to be for me; I had only let a select few know of my whereabouts. Imagine my surprise when I heard Anna's voice on the other end of the line saying, 'So this is where you've got to.'

'Oh hi,' I spluttered. 'I was meaning to call you,' I lied. While she was speaking I was mouthing to Gary that it was my ex I was talking to, and he burst out laughing.

Hearing the giggling in the background Anna asked, 'What's all the laughing about?'

I was now a total gibbering idiot and answered, 'It's just something funny on the TV.' Unfortunately the theme music to Panorama was playing. She ignored my obvious blatant lies and informed me that she had got me something for Christmas. Curiosity and the fact that I had not had female company in quite a while weakened my resolve to a strength similar to the breaking strain of a Kit Kat.

We spent a very pleasant evening together; I can't remember the present she got me, I remember the one I got her, nothing. I did toy with the idea of giving her, as a joke, one of the re-plantable Christmas trees that were left over and sitting in pots in Gary's back garden, awaiting next year's festive season, but I feared that my sense of humour might be misconstrued as a mental disorder. I did, however explain the reasons why I didn't want to get into a relationship at that time. This stance had been even further strengthened by a horrendous New Year's Eve encounter with Adele in Holywood. Anna, to her credit, or perhaps she was beginning to realise that I was not the catch she originally thought, accepted my reasonings with good grace.

The band was back up and firing on all cylinders; Gary and Clive were fitting in very well. I moved into the latter's flat in Green Dragon Lane, Brentford. Whereas Chiswick was definitely the place you would want your 'des res', Green Dragon Lane was not. We lived in a council tower block that had massive spotlights shining all night from the roof to try to prevent drugs being sold around its base. All it did was make sure that the dealers had enough light to count their ill-gotten gains. It also fooled the local bird population; they thought it was daytime around the clock and would still be twittering at 4 o'clock in the morning. There were always dead bodies of our feathered friends lying on the ground as we came and went; I think most of them died from exhaustion.

Fatal instinct

Rehearsals were taking place in a studio in Acton, which was quite a distance away, but it was the only place we could get at a reasonable price. One evening following a productive session, we retired to the pub around the corner for a well-earned thirst-quenching pint.

We settled down to discuss song structures etc. when I spotted Anna sitting in the corner on her own. I was completely taken by surprise; she also lived nowhere near Acton. I asked her to join us, which she did, but when she sat down Ken asked if he could speak to me in private. I thought it a bit rude leaving someone's company before even getting them a drink. I said, 'In a wee minute.'

Ken responded by saying, 'I need to speak to you right now.'

'Alright, alright,' I said.

We convened to a quiet secluded area of the bar, namely the bogs, where Ken grabbed my arm, spinning me round and startling me with the question, 'Have you seen Basic Instinct or Fatal Attraction?'

'What?' I said.

'She's a bunny boiler,' he went on.

'Don't be stupid,' I laughed.

Ken then proceeded to point out that she had been able to get my phone number, when very few people had it and those that did were told not to give it out to anyone. She was now sitting in a bar that was miles from where we or she lived; she couldn't have known that there was a rehearsal studio there without following us; and how did she know that we were going to have a drink after rehearsal when we normally didn't, well not there anyway. I must admit he put up a very convincing case, causing me to wonder why I shouldn't just run out the side door, thus avoiding the family pets being fricasseed, or worse, in my opinion but probably not in the family's, getting an ice pick through the head.

Laughter and giggling greeted us on our return to the table. 'Merry it up,' I thought, 'you won't be laughing at my funeral.' Ken sent me a knowing glance and a wink. At least someone would be able to point the accusing finger following my demise, which would be a small comfort to my family. I couldn't help staring at Anna – the conversation carried on as if she didn't have care in the world. I thought, 'It's always the ones you least expect, isn't it?' For the moment I was safe: there were no sharp implements to hand and she didn't look like she was carrying a weapon, although it was hard to tell as she was wearing a long baggy coat.

'A bit out of your way?' I blurted into the middle of the conversation, stopping everyone in their tracks, apart from Ken of course, my lifelong friend and protector; he knew what I was at.

'Sorry?' she responded.

I said, 'It's a bit of a trek from your place for a drink, isn't it?'

'Is it?' she countered. I looked over at Ken, he knowingly nodded his head, we had her on the ropes, and we were on to her little game.

'And another thing, how did you get my number?' I asked. Again she played dumb.

'What do you mean?' she asked.

'My number, my number!' I shouted. 'No one but my close family and the people around this table had it so how come you were able to get in touch with me?' There was an uneasy silence descending, which was mixed with embarrassed shifting in seats. I didn't care – it was my head that was going to be chipped at like a block of ice, embarrassment I could deal with.

'Abi gave it to me,' Anna said looking majorly pissed off.

'What?' I asked, slightly taken aback.

'Abi got the number from Xan,' she said. Guiltily the big bass player shrugged his shoulders. Anna then said, 'I didn't realise you didn't want to be contacted, nobody said to me.'

'A likely story,' I thought, but the seeds of doubt were setting in; what happened next would cause them to burst into bloom.

The door opened and a tall handsome guy walked in. He was disgustingly well dressed and had a tan that could only have come from the Bahamas or some such place. He looked around the room, spotted Anna, then walked over and kissed her on the cheek. 'Hi darling, I'm sorry I'm late. I got held up at the office, I went to the flat and you weren't there, so I suspected you'd be here,' he said.

'That's OK, Pamela hasn't arrived yet either,' Anna says while still staring at me with a look of disgust.

'Are you going to introduce me to your friends?' 'Tom Cruise' asked.

'Yes, of course, I'm sorry, this is Xan, Abi's brother, that's Ken, Gary and Clive. They're all in Xan's band, you know the one I told you about.' She then turns to me and says, 'And I'm not quite sure who this is anymore.'

I spun round to get some reassurance from Ken but he had made a hasty retreat to the room where the conspiracy theory had begun; I followed him, looking around for an ice pick to stick in his head.

High-rise to hell

Whilst living at Green Dragon Lane I contracted a really bad case of tonsillitis. It was so bad that I couldn't even get out of bed to attend the doctors so Clive had to go and get me antibiotics, pretending that he had a dose as well. I wish I had been a fly on the wall in that surgery.

'Open up and say ah.'

'Ahhhh.'

'Are you sure you have a sore throat?'

It took a couple of days for the antimicrobials to work and at night the infection, temperature and the constant bloody bird song made me quite delirious. I was seeing all manner of things in the room; the hours to daybreak lasted longer than a Mormon's goodbye.

Eventually I started to feel better, but was still unable to make rehearsals, so the boys carried on without me. One night Clive returned saying that in my absence there were rustlings of discontent and they were all aimed at Big Xan. Clive then said that the bass player's behaviour and attitude were less than ideal. I couldn't understand it: Xan had always been the band member that I could rely on the most. What could be the reason behind such a change in mood? I vowed that I would get to the bottom of this ASAP, just as soon as I was back on my feet.

When quizzed Xan went on the defensive, but after further probing he confided in me that his new accommodation was the cause of his negativity. He had recently moved into a flat belonging to a friend of Gary's. Baz was a Turkish, wheelchair-bound lunatic who drove a Rolls Royce and kept a shotgun under his bed. This last fact made us decide that we wouldn't ask him how he ended up with spinal injuries. Because he drove such an expensive car we had believed that Baz's abode must be quite salubrious. How wrong we were. When Xan was shown around his prospective new home, he should've turned tail and run, but he was desperate. Was he really that desperate?

Xan's room, in a ground-floor council flat, contained nothing but a urine-stained mattress. When he voiced his concerns about his bed facilities he was told he could either take it or leave it by our four-wheeled charmer. I was beginning to dislike this guy big style.

Beggars can't be choosers however, and Xan, who hadn't, just, taken to sitting outside Embankment Station with a Styrofoam cup and a dog on a piece of string, moved in.

Living in that dump nearly broke the big lad and his spirit. When I tell you some of the things that happened there, you will understand why. First of all Baz's horrible, vicious cat would sneak into Xan's room and piss on his bed. Pigeons would fly through the broken windows, probably chased by that bastard of a cat, injuring themselves and leaving blood and feathers everywhere. Shady characters would arrive at the door at all hours wanting to speak to Baz and would leave after a short conversation with small bags of stuff. If the visit was after Baz had retired for the evening he would pull the guilt trip and get Xan out of bed to greet his customers, sorry gentlemen callers. Knowing about the gun under the bed probably made this a terrifying experience for Xan. God knows who was a calling; Baz certainly wasn't going to risk himself when he had a well-intentioned fool to take the next bullet.

But the worst, and in my opinion, the funniest thing to occur at 'Chez Nightmare' was that Baz would call Xan into the bathroom while he was sitting in the tub. Then, pulling the guilt trip again, he would ask Xan to shave the parts of his body he couldn't quite reach. As funny as I found this it obviously had our bass player in a state. I assured Xan that things would sort themselves out shortly and he would be out of there soon.

After Xan's revelations I went to bed that night feeling a whole lot better about the band, I think we were over the worst, and a bit better health-wise. However there still must have been a drop of the old bacteraemia coursing through my blood vessels because that night I had a nightmare that went something like this.

Xan was sitting on his body fluid-saturated mattress trying to revive a seriously injured pigeon while in the corner of the room a cat that looked like a feline version of Grace Jones licked its lips and waited for the big fella to fall asleep. Just then Baz's voice wafted into the room summoning Dr Dolittle to the bathroom. He shuddered and put the pigeon into a drawer. On entering the room Xan couldn't help but notice that there was soft music playing; it was a tune he knew but just couldn't put a name to. Scented candles caused romantic shadows to dance upon the walls. Baz was sitting in the bath, a flannel, that was supposed to cover his man giblets, bobbing along on the crest of a wave and revealing glimpses of what looked like a little soldier between two sand bags. The bather looked up with big puppy dog eyes and asked Xan if he would be so kind as to shave his hairy back and neck. Sitting behind Baz, Xan winced as he dragged the razor through what looked like a foam-covered hair vest. With each stroke and tapping of the blade on the side of the bath the water became a floating quagmire of gentleman's fuzz. It was at this point that the song being played became all too recognisable. Baz sighed a contented sigh and gently hummed the melody to 'Oh Sweet Mystery of Life at Last I've Found You'.

I woke from the dream, the tears streaming down my face, but soon realised that my cheeks weren't moistened out of concern for my mate and his ordeal but through uncontrollable laughter. I rolled onto my side and set off for the Land of Nod again, only to find this difficult due to chuckling. Then it came to me – I could sing a lullaby to get over. As my eyes grew heavy I heard myself softly mouthing the words 'Oh sweet mystery of life at last I've found you'.

Unfortunately my rest was short lived. Again I woke, only this time it was due to what sounded like a motorbike being ridden around outside our front door. 'Impossible,' I thought, 'we're fifteen floors up, close your eyes, you're getting delirious again, it will go away soon.'

Just then my bedroom door flew open and in runs Clive shouting, 'Get up, get up!'

I pulled on my clothes and followed him to the now open front door, just in time to watch a guy, with a still running chainsaw in his hand, pushing a TV into the lift. I looked across the hall to where an elderly gentleman was standing on his front door, which had been neatly removed from its frame with all the precision of a surgeon wielding a scalpel. 'Do something!' he pleaded. Clive, a black belt in karate, was not afraid of many people, but even he knew that to try to disarm someone who was carrying a chainsaw could mean being, literally, disarmed yourself. We could only stand and watch as the old man's most precious possession descended, in the lift, to the nearest pawnshop. I had a funny feeling that, seeing as the urban lumberjack had seen our faces, my stay at jolly old Green Dragon Lane would be coming to an end sooner than I thought.

Breaking the law? Breaking the law?

Gary was a gem of a guy, a rough diamond, but he also had a weak constitution and he was constantly getting infections. We even played the Stick of Rock on one occasion with him suffering from a severe bout of shingles. He must have been in agony, but he didn't complain once. I think he knew he was frail as far as his health was concerned; each new infection became harder to get over. He did everything to keep himself well by exercising, eating well, avoiding alcohol and only smoking the odd herbal relaxant. But deep down I think he knew his lifespan was not going to achieve the national average. This may explain a lot.

Alex broke his leg and that put an end to my visits to Nomis. All operations were switched to the rather boring surroundings of his front room. I mean how inconsiderate was that? I could've been partying my liver away; instead I was expected to work for my living, oh the shame of it all. Alex would lie on the sofa like some Roman Emperor and issue orders; he even had me do his shopping. If he was entertaining a lady client (ahem!) I was expected to carry on the work in the office he had procured at D & R Autos. With it only being a couple of doors away I would carry the books and stuff along the street and set up there while Alex finished his balancing of the sheets, so to speak.

It was the dead of winter and as I sat in the freezing cold, windowless room, pawing through hundreds of touring receipts, I longed for the days in Earls Court, where I would invite Inky, Xan and Ken around for a couple of cocktails before we took in the theatre, an art exhibition or rocked our arses off at the Hippodrome on Wednesday nights. We even watched the Rangers vs Leeds 1992 European Cup second round match in John Weller's office. For some reason that night John Lukic decided that it was good goal-keeping practice to punch the ball into his own net. We had a great time even though it was one of the most depressing results in football history.

The garage not only provided Alex with office space but also provided him a storage space for his battered old Cadillac. Gary had taken a keen interest in the gas-guzzler, and as I said before he wasn't going to let a small matter like the law deter him from providing for his family should anything happen to him. One afternoon Alex and myself were sitting in his front room working, or should I say I was, while he flicked through the TV channels. Anyway Alex had his back to the window, whereas I was able to look out over Chiswick Common. My vantage point enabled me to witness a trailer, weighed down with Alex's convertible American automobile, pass by. Gary was sitting in the passenger seat looking straight at me, smiling, with his finger up to his lips requesting my silence. What could I do? He was the new drummer in the band, we had gigs to do and no time to replace him if he were sacked by the manager, which he surely would have been if Alex had known that his pride and joy had just been sold under his nose and without his consent. I also knew Gary's behaviour was fuelled by a desire to put bread on the family table while he could, so I did the totalitarian thing and I kept quiet.

About an hour after he had thieved Alex's car Gary called around with the terrible news that someone had stolen it from the garage. He was very reassuring when he told the devastated owner that he shouldn't worry about it because he was insured. Alex was beside himself with grief. I was beside myself with admiration; Gary didn't even skip a beat or display a flush of the cheek as he delivered a barefaced lie. I would've been a shaking, purple wreck if I had attempted the same thing.

Gary's liberation of Alex's funds didn't end there. Once when Alex was away on business in the USA, he left me the keys to his house to carry on working on Weller's touring accounts. He was due back on a Monday; on the Friday before his return Gary, unexpectedly, arrived at my house announcing that he needed the keys to carry out some DIY which Alex had asked him to do before leaving. This just didn't ring true so I phoned Alex from another room and was informed that indeed he had asked him to do a few things around the house. Satisfied that all was well I handed over the keys and let Gary get on with whatever he had to do over the weekend.

I met Alex at Heathrow to help him with his bags and we headed back to Chiswick by tube. We walked, sorry I did, he hobbled on his crutches, across the Common. In front of Alex's house we could see the familiar figure of Gary sitting on his wall. 'Wait till you see what I've done for you,' he beamed as we reached him. What he had done defied belief.

Alex had the smallest backyard I have ever seen: it was about six feet by four feet, it was paved and only had enough room for one small bench. Gary had kindly removed it and in its place he had sunk a fibreglass pond; one of his 'business' ideas. There was no room to walk around the pond; it came right up to the edges of the walls. Alex couldn't believe his eyes: one step out the back door and he would be up to his arse in algae-infested water and lily pads.

'What the fuck have you done?' Alex squealed.

'What do you mean?' Gary said and then asked, 'Did you not admire the one in my back garden?'

'Yes I did, but I didn't say I wanted one,' Alex shouted, his face turning crimson.

'Oh didn't you, I thought you did. Anyway it's going to cost you £500, I've given you a bit of discount,' Gary said, adding insult to injury. Knowing Gary's temper Alex handed over the cash.

Gary's erratic behaviour became a distraction and quite frankly a terrifying thing to deal with at times. He was sometimes consumed with an anger that I think stemmed from not being able to get himself well no matter what he did. I was in the car with him once, travelling from Brentford to Chiswick, when he jumped out and with a wheel brace in his hand smashed all the windows of a car driven by a massive black guy, just because he had cut him up. Gary then calmly got back in beside me and carried on the conversation he had left without a word of explanation. We were so frightened to sack him that we took the coward's way out and told him and Clive that we were disbanding. We decided for the foreseeable future that the three amigos – myself, Ken and Xan – would just carry on as a recording entity and get in other musicians for gigs if needed. We changed our name to Social Idiot, no explanation needed.

CHAPTER FIVE

Social Idiot

Every picture tells a story, don't it?

I had been asked to write some songs with a guy called Kuma Harada who was the ex-bass player with the Tourists (Annie Lennox's old band), Snowy White (ex-Thin Lizzy) and Mick Taylor (ex-Rolling Stones). As you can imagine I was going to jump at the chance. Kuma's studio was near Old Street Station and Alex arranged for me to go along and meet him. We hit it off quite well and I said I would write some stuff and let him hear it with the provision that if he liked it then maybe we could record something together.

At the time I was living at Ken and Elaine's flat, having left the high-rise hell in Green Dragon Lane for the sake of my physical and mental health. One evening I got a call from Alex. He sounded really worried, and he asked me if I could call over to see him ASAP. He said he was in a spot of trouble but I wasn't to mention it to anyone. I told Ken that I was going over to Chiswick and would probably stay there as it was getting quite late.

Alex answered the door, shaking. Clearly he was distressed. I asked him what the matter was; he invited me into the living room and was just about to spill the beans when a knock came to the front door.

'Who could that be?' I asked.

'I don't know,' Alex said, and then with his voice trembling he asked me to answer it.

Reluctantly I went to the door to be confronted by God knows what, I mean what could have Alex in such a state? I slowly opened the door a fraction and peered out, fully expecting to be set upon by some thug or other or one of Alex's dissatisfied clients – and I don't just mean the ladies here.

To my surprise Ken was standing on the doorstep. 'What's going on?' he demanded.

'I don't know,' I truthfully said.

'Is it something to do with Kuma?' he asked.

'What?' I shouted.

'Have you signed a deal with Kuma behind mine and Xan's backs?' he blurted out.

'I don't know what you're talking about,' and I really didn't. He pushed in past me. When he saw Alex I think he knew that the reason for my clandestine visit had nothing to do with music.

Alex had known me for many years by this stage, not only professionally, with our work with the band and the stuff I did for him as part of Paul Weller's organisation, but we were also good friends socially. Although he obviously knew Ken very well they were not close like he and I were. Alex looked a little reluctant to discuss his problems in front of Ken. Seeing as I had known Ken most of my life I assured Alex that anything he could tell me could be said in front of Ken and it would be treated in the strictest confidence and seriousness. What he was about to reveal would shock even us – and we thought we had heard everything as far as Alex was concerned.

Alex had been going out with a girl who was, let's just say, very heavy boned (ahem!). He had shown me photographs of her that he said were taken when she was a model and before she had developed a gland problem. I couldn't help but think she must have been eating the glands. Anyway I was never convinced that the girl in the picture and the horror picture Alex was dating were the same person. The nose was not the same shape and the eye colour was different for Chrissakes. I had voiced my concerns on the matter and was ignored outright. One of the reasons I think Alex dismissed my misgivings was that she ran a glamour model agency, and to go back to when Alex and I first met, and the reason why I never saw him with the same girl twice, he enjoyed the company of some of the so-called talent, if you know what I mean.

Anyway not only had 'Twiggy' given Alex the dodgy photos but she had also told him that she had cancer in the aforementioned glands and was dying. Again I was not convinced and again I told Alex this. To his credit and foolishness he said he was going to help out in whatever way he could. He contributed to paying for her house and had bought her a car, which was very commendable. Unfortunately the whole thing was a crock of bullshit. Alex was informed of this by one of her friends who she had a falling out with. Obviously he ended the relationship, as any sane individual would have.

The band were glad to see the back of her; we thought she was a rather unsavoury character. She had tried to get involved with the management of the band, even organising an ill-advised photo shoot with some of her 'models' at the launch of the 'Is this Face Free?' EP. The laugh is that our girlfriends were far better looking and far classier; we should've just had our photos taken with them. Unfortunately bad pennies have a habit of coming back and she was the reason why I had been invited to Alex's house. Finding out that the money cow had been taken from her, 'Poison Ivy' had decided to blackmail Alex.

'How is she blackmailing you?' I asked on hearing this bombshell.

'With photos that she says she is going to send to my elderly sick mother and father,' Alex answered, his eyes filling with tears.

Reluctantly I had to ask the next question. 'What are the photos of?' and I heard the phrase that I didn't want to hear.

'I'll show you.'

What we were shown was very hard to make out but it looked like Alex had taken up some sort of Mexican wrestling. He could be seen in numerous pictures wearing a hood and there were ropes and things involved. The costume he had on while participating in his new sport (a word Alex was normally unfamiliar with) seemed to be on the fragile side as the crotch had obviously ripped and his religious heritage was exposed to the world. Another thing I couldn't understand was that this didn't seem to be a very fair bout; he was obviously fighting a shapely lady. His opponent's costume must have been bought at the same shop as it was just as flimsy: bits of her were hanging out. As we came to the end of the photos I tried to offer some sort of assurance by declaring that at least his face couldn't be seen; unfortunately the last one had a picture of Alex without the hood and he had obviously won his match for he was grinning from ear to ear.

Ken and myself treated the gravity of the situation with the respect it was due: we rolled around the carpet crying with laughter. At this point I think Alex knew he had made a big mistake in confiding in us. To find a solution to the problem we decided that a few drinks could provide the necessary mental fortitude. Alex got a few beers from his well-stocked fridge. After a few more beer runs we were warming to the situation, and following the revelations that the witch was demanding that Alex sign his house over to her and also pay a lump sum of £40 grand we decided that the best thing to do was to involve the law. Alex was at first reluctant but I persuaded him that if anything should happen to him then it would be beneficial for the whole sordid affair to be recorded somewhere.

A male and female cop arrived at the door about an hour after the phone call requesting their assistance. Ken answered the door and gave them a clear indication of how their evening was going to go when he said, 'Alex will be with you in a minute – he's just tied up at present.'

A shout of, 'You bastard!' came from the living room in response. I must admit that the lady in blue was a bit of a stunner, the guy I can't remember.

Anyway, Ken and myself were dispatched to the kitchen while Alex was making his statement. A quick rifle through the cupboards and we found a bottle of Rebel Yell bourbon, which we decided would look better empty.

When we were invited in to make our statements we were four sheets to the wind and a little giddy from all the laughing we had done at Alex's expense in the kitchen. The male cop asked Alex if he had any photos of the culprit that were actually of her and not some beauty that she was pretending to have been. The two of them went up the stairs where Alex said he thought he had a few. I prayed they weren't of the same nature as the ones I had seen previously as the thought of her in similar attire could scar an innocent young thing like myself for life.

With them out of the room it left me free to flirt mercilessly with 'Juliette Bravo', which I did. She must have been gay as she didn't seem to be impressed with my ability to slur the lines of a few of our songs, sung in the attempt to persuade her to come to one of our gigs. Ken accompanied me by slapping his thighs, out of time, and falling off the arm of the chair.

After the cops left and my phone number had been rejected by 'Ms Plod', we settled down to finish off the Kentucky sipping whiskey and make ourselves comfortable for the night; it was way too late to get back to Hainault. Alex seemed to be a little more relaxed; we however were determined that this should not last. With a twinkle in his eye Ken told our now tipsy host that for a fraction of the money he was being blackmailed for he could make a phone call home to the old country, make enquires with a few connections he had and have the problem erased permanently.

Alex nearly choked on his drink and asked, 'You mean kill her?'

Ken touched the side of his nose with his index finger and said, 'Did I say that?'

Alex was now looking a little bit frightened and said that surely murder wouldn't be necessary and that we should let the police take care of it. Ken then leaned forward and in a hushed voice told Alex that he could probably pull in a few favours and get the job done for free.

'No! No! No!' Alex started shouting, 'please, no more help from you two, I don't think I can handle any more help from you two.'

'Go on, all I'll need is her address, and you to sit in the car and give the nod when you eyeball her,' Ken went on.

Alex looked at me for some reassurance that Ken was taking the piss. I just nodded my head falsely confirming his worst fears. Our hapless victim left to go to the bathroom; I assume to splash water on his face or maybe the fear had necessitated another reason for the visit. We again went into convulsions of laughter.

As Alex re-entered the room he said, 'Look, I don't want anybody hurt.'

Ken was sitting with the phone up to his ear and was saying, 'Yes, just the one and that's us even.'

Alex lost it at this point and shouted, 'Put that fucking phone down!!'

Ken said into the receiver, 'Hold on a minute,' then turned to Alex and said, 'Jesus, you try to do a mate a favour.' He returned to his conversation, with the dialling tone, and said, 'Cancel that – and you still owe me one.' He gave Alex a steely look and said 'Are you really sure about this? They won't find the body, I mean, I know she's a big girl and all that but she's not the size of Shergar and they never found him.'

I just couldn't take it any more and I burst out laughing, wrecking the bullshitting in the process. Alex for a moment looked relieved but in a split second he threw a dickie fit, calling the both of us bastards.

It took ages to calm Alex down and to see a bit of the funny side; he had after all suffered a bit of a shock. He decided that it was time to end probably the worst day of his life and retire to bed. I can't help but feel that we may have contributed to his suffering in a small way. OK, we probably caused most of it, but hey, opportunities like that don't come along all that often and you must seize them with both hands. As he was walking out the door Alex turned back and said, 'Seriously, you won't do anything stupid will you?' We just smiled. I don't think he ever really knew for sure if we were serious and after the police had cleared up the real mess he never mentioned it again, unsurprisingly.

Social Idiot was put on hold when Alex decided that the chance for me to write songs for Kuma was too good an opportunity to miss. Ken and Xan agreed; after all if this was successful it could be a launching pad to restart the band. Alex also thought that if I was going to take the songwriting seriously I would have to leave the temptations of London behind, or maybe he was just looking to get rid of me. He suggested I go somewhere quieter and more serene, somewhere where the pixie dust of inspiration could settle upon my head and raise me to plateaus of artistic euphoria. Thus I was packed off to live with my friends Gail and Richard in Magaluf. Frying pan and fire.

Spanish flies

I arrived in Palma airport at the start of February 1993; Gail and Richard Martin, who were in the process of opening a bar in Magaluf, met me. It was great to see them again, as it had been about six months since they had quit London for the sunny climes of the

Balearics. The idea was that while I was trying to write songs for the Kuma project I could play in their Rock bar, Route 66, and maybe drum up a little trade. The place, however, was not open yet and there was still a lot of work that needed to be done before they could start rocking the eardrums of the locals and tourists whilst selling them ice-cold San Miguel.

Their apartment was in Palma Nova, opposite a large fast food restaurant. It was very comfortable and overlooked the beach. I was provided with a lovely room of my own. These were very generous people whom I had known for many years, but not enough years for them to be this generous. Gail had been a work colleague of Adele's and through coming to see the band we had all become good friends. There was a chance that after the split a custody battle would ensue over our joint friends. I needn't have worried, it didn't develop into a Kramer vs Kramer situation and we both kept Gail and Richard as mutual friends.

The Martins were doing a lot of the work on the bar themselves; the night after I arrived was no different, so I was left to my own devices. It was low season and most places were still closed. However a salubrious little watering hole, emphasis on the word hole, called Cheeks was open for business. It was an English-run theme pub; I think the theme was just how shitty can you make one place be. Anyway, beggars can't be choosers and I settled down and marvelled at the pink décor and the plastic palm trees. I ordered a beer, and out of curiosity I enquired as to the origins of the establishment's moniker. I was told by a barman who had all the giddy exuberance and class of Timmy Mallet, that it referred to buttocks. Oh how he laughed, pointing to the hanging sign outside that depicted a large pink pair of gluteus maximus muscles. Yes, that's right folks, I was sitting in a bar that was named after an arse, run by one and I felt like a right one myself.

The night however, was to take a turn for the better when a group of about thirty Danish girls walked in and proceeded to rattle out a few tunes on the obligatory Karaoke machine. God they were awful to listen to but to look at was a different matter. They were all tall, blonde, blue-eyed, muscular and drunk, and you can't ask for much better than that when you're feeling lonely in a strange place.

I bided my time refusing many offers to join in the caterwauling that was masquerading as singing. When the night was nearly over I strategically gave in to their offers. I explained that I wasn't very good at this sort of thing but I would give it a go. I picked the track 'Addicted to Love' by super crooner Robert Palmer, the closest thing to Rock in the grubby, beer-stained, little songbook that had been passed around. I belted out, if I may say so, a cracking version, much to the delight of those present. Of course I was called back for encore after encore of the crappiest songs imaginable: 'Yellow Submarine', 'Green, Green Grass of Home' and (may the little baby Jesus forgive me) 'Lady in Red'.

The adulation from the Viqueens would have swollen anyone's head had the competition not been so bad: the Elephant Man singing 'I've Got a Lovely Bunch of Coconuts' through his hood would've had him being carried shoulder high around the place and declared the new Pavarotti. When my public finally let me finish, one very striking great Dane sidled up beside me and in a heavy Scandinavian accent said, 'You are very good.' She walked me back to the apartment just in case I was attacked.

When Gail and Richard returned and saw 'Brigitte Nielsen' sitting on the sofa they must have thought, 'Jesus he's only been here a couple of hours, what have we done?' Unfortunately such pleasant occurrences were few and far between and even fewer when Ken arrived. I had invited him over to join me playing in the bar and because I missed his craic. With him being betrothed and therefore unavailable he prevented himself from being left on his own for the evening by telling anyone I was getting friendly with that I was gay. I only found this out many years later, and annoyed as I was, I couldn't help but feel slightly relieved. I mean even John Major and Bernard Manning could've touched in Magaluf at that time; what with the big smooch-inducing hits 'More than Words' by Extreme, 'Everything I Do' by Bryan Adams and 'To Be With You' by Mr Big, I couldn't fail. I, however, was avoided like I had a wee touch of SARS.

Ken arrived late one Saturday evening unannounced. We hadn't been able to secure a phone line so we weren't able to give him exact directions, he was just aware of the whereabouts of the bar and the fact that the apartment was opposite the golden arches. He got a taxi straight from the airport to Sodom and Gomorrah, aka Magaluf. He was unaware that the bar, due to the brewery not being able to supply the most essential of all ingredients to run a hostelry, beer, hadn't opened yet. He made a few enquires in a taverna that was situated close to the padlocked Route 66. Ken's grasp of Spanish ran as far as being able to order a beer, not by saying anything but by pointing and making a clicking noise with his mouth. Thankfully the barman had a reasonable grasp of English and was able to inform Ken that Gail and Richard were always about. Unfortunately this particular night saw them taking an enforced night off, so they decided they would use their time productively by going to Santa Ponza on a recce to ascertain if there were any Rock bars there providing live music.

I had been unwell for a while with chest pain and nausea. This necessitated a visit to the local quack who diagnosed stress, lifestyle and a chest infection; he prescribed antibiotics and rest. He charged me £300 or the equivalent of in pesetas, or should I say he charged Gail and Richard, I was skint. I promised to pay them back but never got the opportunity; it still causes a pang of guilt to this day. When we returned from the medical centre I informed my benefactors that I was going to take it easy for a few days and would therefore not be accompanying them to Santa Ponza.

Ken carried on drinking in the taverna awaiting the arrival of Gail and Richard, which wasn't going to happen. At one point the barman asked him if he was English. This is a very touchy subject as far as Ken is concerned, so he made it quite clear that he was Irish. The barman then said, 'Ah, Dublin.'

Ken said, 'No, I'm from the North.' His host looked a little confused, so Ken, spotting that there was a lot of football memorabilia adorning the walls, came upon a brainwave to explain the origin of his birthplace.

He put his finger in the air for dramatic effect, and shouted 'Gerry Armstrong.' Seeing as the big striker had been the goal scorer that had put Spain out of the 1982 World Cup, Ken was encouraged to leave by being thrown out the door, his bags following shortly afterwards. Only a couple of hours on foreign soil and banned from one bar already, not bad even for a seasoned professional of the 'chuck out' like old Ken.

Ken didn't really have too many options remaining, it was getting late and there was still no sign of Gail and Richard so he decided to go to the only other point of contact that remained, McDonalds. The beef patty emporium was closing when he arrived. Settling down in the doorway Ken waited for the staff to leave. He knew we were within touching distance but he wasn't brave enough to knock on doors at that time of night. He was acutely aware that the Spanish viewed home security quite simply: your house was proportionately safer in accordance with the size of the dog you owned.

I was in bed tossing and turning thanks to a fever, the result of my chest infection. I woke many times dripping in sweat, my head still full of vivid nightmares. Things were so bad that I was beginning to hear voices. Someone was calling my name – it was a voice I knew. I closed my eyes, reached for a paper bag by the bedside, covered my mouth and took deep palpitation-resolving breaths. I longed for the first light of day.

Unknown to me Ken was longing for the same thing; he had used his last trump card by shouting my name repeatedly into the dark, but had to give up when the local Guardia Civil started taking too much notice of him; he didn't want to round off an already disastrous day in the cells. The essentials in life, a bag of clothes and a guitar, were all the possessions Ken had with him. I had, in the brief conversation we had had weeks previously, suggested that when he finally came over he should bring his four-track recorder and drum machine. This was to enable us to record backing tracks to play over when we took up residency in the bar. These items took up a little bit of space in his bag, so he made space by cutting down on the toiletries. Who needs anti-perspirant in this heat anyway?

With only his holdall as a pillow Ken lay down behind a wall beside the restaurant and tried to get some sleep. This, however, was nigh on impossible due to the repetitive drum beat pounding from what must've been a nearby night club. He spent his first warm balmy night in paradise, wishing he had never left Hainault, cursing the crap that was dance music and hoping not to be arrested for vagrancy.

The next morning I arose a new man – the antibiotics must have kicked in. Gail and Richard were already up and preparing break-fast. We were short of milk, so Richard said he would get some while he was walking Kim, their dog. I contented myself that it would be at least half an hour before I got my morning cuppa, and I settled back with the local ex-pat newspaper. Two minutes later the door flew open and Richard came in shouting, 'Look what I found outside!' What walked in behind him can only be described as the sorriest sight I have ever seen; Brian Keenan had looked fresher the day he was released from four and a half years' captivity. As bad as he looked I was delighted to see my old partner in crime.

The San Miguels were cracked open and we toasted the start of a new adventure. As we were clinking our cans together I could hear what sounded like music coming from Ken's holdall. I asked him what it was. Not knowing, he bent down, opened the bag and the thump, thump, thump got louder. What emerged was the drum machine, which he had accidentally switched on when he laid his drunken head on it outside McDonald's. The banging that had kept him awake all night wasn't a disco churning out dance music but was his own beat box. Priceless.

Due to the fact that Ken and myself were skint, we were reliant on Gail and Richard for means of nourishment until we got playing and became self-sufficient. Ken Heaven has an appetite that would put a sumo wrestler to shame. I remember him having curry-eating contests with an old mate of ours, Michael Smiley. Ken would win hands down, demanding another helping. Our hosts provided three meals per day, which for a normal person should've been sufficient; unfortunately Ken needed at least five feeds in a twenty-four-hour period. The result was that he was always starving, but too much of a gentleman to ask for more food.

One day we were taken to what was the Spanish equivalent of a working-man's café. We were told that it was a set menu and that we could have whatever we wanted from a large serving counter. The table was weighed down with tons of delicious-looking fruit and vegetables. There was only one problem – Ken hated salad. The only thing that he was able to eat, from the choices available, was egg mayonnaise. Not knowing where the next meal was coming from he piled his plate high with about twenty hard-boiled eggs. When he returned to the table I couldn't help but notice the look of disbelief on Gail and Richard's faces. Ken started to wolf the eggs down, much to the amazement, nay amusement, of all those other diners who were nibbling on lettuce leaves and olives.

Halfway through the oesophagus-clogging feast Ken needed to take a break, stretch his legs and drink some water. There was a beading of sweat on his forehead and an unsteadiness to his gait. He pulled himself together and returned to the table and polished off the remainder of his meal. When he was finished I half expected to hear a round of applause from the slack-jawed audience; instead there was a stunned silence. Just then the waitress, who had obviously been waiting for the floorshow to reach its climax, came over and asked if we would like the baby spare ribs with saffron potatoes or the special paella for our main course.

Ken said, 'Sorry?'

The waitress repeated herself.

Then Ken said, 'But I thought we could only have what was on that table.'

'No,' she said, 'you can have anything from that table as your starter.'

Ken's face was a picture; he had passed up the opportunity of a cracking feed, which to him was almost like committing a sin. Even he, who considered himself a hungry Horace, couldn't face any more food, so he sat and watched the rest of us devour a beautiful meal followed by delicacies from the crowded sweet trolley. There was a slight green tinge to Ken's face as we ate; it could've been envy, but I think, realistically, it was a nausea brought on from a hard-boiled egg overdose. He would however, get his own back later when he filled the room we shared with the overpowering sounds and smells of someone trying to digest and expel a meal that sat as heavy as a wet hay stack.

Now that the gruesome twosome was back together there was plenty of scope for mischief-making. But first we had to get down to some work and record the backing tracks for our debut performance at old Route 66. We wrote out a list of songs that we would like to play and discarded the ones that had too many intricate bits; they just wouldn't lend themselves to a drum machine. Each track was recorded in this order: firstly the drums, then rhythm guitars were added and lastly lead parts for harmony solos. There was however no bass which we thought we could get away with, but without it the sound was terrible. We didn't have access to a bass guitar so we had two options: one, cobble what money we had together and purchase a very cheap one from the one music shop on the island in Palma, or two, contact Xan, and invite him over with his bass and a shareable amount of spending money for a holiday. Ole big fella, welcome to the Balearics.

Xan was to stay for two weeks of sun, sea and session work. Before the frivolity could begin he was put to work on laying down bass lines on the songs he knew and Ken would provide the rest. Recording finished, we were ready to entertain the drunken revellers of Magaluf town.

The bar had been open for a couple of weeks and trade was slow. The location wasn't great – it was situated down an alleyway in a small square between a shoe shop and a strip club, with the exotic dancers being some of the best customers. Gail and Richard were hoping that Electric Soup, for that is what we called ourselves, after the name given to Tennent's Super by the bums in Glasgow, would attract a bigger, classier crowd. Don't get me wrong, I'm not being snobby here, but I'm sure that when they bought the bar they never imagined they would be the hosts to a varied selection of strippers, a one-eyed salty old sea dog who smelled of fish and a Norwegian madman who thought he would prove what a Viking he was by drinking as much as he could, then throwing himself down the stone stairs that led to the toilets.

The mad Norse had performed this stunt on many occasions during his vacation but on one of the nights he slightly overdid it, sustaining numerous injuries that required hospitalisation. He also left large amounts of blood on the walls, floors and ceilings that needed at least an hour's work to remove. Thor couldn't understand why when he returned the next evening, swathed in bandages, he was no longer welcome. He was asked to leave and became very animated. There were four boys from Newcastle upon Tyne who were on a month-long golfing holiday, a break from their day jobs as nightclub bouncers, if you can have such a thing. They offered their assistance but by this stage our Viking hero was a quivering sobbing mess, so Gail and Richard took pity on him and let him let stay. He visited the toilets in the conventional manner from then on.

We were to play on a stage constructed from beer crates and a large piece of wood balanced on top. I have always sung with a band and have become used to the idiosyncratic time changes and mistakes that can occur in the process of live performance. Singing to a backing track is a very different kettle of fish altogether; there is no room for manoeuvring. If you miss the cue to go into the chorus from the verse, there is no one to go with you until you have found your feet again, you are just left faffing about until you recognise a piece of the music that will steer you back in. And that, of course is what happened on our very first song on the very first night.

To enable Ken and myself to get into the tunes at the same time as the backing tracks, we had a click track count of four; this was all well and good if you could hear it. With the hubbub in the place this proved impossible. Our first all-important, nerve-settling, impression-making song was 'Black Magic Woman'. It started like this. Click click click click, backing track, one beat later guitar, and one beat after that the vocal: effectively all three components of the song were playing totally out of time with each other. The backing track, being a machine, was stubbornly sticking to its preprogrammed course, therefore it was left to the two human elements within the equation to catch up with, firstly each other and then the machine. I didn't fancy our chances.

Ken, as he would've done in a conventional band, held back for the singer. I in a panic tried to catch up with him causing us to swap places; the machine kept calmly plodding away. There was a collective look of confusion on the assembled faces. We had been advertised as a Rock band; what they were hearing was more like avant-garde jazz.

The Geordie bouncers, strippers, holiday makers and especially Gail and Richard all stood open-mouthed. The proprietors added a look of horror: after all they were hoping that our musical endeavours would bring punters in, not drive them away. The backing track reached the lead break a good two seconds before Ken and myself; we had only just caught up with each other at this point. Carlos Santana in my opinion is a very overrated guitarist but even he would've sounded better with one hand tied behind his back and using a dinner plate as a plectrum, than the gibberish Ken was producing. Don't get me wrong, he was playing all the right notes, but as Eric Morecambe famously said 'not necessarily in all the right places'.

We somehow made it to the end of the feckin' song, and we were greeted with only the mad Norse showing appreciation. His clapping was so out of place it sounded like someone slapping the bottom of an HP sauce bottle in an Egon Ronay five-star restaurant. He was so drunk that we could've done 'The Flight of the Bumblebee' on tracing paper and combs and he would've applauded enthusiastically.

Richard looked like someone who had been waiting for a liver transplant being informed that an organ had become available, only to then be told it was George Best's. To say he and Gail were disappointed would be putting it mildly. I have never been so embarrassed in all my life; I had spent the last couple of weeks bumming and blowing as to how magnificent we were going to be. The rendition of our first song made me out to be a liar at best or a tone-deaf moron at worst. We had to quickly regroup to save the set, the customers that stayed and our tarnished reputations. I announced that we would be taking a very short break to sort out some technical problems and we headed to the bar for a long drink and a short chat.

After a stiff libation and a quick discussion it became clear that the reason that we both came in at the wrong time was that we couldn't hear the click track properly. The solution was obvious – we would need to turn it up slightly, geniuses the both of us. We took to the stage determined to make amends. And that is just what we did – the adjustment worked and we were able to complete a full set with only a few minor hiccups. We rounded the evening off with a storming version of 'Freebird'. The lead break enabled me to go to the bar and leave the stage to the maestro. He was so good that one idiot at the bar claimed that he was miming, so I had to forcibly drag him to the stage and stick his head against Ken's amp. I think he got the message. We had grasped victory from the jaws of defeat and were hailed as rock stars, the drink flowed and all was well on the Balearics. Of course it would never last.

The prisoner

Flyers had been printed to try to promote the coming week's entertainment by Electric Soup. One of the most annoying things about Magaluf are the PR terrorists that try all manner of bullying tactics to entice you into whichever den of iniquity they were in the employ of. Ken and myself felt we were too classy to drag people off the streets, so the flyers sat on the bar. That is until Big Xan took it upon himself to politely hand them out to anyone who looked like they enjoyed a little Rock on the heavy side. Cue the big lad getting arrested when he presented the very first leaflet to an undercover cop. We were actually playing at the time and were totally unaware of what had happened. As the hours went by we thought that Xan was just taking in the many weird and wonderful sites of the town.

Our old bass player was taking in sights of a far more horrendous nature, one of which was the communal stripping and beating of those that the cops suspected of dealing in drugs. Xan, who has a chronic back problem, was beside himself with fear. He thought that if they even gave him the slightest of taps with one of their rubber tickling sticks he would collapse in agony. They, in turn, he feared, might think he was acting up and give him a couple of whacks to toughen him up a bit.

Xan was asked to strip naked in front of laughing policemen, which is a horrendous thing for anyone to endure. He was then dealt the ultimate indignity. He was asked to lift his todger in case he was concealing drugs behind it. Fear had reduced its size to that of a chipolata; all that could've conceivably been hidden there was a Tic Tac. As all this was going on he was praying that he would not hear the snap of a rubber glove and the feel of a latex finger in his inner sanctum. At least he had the comfort of knowing that his old band-mates were searching frantically for him and that at any minute they would burst through the doors to save him from this 'Midnight Express'-style ordeal.

Back at Route 66 we were having a whale of a time. The set had gone really well and we were being bought drinks by anyone with a spare peseta burning a hole in their holiday pocket. It was just a pity that Xan had missed it, but hey, he'd catch the gig tomorrow. As the night started changing to day we did start to become a little concerned as to the whereabouts of our old mucker; after all there were a lot of assholes in England football tops about.

We left the bar and walked to the front of the main strip where we looked up and down. There was no sign of him. I suggested that we split up and visit all the bars to track him down. Just as we were about to set off, the barman that Ken had insulted with his Gerry Armstrong comment, came out of his taverna cleaning a glass on his stained apron.

He said, 'Your friend he gone.'

I asked, 'Where to?'

He replied, with a gleeful grin on his face, 'Guardia Civil.'

Panic set in as we ran back to the bar to seek the assistance of Gail and Richard. At least they could speak a bit of Spanish. Richard nearly choked on the beer nuts he had just stuck in his mouth when we told him Xan had been arrested.

'What for?' he coughed, spitting out small flecks of salty pulp.

'God knows,' I said. But at least we now knew where he was. It was decided that I should accompany Richard to the Police Station, I think for moral support, as I don't know what other useful purpose I could've served.

When we arrived we went to the information desk, Richard asked if a Xan Phillips had been brought in. He was told that yes, indeed, a man of that name had been arrested earlier that night and was in a holding area. We were shown through an armour-plated door into a room that looked like a scene from 'Hill St Blues'. There was all manner of life's flotsam and jetsam wandering about. Junkies were rubbing shoulders with drunks who were in turn chatting up the local prostitutes. There was an atmosphere of restrained violence with many there sporting headwounds and black eyes, probably a yobbish gift given to each other.

A man had decided that the effort of making it to the toilet he was standing beside was too much. He started urinating onto the floor, much to the annoyance of one of the officers who showed his disgust by beating the drunk around the buttocks with a nightstick. There was a smell of urine, blood, sweat and tears: anyone subjected to this place for too long would be removing their shoe laces and looking around for the nearest beam or pipe that would successfully take the weight of a dehumanised being. And there in the middle of all this mayhem and filth was the gentlest man you could ever meet sitting on a bench with his head in his hands.

It transpires that the heinous crime that Xan had perpetrated and which had elevated him to the status of public enemy number one, was to hand out advertising literature without a licence. No problem, we could just explain that he had done it off his own bat and was just trying to help out a couple of old friends in a band. The explanation brought gales of laughter from the other leafleteers who had been scooped that night: after all, who in their right mind would do such a demeaning job for anything other than the pittance that it paid. The cops were not impressed; they kept saying he was working without being a national, which at that time, unlike the rest of Spain, you still had to be.

While Richard was arguing Xan's case another Guard came over, having overheard that the big lad had been handing out flyers for my band, and enquired about my national status. Richard's blood suddenly turned ice-cold; he knew he was in for a massive fine if he had been caught employing a couple of wandering minstrels who didn't have licences or citizenship. He started stammering that I, of course, had the proper documentation. The cop looked unconvinced and told me to stay put while he went off somewhere, probably to measure up a nice bit of rubber hosing with which to beat me.

Richard was then asked by cop numero uno to present Xan's return plane ticket to prove that he wasn't planning on staying. After asking where it was, Richard said he would come back with the evidence from the apartment. He was led back to the large reinforced security door, it was electronically operated by someone on the other side, and as it swung open and seeing as no one was watching me I decided to make good my escape. I nonchalantly tagged onto Richard. I found myself walking back through the foyer, and out the front door to be greeted with the sweet smell of tapas and freedom.

We ran like a couple of Harrison Fords in 'The Fugitive', keeping to the back streets and staying in the shadows. Richard kept shouting, 'Fuck, fuck, fuck!!' which I thought was a bit strange for someone who was trying not to draw attention to himself. When we reached the apartment it was decided that I should go to the bar while Richard took back Xan's ticket to freedom. I agreed of course; I didn't want to become a guest of the Bangkok Hilton. We agreed that Richard should say, if asked, he didn't know of my where-abouts, stating that the last time he saw me I was still incarcerated. The plan worked and Big Xan was released, with a stern warning that should he break the law again there was a piece of piping with his name on it.

Xan entered Route 66 and was greeted like our very own wee Ronnie Biggs. Drinks were on the house, which eventually helped with his nerve-wracked state. Due to my now 'on the run' status it was decided that at the next available opportunity Ken and myself were to become Spanish citizens, Hose A and Hose B.

The following day Gail and Richard made enquires and discovered that we needed to have a medical before the relevant documentation could be submitted; an appointment was booked with a GP in Santa Ponza for the next day. In the meantime we decided to spend the free time we had – we couldn't play in the bar until we were legal after all – drinking cheap sparkling Spanish wine, sitting on the balcony with binoculars and observing the local wildlife, that is when the beautiful topless sunbathers weren't getting in the way.

We took to calling ourselves Fingal (Xan), O'Flaherty (Ken) and Wilde (me) after the great Irish wit and child molester Oscar. We drank ourselves into a Cava-induced giggling mess. The blazing sun, as it always does, was not helping with the intoxication and potential sunstroke. We staved off headaches by drinking more dehydrating alcohol and running to the toilet. While Xan was away at the bathroom reducing his kidneys to sun-dried prunes, Ken revealed a cunning joke to play on the just-released prisoner.

Returning after draining the spuds Xan was presented with the binoculars by Ken, who had been hogging them, and told it was his turn. He even suggested that there was an area of natural beauty that was on the beach and situated in front of some rocks. Big Xan was only too keen to take in the vista and scanned the area, adjusting and readjusting the focus so as when the subject came into vision he could benefit from a clear view. When it did he announced that indeed the view was spectacular. What he didn't know was that Ken was waiting for the next police car to drive past, which they did every fifteen minutes or so. When it appeared he whispered to 'Peeping Tom' that the cops always kept an eye out for lechers ogling the ladies on the beach. Xan pulled the binoculars away from his eyes only for a police car to come into his vision.

Having spent the previous evening basking in the warmth of the Guardia Civil's hospitality and not wanting to partake of it again any time in the next century or so, Xan ignored his bad back and dropped to the floor in an attempt to get out of sight. He dragged himself across the tiles on his naked torso; the suntan lotion made a squeaking sound and picked up the dust, dirt and dog hairs off the floor. His chest and back now looked like that of a Greek waiter. The car, of course drove on. Xan, however, was informed that they had stopped, with the Guards getting out and making their way towards the apartment. Xan was now frantic and while still doing an imper-sonation of Christie Brown in 'My Left Foot' he rolled and pulled himself over to the sofa where he stuffed the binoculars under the cushion.

'Where are they now?' he shouted.

'They're nearly at the front stairwell', he was told. Ken shouted that he should hide in the toilet; he was then informed that we would put them off his trail.

While Xan was sitting shaking in the bogs Ken went over and knocked on the front door, he then opened it and said, 'Sorry, no speaky Spanish.'

I then said, in my best broken English, 'Haf you sin a tall blanco mein wit tha looking glasses?'

Ken answered, 'No no, you've got the wrong place, there is no one here with binoculars.

I then went on, 'We see a mein wit a mucho grande nose looking at tha senorittas.'

Ken again denied all knowledge of the big-hootered letch.

I then said, 'We haf trouble wit hem before, his nam is Sam Fliplips.'

From the toilet there came a cry of 'You bastards,' as the penny he wasn't spending dropped.

Dude looks like a lady

The next day we were horrendously hungover which was unfortu-nate as we were to have a medical that would determine if we were allowed to stay on the island or not. As we had arisen late and the medical was at noon I didn't have time to shower or shave so I just tied my hair back into a ponytail and hoped that this would be enough respectability to drag me through.

We arrived in Santa Ponza by taxi and looked around for the medical centre. What we found was a converted garage with the shutters pulled down and nobody about. The sun was directly overhead and there wasn't the slightest shade. Well that's not strictly true: there were bars about one hundred metres away, too far to walk to without missing the doctor, and with names like, 'The Easter Rising Arms', 'The Michael Collins Inn', 'The Remember 1690' and 'King Billy's Big White Horse'. You wouldn't set foot in them anyway for love nor money.

We watched the Persil-white bodies of the Paddys and Billys walking to the beach wearing only scrotum-revealing, skin-tight swimming briefs, white sports socks and black slip-on shoes. Each of them carried on their shoulders twenty-four cans of cheap Spanish lager warmed to perfection and still in the box; it would be their only absorption of Spanish culture. Those wimps who decided to cover their torsos from the blistering sun wore either a Celtic or Rangers top, just to let everyone in 'Johnny Foreigner Land' know what particular flavour of bigot they were. Flying their colours also enabled them to identify the next victim for a glass in the face, Heaven forbid that they disfigured one of their 'own sort'. Here's a thought – would it not have been easier and a lot more relaxing to leave their disgusting hatred at home? But hey, where's the fun in that.

Around 2pm and with sunstroke just on the horizon a big white Mercedes pulled up and out of it got a man still dressed in his golf attire. He announced that he was the doctor while hurriedly pushing up the shutters from the door. We were ushered in by being gently shoved in the back. Once inside the dimly lit waiting area, he greeted us with an outstretched palm and the word 'passport'. Richard cordially shook his hand. The medic violently pulled his away as if he had had a dog shit placed in it. 'No, you fool,' he said in surprisingly good English, 'where are the passports?' I really didn't like this guy; we were obviously an inconvenience, probably just a quick buck before he started the back nine, followed by Sangria at the clubhouse. He, however, had us by the short and curlies; we needed him more than he needed us.

Both Ken's passport and mine were handed over; the doctor looked at them then motioned for Ken to follow him into a small examining room.

'How is your heart?' Ken was asked.

'Fine thanks,' he replied.

He was then asked, 'And your wife's?'

Ken couldn't think as to why he was being asked about Elaine, maybe the Doc thought she would be following him, so he just said, 'Oh she's fine too.'

This went on, with the quack asking about all manner of organs and orifices, each time enquiring as to Elaine's welfare. After about ten minutes he stood up, stamped and signed a couple of forms, passed them over and held his hand out. Ken shook it, again Dr Kildare ripped his hand away and shouted, 'El dinero'. Ken pointed to Richard who was going to pay for this shambles.

Richard counted out the fee requested and the doctor pointed towards the door with a shooing noise. Richard then, in his limited Spanish, said that I needed to be checked out as well. The medic then said, 'No, only two.'

Richard said, 'Yes, uno, dos,' pointing to Ken and myself.

The doctor looked very confused and he asked to see the passports again. He gazed at the photograph of me and then in my direction. He then turned to Ken and said, 'This is not your wife?' pointing to my snap, which had me clean-shaven, my hair looking its luxuriant best.

'No it feckin' well is not, ya cheeky bastard,' Ken said indignantly, 'that's him there,' nodding towards me.

It transpires that the doc had thought, after seeing the photo, that I was a woman; he also assumed that I was Ken's wife. I, folks, had been for a full medical and declared a female, I even had my documentation stamped and named Senorita Nancarrow; the shame would haunt me forever. That night the three Geordie bouncers, Xan and the regulars enjoyed the evening even more having been given the opportunity to wolf whistle and shout 'give us a kiss love' in the direction of myself, the feckers!

Born in the USA

When Xan's two weeks were up we bid him a fond farewell. We didn't know how long it would be before we would see him again, so it was sad to see him go. He, on the other hand, having been arrested, stripped naked, made to reveal the underside of his member, threatened with physical violence, nearly deported and branded a pervert, probably couldn't wait to see the back of us. O'Flaherty and Wilde would just have to get along without Fingal.

We changed the name of the group, mainly to throw the cops off our trail, to the Crawford Huey Duo (it would take too long to explain), and carried on playing. Trade was very slow; America had become financially more accessible, with many who would have normally travelled to the sunny parts of Europe deciding that Florida was a cheaper and more exotic option. Gail and Richard were starting to feel the financial strain. Rescue, however, was quite literally sailing over the horizon. The US fleet would dock in the harbour in Palma, the sailors and marines would decant and set off in search of night life, and the lure of the strip bar next door would send them and their pocket-burning dollars in our direction.

While the US Navy was in town trade was excellent. What will we do with the drunken sailors? I'll tell you what, rock their asses off. Our set was going down a storm; each song was rewarded with a-whoopin' and a-hollerin'. A quick prompt that we were parched from the stage initiated a barrage of bottles of ice-cold Mahou being sent our way; we couldn't lose. That is until one night this little redneck from somewhere down South started shouting, at the end of every song, 'Play some God damn white man's music!'

I was getting really pissed off with the little KKK prick so when he approached me, while I was standing at the bar during a break, and demanded that we, 'Play some good old Country and Western and no more of this nigger shit,' I leaned close into his face and told him I was going to sing 'The Crystal Chandeliers' by Charlie Pride, the only black Country star I could think of.

A small, racist marine grabbed me by the throat, obviously trying out his unarmed combat training. Unfortunately for him I never took too kindly to bigots, bullies and people who think they are hard because they are wearing a uniform. I punched him a couple of good whacks in his Southern fried face. He was taken aback slightly: obviously his martial arts instructors hadn't told him that when he was forcing democracy down the throats of people in their own country they might not take too kindly to America's foreign policy and they might just fight back.

When only a few of his mates tried to join in the Geordie bouncers quietly and efficiently dealt with them. Most of the sailors and marines were obviously pissed off with their slack-jawed shipmate's behaviour, for instead of coming to the aid of their comrades in arms, they cheered us on. In the blink of an eye the bar was flooded with Military Police, and the bruised and battered heroes of the good old US of A were dragged out to spend the rest of their shore leave peeling spuds in the brig.

I was feeling a little shaken after my confrontation with Mr Trailer Trash. I considered myself a lover, given half the chance, more than a fighter. One of the strippers from next door who frequented the bar and who had a bit of an eye for me, I think it was the glass one, ordered me a nerve-soothing large brandy. I accepted most gratefully. Ken, spotting an opportunity, approached her, and informed her that I was his best mate and that the whole ugly incident had left him feeling a little unsettled. She laughed and ordered another brandy, a small one.

Not even the US fleet could save Route 66; trade slowed again after they left and an idiotic ruling from the local council declaring that Uranus, as we were now called, couldn't play after midnight didn't help; no one leaves the house in Spain until after this time. I had a feeling that there might have been a bit of skullduggery going on. A brown envelope or two stuffed with used 5,000 peseta notes may have passed hands from the local bar owners to the officials at City Hall, because they seemed to be able to carry on with music into the early hours of the morning without the raising of a civil servant eyebrow. Anyway we started to become a financial strain on Gail and Richard's funds, so we decided that it would be best for all concerned that we return to London. But before we did Elaine was invited over for a holiday; the plan was that we could all travel back together.

Now that we were not gigging there was nothing stopping us from having a few drinks in the early evening, so that's what we did, and we carried on into the early hours of each morning. We had become quite well known in and around the main drag; we were given free drink in nearly every bar we frequented and of course in Route 66, which really helped as we were relying on the little money Elaine had brought over.

As a source of income Ken would give guitar lessons outside the bar. This was great fun, especially when we told those that partook that I was Swedish and Ken was Spanish. Keeping up the accents became harder as the drinks went down. On one hilarious occasion Ken tried to keep the pretence going with someone who was actually Spanish. I can only assume that his ola-ing and si si-ing made the guy assume that he was dealing with an idiot savant, similar to the Dustin Hoffman character in the film 'Rain Man'. Ken obviously had God-given talents but was sadly hampered by being a corkscrew short of a Swiss army knife.

The 12th of July and for once it was sunny

It just so happened that the glorious 12th of July fell while Elaine was over. We hadn't realised because each day blended into the next and it felt like a permanent weekend. It was the sight of a guy draped in a Union Jack, singing 'Who's in Derry? We're in Derry, fuck the Pope and the Virgin Mary', that brought the realisation that we were missing out on the jollifications. It also brought back the memories of my family peering through a crack in the curtains, while directly outside our window, no more than fifty feet away, a bonfire burned with a effigy of the Pope and a Tricolour on top. Oh, how we laughed, as did the few other Catholic families that had been placed by the council into our estate. The upshot is that I never really had much affection for the annual celebration of all things Orange. Don't get me wrong, everyone to their own, each side has their celebrations of hating each other, but you can't expect people who are having symbols of their religious beliefs and national identity set on fire in front of them to join in the hurrahs.

My mate Fish can be a wee bit naive at times, but obviously not as naive as myself for when he suggested, one year, that I should join him, Lado and Ken at the annual 11th night bonfire, I foolishly accepted. We were sitting on a grass bank down the shore in Holywood drinking bottles of cider. Everything was quite jovial until a gang from my old estate came sauntering past. One of them recognised me, pointed me out with an outstretched finger and shouted, 'There's a Taig that's gonna burn well on the old fire tonight!' At first I thought that he was joking, after all this was a cultural celebration, wasn't it? But patriotic venom, bigotry and Buckfast fuelled these boys – they wanted blood. Ken could see the situation starting to turn nasty so he turned to me and simply said, 'Run.'

I didn't need telling twice, I was up and on my toes before the first of their grasping hands could get to me. I ran, maybe foolishly, in the direction of the bonfire. I knew there was a pedestrian walkway just beyond that would take me up onto a main road and into view of passers-by and hopefully a patrolling police car.

There was no way I was going to let the mob catch me: I was an athlete. I held the record for the high jump in my high school, I always won the triple jump and long jump and was only denied winning the 100 metres and 200 metres every year by an exceptional sprinter called Kieran McKee. These guys were low-life drunks, not fit enough to keep up with me. I made it to the main road and ran in the direction of the High Street. I was just reaching Ned's bar, when from around the corner came another gang of hoods, who were alerted to my escape mission by the shouts and hysterical screaming of the chasing pack, well by those that hadn't stopped for a cigarette or to throw up.

My new adversaries fanned out in front of me to ensure that I would get the kicking my family background entitled me to. I resigned myself to my fate; young Protestant and Catholic men had in the past found themselves outnumbered and kicked to death in similar circumstances in our wonderful country and as I write this it is still happening unfortunately. From behind the horde blocking my way to the safety of my Ma and Da's, someone emerged.

Ken had run in the opposite direction to me, knowing that I needed to double back to get home. He pushed his way through, stood his ground and shouted that if anyone was going to hurt me they would have to go through him. The odds were stacked against him big style, but what he had on his side was his family's reputation. There was a stand-off for a second then the line of hate parted and allowed me to walk through. Their bravery was similar to those upper-class low-life that chase a fox to the point of exhaustion, for it then to be hysterically ripped to pieces. This fox got away, not through any cunning, but thanks to his Protestant best friend and his loyalty, not to Queen and country, but to his Fenian mate.

Elaine came from the Protestant side of the religious divide. Ken came from a similar family background, but because his mum was a Catholic, and to wind the rest of the family up, he called himself a Nationalist, which I believe he really is. But that 11th night in Mallorca he decided, for fun, to resort back to his planter roots. He and Elaine thought that it would be great craic to kick a Taig at midnight, just to welcome in the glorious 12th. Seeing as I was the only thing that loosely resembled a Catholic I would have to fit the bill. They goaded me most of the night that on the stroke of twelve I would be expected to offer up my arse to their boots in celebration of the famous victory at the Boyne River.

When the time for commemoration arrived I had forgotten all about it, probably due the patron Saint of beer Miguel. We were walking along the footpath, me slightly in front of Ken and Elaine, when I heard a rustling; I turned to see them advancing with 'kicking legs' pulled back in preparation. I suddenly remembered my date with destiny and fearing a haemorrhoidectomy from a couple of good stout Orange marching brogues, I turned and ran straight into a palm tree no more than two feet away. Luckily, for the tree, my head missed the trunk, but my left shoulder made full contact, spinning me around and dumping me flat on my arse. I lay on the ground slightly concussed while my assailants pretended to give me a good kicking. A passing police car stopped and it took all our powers of persuasion to convince them that I was not being assaulted but was taking part in a traditional Northern Irish custom.

After the sectarian shoeing we headed back towards the apartment but stopped, as we always did, at a taverna that sat in the middle of the footpath. We purchased our last beer of the night and ordered a bite to eat. Ken and myself were still laughing and talking about the '11th night kicking incident' when Elaine went to the bathroom. Ken said I was lucky that the tree had saved me from the beating I deserved. I told him to 'feck off' and he threw a chip at me; I retaliated by doing the same. Ken upped the ante by picking up the plastic ketchup bottle and squirting sauce all down the front of me. He seemed a bit shocked that I wasn't reacting the way I normally would have, by giving him a slap around the ear. I just sat there and let him do it.

Elaine returned from the toilet and I greeted her with, 'Remember that shirt you lent me?' I just pointed to the condiment-saturated garment and then to her partner. Ken's face went pale, he was speechless. He turned and ran, Elaine in hot pursuit. I was just glad that it was his turn to be chased under threat of violence.

Adios

All good things must come to an end and so it was that our time in Mallorca was over. We spent an emotional final night at Route 66 while we waited for a taxi to take us all to the airport. We bid Gail and Richard a bleary farewell; I was also saying goodbye to a Dutch girl I had been seeing, on and off, called Monique. Ken insisted on calling her Monica, much to her displeasure. In the cab I actually got a little tearful – I felt that this might be the last time I would ever see Gail and Richard, and so it proved. Shortly after we returned to London they split up; probably the pressure of running a loss-making business didn't help. Gail went back to England, Richard stayed on in Spain. I lost contact with both of them and have never heard from them since. I'd say they are probably quite glad of that. I, however, am not – they were a lovely couple that I probably caused more stress to than they deserved.

At Palma airport Ken, Elaine and myself had a few drinks that we didn't need. Elaine's flight was about two hours after ours due to a ticket-booking problem. I kept asking Ken the time to make sure we didn't miss the plane; he kept assuring me that we were OK. I should've checked myself.

As I was walking to the toilet I glanced at a clock. To my horror we only had fifteen minutes to boarding and we hadn't even checked in. I ran back and dragged Ken to his feet, shouting that we were going to miss the flight. As we ran along the concourse, pushing the trolley with all our bags and musical equipment on it, the tannoy blared out our names: the plane was about to depart. When we reached the check-in gate the staff started laughing – we had no chance of getting to the departure gate in time. Just when all hope was lost a miracle happened.

The plane had actually stalled for some reason, and the word came back that we could get on board if we could make it out to the runway. This is not a word of a lie, and remember this is many years before 9/11. We were whisked, luggage and all, out a side door, put onto one of those baggage buggies and driven at high speed up the tarmac to the hastily repositioned steps. Our gear was thrown into the hold as we ascended the stairs. We were greeted by bemused flight attendants and even more baffled passengers who were wondering who could be so important that a plane had been stopped on the runway for them to get on. Imagine their indignation when two long-haired drunken Paddys appeared, a little shaken, but mighty relieved all the same.

The adventure was, unfortunately, far from over. Now that we were safely in the air, we had a discussion about whether we had enough money to buy a couple of in-flight drinks. We came to the conclusion that because we were flying into Stansted and would, therefore, need all the money we had for train fares back to London, we couldn't really squander our last pennies on booze. So of course we spent it anyway, with the reasoning that Elaine's friend Donna could be phoned and persuaded to pick us up. We didn't even know if she was free to carry out this mission of mercy. Beers and spirits in hand we settled down for a pleasant journey home. I promptly fell asleep.

I woke choking and gasping for air. For a second I didn't know where I was – what I did know was that if I didn't get oxygen into my system ASAP I was going to die. Something was blocking my airway, so I started coughing violently in an attempt to remove it. Ken, who had been watching me bug-eyed, eventually leapt into action. The punches rained down viciously on my back; I thought my ribs were going to snap. I thanked Ken for his kind assistance by throwing a punch at him. The flight attendants started running towards us thinking that we were having a mid-air dust up. When they realised what was happening one of them stood me up, turned me around, put his arms around my midriff and commenced the Heimlich manoeuvre. All those who had fallen asleep were woken by the sights and sounds of what looked like a little bit of gay loving by the steward and his purple-faced partner.

I eventually coughed up the object that had edged me towards the teeth of death. I gasped in lungfulls of bacteria-heavy compressed air, while trying to thank and remove the steward from behind me. I had a funny feeling that he was lingering a little longer than he should have. I didn't really care; we could get married if he wanted, I was that grateful to be alive. I sat down and wiped the sweat from my brow. I looked down at the lump of goo that was still lying on the floor. I asked, 'What the feck is that?' Ken looked a little sheepish then explained.

'The free meals arrived and seein' as you were asleep I ate them both, but I felt a bit guilty and knowin' that we were goin' to have a long wait tomorrow mornin' with no money, I decided to stuff a bread roll into your mouth and . . . well . . . you know the rest,' Ken said.

I was, to say the least, speechless: my best mate had nearly killed me in an attempt to make sure I wasn't going to be a little peckish the next day. Calmly I said, 'Would it not have been better to wait until I was awake before you foisted your kind offerings upon me?' He said that if he had waited, the temptation would have resulted in him eating it himself and he didn't think that would've been fair. Folks, you have borne witness to the logic of a confused mind.

We arrived in Stansted at 5am; we collapsed onto a couple of rows of seats and fell asleep, knowing that it would be at least another four hours before we could phone Donna. Thank goodness she was able to, reluctantly, pick us up. Ken had persuaded her by telling her that we would pay for the petrol and also give her £40 for her services on our arrival home. Elaine was flying into Heathrow and we assumed, due to our self-imposed lack of transport, that she would be home before us, and she having money meant that we could repay our debts to Donna – problem solved. When we got back there was no sign of Elaine. The flat was locked: we would have to break in.

We stepped over the remains of the front door to find the phone ringing. Ken answered it and was greeted by Elaine's dad who was a little irate; he had been ringing for hours expecting us home ages ago. The reason for his call was to tell us that after we had abandoned his only daughter in a foreign country, she had fallen asleep and missed her flight, with the next available one being five days away. She had to go back to Gail and Richard, after wishing them a fond farewell, and ask if she could stay with them until then, which of course, being the decent people that they are, they said she could.

Later that night we were able to scrounge up the £40 from a neighbour with which to pay Donna. We then spent the money on a

Chinese and beer. As we sat discussing and retelling the adventures that we had just experienced, Donna walked through the hole where the front door used to be looking for her taxi fare. We had nothing, she had a wild temper, so she lifted one of the full cans of beer and whacked Ken about the head. The result? Abrasions, bruises and lacerations. It was good to be back in Old Blighty.

At this point you are probably wondering about the songwriting that had initiated my exodus to Mallorca in the first place. Well basically I didn't come up with a single note or lyric the whole time I was there, preferring instead to do my bit as the cultural attaché to Spain for the drinking classes of Ireland. As it became obvious that we would be moving back to London there was a girding of the loins and a kicking up the arse. I wrote a whole album's worth of stuff in the last week that we were still soaking up the sun. I have always found leaving things to the last minute worked for me and again in this case the pressure of having to get something together before the plane took off resulted in eleven songs that were crackers, even if I say so myself. Alex would be impressed when he heard the fruits of my labours, thinking that I had spent the best part of a year toiling away at my chosen art form, abstaining from the pleasures of the flesh and the nectar of the hop. He would never know about the sheer unadulterated, unholy and unhealthy shenanigans that unfolded under the blazing sun of the Balearic Sodom and Gomorrah. But we do, don't we folks?

The end of an era

Now that I was back in London it became apparent very quickly that anything that I had worked for was gone. Alex announced that any further collaboration with Kuma was a no-no. I was told it was due to ill-health, but this may have been another of Alex's ever-increasing economical policies with the truth; I bumped into Kuma a couple of months later and he looked in fine fettle. Alex had always used the term 'slowly, slowly catchy monkey' when referring to the Nellies getting a record deal. I'm afraid that we had missed too many opportunities to get signed by acting so slowly that the monkey was away on its toes by the time Alex got round to doing the business. I had to come round to the fact that we were never going to make it.

I sort of went off the rails a wee bit and partied till I dropped. Don't get me wrong, I'm not complaining, I had a whale of a time and there were some memorable nights of Rock and Roll mayhem with Inky in Camden. We also became residents of the Tuesday Rock Night at a Leicester Square bar – the name escapes me – where Ken's and my head banging routine to 'Turbo Lover' by Judas Priest became the stuff of legend.

It was also the scene of one of the funniest things Xan has ever done. The big bass player had been getting gip from his parents about the length of his hair. His father, a lovely man at the end of his tether, disapproved with great enthusiasm, branding his son a long-haired hippy, which I think is hilarious coming from someone who named his son Xan. The pressure must've got to Xan; he decided that he would have to do something about his locks.

He arrived at the bar for our midweek rockathon with a hairdo that looked like a mix between Emo Philips and Pam Ayers. It basically was a bob with a fringe that was halfway up his forehead and looked like it had been cut with a pair of plastic scissors, the kind a child would use to prevent injury. The back was shorter than the side bits, which curled up until they touched the sides of his mouth. It was a trichiological catastrophe akin to the time that that temptress Delilah persuaded Samson that a short back and sides might loosen her toga. I thought, 'He's a feckin sight.' Then I realised that the demise of the Nellies might've had a slightly deranging effect on his fragile mind. To save his feelings I told him that his hair was 'different'. Ken was his usual compassionate self, saying he looked like a brunette version of Joanna Lumley, when she was in the New Avengers; only he had better legs and a more ample bosom.

At that time we had a small but willing set of female admirers. That night a few were present; one of them happened to mention that she thought that Big Xan's hair was, in her words, a 'fuckin mess'. I just wouldn't have it. Don't get me wrong, I agreed with her, in fact, I would've gone further declaring it a natural disaster of World Health Organization worrying proportions, but no one took the piss out of a Nellie.

'I think it's cool, he's making a statement, he isn't pandering to what a Heavy Metal musician is supposed to look like,' I lied.

'Well I think he looks gay,' she countered.

'How dare you, have you never heard of Freddie Mercury?' I asked, while hoping that Xan wasn't going to go the whole hog and brandish a yard-brush bristler of a moustache similar to the one sported by the queen of Queen.

As the night went on and the beer went down I actually started getting used to the inverted bird's nest adorning Xan's head. I didn't like it, hell no, but it was growing on me like a verruca. As night turned to day we tumbled out onto the streets in search of the last night buses home. At Trafalgar Square we huddled together before setting off for our respective bus stops, but before we could say our goodbyes Xan reached up to his head and whipped off the toupee that he had been wearing all night as a joke and with no regard for my blood pressure. Hook line and sinker, we had all been done up like a kipper, it was a classic.

Xan played the same trick on his mother and father. They were so aghast at the vision of what their son's hair could turn out like if he got it cut that they never mentioned its length again. Genius really.

I think the hedonistic lifestyle reached its zenith when on my 27th birthday Paul Taylor and myself spent a drunken day in Soho, the culmination of which saw us visiting a tattoo parlour in Ilford and me getting inked. The next morning I woke on Ken's sofa wondering why the top of my right arm was aching, having forgotten about the whole incident. When I visited the bathroom and looked in the mirror I was somewhat perplexed at what I saw. Being a Rock God it was only natural that I would've chosen a snake, fire-breathing dragon or at least a bleeding skull to be my first tattoo, but oh no, not me – I chose a picture of Mickey Mouse to scar my skin for life. Ken nearly wet himself laughing.

Things were changing at a pace, time never sits still, and Steve Bruce had even sold the Stick of Rock. A consortium of skinheads were the new proprietors; they probably considered it the thrill of a lifetime to be running a bar that had been owned by a member of Cock Sparrer. One night Inky and myself decided, seeing as we were in the Bethnal Green area, to pop in for a pint.

The place was a mess: the lighting was abysmal, bulbs that had blown had not been replaced, the floors hadn't been cleaned in weeks and the clientele looked absolutely delighted that we had arrived – it gave them someone other than each other to glare at. I ordered a pint of Guinness to be informed that it was lager or nothing. Inky only drinks cider so the barman blew the dust off a couple of bottles sitting on a switched-off cold shelf, and poured the chilled to room temperature contents into a dirty glass. Warm Strongbow is disgusting; Inky asked if he could have some ice. He was told that they didn't have any.

As usual I thought I would add a little humour to the situation so I asked the four-brain-celled bar steward if he had forgotten the recipe for ice. He didn't smile but pointed a gold sovereigned finger at the door. The punters around the counter kicked back their seats and stood as one; they were probably hoping we would refuse to leave and we would have to be persuaded gently out onto the street with the ox-blood leather of a fourteen-hole DM boot. We really didn't need that much encouragement; there were park benches more inviting than the newly refurbished Stick of Rock.

Outside I saw red. 'Those bastards have just forced me out of a place that up until recently I called my home,' I shouted. I decided to go back in and take my chances. Inky, in turn, decided that this was a slightly foolish idea; he jumped on top of me, wrapping his legs around mine. If we were to have a fight, which would never happen, I know for a fact that Inky would last about two seconds. This is not a boast: it's just that he is too much of a pacifist to lower himself to the ugly brutality of macho, bullshit violence. I just stood there until I calmed down with what looked like a hairy scarecrow hanging from me. We laughed a lot on the walk back to his flat.

It was sad to witness a great little boozer like the Stick lose its soul, but its degradation was not to last for much longer. It closed its doors for the very last time only a couple of weeks later. It was rumoured that it might have been mismanagement although I find that hard to believe. As a final insult the decorative tiles, depicting street scenes of 18th-century London that ran the length of the back wall were chipped off and sold. They had been listed as a national treasure valued, then, at £250,000. Who it was I wouldn't like to say, although one of the last owners, it is alleged, made a hasty move to America. I'm sure the two weren't connected M'lud.

The closing of the Stick seemed to symbolise the end of an era. Things were changing, shit we were all changing. Relationships were being built or destroyed, people were getting older and wiser; others were getting older and madder. There were no conscious decisions made: we all just followed different courses, things would never be the same. I started to get itchy feet. I was restless and burnt out; the Rock and Roll Capital had taken its toll; it was all self-inflicted; something had to give.

CHAPTER SIX

Strictly No Ballroom

The return

I came back to County Down at the start of 1994 for a couple of weeks rest and reflective analysis on what the feck was I going to do next. I had spent the last couple of months of my eight and half years in London dossing on the sofas of Paul Taylor, Inky and my sister Roisin. I had also made use of the flat of a beautiful Spanish girl called Anna Fernandez. Alex Balkin had introduced us to each other at an awards ceremony, which one I just don't remember. He was in the process of trying to romance her. She was stunning, so I did the gentlemanly thing and stole her from him while his back was turned.

As well as her inherited beauty Anna was also in possession of genetic material that would see her developing cancer: a tumour would require horrendously painful reconstructive plastic surgery. So as well as sharing her Brixton abode I shared in her battle to beat the big C. it was not, to say the least, the best way to develop a relationship. Added to her medical trauma, we were also skint which didn't help – I would have to scrounge money from friends and family just to get the fare to visit her in the Royal Marsden Hospital. For somebody who had vowed to stay clear of the DHSS I found it very depressing, after all this time, to have to sign on again.

Thankfully Anna made a full recovery and got the all-clear, which made the world a much brighter place. For a while things were ecstatically rosy in the garden, as you can imagine having faced down the spectre of death and winning. But Anna was a bit of a mystic: she practised yoga, meditated, believed in the power of crystals and that you could cure all ills by rubbing lavender on the backs of your knees or something. Hey, she beat cancer so why wouldn't she believe? I, on the other hand, as anyone who knows me will attest to, do not believe in anything spiritual. In this respect we were not a good match; we never argued, we just didn't happen.

While visiting Roisin in Hounslow one day I poured my heart out, which was a rarity for me. I think I was depressed without having it officially diagnosed. I had given up my job, I had split up with my long-term partner Adele, the Nellies were no more and I had nowhere to call home. Furthermore a genre of music called Grunge had exploded out of Seattle and had all but destroyed and ridiculed the music I loved and was writing. I felt redundant. Roisin suggested I go back to Belfast to get my head together and return to London when the mists had cleared; I calculated that this would take three weeks tops. I'm still here seventeen years later.

My Ma and Da had downsized their house; most of the chicks had flown the coup. Myself, Elish and Roisin had all moved to London; Marie was still in Italy. The shop had become too much of a handful as their workforce dwindled through migration. The house, with its six bedrooms, was way too big; they decided to buy a smaller home close to the shores of Belfast Lough. Only my brother Mark and my sister Louise remained at home. Everything was perfect as far as accommodation was concerned – perfect, that is, just as long as none of the rest of the kids came back.

I returned to a family home that I had never lived in and which was too small for another body. My Da suggested that I slept in the half-finished yacht he was building in the garage – to this day I still don't know if he was joking or not. Even though the offer of laying my weary head down on the damp floorboards of a boat and breathing in sawdust all night was very tempting, I passed on his kind offer, especially when I was told that there had been sightings of a rat that was described as being as big as a cat. Luckily my old friend Colin Shiels was living in a beautiful house just outside of Holywood and he was kind enough to offer me a room there. It was a no-brainer.

Colin is a bass player, our old friend Mixi McMillan is a guitar player and I'm a singer of sorts. We're all mates and drinking buddies and the inevitable happened, we formed a band, just for a laugh while I was waiting to return to London. We needed a drummer so I contacted Roger Davidson who was in the band

70% Proof, the one that No Hot Ashes had drawn with in the battle of the bands competition in the Co-op Hall all those years ago. Roger's and my paths had crossed one other time after my move to London. It happened when the Nellies had been on tour in Ireland and we had played a place called Charlie Heggarty's in Bangor, Roger's hometown.

The gig was an unmitigated disaster: the place was packed with British soldiers, who didn't want to hear anything remotely Rock and Roll, and they showed their disapproval energetically. While we were playing Inky was sitting at a stall with the intention of selling the freshly released, 'Is this Face Free?' EP. To his amazement the off-duty 'mummy's little heroes' started buying the record in great amounts. At first he was delighted, but this gave way to horror when the bastards started using them as Frisbees, firing them at the band. Not since Van Gough cut off his own lug with his palate knife, have a bunch of artists been so close to losing body parts by means of instruments of their own art. Punches were exchanged; boots were delivered from the stage to regulation shaven faces. The bouncers were eventually called upon to toss the cannon fodder out the doors. I had a feeling in the years to come that this would be one of their more comfortable fights.

Military coup over, we carried on playing to those that remained, one of whom was Roger, who was there with members of his own band and guys from a rival band. At the end of the show we packed as quickly as we could in an attempt to get away before we bumped into the soldiers who would be emptying out onto the streets from the watering hole they had retreated to.

One of the boys with Roger started giving us verbal abuse, demanding that the now packed up gear be reassembled so they could show us what a good band sounded like. I had words with him; he was talking when he should've been listening and it was going to get ugly. Up stepped Roger and asked what was going on. 'This prick here won't put the gear back up so we can play a couple of songs,' the drunk said pointing at me. Roger turned to me and asked if this was true. I told him that his asshole friend was correct and did he have a problem with it.

Instead of attacking me Roger, without warning, gave his mate a couple of sobering right hooks to the side of the head saying, 'Wise up, you dick.' I got the feeling that there must've been a bit of previous between these two, probably band rivalry or something, because Roger seemed to get quite a bit of pleasure from the physical assault he had just administered. Without batting an eyelid Roger turned to me and said, 'If you ever need a drummer give me a call.' Five years later that's just what I did.

Roger answered the phone and seemed slightly taken aback that he had been asked to join a band by someone with whom he had only had a passing acquaintance. The bastard turned me down. I returned to the living room where Mixi and Colin were waiting for me to come back with the good news that we had filled the vacant drum stool. They were slightly surprised that we had been rejected; after all we had decent reputations on the local circuit. I suppose we would just have to put plan B into operation; there were a few other drummers we could consider. I flicked through my address book and reached for the phone just as it rang.

Roger was on the other end of the line. He had spent the last thirty seconds analysing his options and realised that this was the chance of a lifetime; oh, the poor misguided fool, he should've taken another thirty seconds and stuck to his original decision thus saving his hearing, liver and renal function.

While staying at Colin's I was privy to the sheer madness that is his mother. Don't get me wrong, she didn't live in the house with us, thank God, but she may as well have. On the odd occasion that I ended up with a little female company, she had a perfect knack of calling round just as I was about to send my soul to hell; I think she had a hotline straight to the Vatican. She also had a little dog called Teddy that she would walk twenty-four hours a day past the house. To ensure her son was safe and free from sin, she spied through the big front window. We got so used to the metal frames of her glasses shining on the double glazing that one evening, when there was a party going on, and the goggles appeared, Colin encouraged everyone to give a liberal display of the middle finger and the more traditional two-finger salute. It was hoped that this would encourage her on her busybody way.

The next day Colin, a devout Catholic, was slightly dismayed when he was told by his next-door neighbour, that the Parish Priest had called to our house. Unable to get an answer at the door, due to the abominable music emanating from the stereo, the poor Padre had gone to the front window and peered through. He was confronted with the sort of greeting that is only afforded to murderers, rapists and Protestants.

Colin's mum had told me that his brother Gary, before migrating to the States, had left some clothes at the family home. She thought, through the goodness of her heart, that I could maybe get a turn out of them. The fact that I was about two foot taller than Gary didn't seem to dissuade her. One sunny day I was out doing something in the garden, as were all the neighbours – in Ireland you try to make the most of the annual day of sunshine – when Mrs Shiels and Teddy walked past. Much to the amusement of the curtain-twitchers she shouted, 'Anytime you want to, you can call round and get the jeans off me.'

Returning to London just started to become an option I didn't want to take. Don't get me wrong, I adore the city and in some ways I still consider it my home. I met and fell in love with some of the finest people in the world there, but now I was having a ball with my new bandmates. My family, Colin, Roger and Mixi's generosity, friendship and craic are the reason I stayed. Knowing that I was not going to return to London meant that I had to face up to the realisation that I was never going to make it as a rock star.

I was also giving up the friendships I had revelled in. I would miss all my mates especially Ken and Xan. We had shared a dream and made music together; there is no stronger bond between friends. It still pisses me off that the quality of our songs was never given the chance to be appreciated by more people. We were close on a few occasions to becoming a success, but we were unlucky. Then again, another way to look at it is that we were extremely lucky to have found each other – by Christ we had a ball.

The Strictlys

With the core of the new band now established there was an urgency to get a second guitar or keyboard player in to fill out the sound. It was so urgent that we decided to go on the piss in Belfast instead. After a few quarts of the devil's buttermilk we visited a burger van, leaving with portions of chips and somehow, the name of a guy who could play guitar and keyboards. I really can't remember the exact ins and outs of how this actually happened but the next day we had Eamonn 'Keyser' Keyes in the band. What he brought was exceptional musicianship and the ability to give me cluster headaches. He was, and I assume still is, one of the most talented people I have ever met; he is also one of the most stressed people on the planet.

There were now five of us. All we needed was to find somewhere to rehearse, to get a set together and persuade someone to give us a gig. What we also needed was a name. I had always chosen the moniker, apart from No Hot Ashes, for all the bands I had been in; this I think may have contributed, in no small part, to us never making it. I was not going to let this gift go to waste so I came up with a short list of three names. 'Ghenis Can't', 'The Pretty Ugly Oxymorons' and 'Strictly No Ballroom'. The latter got the least aggressive 'feck off' from the other band members so that was that settled.

We started rehearsing in this massive abandoned linen mill just off the Beersbridge Road in East Belfast. A guy called Maurice McNab, who would later become the local DJ Maurice J, ran it. He had also been in one of the support acts that had been spat on at my last No Hot Ashes gig. Knowing that bands need tons of equipment to function, the sensible thing would be to have the rehearsal studio on the ground floor, thus avoiding musicians developing inguinal hernias. Unfortunately, for some inexplicable reason, the practice area was on the top floor of the five-storey building. Maurice assured us that this was not a problem, there was a lift, however each time we arrived it was mysteriously out of order. I have a slight suspicion that Maurice may have been getting his own back for being speckled with phlegm at the School Aid gig.

Our first full rehearsal was to begin on a Saturday morning, which seems like a reasonably good time, unless of course, all five band members hadn't spent the previous night getting absolutely legless. What with the raging hangovers and the ten flights of stairs to carry all our gear up we were all feeling a little under the weather when it was time to play the first song. This could've spelt disaster.

Del Amitri were a band that we all admired so it was a unanimous decision to make their song, 'The Last to Know' the first tune Strictly

No Ballroom ever played. As the last notes hung in the air we all looked at each other. There were smiles all round: it had been played a little rockier than the original, but note perfect. Each song after that just got better and better, and hangovers were forgotten as the realisation dawned that this band could be shit hot.

We needed a gig to get some attention. By chance a friend of ours, Pat Catney, who owned the Kitchen Bar, situated in the city centre of Belfast, invited us to play there. It was a truly wonderful place, catering mainly to daytime trade; it attracted workers during their lunch hours, with an excellent selection of beers, the horse racing and the delicious board of fare. Which reminds me of a hilarious story which happened to a few Filipino friends of mine.

Being new to the country they had asked me where would be a good place to go to absorb some Irish culture. I, of course, pointed them in the direction of the good old Kitchen Bar. I had advised them to order the 'Paddy Pizza', which was a large home-made soda bread topped with all sorts and then smothered in melted cheese, a favourite with the lunchtime punters. On entering the bar they told Pat that I had sent them and they were shown to a table straight away, which at lunchtime was a rarity – you usually had to wait in a queue.

A waiter took their order and they requested the Paddy Pizza as instructed. He then asked them if they wanted anything else and they asked for fries, one portion each. When the pizzas arrived they couldn't believe the size of them. What they also couldn't believe was that five plates containing bacon, double sausage, double egg, tomato, mushrooms, soda bread, potato bread, black pudding and white pudding arrived as well; the table was groaning under the strain.

These people were small in stature and certainly in no anatomical state to consume the pile of fat and carbohydrate set down in front of them. One of them called the waiter over saying that there must have been some mistake – they hadn't ordered these second plates of food. He told them he was sure that they had, he had it written on his pad. There on the page in blue biro were the words, 'Five Ulster Fries'. If only they had asked for chips instead this whole diplomatic incident need not have happened.

The Kitchen Bar is a lot smaller when you are trying to set up a five-piece band that includes a guitar player who also plays keyboards. Pat had assured us that there would be a stage provided, and there was. However, it was only big enough to put Roger's drum kit on; the rest of us had to be content with the floor. The space was so limited that all the amplifiers had to be piled on top of each other at one side of the stage, as opposed to the traditional set-up of each musician having their own gear behind them. This meant that the full sound of the band would be coming from behind Keyser, which was great for him but a disaster for the rest of us who wanted to hear what we were playing and singing. There was no other alternative so we just had to make do.

We were worried that nobody would turn up. Don't get me wrong, we had begged and bribed every family member and friend we could think of, but that area of Belfast was still quite rough and desolate at night. It was so bad that we had to get security men to open 'anti-terrorist' gates to enable us to get the van near the bar. Thankfully everyone turned up. There were, in fact, far too many for the small front bar so the restaurant at the back was utilised. They even opened the windows in the wall that ran the length of the alleyway at the side of the bar so that a large section of the crowd could stand outside and observe the shenanigans within. It was so packed that my family, including my Ma, Da and Auntie Lilly, were allowed to stand behind the bar counter so they wouldn't be crushed. At one point they even helped the overstretched bar staff to pull pints.

Despite the rather unorthodox stage set-up we sounded pretty good, but it was the sheer energy coming from the band that lit up the room. We were having the time of our lives and it was as infectious as head lice in nursery. The place went wild; punters were dancing on the chairs, tables and quite literally in the street. It was an absolute triumph; a success beyond our wildest dreams. We could be confident now that we were ready to play the established gigs in Belfast, that is, as long as we could persuade someone to book us.

As a postscript to the Kitchen gig: my Ma had put her brand new suede coat under a chair for protection. Unfortunately an over-zealous dancer had kicked over a bottle of bleach, which had been stored under a bench next to the chair, in a rather health and safety conscious, carefree sort of way. The person with the size nines then proceeded to jig upon the bottle until it exploded all over the Ma's coat. She was unaware of the damage until the end of the night when she returned to retrieve the hypochlorite-smelling soggy garment. Pat

Catney, when he saw what had happened, walked over, asked my Ma how much it had cost, took the money from the till, with a little extra for the inconvenience and handed it to her. A real gent, I think you'll agree.

Having only been back in Belfast for a few months, I was not that familiar with all the places that bands could play, so one night we decided to do a recce around the town to see where the best venues were and to make contact with the people who booked the bands. The rest of the boys were well aware of all the gigs so they escorted me from place to place.

Being used to playing places like the Stick of Rock, the Marquee, the Fulham Greyhound, the Brentford Red Lion and the Ruskin Arms I found it very disappointing that Belfast had not changed since I left. Musicians were shown little or no respect, in that they were expected to set up in places like in front of the toilets and provided with only one power supply. It looked like designers had pumped all the money into the décor and the band area was an afterthought, which is a terrible shame seeing as how much of Irish culture is based on music.

I was just about to give up when we stumbled, quite literally, upon a bar as we were walking past Botanic Railway Station. The building resembled an old church, which was funny because that's exactly what it was. There was music blasting from a cellar bar so we decided that it was only right and proper to spend the taxi fare home on beer and investigate.

It was perfect. The Empire was exactly what I was looking for – it was dark, untouched by interior designer terrorists, it had a crowd that fitted like an old leather biker jacket and best of all at one end, not around a corner, not in front of the kitchens, not in front of a fire exit, was a stage that was big enough to offer the performing bands the dignity of not having to play on the ground.

The band that night were called Boardwalk Blues and they were very good. I think they used a drum machine which as far as the blues is concerned is a bit of a paradox, but the crowd didn't seem to mind and were lapping them up. When I say they were very good, they were, but I knew deep down in my arrogant soul that we were better. I asked one of the bar staff if I could speak to the manager.

A rather handsome guy with a Saddam Hussein moustache was

presented to me. I proceeded to bend his ear for about ten minutes, saying how good we were and that if he booked us we would pack the place with thirsty punters. I could see he was getting a little miffed at having to listen to a drunken, bigheaded little shit, especially as I was shouting to be heard over the music. Eventually he surrendered and asked me, for the sake of his sanity and his hearing, backstage.

Once there, he was a captive audience to my egotistical rantings. After a while he held his hand up and said, 'Enough, enough. We have just had a cancellation for two Saturdays from now – if you play a gig as well as you talk a gig then we'll see about booking you again.' I assured him he was making the right decision and shook his hand while asking him his name: always best to know whom to speak to the next day in case he has had reason to change his mind. 'Mike Gatt,' he said. I returned to my fellow band members triumphant. We were about to play the best gig in Belfast, a place where bands had to wait years to get into. I raised my glass to the rest of the boys, looked around the place, and then nearly threw up. How the hell were we going to fill this place with only two weeks' notice?

The two weeks flew by in a haze of rehearsing – at that point we didn't have enough songs to fill two one-hour sets – and phone calls to relatives and friends encouraging them to come along to the event of the year. We were all sick with nerves on the night. We did our sound check at 7pm and went to Lavery's Gin Palace for a few nerve-steadying libations. At 10pm we took the short walk back to the Empire where we were due to start playing a half-hour later.

We couldn't believe our eyes: there was a queue around the block of people who couldn't get in, the place was that packed solid. This sight, as gratifying as it was, was also disturbing; there were a lot of the people we had invited along being denied access. When they saw us they started shouting for us to get them in. Some we were able to, after we told the bouncers that they were members of the band. The door staff, however, soon caught on that we were not the Belfast Symphony Orchestra and put a stop to this. A few of our friends didn't make it: we all felt a bit shitty about this, but hey, when you're popular you're popular; they would just have to turn up a bit earlier the next time.

If there was going to be a next time. We had certainly done

ourselves no harm in the crowd department – the place was heaving and the queue for the bar was ten thick. The staff were under-resourced; maybe Mike had decided that he couldn't risk putting on extra staff due to the drunken ramblings of a nutcase. He was actually serving behind the bar, something that had never been seen before (or since). To ensure another gig we would have to rock the joint, and that's what we were there to do.

Na nana na na, Na nana na na, Na nana na na, was the opening riff of 'The Last to Know'. Mixi had played it over and over at every opportunity at each rehearsal until we were going to kill him. Now it sounded immense, especially when Keyser's keyboards came in on the fourth progression. 'So you're in love with someone else, someone who burns within your soul and it looks like I'm the last to know' – the first line I ever sang in the Empire. It was a little ironic, in that I was back in the same city as Adele and she was now happily married. My family and friends had kept this information from me until I had been, indeed, the last to know. Why they did this I'm not quite sure – I was genuinely delighted for her. Maybe they thought I would be hurt, but I was happy being single and had no intention of getting serious with anyone anytime soon. As the song came to an end the place went mental, everyone was on their feet and clapping and cheering, including the bar staff, one of whom I thought was very pleasant on the eye. I made a mental note that I would intro-duce myself once we had shaken the Empire to its foundations.

Demolition job over, the crowd were exhausted by an encore of 'Honky Tonk Woman' which they sang until they were hoarse. We were offered every Saturday for the next month by a 'cream cracker'd' Mike Gatt. He would make sure there were more staff on the next time we played. We were over the moon, we couldn't ask for more. To round the evening off perfectly I looked around for the beautiful barmaid I had noticed earlier; she had left with her boyfriend.

Before the next Empire gig Paul Weller had played a gig at the Ulster Hall. Celestine, his beautiful secretary/PA and giggle merchant, met me in Morrison's Bar, where we hugged. It was great to see her again; we had spent many afternoons at Nomis laughing our heads off when we should've been working. She had also been responsible for rescuing me after I had fainted following two days of partying with no food or sleep.

I had been on the phone in John Weller's office when I started getting these feelings of déjà vu, then everything went black. The person on the other end of the phone raised the alarm. He thought, after hearing the crash, that I had been whacked over the head or something. I had fallen from the chair, which for some reason John kept with its back to the door, and I was now blocking anyone trying to get in. Celestine had to get some of the boys from reception to help her push the door and me across the floor.

Alex was furious: how dare I try to kill myself in the boss's office (where of course, I shouldn't have been). Was I not thinking about the consequences to him, he might have got the sack? He was all heart sometimes old Alex. Nothing like this had happened to me before so I phoned my Ma to keep her informed in case it was something more serious. I didn't mention the partying but said I thought it was down to low blood sugars with me being far too busy doing important business to keep regular meals.

My Ma was obviously unaware of the Rock and Roll image that I was trying to portray for on hearing of my medical drama, she suggested that, when I was out and about, I should carry a packet of McVittie's digestives with me. How cool would that have looked, me propping up the bar at the St Moritz in my coolest threads, a packet of dunking biscuits hanging out of my pocket.

Anyway back to the Ulster Hall. I had quite a few friends with me and Celestine graciously got us all on the guest list. My only regret after the gig was that Paul had to leave straight away: I would've loved to have seen his face when he saw me, the long-haired loon that hung around Alex's office, turned up to every party going and really didn't seem to have that much of a purpose. But in a way I was kind of glad that I didn't go backstage that night as Kenny Wheeler may have, in the interim, found out where the supply of booze, left over from the Christmas party and stored in his office, had gone, and he just might have tried to extract the equivalent value from my hide.

Bella Donna

The second night we played the Empire, to my delight the barmaid, (sorry I mean bar person; must try to be politically correct) who had caught my eye was working again. She was even more beautiful, tall and elegant than I remembered. She was a Celtic vision, and to round the whole thing off, quite literally, had a lovely backside – stuff PC!! Normally when I'm singing I don't see the crowd due to the lights or trying to concentrate on the vocal but in her case I made a conscious exception. After the gig I was suitably refreshed enough to approach her, something I would not have done if I hadn't been as tired and emotional as a newt.

I asked her if she was married she said no (good). I asked her if she was engaged she said no (excellent). I asked her if she was seeing anybody she said yes (shit – 2 out of 3 is just not good enough Mr Loaf). She then enquired as to why I was bothering her with all these questions. I told her that if she had been single I was going to ask if she would like to go for a drink sometime. I don't know if her laughter was that of delight – because I'm sure her idea of a great end to a busy night is some sweaty, balding drunk coming up and more or less proposing marriage – or hysterics, you know the type, uncontrolled and brought on by fear. Either way I withdrew from her company a beaten man.

A few months later 'Mad' Mixi McMillan and myself were doing one of our traditional nights out. Our week went like this. Monday out for a drink to recover from the weekend. Tuesday was the Comedy Club at the Empire. Wednesday we would have a night in. Thursday, Rab McCullough's blues night. Friday out because it was the weekend. Saturday, we would be gigging or going to watch another band to slag off. Sunday, Eddie Friel at the Empire for a relaxing couple of pints of Murphy's stout, while Ed tinkled on the old ivories. Oh and sometimes we would go out on a Wednesday.

I don't recall which night of the week this was but on our arrival at the door of the Empire the object of my desires was taking the entrance money; we didn't pay as we were the stars of the Saturday night extravaganza, don't ya know, so I wasn't even afforded an excuse to talk to her while handing over the well worth it £3. But a strange thing happened as I walked past: I heard the question, 'About that drink?'

I turned to see if Mixi had had a sex change and whether the castration had perhaps raised the tone of his voice an octave or two, but no, he looked the same, maybe slightly less jaundiced, but definitely manly. He, seeing my confusion, nodded in the direction of the now even more confused young lady.

'Excuse me?' I mumbled and she repeated, 'If you want to go for that drink you suggested I would be delighted.' I then said, 'What do you take me for, keeping me hanging on for months on end like a puppy dog begging for a biscuit. I will not be taking you for a drink because since the time I asked you out, I have been on numerous dates with many different beautiful women and I'm in the process of vetting them to ascertain which one comes up to my very high standards, which quite frankly I don't think you would reach even if you had a step ladder with an extension.' As you've probably guessed I didn't say this at all; all I could muster up was a 'Yes please.'

Then came a problem. I didn't know her name which I felt might make her feel a little unflattered, she probably would think that I couldn't even be bothered to ask what she was called. In my defence, following that first disastrous conversation, it didn't cross my mind. I felt that there was no hope for me. But salvation came in the shape of her cousin, an Aussie called Martina who also worked in the Empire. I played it cool, my Da had once told me of a way of getting out of forgetting someone's name, so I used it.

The conversation went something like this.

'I'm going on a date with your cousin but I can't remember her name.'

Looking horrified, Martina snapped, 'Her name is Donna actually.'

As quick as flash I replied, 'No, not her first name, silly, her surname.' Job done, or so I thought.

Martina then says, in her Melbourne twang, 'McDonna.'

This took me by surprise and I burst out laughing. She obviously was onto my clumsy attempt to get her cousin's name and had tried to turn the joke on me. I was having none of it, but at least I had succeeded in getting her first name.

Later on, as I passed Donna on my way to the toilet, I sniggered, 'Your cousin's a hoot. She has just told me that your name is Donna McDonna, I mean what mad, sadistic parents would inflict such an idiotic name like that on a poor child.'

'Mine,' she says. 'What?' I says and she says, 'Yes my mad,

sadistic, idiotic parents called me Donna McDonagh' (different spelling but roughly the same pronunciation).

I says, 'We still on for that drink?'

She says, unconvincingly, 'I suppose so.'

We were to meet at Botanic Station the next Wednesday night. It was pouring with rain and I stood in the doorway waiting for two and a half hours. Why? I can't answer that, as I would never have done it before. I can't abide anyone being late, and it became more and more embarrassing as people walked past me on the street to do whatever they had to do and I was still there when they came back from doing it. People who had passed me to get on the train were passing me again having made their return journey. I was now getting dirty looks from some who must have thought I was an undercover ticket inspector. I could see their point – who else would be standing in a cold damp railway station for hours on end unless they were getting paid for it – or worse still, maybe they thought I was a loitering pervert of some kind.

Just as the mortification was about to finally force me home, across the road came Donna with what looked like a beret on her head – very strange.

'Hi there,' I said, 'I'm sure we said 7 o'clock didn't we?' hoping that I had got it wrong and that it wasn't that she just couldn't be bothered rushing herself to see me.

'That's right,' she said, 'I just lost track of the time.'

'Sweet heart of Jesus,' I thought, 'she's fitting me in between East-enders and Brookside.'

We went to a great wee bar called the Fly that has in recent times turned into a yuppie atrocity. That night however it was the way a good Irish bar should be: dark, slightly grubby looking and playing good music. Incidentally a football match was on the TV and I think it was Man City against Man Utd and to my horror I think Man Utd won 5-0. Could it get any worse?

Well, yes it could. All my life I swore I would never go out with anybody who smoked and one of the first things Donna did was take out a packet of tobacco and rolling papers. She proceeded to manu-facture what can only be described as a dirty soggy little piece of rolled up toilet paper with the remnants of my Da's compost heap poking out of both ends. She then produced a Zippo lighter with the words 'With love, Rab' (her ex) engraved on it and lit it, sending clouds of noxious fumes in my general direction. She then says, 'Oh my manners, would you like one?' I declined her delightful offer and spent the next few minutes watching her remove pieces of tobacco from her tongue with her fingers.

I fell in love with her right away. Why? I hear you ask. Well she is totally beautiful and that night she was wonderful company; oh, and I have mentioned her bum, haven't I? To stand any chance of this going any further I felt that I needed to impress her. I started to transfix her with some of my stories and a list of my attributes. I have achieved many things in my life – modesty and space prevent me from listing them here (ahem!) but for some reason they just didn't seem enough. I spun a few silvery strands of a web that I thought would catch her educated brain: Degree and a Masters, well excuse me!

For some reason I told her that following my time living in Spain I had become fluent in Español (false). I also told her that my sister Marie had lived in Italy working for Nikki Lauda for many years (true) and that I had also become fluent in Italiano through visiting her on many occasions (false). Where was the harm? Living in little old Belfast I would never have to prove these claims. Cue our Marie inviting us over to Milan.

We were to fly out of Dublin Airport on All Ireland Gaelic football final day. The flight had been delayed and we were summoned to the bar for complimentary drinks, which provided us with the opportunity to watch the match, which was great craic. I can't remember the result of the game but the result of the free drinks was that I was feeling no pain when we were finally called to board the plane.

We were expecting a normal aircraft: what we got was a Lauda Air private jet, how impressive was that? An additional surprise was that Marie was on the plane and we were greeted with glasses of champagne as we boarded. 'I could get used to this,' I thought, my humanist/socialist soul being left on the tarmac. The flight was most pleasant with even more champers, and a delicious meal with linen napkin, porcelain dishes and real cutlery, if you don't mind. I had had enough of the high life and as Marie and Donna chatted I felt the need to rest my eyes. I fell unconscious and threw in a snore or two for good measure.

When we arrived an elbow to the ribs rudely awakened me. 'Thank you dear,' I said and weaved my way down the aisle still chasing the drunken sleep gremlins from my head. We got to the terminal but something was distracting me. Out of the corner of my eye I could see something stuck to my boot so I tried, without success, to kick it off. I increased my efforts with what must have looked like a demented version of the River Dance to the machine-gun-toting police who, knowing I was not Michael Flatley, came to the conclusion that I must be a threat to national security. It was only swift intervention from my Italian-speaking sister that stopped me from being arrested.

'He's Irish!' Marie shouted and much to our nation's shame this seemed to be enough to call off the code red. I was embarrassed and annoyed with myself until I found out that while I had been sleeping Marie and Donna had decided that tying the red ribbon from the linen napkin to my laces would be a good idea. Oh how I would've laughed in my prison cell had the drunken reputation of the Emerald Isle not saved my bacon.

While in Italy we used our time productively visiting as many places as possible. My fluent Italian(!) came in very useful when I accidentally put us on board an express train to Munich. Thank goodness it stopped once before the border – we had no passports with us – at beautiful Lake Como. Of course I took full credit for this, I obviously knew all the time that this was going to happen. My lack of knowledge of Italy and its language was finally blown when we returned following a wonderful day in Venice. On arrival at Garibaldi Station I phoned Marie and informed her that we were ready for collection. She told us that she would pick us up from a little café situated right in the middle of the road just outside the station.

I ordered the drinks and spotted a selection of delicious-looking treats on the counter; here an opportunity to impress presented itself. I took a small dish and filled it with some of the contents from a bowl sitting at the end of the bar; the waiter looked at me quizzically as I brought them over to Donna.

'These,' I announced, 'are capers or as they call them here capre, and during my time living in Spain I devoured them.'

'What are they?' Donna asked.

'Little green crunchy peppers,' I replied, 'go on, try one.' Donna popped one into her mouth just as my sister entered.

I went to the bar to get Marie a drink. While I was away Donna asks her, 'Are these meant to be so hard?' pointing to the objects in the dish. On my return from the bar Marie was looking a little confused and Donna was looking a lot uncomfortable while still chewing hard on the pepper.

'Where did you get these from?' Marie enquired, pointing to the gastronomic delights.

'Over there at the end of the bar,' I replied.

'My God, Eamon, they're the stones from the olives that those old men are spitting out!' Marie squealed. Donna's face, in the words of Procol Harum, 'at first looked ghostly, then turned a whiter shade of pale'.

Now that Donna was under my spell I thought it would be a good idea to take her to London to visit all my friends. She was blown away by the hospitality of the likes of Ken, Elaine, Xan, Inky, Steve and Ness. Gary and Ann were high on my list to visit and we did just that. When we arrived at the door Gary answered. He could see by the shock on my face that I had clocked that his appearance had dramatically changed, so much so that Donna didn't recognise him from the photos of the band I had shown her. There was a new addition to the family, a baby girl, Zoe, who Gary was obviously hugely in love with.

They seemed in good enough spirits but I sensed an air of defeat. Gary no longer went to the gym due to recurring chest infections and had lost about four stone. Ann put a brave face on it and was talking excitedly about what the kids were up to. When Gary went to the toilet she confided that she was very worried about him. I could see why. When we left I said to Donna, 'I think that's the last time I'm going to see him.' She offered no argument.

Back in Belfast, Christmas came around, and Donna and myself had a brilliant time. It actually snowed on Christmas Eve just as Christmas Day was arriving. Everything was wonderful, I had a new band and I was in love – what could be better? The day after Boxing Day the phone rang. Ann was on the other end of the line. She told me my old drummer and friend had passed away due to pneumonia on Christmas Eve Night. She hadn't phoned me earlier because she didn't want to spoil the holiday, how human is that? She hung up and I knew I would never hear from her again. I also knew that that was what she wanted, perhaps a fresh start was the order of the day. I sat on the stairs for a while just thinking about the great times and the mad times we had all had together and I couldn't help wondering if those bloody Christmas trees were still alive in Gary's back garden. I smiled and hoped so.

You couldn't make it up

I was back in London sooner than I thought I was going to be. Ken decided to make an honest woman of Elaine, he asked her to marry him. It reminded me of what Leslie Crowther said when Phil Lynott had asked for his daughter's hand in marriage: 'You may as well, you've had everything else.' Ken asked me to be his best man. I hate public speaking and as gratifying as it was that someone thought enough of me to bestow such an honour it was probably the worst thing anyone could've possibly asked of me. I told the 'groom to be' that I was chuffed to be asked, but I would have to decline. I didn't want to spoil their big day by soiling my underwear in front of their family and friends. Ken said I wasn't to worry myself, it wouldn't be your traditional sit down, top table, affair anyway, all I would be expected to do was read out the cards of congratulations from those that couldn't be present. This I thought I could just about do, so I reluctantly accepted.

As the date for the hitching approached I found myself facing each morning with a nervous stomach that, on occasion, nearly made me hurl. Even though on the face of it there would be very little for me to do, the thought of me standing up and mumbling my way through dozens of cards, while everyone was expecting me to reel off a load of funny anecdotes about Ken, filled me with terror. Don't get me wrong, as you should be well aware by now, there were many tales to tell, but writing them down is one thing, pretending I was a great orator in the mould of Peter Ustinov is a different kettle of haddock altogether.

Then there was the stag night, which I was supposed to arrange, and I was also expected to protect Ken, as per Elaine's instructions, from anything horrible happening. Stupidly and just plain asking for trouble it was to be staged the day before the wedding. Ken's family, as you may have gathered, were a little unorthodox, and thirsty with it. I didn't fancy my chances of dissuading Ken's brothers from shaving off his body hair or any other such ritualistic torture that men on such occasions inflict on someone they are supposed to love. I was literally worried sick. The result? An ulcer.

I flew out to Heathrow looking forward to seeing all my old London mates but not looking forward to my responsibilities. Ken had suffered the recent tragic loss of his beautiful sister Ann; it was the first time since her passing that a lot of the family had come together. The result was that it was already an emotionally charged atmosphere to begin with. There were a lot of tears, both of grief and joy, a strange mix but in a way a nice one. Ann's memory would be celebrated on a day that brought two people that she loved and who truly loved each other together; she would've smiled at the thought. In this cauldron of emotional turmoil I was supposed to provide a drunken night of frivolity, male bonding and alcohol abuse.

Thankfully, for me, the stag night was only to consist of, by mutual consent, a drinking session and a few games of pool. It was decided that we shouldn't stray too far, we would use the bars in the Hainault area including a rough-looking shit-hole that was situated next door to the Bald Hind, the venue for the reception the following day. Surely nothing untoward could happen in these circumstances.

All was going well, the boys were having a good time, drinking and playing a little eight ball. They were loud but not doing anything to cause offence. However, there was group of Essex wide boys playing at a nearby table who obviously thought that their Alpha male territory was being invaded. They kept sending over dirty looks accompanied by, under their breath, snide remarks that resulted in bursts of laughter. There were also, barely audible, Mick and Paddy jokes. They must have really fancied themselves, and believe me if I had been on my own I wouldn't have hung around; they were definitely thugs. But I was with a different class of hard men.

The Heavens were as tough as nails and let's just say that they had histories that made your average gangster look like a Seventh Day Adventist. Feeling that they were having the piss taken out of them my companions went on the offensive and started to take the Mick, if you'll forgive the irony, out of the wannabe Krays. One of them was singled out for a special ribbing: he appeared to be the top guy, the leader of the pack, and unfortunately for him he was wearing the most obvious syrup since Burt Reynolds decided to cover his balding pate with the pelt of a ginger Tom.

Harry walked over to 'Wiggy' and challenged him to a game of pool. When he said, 'Fuck off Paddy,' Harry said, 'Keep your hair on,' which brought much cheering, and laughter from our lot. Knowing he was under pressure to flex his ego muscle the challenged said, 'Alright, how much?' Harry pulled out a wad of notes that would have choked a donkey. The colour drained from his opponent's face; it also drained from mine. Harry was now laying down on the table the whole kitty for the night's drinking. Game on ladies and gentlemen; well it was once the wide boys rustled up the rest of the readies to cover the bet.

Harry was an excellent snooker player, the result of many wasted years on the tables of the Holywood Social Club. Now all he needed to do was to transfer his ill-gotten skills to the smaller pool table. This he did with great aplomb, handing out an arse-kicking of biblical proportions. It was supposed to be the best of three but only two games were played. What followed the downing of the final eight ball was a lot of pushing and shoving, but I think that the barrow boys could see that they had bitten off more than they could chew they backed off quick smart. There is a look in the eye of someone who has no fear: the Heavens have that look and when someone who is acting the hard man sees it they realise their bluff has been called. Game over, we were off to the next bar, with double the kitty. More drinking money was the last thing we really needed.

After the cash had all gone we started to head back to Ken's place, but before we could settle down for a good night's sleep in preparation for the forthcoming nuptials, the groom had to be subjected to some sort of humiliation. This was to take the form of stripping him naked and tying him to the railings of the local primary school. Ken wasn't for having this and objected by throwing punches and kicking like a mule. Those of the assembled party who were not used to the Heavens must have thought that they were having a full-on scrap, but in actual fact, all I saw was a little bit of bone-breaking, teeth-loosening, horse play.

Job completed, Ken was now staving off the chill of the night air with just his pubic hair and the ropes securing him to the fence. I was instructed that if I didn't want to be the recipient of a little bit of tomfoolery Heaven style, I was to leave him there. Everybody started to make their way home congratulating each other on reducing a loved one to a nude, nervous wreck. What they weren't aware of, and I was, having lived there, was that the area where they had left their relative was a haunt for gay cruising.

I hung back until I was out of sight and ran back to where Ken was advertising his wares. I really didn't think that a Rogering, on the night before your wedding, was the best way to prepare for married life. I started to undo the ropes hoping that passers-by wouldn't think we were indulging in a little light on the loafers bondage.

Thank feck no one was about and after about ten minutes – obviously his family didn't want Ken to free himself – the ropes came away. Now we had the problem of finding some sort of garment to hide Ken's blushes. There was only one obvious solution at hand. I was wearing the jacket of a suit that I had borrowed for the big day from a friend. I took it off and offered it to the now shivering groom, who proceeded to wrap it around himself like some sort of toga or polyester nappy. Walking back across the muddy grass Ken, for good measure, threw in a few drunken falls, just to round the evening off. I made a mental note that when I returned the suit I wouldn't mention this bit to the owner.

The next day there were thick lips and even thicker heads. Hangovers were postponed with large slugs of whiskey. Despite the chemical state of those present everyone looked great, all done up in their best bib and tucker, that is except me. I looked resplendent up to the waist but from there on up I looked like a tramp. The on-loan jacket appeared like it had been used to cover a dog's genitals, while it dragged itself along the grass trying to dislodge it from its arse, which is pretty close, when you think about it, to what actually did occur.

We made our way to the register office where the ceremony was to take place. I was to sign as one of the witnesses, which seems like a pretty mundane thing to do but due to the nervous state I was in, waiting for the reception and the drink from the night before, I can be seen on the wedding video shaking like a leaf. A few comments were made from the congregation such as, 'Who's getting married today anyway?' and, 'Jesus he's not a surgeon is he?' followed by much laughing and reddening of my cheeks.

Following the legalities we all proceeded to the Bald Hind for the dreaded reception. The meal was supposed to take place at 2pm followed by the bowel-loosening speeches. This, however, was a Heaven wedding, therefore there just had to be hiccup with the catering. The meal was three hours late with most of the guests putting in the time constructively by drinking. By the time I was to do my little bit the wedding party was now a baying pack of drunks. I read the cards as best I could. Those English in the crowd kept shouting that they couldn't understand me and there were a few Irish ones who joined them.

The cards over, I looked up to see the expectant faces of a group of people wanting to have their sides split by the best man's witty repartee. My mouth went dry. I really should've cut my losses and just sat down, but like a fool I tried to rise to the challenge. I scanned the room and my gaze fell upon the baldy head of Harry Heaven. Clutching at straws that were as thin as his wispy hair I said, 'I would just like to thank Harry for coming, he's the only one here that makes me look like I have a full head of hair.'

To my amazement there was much laughter and cheering. What there was also was the sight of Harry leaving the premises. I thought, 'Shit, he's going to kill me.' But I didn't care, I was on a roll; surely I should be able to generate a few more beatings for myself by insulting other people for laughs. Just as I was about to wow the hordes, the door Harry had left through swung open and in walked the man himself wearing the wig of the gangster from the bar next door. All hell broke loose, how could I follow that? I'd been upstaged by a man who had risked a stabbing, or worse, just to get a laugh. It was time to sit down, let the master take over and watch the mayhem unfold.

This is the end beautiful friend

Back in Belfast I got a phone call one day from Arty Magee, Stephen's brother, to inform me that their mother, a wonderful woman, had passed away. I had grown very fond of her over the years that her son had been managing No Hot Ashes. She was a feisty woman who had no sorrows to seek. She had brought up six children virtually single-handed and also worked tirelessly for the homeless charity The Simon Community. I always remembered her chesty laughter as she listened to the absurdities that were talked around her kitchen table by the would-be rock stars. So I was deeply saddened to hear of her death and prepared myself for her funeral. What I would also need to prepare myself for was the first face-to-face meeting with Magee since that horrendous visit he had paid me in London all those years ago. I needn't have worried.

We embraced each other like estranged family members reunited. I asked him how he had been and had he wised up. Magee told me that he had changed his life around. He had moved to Manchester where he was involved in setting up a recording studio, with his brother, which offered kids from the inner cities the opportunity to produce music free of charge. He had spoken at the European Parliament about this project. He travelled the world and had met a beautiful woman who he married and had two wonderful children with. He became a much respected teacher in Bexhill-on-Sea and through his love of the arts, literature, music and his life-long hatred of bullying, he made a massive difference to a lot of children's lives. He then informed me that he hadn't had a drink or drug in fifteen years. I was as proud as punch of him and promised it wouldn't be as long, or in such tragic circumstances, until I would speak to him again.

A short while later and many years after that cathartic day in Kensal Rise, when Magee's addled state nearly destroyed my career and caused him to reassess his life, addiction's dog of two heads, temptation and greed, came back to bite. I got the news one cold, wet November morning. I flew out to Gatwick the next day for my friend Stephen Magee's funeral. He died at the age of 43. I watched his two children throw soil on his coffin. As I said way back at the start of these ramblings you could forgive Stephen anything, but in this case I'll have to make an exception. He has robbed his family and the world of a kind, intelligent, funny, exceptionality gifted human being. As a humanist, I don't believe in 'the after life', but I do believe that the dead live on through love. Many people loved Stephen, myself included. So live on my friend, I miss ya.

A public health warning

I had moved out of Colin's house to give him a bit more space and privacy with his soon-to-be wife Cathy. I gave them enough space, in fact, to marry and divorce. The first place I stayed in was a house owned by a friend of ours, John Ball; it was situated at the lower end of Dunluce Avenue just off the Lisburn Road in Belfast. My room had no carpet and no heating. One day when Mixi called I was having a snooze. He came up to get me and couldn't believe that I was lying on a mattress on the floor, barely visible hidden by the steam from my breath. He was further shocked to see that there was ice on the inside of the windows. To be honest I wasn't that worried about the conditions: all I needed was somewhere to rest my head, and the house had the advantage of being smack in the heart of Belfast; a short walk would find me in Shaftsbury Square and waiting for my old drinking buddy Mixi.

Mixi's suit was always in situ on our Friday night drinking sessions. He would go for a few drinks with his friends from the office and then meet me to further disable himself with alcohol. By the end of the night he would be on the dance floor, tie over one shoulder, while doing what can only be described as the gyrations of someone suffering from St Vitus' dance.

I would always start the evening with the intention of staying at his Claremont Court apartment. When I say I intended to, it was just that sometimes Mixi would go to the toilet and not return to the bar. Instead he would make his way home, leaving me out on the street or spending two hours banging on his door with him being clearly visible through the letterbox passed out on the floor. On the nights when his stamina actually got him to the end of the night we would visit our favourite kebab shop and purchase two goat meat beauties for the consumption of when we got to his place.

One winter's Monday I met Mixi after work for a wee drinky poos. As always he was resplendent in his suit. As we neared the Crown Bar I became aware of a terrible niff that seemed to be emanating from my old mate. I asked him if he had showered that morning. Disgustedly he assured me he had. I asked, 'What the hell is that smell?' He said that he had smelt it all day in the office, and his co-workers had complained bitterly, even going as far as opening all the windows despite the freezing conditions outside. Mixi assumed that he had picked the smell up on his clothes from his working environment. At the doors of the bar an icy wind got up causing Mixi to pull the collar of his jacket up and dig his hands deep into the pockets.

'What the feck is this?' he shouted stopping dead in his tracks.

'What's what?' I asked.

'This,' he said producing a white soggy paper bag from one of his pockets. I cautiously stood over him as he peered into the package. There, gently giving off the gases of hell itself, was a three-day-old doner kebab, garnished with salad, chili and garlic sauce.

Even when Mixi made it home on his own and in one piece he had a knack of keeping the emergency services busy. One such occasion saw him take a packet of bacon, with which to make a sandwich, remove the rashers, throw them in the bin and then place the plastic wrapper under the grill. He settled back upon the sofa to wait the minute and a half for the pig meat to become crisp and begging for HP sauce; he then promptly fell asleep. He woke upon the landing with a burly fireman trying to give him the kiss of life

Mixi's flat became a haven of love for those of us, at the time, who were single and playing the field. Unfortunately there was a three-month period where even the hardiest of Casanovas were being put off romantic conquests by a smell that was both sickly and sweet. Jokes soon ensued about the smell of death curtailing our love lives; we assumed that there must have been a dead rat or something under his floorboards. But as the days and weeks went on the stench became almost unbearable, and we no longer invited members of the fair sex back for fear of repulsion. However we still spent the evenings before the gigs there with the windows open and twenty scented candles bothering the smoke alarm.

One morning Mixi rose to the sight of men in white boiler suits entering a flat just below his. They discovered the body of an old lady who had been dead for nearly four months; her remains and residues had decomposed so much that she had spread over all surfaces and it took weeks to finally rid the place of the smell. All together now, 'Neighbours, everybody needs good neighbours.'

Many of our Saturday night gigs were nearly disabled by the hangovers that all of us would be nursing following our traditional Friday night session. One particular gig, Morrison's, was almost unplayable due to the fact that the fan on the ceiling of the downstairs bar was vibrating so strongly it caused the stage to undulate. This, mixed with the nausea from the alcohol of the previous night, nearly caused all of us to throw up.

The same night the manager asked me, in a very threatening manner, to refrain from swearing on the stage. All I said was, 'Let's feckin' Rock and Roll.' I asked him if my disgusting language was putting his rougher than rough clientele off their puking in the toilets. My attempt at humour led to us to being banned from the place. But before we were thrown off the premises Roger demanded that they sell him a carryout. Seeing a quick buck the manager was more than happy to take back some of the fee he had reluctantly just given us before turfing us out.

Believe me, Roger is no connoisseur of lagers, so it came as a surprise to all of us when he threw an absolute dickey fit when he was presented with eight cans of Oranjeboom lager for a tenner. 'Fecking Oranjeboom, fecking Oranjeboom? Are you serious? You're offering me eight cans of fecking Oranjeboom lager for a fecking tenner, I wouldn't drink that crap if you *paid* me a tenner,' he screamed at the barman.

The bouncers were called upon to drag our drummer from the premises. He was still remonstrating on the street outside until he realised that he was, in fact, carryoutless (is there such a word? If not I suggest there should be because there are definite occasions when you find yourself carryoutless – the best example of this is Boxing Day). Anyway finding himself in a position where he might not be able to quench his post-gig thirst and therefore panic-stricken he said, 'OK, OK I've calmed down now, if it's alright with you gentlemen I will take the Oranjeboom please.'

After about two years it was time for Keyser to move on. He had become dissatisfied, he says, with the direction and dedication of the band. To be honest it was the best for everyone all round. He had, towards the end, even made a suggestion that we should stretch ourselves a bit by playing Funk Rock. I couldn't believe my ears – we were packing the Empire and other venues every time we played. The people that were coming along were obviously happy with Rock otherwise they wouldn't have been there. I couldn't see the sense of alienating them and ourselves by playing a type of music that I for one didn't even like.

To be honest Keyser has publicly said, more or less, that we were 'lazy'. Well, maybe we were, but we're just as lazy now, still packing the Empire night after night and have released two albums. I have always been of the opinion that if a footballer isn't happy, put him on the transfer list, let him go, before performances start to slip. It was a big loss to lose someone as talented and versatile as Keyser, who we hoped would go on to something artistically more fulfilling for him than playing in a good time covers band with friends, but hey, as I said, it was best for everyone's health and sanity. The headaches stopped.

A day at the races

With Keyser gone we needed another guitar player. The choice was obvious: I would just get Ken in. Well actually, like all things concerning my old mucker it wasn't easy at all. Let me explain, I knew Ken would jump at the chance of joining the Strictlys, he had made no secret of wanting to return to Ireland. Elaine, on the other hand, knowing the alcoholic temptations that old watering holes provided, was less than enthusiastic; in fact, she was dead set against it.

At one time Ken had tried to break the deadlock by coming up with a cunning plan, which was simple and foolproof. He reasoned that if he had enough money to make the transition from London to Holywood it would change Elaine's mind. Money after all is the spoonful of sugar that can make the bitterest of pills palatable.

Ken considered himself a connoisseur of horseflesh, and I don't mean he was fond of the odd boiled German sausage. He had studied the form for many years and put many bookies' children through college. His family's triumphant return to Ulster would be facilitated by him removing, from his and Elaine's joint account, their life savings, the sum of £500, which he was to put on a dead cert at 100/1. What could be easier?

The mule trotted in last. It was so slow that it won the next race by a nose, after a photo finish and a steward's enquiry. Elaine threw a fit of epileptic proportions when the green luminous letters informed her that she had insufficient funds to complete her transaction.

Once Ken had released his private parts from his wife's vice-like grip, he explained that he hadn't frittered the money away, he had, in fact, had to lend it to someone close to him who had got himself into a spot of bother. This mysterious blaggard would have to remain nameless so despicable was the pickle he had got himself into. Elaine put two and two together and for some reason, calculated that I must have been the recipient of her family's nest egg. She lifted the phone and spoke to Ken's family, instructing them that I was to be found and persuaded to return the monies post-haste.

My brother Mark just happened to be in the bar when the Heavens entered, providing them with a point of contact to public enemy number one. He phoned me and told me that I needed to get to the bar ASAP with the money that I had swindled from Ken and Elaine. Apparently, it was surmised that I needed the money to pay for an abortion after getting some poor girl in the family way; funny how these things snowball isn't it? Well actually it wasn't in the least bit feckin' funny. My reputation, for what it was, would've been ripped to shreds, my Catholic Ma and Da would've been horrified in the extreme and Donna, who I was still in the process of falling in love with, would've been somewhat miffed to find that I had been messing about with other women. The strange thing is that I actually prided myself on having been very frugal with my affections. I had not once, in all the relationships I had been in, strayed, so it was a tad irritating to be painted in such a bad light.

After setting the record straight with the Heavens I phoned Ken and had it out with him. He spilled the beans but swore me to secrecy; he knew that if Elaine found out about his equine fiscal dalliances it would be the end of his marriage. What could I do? I bit my lip and never said a word. Until now of course and only after Ken finally 'fessed up just a few weeks ago.

With all this in mind I suspected that if I asked Ken to up sticks from London to Belfast, with only the prospect of playing once a week in a covers band, that it could've caused Elaine to leave him. I voiced my concerns with Donna, when Ken expressed, off his own bat, an interest in joining the band. She said I should do what I thought was the right thing, bearing in mind all the circumstances.

With a heavy heart, I mean I loved the guy, I deliberately made it difficult for him to join. I told him that I couldn't make the decision on my own, the rest of the band would need a say; not totally true. I also told him that backing vocals would play a big part in the decision-making process, which was the truth, but Ken was such a good guitarist that I'm sure we could've done without the harmonies. I therefore told him that he would have to audition; he was too good for that.

I knew I hurt Ken but I just couldn't have the disintegration of a family I held very dear on my conscience. Ken and myself would never play in a band together again, a damn shame. We had been friends for nigh on twenty years. We were close, very close. I remember Ken once jokingly saying that if I ran off with Elaine he would miss me. This still makes me laugh even today.

Cometh the hour, cometh the man

The race was on to find a replacement guitar or keyboard player. We wouldn't be able to get someone who could do both, they were like hens' teeth. With that option closed to us it was the consensus that, seeing as we were definitely moving in a more Hard Rock direction, a second guitar player was needed, but he would have to be able to sing harmonies. How hard could it be? An advert was posted in all the music shops in Belfast. 'Lead guitar player wanted for Hard Rock covers band, backing vocals essential,' it read. Oh my God, the nutters that auditioned for us were unbelievable. All of them wanted to be Eddie Van Halen but lacked the talent or charisma and none of them could sing. One of them even asked, 'You know the way your advert said backing vocals essential, how essential is essential?' Give me strength.

We had just about given up hope of finding someone when a colleague, who was working as an research fellow in the rheumatology department of Musgrave Park Hospital, where I had taken a temporary job, approached me saying that he had heard that I was in a band and that we were looking for a guitar player. Paul Kane thought that he could fit the bill.

The Strictlys all had long hair and a Hard Rock image. Paul had short hair combed into a quiff and wore glasses; he looked like a cross between Vegas Elvis and Benny Hill. 'He won't fit the bill,' I thought. I gave him the titles of three songs, which I must admit I chose for their lead work difficulty factor. To my shame and in my arrogance I assumed by his appearance that this hucklebuck head couldn't possibly cope with the technicalities of Metal. Keyser was still serving his notice and to his credit he was honouring the gigs that we still had booked. Paul is a smart cookie so he hid in the shadows of the Empire and watched us playing the songs that I had requested him to learn.

Paul's audition took place in a converted barn just outside the North Down town of Newtownards. Before he arrived I had voiced my reservations about him to the rest of the band. In a way I was trying to get myself off the hook, wasting everyone's time, inviting someone who I described as 'a bit of an overweight Teddy Boy that wore goggles'. With my prejudices running around the rest of the band's heads, Paul plugged in his guitar and asked what we wanted to try first. 'Boys are back in town,' I said.

Perfect was how he played it. He also went on to play not only the songs selected but also the rest of the numbers in our set, note perfect. We couldn't believe it. How could 'Shakin' Stevens' know all these Rock classics? Little did we know that he had taken note of everything we played that night at the Empire and learned them all. It would be a few years before he let us in on his secret. Not only was his guitar playing exceptional, he also had no fear of the mic; his backing vocals hit the spot. We welcomed him into the Strictly No Ballroom family and he has been a brother ever since.

I think the first or second gig we did with Paul was a 40th birthday party for a local, self-made millionaire. It was to be held in a marquee at the side of his mansion just outside the County Down village of Killyleigh. Normally we wouldn't do this sort of gig, we never did weddings or anything like that, but he was offering us a fortune, so why not? Well I'll tell you why bloody not, a Metal band

and the acoustically non-absorbent nature of the walls of a big tent do not good bed fellows make.

We should've known we were slightly out of place when we arrived and saw the TV chefs Paul and Jeanie Rankin doing the catering. The only contact any of us had previously had with these bastions of culinary excellence was when one night a drunken Roger decided that it would be a good idea to enter their swanky restaurant, Roscoffs, walk to the reception and order a gravy chip to go. He was asked to leave in a manner befitting of an inebriated oaf.

Our alienation at the party was further compounded when we saw that the guests were attired in the best of Armani. We were, as usual, wearing our regulation jeans and assorted band T-shirts. The host greeted us with open arms; he had seen us on many occasions in the Empire and was a bit of a fan. He also provided us with a case of white and red wine. There were only four of us drinking, Mixi was driving, it was going to get messy.

'I say, would you mind turning that down?' a woman in what looked like one of Clint Eastwood's ponchos said just after we completed the first song. Normally we would do the gentlemanly thing and ignore the old crone, but we were on foreign soil, so to speak. We realised that we were not the main attraction, I mean these people hadn't come to see us specifically, as would have been the case at the rest of our gigs. We were, in fact, employees, and as the old saying goes 'he who pays the piper calls the tune'.

The amps were turned from 10 to 8, then from 8 to 6, then from 6 to 4 and finally after a visit from the local peelers from 4 to 2. I was able to sing without a mic and was still louder than the band. Roger was playing his kit with cushions on the drumheads, which is not a good sound. We were becoming more and more frustrated as the night went on and even the thought of the huge wedge we were going to get couldn't console us. What did ease the pain was that we had dispensed with the glasses we had been provided with, and were openly swigging from the bottles of wine that littered the stage.

About a week before the gig I had dislocated the little finger on my right hand playing football. Strong painkillers and alcohol do not mix unless you're a member of Aerosmith in the 70s, so by the time we were finished I was feeling a little vague to say the least. Our host was over the moon as far as our performance was concerned, God help him he must've been feeling as spaced as I was. He was so delighted with us that he led us to his kitchen which had cases of wine stacked to the ceiling, and told us to help ourselves to the vino.

Never a band to look a nag in the gnashers, we waited for our more than generous host to return to the party and then took a case of wine each. Greed is a very unattractive trait. Colin then said that, in theory, Champagne was a wine, so we set down the 'peasant juice' and lifted a case of Moet & Chandon each. Under cover of night we ran up the archway through the middle of the mansion to Mixi's car, which was parked beside a brand new top of the range Aston Martin. With the boot of Mixi's old Audi heavily laden down with 'millionaires' lemonade' we climbed in to make good our escape.

The gravel of the newly laid driveway skipped up under the spinning wheels of our sober guitarist's car as we sped off. In the rear view mirror Mixi could see the figure of the birthday boy running after us.

'He's chasing us!!' Mixi shouted. 'What will I do?'

'Drive on,' the drunks in the car shouted in unison.

Mixi being untainted, that night anyway, with the demon booze, ignored our advice and turned the car around. As he drew level with our pursuer, he sheepishly wound down the window and asked, 'Everything OK?'

'Yes yes,' the out of breath, just turned 40-year-old, said. He then asked 'I was just wondering did you happen to lift any champagne?'

Mixi, too quickly for comfort, stammered, 'No, no, we didn't.'

To which, a decent man who deserved better, said, 'Come with me and I'll get you a couple of bottles.'

Back in the kitchen we held our breaths, hoping he wouldn't see the gaping hole in his Moet collection. To our relief he just opened a fresh case and handed us a bottle each. We thanked him while feeling shit, and walked back to the car, the motor still running like a getaway car employed by lowlife robbers, which is what we were really.

It was a midsummers night as we drove towards the village of Killyleigh; there was still enough daylight for the birdsong of thrushes, blackbirds and starlings to fill the pollen-fragrant air. As this was the North Down peninsula there was also the jovial rat-a-tat-tat of side drums and the piercing squeak of badly played flutes.

A 'kick the Pope' band was making its way back home from some parade that commemorated something that happened hundreds of years ago and probably resulted in people being, 'up to their necks in Fenian blood'. I think they were called 'Ulster's Young Defenders' which made me think, why were there never any flute bands which celebrated Ulster's young forwards or midfielders? Just a thought.

The Strictlys were religiously mixed; we had two Catholics, two Protestants and myself, an atheist. Not once had there ever been an angry word about religion or politics, but all of us were now pissed off that we were held up in traffic on the village High Street by what looked like a load of drunken louts in American Revolution military uniforms. As the minutes went by the hackles started to rise on the back of our collective necks. All of us being seriously sozzled, apart from Mixi, didn't help. Colin, for some reason, that didn't involve reason, decided to roll down his backseat window and shout 'Tiocfaidh ar la,' meaning, 'Our time will come,' a well-known phrase of Irish Republicans.

A crowd of about forty attacked the car, fists thumping on the roof and windows. Mixi had to mount the kerb and drive down the footpath scattering pedestrians to escape the hoard. As we reached the outskirts of the town and relative safety I saw red. I slipped from my seat-belt, turned round in my chair and threw a right hook at Colin's head, completely forgetting about the plastic cast on my injured hand. The blow glanced off the side of Colin's noggin and hit Paul on the side of his face, knocking his glasses off. There must have been alarm bells ringing in our new guitar player's ears and what he thought of his first gigging experience with the Strictlys doesn't bear thinking about.

I was more accurate with the second punch, although I did change hands, catching Colin a good 'un, however in the process I knocked the bottle of champers out of Roger's hands and it ended up rolling around the floor. Mixi was shouting for me to sit down; he was finding it slightly difficult to control a car being driven at high speed with a fight going on inside it. I returned to my seat, still fuming. Colin was ranting and raving in the back, claiming that his attempt at having us ripped to pieces was only a 'wee joke'. I turned the stereo up as loud as I could to drown him out. As I calmed down I was aware that there was a bumping against the back of my seat. I turned round to see one of the greatest acts of lunacy ever witnessed within the tight confines of a packed car. Roger was trying to open the bottle of champagne that had been knocked over in the fracas.

There is a demon among us

Unfortunately this mentalist episode of Colin's was not an isolated incident; he has a reputation for flirting, arguing and causing mayhem. Colin Shiels, I have to say, is one of my best friends but he is feckin' nuts. Don't get me wrong, he isn't a half-wit or anything, in fact, he is very well read, highly educated, well travelled and has a general knowledge second to none. He just has a wild streak about him that has seen him throwing a lighter onto the open fire of the new house of a friend of ours. The resulting explosion propelled burning coals around the room and onto a hearthrug, nearly razing the new home to the ground. In the same house he decided to try to run up the plasterboarded wall like Donald O'Connor in 'Singing in the Rain', only for the flimsy material to give way. Colin entered the adjoining room in a cloud of dust and left a gaping hole in the wall.

There was also the time that Colin covered a drunken, sleeping Mixi from head to toe with three cans of shaving foam and then for good measure sprinkled him with a box of Rice Krispies. His victim woke and opened his eyes, introducing scented foam to the sensitive mucous membranes of his peepers. He started screaming. Mixi resembled a mix between Peter Gabriel's 'Slipperman' character and the 'Singing Detective'. He had to shower fully clothed in an attempt to minimise the damage to his carpeting. When he was foam-and-breakfast-cereal-free he threw Colin out of his flat. Colin, not knowing when to call it quits, kept opening the letterbox, peering through and shouting, in a whiny childlike voice, 'Mixthi, pleath let me in I'm shorry.' Mixi reached for an aerosol can of Lynx deodorant and a lighter, and sent a jet of flames through the letterbox, singeing Colin's hair and eyelashes.

One of Colin's other favourite tricks was to change the message on answer phones to something quite disgusting, then sit back and laugh his 'Jacksons' off thinking about the repercussions. A case in point occurred when Mixi was in the company of a young lady in the bedroom of his flat. Colin changed the pleasant recorded missive to, 'I can't come to the phone right now, I am taking part in a mixed-race orgy in the honour of the one true lord Satan.' Which was actually quite tame for Colin. The next morning, while Mixi was finishing off what he couldn't finish the night before, the phone rang. Being otherwise engaged he let it ring.

When the greeting from hell came on Mixi was thrown off his stroke by the all-too-familiar tones of our very own Jeremy Beadle blasting from the tinny little Amstrad speaker. Mixi withdrew from the situation a little too quickly for a true gentleman and bounded into the living room, waving without using his hands. He was just a fraction too late to save his poor mother from the horrors of finding out that her son was a ritualistic devil worshiper. As he unsuccessfully tried to convince her, and in turn his Presbyterian Minister father, that it was all a joke, he turned, still in a state of rigidity, to discover that myself, Colin, Roger, Paul and a few other assorted hangers-on had all stayed over and were now bearing witness to our friend conversing with his dear old mum while still physically displaying his fondness for the female form. Breakfast didn't go down well that morning due to a mixture of revulsion and hilarity.

The point of me telling you all these tales is that if you should ever find yourself in the company of one Colin Shiels, always be on your guard. Don't let the Dorian Gray youthful looks fool you, he may not be able to shave but he can rustle up a whole mess of madness that would put Motley Crue to shame. If evidence were needed ask one of his regular victims, Mixi. He will regale you with tales of physical harm and mental torture, including the time that he had fallen asleep in Colin's house during a party and on waking found that the summer sun had just risen so he decided to take the beach walk back to his own house. Halfway home he bumped into one of his bosses out walking his dog. They had a long chat about the implications of oil prices on the value of the dollar. Unfortunately, unknown to poor Mixi he had 'I love Satan' and '666' written across his forehead and cheeks with a black marker. he didn't speak to Colin for weeks. Be afraid, my friends – be very afraid.

Ladies and gentlemen, can you be upstanding for the brides and grooms

Paul quickly became the heart and soul of the band. All of the boys were exceptional musicians; Colin is a phenomenal bass player who knows how to throw shapes on stage of Pete Way and Steve Harris proportions. I always thought that monitors were to hear the vocals and instruments on stage until Colin showed me that they were, in fact, something to rest your foot on while thrusting the bass into the faces of the crowd. Roger is a powerhouse of a drummer who rarely misses a beat and even rarer still keeps a set of sticks intact for a whole gig – even the graphite unbreakable ones. Mixi is a brilliant melodious soloist and on stage has the swagger of a wasted Joe Perry.

Paul was joining a band that was comfortable with their musicianship and with each other, so it could've been difficult for him to blend in. We needn't have worried: he slipped in like a well-lubricated suppository. His musicality was second to none. Whereas the rest of us were influenced by Hard Rock and Heavy Metal, his grounding is in the Rock and Roll and Rockabilly genres. He made us boogie. He is also a great singer, which meant that his pristine harmonies gave our songs a sheen that had been absent. Paul sang lead vocals on such songs as 'Pretty Woman' and 'Rock this Town', giving me a beer break. Result all round really.

Paul's dedication and love of the band was never more evident than on the sad occasion of his mother's death. Her funeral was to be held on one of the Saturdays that we were to play the Empire. It was just assumed that we would cancel the gig, something we had never done, even when one or all of us were horrendously hungover or ill. But much to Paul's credit and bravery we took the stage that night, a little tearful but proud as punch.

Through the band we have all met our better halves and Paul was to be no exception. Soon after joining, he caught the eye of one of a troupe of dancing girls that would shake their stuff to our Metallic outpourings on the left-hand side balcony of the Empire. From what I remember, Lesley, for it was she, had had a bit of competition for Paul's affections from one of the other dancers, but from the start Paul knew who he really wanted. His other admirer had to settle for a member of a more inferior band – oh, scratch my eyes out and call me Joan Collins.

Paul and Lesley decided that it was time to cement their love by getting 'Happy Harried'. The ceremony took place at Belfast City Hall and the reception in an old venue of ours, the Errigle Inn on the Ormeau Road. Folks, I have never been one for fashion, as the many photos of me through the years will attest to, so I had to kit myself out for the special occasion. I wasn't going to go overboard because I knew that the chances of me wearing the same clothes again were slim. I had survived my whole life never owning a suit. I borrowed one from friends and family on the very few occasions that I needed one – job interviews, weddings, funerals etc. The day before the special occasion I headed for Forestside Mall to carry out the activity I hate the most, shopping.

To cut down on the amount of time that I would spend crashing into the back of people who stop dead in their tracks in the middle of the aisle, I grabbed the first things that came to hand that fitted. This included a brown pair of brogues that a science teacher with corduroy patches on his sleeves wouldn't even wear. Although the clothes I bought were purchased in haste Donna thought I looked really smart; I think it was the novelty of seeing me in something other than jeans and T-shirt that did it.

It takes very little to get the Strictlys into party mode; a special occasion such as the lead guitar player getting hitched was a recipe for unrestrained merriment and lunacy. For such an important outpouring of glee we needed someone to lead the line, and boy, we were not disappointed by our drummer.

Roger and his beautiful under-age fiancée, Tracy, were turned out to perfection. It was evident that a lot of effort had been put into their appearance, so much so that Roger had regaled us with a tale of the morning's shenanigans, which involved him hovering over Tracy while she ironed his rather expensive designer shirt. He was panicking in case her age and therefore lack of experience might result in her burning a hole in his prized possession. He need not have worried: you could've sliced cheese with the creases in the sleeves. Why he didn't iron it himself is anyone's guess. Anyway they looked resplendent, as did everyone connected with the band. Even though it was the tidiest I had been in many a year, Donna still put me in the shade, she always did, natural beauties do that sort of thing.

After the formalities at Belfast City Hall and while the photos were being taken we all retired to a bar across the street to toast the happy couple. A few swift ones later we caught the bus up the Ormeau Road to the Errigle for the reception. The bar is a well-known music venue that we had played on many occasions; we only stopped doing so when they introduced a noise limiter which meant that the bands couldn't play above a certain volume – we didn't get beyond the first note. The bride is a close friend of Rosie McGurran, the proprietor's daughter, so it was an excellent choice for what was to be a hoot.

After the meals and speeches, one of which was from Colin and was cruel, touching and hilarious in equal measure, the real festivities could begin. Instead of a band, Mr and the new Mrs Kane had decided a DJ would eliminate the risk of the Strictlys hijacking the whole thing, thus stopping us commandeering the stage, and reducing the day to one of a display by drunken people who believe, with their whole hearts and souls, that the celebrations wouldn't be complete without their alcohol-hindered exhibitionism. Good plan in theory.

The 'Deck Demon' was instructed to play huge quantities of Rock and Metal to placate those who were there and believe that these genres of music mean everything; cue disintegration into mayhem. From the first strains of AC/DC's 'Highway to Hell', the dance floor was packed with no one except the Strictlys. We huddled together headbanging like a bunch of tourists at the Wailing Wall. Roger had taken to wearing Donna's straw hat, which had a lovely little ribbon around it, and opening his shirt to the naval. After a couple more Rock classics the DJ took pity on the rest of the guests and put on something by Buck's Fizz, which drove us back into the arms of our loved ones and the sweet caress of Jack Daniel's.

All the fluid we were taking onboard, to avoid dehydration of course, resulted in an urgency to relieve my bladder. I walked towards the toilet aware that there must be something like a piece of paper stuck to the sole of my shoe. I did a little dance in time with the music to try and remove it; this proved to be unsuccessful. I reached the bathroom, where the light was much better, and looked down at my right foot to identify the cause of the flapping. To my dismay the whole sole of my shoe, as far back as the heel, was hanging off. I did a quick root cause analysis to try to establish the source of the damage and came to the conclusion that it must have been Status Quo.

In case you were wondering, Francis Rossi and Rick Parfitt weren't guests, but their classic 'Down Down' had been one of the tunes played in the opening salvo by the DJ. In a fit of unrestrained euphoria I had dropped to my knees, during the breakdown section which follows the second chorus, and obviously put more strain on the glue keeping my shoes intact than the manufacturers had anticipated. As I stood in the bogs looking down at the mess I moved my foot back and forward and for a second it looked like my brogue was talking to me.

Returning to the table I said to Donna, 'I have a little predicament.' She said she'd already seen it and not to worry, she still loved me. I said, 'No no, not that, my shoe is falling apart.' It was still very early on in the day; the flapping sole could pose a health and safety issue, especially the way the grog was going down and the music was cranking up. I looked around the stage and to my relief found a whack of gaffa tape that had been stuck to the floor some time in the last decade or so, maybe even by us. I ripped it off and attempted to do a little bit of cobbling. Donna was not pleased. In one swift movement I had turned from a dapper gent about town to a street bum – all I needed was a piece of string to hold up my trousers and a Styrofoam cup with which to collect small change. I was dragged across the road to the local cab office and in the blink of an eye we were on our way back to the shop where I had purchased the shoes the day before.

The faulty footwear was replaced, although I did refrain from mentioning the Quo incident when I was asked what had happened to them by the rather perplexed shop assistant. On arrival back at the reception the sight of Roger skidding along the floor on his knees greeted us. Tracy was sitting at the table, her head in her hands, looking a little horrified. Seeing her pain I had a quick word with our drummer and persuaded him to return to the table. He sat down and on seeing Tracy's tormented face he asked, without a hint of irony, 'Why don't you love me any more?' Just then the opening riff to

'Paradise City' erupted from the speakers. Roger didn't even wait for Tracy's answer to his heartfelt question, he leapt to his feet, ran towards the stage and jumped up, hands outstretched. He was attempting to catch hold of a bar that ran the length of the ceiling. In his mind's eye he was going to swing like the man on the flying trapeze.

Shards of glass filled the air and the dance floor as Roger came crashing down to earth. The bar was not metal, in fact it wasn't even a bar: it was a fluorescent light tube. As Axl sang 'I'm a hard case that's tough to beat,' Roger was rolling around the floor on the broken glass. In the meantime Tracy was excusing herself and leaving the reception and her fiancé for good. Roger caught the love of his life exiting out of the corner of his eye and he was after her like a greyhound out of the traps. Alcohol, injuries and a lower centre of gravity than most caused him to resemble Groucho Marx sprinting on his honkers.

Donna and myself went after them and found them having a loud chat in the foyer. We were able to persuade them to return to the party. Roger spent the rest of the night glued to his seat and looking into the eyes of his betrothed telling her how much he loved her.

Because Rog and Tracy lived in Bangor, an extortionate cab ride away, I invited them to stay in our Elish's house; we were looking after it while she was overseas. Seeing as Roger was still heavy with drink we got a fast food carryout with which to soak up the alcohol and to try to prevent a worse hangover than he was going to have anyway. Roger covered his burger with ketchup and mayonnaise – he may as well have poured it down the front of his clothes for that's where it ended up. The next day Roger surfaced late. Tracy, Donna and myself were sitting in the living room drinking tea when he walked in holding a shredded, blood- and condiment-splattered garment in his hand. 'What the fuck happened to my good shirt?' he asked.

Roger and Tracy's own wedding, a month or so later, was not spared from the shame of the Strictlys. With the very obvious age gap between the betrothed they resembled Nicole Smith and her eighty-nine-year-old husband J. Howard Marshall 2nd, as they walked down the aisle, but they were so happy no one seemed to mind much.

Roger had asked us to play at the reception; possibly a sign of senility. Mixi however had broken his finger in a bizarre skiing accident; apparently he was unaware that you shouldn't really drink alcohol while hurtling down the slopes. He was attempting to stop the ice falling out of his glass of Jack and Coke, lost his balance and fell face first onto the hard-packed snow. His injures were horrific. Thank goodness they didn't change his looks much – some even said that there appeared to be a slight improvement. Anyway, the finger injury curtailed his love life and guitar playing. The former I didn't care to know about, but the latter meant that we would have to play the wedding as a four piece, something we had never done before.

Roger's brother was the best man. However, during his speech his father seemed to think it was he who should be delivering the anecdotes and kept shouting over his son. Very bizarre. This etiquettical misdemeanour set the tone for what was to happen.

The DJ, as with Paul and Lesley's wedding, had been instructed to play lots of Rock music and again it had the same effect, turning some of the guests, us, into raving mad, headbanging lunatics. When it was our turn to play we were drunk and up for it. Can't remember much about the gig but I do recall that we had been finished for about an hour or so and last orders at the bar had been called when, for some reason, and I still don't know why, we decided to get back on stage and do the 'Ace of Spades' by Motorhead.

As we rattled through one of the greatest examples of why you can prove to the 'trendies' that Rock is quite easily the greatest form of popular music without getting an argument, the manageress stood at the side of the stage doing her best impression of Iris Robinson at an Alan Carr gig. 'Get off the fucking stage now!!' she screamed. We ignored her and carried on playing. She promptly sent out a message to security. On their arrival they made menacing signals at us by drawing open hands across their throats and punching the palms of their hands. All of a sudden the line, 'That's the way I like it baby, I don't want to live forever,' never seemed more apt. It must have been one of the only times that the groom, at his own wedding reception, had been forcibly thrown out. The bride bristled with pride and looked forward to their future life together.

Nurse, the screams

While working in Musgrave Park Hospital I became very friendly with a theatre recovery nurse called Michael Canavan. He was a red-haired scouser who had stopped me in the corridor one day to ask if I was the singer in the band he had seen the previous week. I told him that indeed, I was that handsome hero and that Paul Kane was the guitar player. This was to be the start of a beautiful, drunken friendship.

Michael had endeared himself to me when I heard that he had been reprimanded for an incident where he used his initiative to rouse someone who they had found difficult to bring round from the effects of his anaesthetic. The patient was heavily tattooed with images of a sectarian nature adorning each arm. Shaking him didn't work and calling his name was even less effective. They were becoming desperate – they needed the space for a patient who was ready to come out of theatre.

It was decided, by Michael, that they should use a technique similar to the one where relatives talk to coma patients hoping that the familiar voices release the poor individual from the hiding place within their brains. Staff Nurse Canavan pursed his lips and softly whistled, 'The Sash.' There was an instant twitching of the eyelids and the legs started to march; the patient then opened his eyes and smiled. To my mind this was a piece of genius. A passing Sister, however, was of a different opinion and Michael was beckoned with a gnarly old finger to the ward office where he was given a telling off for being funny.

Michael and his girlfriend Barbara, another nurse, lived in a rented attic flat off the Lisburn Road. It was just behind a bar that Donna and myself used to frequent on a regular basis, the Chelsea. Michael had invited us to join them there one Sunday afternoon for a few drinks, which we agreed to. The bar, before it became a yuppie hellhole, was a cracker that had Blues bands on during the Sabbath lunchtime. At that time the licensing laws demanded that the pubs close their doors between 2.30pm and 7pm on the 'Lord's day'. Everyone, I assume, was to return home, bask in the love of their families and the light of Jesus, and then go back out later on to get rat-arsed. The manager of the Chelsea found this to be somewhat of an inconvenience to its patrons so he just closed the doors and let those that wanted to stay on do just that. We did just that.

A lunch for two was stretched out to a supper for four back in Michael and Barbara's flat. They were great company and while we were chatting I happened to mention that I had always contemplated becoming a nurse, but I felt I was too old to do anything about it now. Barbara said that even though I had just turned thirty it shouldn't be a problem, they were letting all ages in now. 'Very reassuring,' I thought, even someone as decrepit as myself could get in. I said I would think about it. Michael said that while I was doing that I could round the evening off with a Baileys and brandy.

I hate Baileys, I really do, but for some reason, maybe it was the good craic, maybe it was the ten pints of Murphy's stout I had consumed in the Chelsea, but my distaste for the creamy Irish liqueur dissolved. I sat back with a half pint of this noxious cocktail and toasted our hosts. After a few more I was becoming rather animated on the subject of God and how I found it inconceivable that anybody with any scientific education could believe in something that there was absolutely no evidence for. I had just got to a point where I was comparing the Almighty to fairies at the bottom of the garden when an urgency to visit the bathroom came upon me.

There is no worse feeling in the world than being in two minds as to which end of you needs to use the toilet first: a miscalculation could result in the soiling of bathroom rugs and the obliteration of friendships. I had to play this one very carefully; I had only been going out with Donna a relatively short while and I felt that messing myself at a social gathering could possibly be the end of something beautiful before it had even started. I pulled my trousers and under garments around my ankles, sat on the toilet and waited for the most urgent of the evacuations to present itself. There was a terrible fear that if I were to feel nauseated first, I could be positioned head down the bowl with all hell breaking loose behind me, and the reverse was just as terrifying. I sat and wondered if it was too late to seek God's forgiveness for my blasphemous rantings earlier, but I was too much of an atheist even to contemplate this in such a time of dire need. These thoughts were tiring and I closed my eyes to rest my aching mind.

I was vaguely aware of a banging noise as I opened my eyes. The room I was sitting in was strange to me but there was a voice calling my name that was familiar. I turned to see that the door, which was now being hammered upon, had a lock that was engaged. I stood up, or should I say I tried to, but my legs had seized up and there were shooting pains from my knees right up to my buttocks. I straightened slowly. Finally erect, I stumbled to the door and opened it. There standing on the other side were Donna, Michael and Barbara.

I was so relieved to see familiar faces, even though there were a variety of expressions upon each one. Barbara had a look of embarrassed disgust; Michael's was one of hilarity and Donna's face held the expression of someone who had just witnessed something that they could've quite happily made it to the end of their lives without seeing. In my Baileys and brandy stupor I had forgotten to adjust my dress. I stood naked from the waist down doing my best impression of the last turkey in the shop. Donna ordered a taxi, helped me into it and put me to bed when we got home. Ahh, the compassion of love in its early stages. If I were to carry out a repeat performance now I'd still be sitting on the toilet the next day with the indentation of the hole in the seat red and raw around my arse and thighs.

The next day I was seriously hungover, so when the phone rang I was in two minds whether to answer it or not. On the other end of the line Michael greeted me with, 'I hope I haven't caught you with your trousers down,' his scouse humour in fine form. I thanked him for his kind remarks by issuing a few expletives. He then informed me that, coincidentally, the advert for the next nursing intake was going to be in the *Belfast Telegraph* that very night and that I should apply. I hung up and made a mental note to do no such thing; I really couldn't see myself starting back into education twelve years after leaving Bangor Tech. As the day wore on and after a phone conversation with Donna that ended with her saying, 'Why not?' I changed my mind and I thought, 'Why not indeed?'

I can have no regrets; I honestly believe that no one makes a bad decision. My rationale is simple – who in their right mind when faced with a fork in the road would choose the path that has the serial killer with the chainsaw waiting at the end of it? The answer, I would hope is no one. For whatever reasons we make the decisions we do, they obviously were the right ones at the time or another route would've been taken. It's no use after the fact rhyming off a load of ifs and buts; it's in the past, done with, over, finito.

Every life decision I've made was, under the circumstances, the right one; it may not have worked as I'd hoped, but tough shit Paddy, that's life. I was now no longer the star-struck kid who idolised Ken Heaven and then a list of rockers from AC/DC to ZZ Top. Don't get me wrong, I still loved them but wasn't going to die, as I thought I once would have, if I didn't get the next issue of *Kerrang*! or the Japan-only release of Journey's 'Captured' live album. Crap, I was growing up.

When I actually really think about it I never had the X factor. I could sing in tune but I was never going to be Paul Rodgers. I could put on a show but I knew that David Lee Roth wasn't going to be quaking in his leather chaps. So as heartbreaking as the realisation that my dream of becoming a bona fide rock star was not going to happen was, the pragmatic lifting of the delusional mists was actually a bit of a relief.

Rock and Roll had laid a varied and exciting path for me and I took each crazy paved twist and turn in my stride and with relish. I had had moderate success but I had never 'made it', in the true sense of the term. There were no platinum discs, no limos, no TVs out of hotel windows – well there was one which I forgot to tell you about – but I had had a ball trying to achieve these hollow status symbols. Through music I've fallen in love and I've made friends that remain dear to me to this day and I hope will always remain so. I felt I needed a new challenge: something that would allow me to put something back into society.

There would need to be a re-evaluation of life. I'm not made from the same material that cockroaches and Keith Richards are hewn from, therefore for me to reach an old age I would need to wise up, knuckle down and better myself. A lot of my lifestyle was unhealthy at best and deadly at worst; I had lost friends along the way remember. My Da, when I told him that I was thinking of becoming a nurse, said he felt like kissing my feet. I'm glad he didn't because with his lumbago he would've been in traction for weeks. All joking aside, he was totally relieved that I was contemplating something sensible and worthwhile. Was I that much of a worry? I suppose I was.

In April 1996, three weeks after requesting an application form from the jobs section of the 'Sixth Tele', I was sitting in a classroom of the Northside College of Nursing in the Ulster Hospital, Dundonald. I was surrounded by four males and about forty females, the majority of whom were considerably more attractive and younger than I was. I looked around me and realised that I was going to be here for the next three years. What the hell was I thinking of? I stretched back in my chair, cupped the back of my head in my hands and had a wee chuckle to myself. Up to that point I had had the good fortune of never being bored; my life had been far from dull. Maybe it was now the turn of nursing to benefit from my ability to live up to a phrase which has been used about my life experiences: 'It could only happen to you.' As I was thinking this I became aware of a glass case in the corner of the room which housed a statue of Florence Nightingale. For a second, while a beam of sunlight shone upon her face, I could've sworn she was laughing. Or maybe she was crying – either way I knew it was time for massive changes and for the next adventure to begin.

But it doesn't end there ...

Are you wondering if Eamon is still singing? Or did the Northan Ireland nursing establishment soothe his vocal chords? Has Ken patented his knob roll? Is he still off the sprouts? And what about all the other characters from Holywood Star? What are they all doing now?

Why not join them on Facebook and see how the story continued ... www.facebook.com/holywoodstar

And to keep your toes tapping and your head banging, various recordings by Nellie Dean have been released as a digital Holywood Star EP. Available from iTunes, Amazon and plenty of other online stores.

Eamon's book is only available online but if you want to sell it in a shop or similar, please send bulk order requests (minimum 24 books) to books@showcaseuk.tv

As soon as Holywood Star is available as a general release, or as an ebook, or if something mad like Nellie Dean reforming ever happens we'll announce it via the mailing list which you can sign up to at: www.showcaseuk.tv

For the book's first birthday we added a new front cover that was designed by Rachel Woodman from The Choir Press, plus a new back photo and this page.

And during the first 12 months we've had tremendous support from many people who love the book. Here is a list of those we'd like to thank in print.

Miles Bailey and his team from The Choir Press for their valued support and advice.

Phil Black and everyone at Rock Radio Northern Ireland, especially Balattys Podcast and the Seatville Show; Dan Renton, Dan O'Gara and everyone from Dorset Rock Online, Strictly No Ballroom, Mari Jackson. The Guitar Rooms Holywood, Phil Allely, Breezy Murray, The Quay Vipers, The Empire Belfast, Jerry Ewing from Classic Rock, Rob White, Neil Jefferies, Jon Kirk, Arthur Magee, Grant Sharkey from Chapter One, (Hythe, Hampshire) the only book shop in the world to stock and sell the book, Rhian French, Slugger O'Toole, Eve Murray, Suzy Wheeler, Bernard Johnston, Malcolm Dome, Donna and Johnston Fleming, Melissa Morgan, Ivan Martin, Maurice J. and of course Fishy.

For their reviews of Eamon's book on Amazon.co.uk: Paul Smythe, Conor Heaven, David Attwood, Amanda and Heath Taylor, Seatzie Seatzieville, Belfast Belle, Lee Brown, Claire Kelly, P.A. Loyer, Clarkie W, Thomas Nancarrow, Mrs Valerie P. Willis, Mr Michael O'Sullivan, Niall Mullan, Fish, the elder, John Jameson, G. Forbes, Mr Daniel W. J. Kendall, Nigel Law, Mr P. Murch, Michael Jeffrey.

And finally thank you for buying this book; if you can buy it for a friend or family member we'd be more than grateful.

Following on from *Holywood Star*, Eamon ventures into the world of children's fiction with *Liono. The little lion who loves flowers*. Published by Showcase UK.

Both Eamon and Showcase UK support the Stroke Association.

Notes
The characters are still contributing to the story.